Test Bank

Sears and
Zemansky's

UNIVERSITY
PHYSICS
with Modern Physics
11th Edition

Young & Freedman

Benjamin Grinstein
University of California, San Diego

PEARSON

Addison
Wesley

San Francisco • Boston • New York
Capetown • Hong Kong • London • Madrid • Mexico City
Montreal • Munich • Paris • Singapore • Sydney • Tokyo • Toronto

ISBN 0-8053-8772-2

PEARSON

Addison
Wesley

3 4 5 6 7 8 9 10–DPC–07 06 05 04 03

www.aw.com/bc

CONTENTS

Chapter 1 Units, Physical Quantities, and Vectors

Multiple Choice Questions

1) The following conversion equivalents are given:

   1 gal = 231 in^3 1 ft = 12 in   1 min = 60 s

   A pipe delivers water at the rate on 35 gal/min. The rate in ft^3/s, is closest to:

   A) 0.078   B) 0.071   C) 0.064   D) 0.057   E) 0.050

   Answer: A
   Var: 50+

2) The following conversion equivalents are given:

   1 m = 100 cm   1 in = 2.54 cm   1 ft = 12 in

   A bin has a volume of 1.5 m^3. The volume of the bin, in ft^3, is closest to:

   A) 35   B) 41   C) 47   D) 53   E) 59

   Answer: D
   Var: 1

3) The following conversion equivalents are given:

   1 mile = 5280 ft   1 ft = 12 in   1 m = 39.37 in   1 hour = 60 min   1 min = 60 s

   A particle has a velocity of 5 miles per hour. The velocity, in m/s, is closest to:

   A) 2.2   B) 1.8   C) 2.0   D) 2.5   E) 2.7

   Answer: A
   Var: 50+

4) A speed of 65 miles per hour is the same as

   A) 24 m/s   B) 29 m/s   C) 32 m/s   D) 37 m/s   E) 42 m/s

   Answer: B
   Var: 1

5) The following conversion equivalents are given:

   1 kg = 1000g   1 l = 1000 cm^3 1 l = 0.0353 ft^3

   The density of a liquid is 0.60 g/cm^3. The density of the liquid, in kg/ft^3, is closest to:

   A) 17   B) 14   C) 15   D) 19   E) 20

   Answer: A
   Var: 50+

6) The components of vector $\vec{A}$ are given as follows:

$$A_x = +5.5$$
$$A_y = -5.3$$

The magnitude of $\vec{A}$ is closest to:

A) 7.6   B) 6.1   C) 6.9   D) 8.4   E) 9.2

Answer: A
Var: 50+

7) The components of vector $\vec{A}$ are given as follows:

$$A_x = +7.4$$
$$A_y = -4.6$$

The angle measured counter-clockwise from the x-axis to vector $\vec{A}$, in degrees, is closest to:

A) 328   B) 148   C) 238   D) 122   E) 32

Answer: A
Var: 50+

8) The components of vectors $\vec{A}$ and $\vec{B}$ are given as follows:

$$A_x = +3.1 \qquad B_x = -5.6$$
$$A_y = -7 \qquad B_y = -3.1$$

The magnitude of the vector difference $\vec{B} - \vec{A}$, is closest to:

A) 9.5   B) 4.6   C) 10   D) 91   E) 1.3

Answer: A
Var: 50+

9) The components of vectors $\vec{B}$ and $\vec{C}$ are given as follows:

$$B_x = -6.1 \qquad C_x = -9.8$$
$$B_y = -5.8 \qquad C_y = +4.6$$

The angle (less than 180 degrees) between vectors $\vec{B}$ and $\vec{C}$, in degrees, is closest to:

A) 69   B) 111   C) 18   D) 162   E) 80

Answer: A
Var: 50+

10) The magnitude of $\vec{A}$ is 6.6. Vector $\vec{A}$ lies in the second quadrant and forms an angle of 60 degrees with the y-axis. The components, A_x and A_y, are closest to:

A) $A_x = -5.7$, $A_y = +3.3$

B) $A_x = +5.7$, $A_y = -3.3$

C) $A_x = +3.3$, $A_y = -5.7$

D) $A_x = -3.3$, $A_y = +5.7$

E) $A_x = -3.3$, $A_y = -5.7$

Answer: A
Var: 50+

Figure 1.1

Vectors $\vec{B}$ and $\vec{C}$ are shown. Vector $\vec{D}$ is given by $\vec{D} = \vec{B} - \vec{C}$

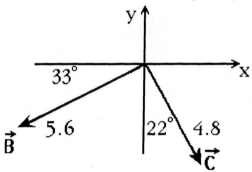

11) In Figure 1.1, the magnitude of $\vec{D}$ is closest to:

A) 3.2   B) 5.3   C) 6.6   D) 8.0   E) 9.2

Answer: C
Var: 1

12) In Figure 1.1, the angle, measured counter-clockwise from the x-axis to vector $\vec{D}$, in degrees, is closest to:

A) 12   B) 102   C) 168   D) 192   E) 258

Answer: C
Var: 1

13) Vectors $\vec{A}$, $\vec{B}$ and $\vec{C}$ satisfy the vector equation $\vec{A} + \vec{B} = \vec{C}$ Their magnitudes are related by $\vec{A} - \vec{B} = \vec{C}$. Which of the following is an accurate statement?

A) $\vec{A}$, $\vec{B}$ and $\vec{C}$ form the sides of a right triangle.

B) $\vec{A}$, $\vec{B}$ and $\vec{C}$ form the sides of an equilateral triangle.

C) The angle between $\vec{A}$ and $\vec{B}$ can have any value, in view of the limited information given.

D) $\vec{B}$ and $\vec{C}$ are perpendicular vectors.

E) $\vec{A}$ and $\vec{B}$ are antiparallel vectors.

Answer: E
Var: 1

14) Which of the following is an accurate statement?

A) The magnitude of a vector can be zero even though one of its components is not zero.

B) It is possible to add a scalar quantity to a vector.

C) Even though two vectors have unequal magnitudes, it is possible that their vector sum is zero.

D) Rotating a vector about an axis passing through the tip of the vector does not change the vector.

E) The magnitude of a vector is independent of the coordinate system used.

Answer: E
Var: 1

15) What is the magnitude of the sum of the following vectors?

$\vec{A} = \vec{i} + 4\vec{j} - \vec{k}$ $\vec{B} = 3\vec{i} - \vec{j} - 4\vec{k}$ $\vec{C} = -\vec{i} + \vec{j}$

A) 7.07   B) 2.00   C) 10.76   D) 6.78   E) 8.12

Answer: A
Var: 12

16) Two vectors are given as follows:

$\vec{A} = +3\vec{i} - 2\vec{j} - 3\vec{k}$ $\vec{C} = -4\vec{i} - 2\vec{j} - 3\vec{k}$

The magnitude of $|\vec{A} - \vec{C}|$ is closest to:

A) 7   B) 6   C) 8   D) 9   E) 10

Answer: A
Var: 50+

17) Two vectors are given as follows:
$$\vec{A} = +3\vec{i} - 2\vec{j} - 2\vec{k} \qquad \vec{B} = -2\vec{i} - 5\vec{j} + 2\vec{k}$$

The scalar product $\vec{A} \cdot \vec{B}$ is closest to

A) zero   B) –20   C) 12   D) –12   E) 8

Answer: A
Var: 48

18) Two vectors are given as follows:
$$\vec{B} = -2\vec{i} - 5\vec{j} + 2\vec{k} \qquad \vec{C} = -4\vec{i} - 2\vec{j} - 3\vec{k}$$

The angle between vectors $\vec{B}$ and $\vec{C}$, in degrees, is closest to:

A) 67   B) 113   C) 39   D) 141   E) 90

Answer: A
Var: 50+

19) A vector is given as follows:
$$\vec{A} = +3\vec{i} - 2\vec{j} - 2\vec{k}$$

The angle between vector $\vec{A}$ and the y–axis, in degrees, is closest to:

A) 119   B) 61   C) 29   D) 151   E) 90

Answer: A
Var: 50+

20) A vector is given as follows:
$$\vec{C} = -5\vec{i} - 2\vec{j} - 3\vec{k}$$

The vector product $\vec{C} \times \vec{j}$ equals:
A) $+3\vec{i} - 5\vec{k}$
B) $+3\vec{i} + 5\vec{k}$
C) $-3\vec{i} + 5\vec{k}$
D) $+3\vec{i} + 2\vec{j} - 5\vec{k}$
E) $-3\vec{i} - 2\vec{j} + 5\vec{k}$

Answer: A
Var: 50+

21) Two vectors are given as follows:

$$\vec{B} = -2\vec{i} - 5\vec{j} + 2\vec{k} \qquad \vec{C} = -5\vec{i} - 2\vec{j} - 3\vec{k}$$

The magnitude of $|\vec{C} \times \vec{B}|$ is closest to:

  A) 33   B) 29   C) 25   D) 21   E) 17

Answer: A
Var: 50+

Figure 1.2
Three vectors are given as shown.

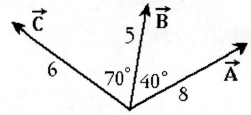

22) In Figure 1.2, the scalar product $\vec{C} \cdot \vec{B}$ is closest to:

  A) zero   B) +10   C) +28   D) –10   E) –28

Answer: B
Var: 1

23) In Figure 1.2, the scalar product $\vec{A} \cdot \vec{C}$ is closest to:

  A) zero   B) +16   C) +45   D) –16   E) –45

Answer: D
Var: 1

24) In Figure 1.2, the magnitude and direction of the vector product $\vec{B} \cdot \vec{A}$ are closest to:

  A) 26, directed into the plane

  B) 26, directed out of the plane

  C) 31, directed on the plane

  D) 31, directed into the plane

  E) 31, directed out of the plane

Answer: A
Var: 1

25) In Figure 1.2, the magnitude and direction of the vector product $\vec{A} \cdot \vec{C}$ are closest to:

    A) 16, directed into the plane

    B) 16, directed out of the plane

    C) 45, directed on the plane

    D) 45, directed into the plane

    E) 45, directed out of the plane

Answer: E
Var: 1

26) An airplane undergoes the following displacements: First, it flies 65 km in a direction $30°$ east of north. Next, it flies 78 km due south. Finally, it flies 100 km $30°$ north of west. Using analytical methods, determine how far the airplane ends up from its starting point.

    A) 61.1 km   B) 62.3 km   C) 63.5 km   D) 59.8 km   E) 58.6 km

Answer: A
Var: 50+

27) A cube is positioned with its vertices at the following points:

    A = (0,0,0)   C = (1,1,0)   E = (0,0,1)   G = (1,1,1)

    B = (1,0,0)   D = (0,1,0)   F = (1,0,1)   H = (0,1,1)

What is the angle of intersection of the planes formed by the triangles EBC and ECD?

    A) $57°$ B) $60°$ C) $45°$ D) $53°$ E) $90°$

Answer: B
Var: 1

28) Which of the following is an accurate statement?

    A) If the vectors $\vec{A}$ and $\vec{B}$ are each rotated through the same angle about the same axis, the product
    $\vec{A} \cdot \vec{B}$ will be unchanged.

    B) If the vectors $\vec{A}$ and $\vec{B}$ are each rotated through the same angle about the same axis, the product
    $\vec{A} \times \vec{B}$ will be unchanged.

    C) If a vector $\vec{A}$ is rotated about an axis parallel to vector B, the product $\vec{A} \cdot \vec{B}$ will be changed.

    D) If vectors $\vec{A}$ and $\vec{B}$ are both rotated through the same angle about the axis, the sum of $\vec{A}$
    $+ \vec{B}$ will not be changed.

    E) When a scalar quantity is added to a vector, the result is a vector of larger magnitude than the original vector.

Answer: A
Var: 1

Short Answer Questions

1) Albert, a person who chooses to live mostly apart from other people, uses as his unit of length (for walking to visit his neighbors or plowing his fields) the albert, the distance Albert can throw a small rock. One albert is 60 meters. How many square alberts is one acre?

(1 acre = 43,560ft^2 = 4050m^2.)

Answer: 1.125 A^2
Var: 50+

Figure 1.3

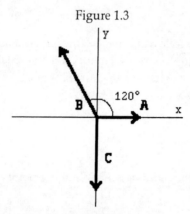

2) Find the magnitude and direction of the sum R of the three vectors shown in Figure 1.3; R = A = B + C. The vectors have the following magnitudes: A = 5.0, B = 7.9, and C = 8.0. Express the direction of the vector sum by specifying the angle it makes with the positive x–axis, with the counterclockwise angles taken to be positive.

Answer: magnitude: R = 1.6, direction: Θ = 312 $^\circ$
Var: 1

3) Two boys searching for buried treasure are standing underneath the same tree. One boy walks 12 m east and then 12 m north. The other boy walks 15 m west and then 11 m north. Find the scalar product of their net displacements from the tree.

Answer: –48 m^2
Var: 50+

4) Find the vector product $\vec{A}$ x $\vec{B}$ of the two vectors $\vec{A}$ and $\vec{B}$, where $\vec{A} = 7\vec{i} + 8\vec{j}$ and $B = -6\vec{j}$ $-3\vec{k}$. Express your result in terms of the $\vec{i}$, $\vec{j}$ and k unit vectors.

Answer: $-24\vec{i} + 21\vec{j} - 42\vec{k}$
Var: 1

5) Find the angle, in degrees, between the vectors $\vec{A} = 3\vec{i} + 5\vec{j} - 2\vec{k}$ and $\vec{B} = -7\vec{i} + 5\vec{j} + 6\vec{k}$.

Answer: 97.1 $^\circ$
Var: 1

8

Chapter 2   Motion Along a Straight Line

Multiple Choice Questions

1) A train starts from rest and accelerates uniformly, until it has traveled 3.3 km and acquired a velocity of 48 m/s. The train then moves at a constant velocity of 48 m/s for 430 s. The train then decelerates uniformly at 0.065 m/s^2, until it is brought to a halt. The acceleration during the first 3.3 km of travel is closest to:

    A) 0.35 m/s^2 B) 0.31 m/s^2 C) 0.38 m/s^2 D) 0.42 m/s^2 E) 0.45 m/s^2

Answer: A
Var: 50+

2) A train starts from rest and accelerates uniformly, until it has traveled 3.8 km and acquired a velocity of 24 m/s. The train then moves at a constant velocity of 24 m/s for 410 s. The train then decelerates uniformly at 0.065 m/s^2, until it is brought to a halt. The distance traveled by the train during deceleration, in km, is closest to:

    A) 4.4   B) 4.2   C) 4.0   D) 3.8   E) 3.6

Answer: A
Var: 50+

3) A train starts from rest and accelerates uniformly, until it has traveled 2.5 km and acquired a velocity of 48 m/s. The train then moves at a constant velocity of 48 m/s for 410 s. The train then decelerates uniformly at 0.065 m/s^2, until it is brought to a halt. The velocity of the train, when it has decelerated for 290 s, is closest to:

    A) 29.2 m/s   B) 27.7 m/s   C) 26.2 m/s   D) 24.8 m/s   E) 23.3 m/s

Answer: A
Var: 50+

4) A train starts from rest and accelerates uniformly, until it has traveled 5.3 km and acquired a velocity of 28 m/s. The train then moves at a constant velocity of 28 m/s for 470 s. The train then decelerates uniformly at 0.065 m/s^2, until it is brought to a halt. The average velocity, during the first 9.5 km of travel, is closest to:

    A) 18.0 m/s   B) 18.5 m/s   C) 19.1 m/s   D) 19.6 m/s   E) 20.1 m/s

Answer: A
Var: 50+

5) A car moving at a velocity of 20 m/s is behind a truck moving at a constant velocity of 18 m/s. When the car is 50 m behind the front of the truck, the car accelerates uniformly at 1.8 m/s^2. The car continues at the same acceleration until it reaches a velocity of 25 m/s, which is the legal speed limit. The car then continues at a constant velocity of 25 m/s, until it passes the front of the truck. The distance the car travels while accelerating, in meters, is closest to:

    A) 50   B) 54   C) 58   D) 62   E) 66

Answer: D
Var: 1

6) A car moving at a velocity of 20 m/s is behind a truck moving at a constant velocity of 18 m/s. When the car is 50 m behind the front of the truck, the car accelerates uniformly at 1.8 m/s². The car continues at the same acceleration until it reaches a velocity of 25 m/s, which is the legal speed limit. The car then continues at a constant velocity of 25 m/s, until it passes the front of the truck. The time interval from the point that the car reaches the speed limit until it passes the truck, in seconds, is closest to:

   A) 4.6   B) 4.8   C) 5.0   D) 5.2   E) 5.4

Answer: E
Var: 1

7) A motorist makes a trip of 180 miles. For the first 90 miles she drives at a constant speed of 30 mph. At what constant speed must she drive the remaining distance if her average speed for the total trip is to be 40 mph?

   A) 45 mph   B) 50 mph   C) 52.5 mph   D) 55 mph   E) 60 mph

Answer: E
Var: 1

8) A racquetball strikes a wall with a speed of 30 m/s and rebounds with a speed of 26 m/s. The collision takes 20 ms. What is the average acceleration of the ball during collision?

   A) Zero   B) 200 m/s²   C) 2800 m/s²   D) 1500 m/s²   E) 1300 m/s²

Answer: C
Var: 1

9) Which of the following situations is impossible?

   A) An object has velocity directed east and acceleration directed west.

   B) An object has velocity directed east and acceleration directed east.

   C) An object has zero velocity but non-zero acceleration.

   D) An object has constant non-zero acceleration and changing velocity.

   E) An object has constant non-zero velocity and changing acceleration.

Answer: E
Var: 1

10) A ball is projected upward at time t = 0.0 s, from a point on a roof 30 m above the ground. The ball rises, then falls and strikes the ground. The initial velocity of the ball is 32.5 m/s. Consider all quantities as positive in the upward direction. At time t = 2.1 s, the acceleration of the ball is closest to:

   A) zero   B) +5 m/s²   C) +10 m/s²   D) -5 m/s²   E) -10 m/s²

Answer: E
Var: 50+

11) A ball is projected upward at time t = 0.0 s, from a point on a roof 80 m above the ground. The ball rises, then falls and strikes the ground. The initial velocity of the ball is 56.9 m/s. Consider all quantities as positive in the upward direction. At time t = 5.81 s, the velocity of the ball is closest to:

A) zero   B) +165 m/s   C) +12 m/s   D) –165 m/s   E) –12 m/s

Answer: A
Var: 50+

12) A ball is projected upward at time t = 0.0 s, from a point on a roof 70 m above the ground. The ball rises, then falls and strikes the ground. The initial velocity of the ball is 67.2 m/s. Consider all quantities as positive in the upward direction. The average velocity of the ball, during the first 2.45 s, is closest to:

A) +55 m/s   B) zero   C) –55 m/s   D) +110 m/s   E) –110 m/s

Answer: A
Var: 50+

13) A ball is projected upward at time t = 0.0 s, from a point on a roof 30 m above the ground. The ball rises, then falls and strikes the ground. The initial velocity of the ball is 87.2 m/s. Consider all quantities as positive in the upward direction. The velocity of the ball when it is 16 m above the ground is closest to:

A) –89 m/s   B) –71 m/s   C) –53 m/s   D) –36 m/s   E) –107 m/s

Answer: A
Var: 50+

14) A ball is projected upward at time t = 0.0 s, from a point on a roof 40 m above the ground. The ball rises, then falls and strikes the ground. The initial velocity of the ball is 44.6 m/s. Consider all quantities as positive in the upward direction. The time when the ball strikes the ground is closest to:

A) 9.9 s   B) 9.6 s   C) 9.3 s   D) 10 s   E) 11 s

Answer: A
Var: 50+

15) A motorist traveling at a constant speed of 150 km/h in a 50 km/h speed zone passes a parked police car. Three seconds after the car passes, the police car starts off in pursuit. The policeman accelerates at 2 m/s^2 up to a speed of 70 m/s, and then continues at this speed until he overtakes the speeding motorist. How long from the time he started does it take the police car to overtake the motorist? The motorist continues at a constant speed during this process.

A) 48 s   B) 56 s   C) 38 s   D) 35 s   E) 99 s

Answer: A
Var: 46

Figure 2.1

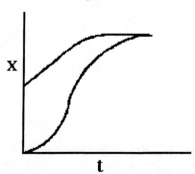

16) Shown in Figure 2.1 is a schematic graph of position versus time for two moving objects. Which of the following best describes what is depicted here?

A) A ball is thrown into the air and a moment later a second ball is thrown, but with a higher velocity than the first.

B) While accelerating in an attempt to pass, Mario Andretti plows into the back of a speeding A.J. Foyt on the back straightaway at the Indy 500.

C) Leading the Indianapolis 500, with two laps to go, Bobby Rahal throws a wheel bearing and pulls in for a pit stop as Tom Sneva zooms by and goes on to win.

D) A rock and a crumpled piece of paper are dropped from rest at $t = 0$ in the presence of air (i.e. friction is present).

E) A speeder races past a parked police car. A moment later the police car starts and takes off in pursuit with high acceleration and siren screaming. He ends up giving the violator a speeding ticket.

Answer: E
Var: 1

17) A test rocket is fired straight up from rest with a net acceleration of 20 m/s^2. After 4 seconds the motor turns off, but the rocket continues to coast upward. What maximum elevation does the rocket reach?

A) 487 m   B) 327 m   C) 320 m   D) 408 m   E) 160 m

Answer: A
Var: 1

18) A child standing on a bridge throws a rock straight down. The rock leaves the child's hand at t = 0. Which of the graphs shown here best represents the velocity of the stone as a function of time?

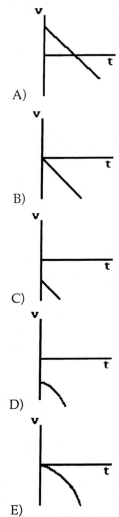

A)

B)

C)

D)

E)

Answer: C
Var: 1

19) A package is dropped from an airplane traveling horizontally at constant speed. Friction is negligible. One second later a second package is dropped. Which of the following is an accurate statement?

A) The distance between the two packages will remain constant as they fall.

B) The distance between the two packages will steadily increase as they fall.

C) The second package will hit the ground more than one second after the first hits.

D) The horizontal distance between the two packages will decrease as they fall.

E) The horizontal distance between the packages will increase as they fall.

Answer: B
Var: 1

20) A toy rocket is launched vertically from ground level (y = 0 m), at time t = 0.0 s. The rocket engine provides constant upward acceleration during the burn phase. At the instant of engine burnout, the rocket has risen to 65 m and acquired a velocity of 50 m/s. The rocket continues to rise in unpowered flight, reaches maximum height, and falls back to the ground. The time interval, during which the rocket engine provides upward acceleration, is closest to:

   A) 2.6 s   B) 2.9 s   C) 2.3 s   D) 2.1 s   E) 1.8 s

   Answer: A
   Var: 50+

21) A toy rocket is launched vertically from ground level (y = 0 m), at time t = 0.0 s. The rocket engine provides constant upward acceleration during the burn phase. At the instant of engine burnout, the rocket has risen to 84 m and acquired a velocity of 80 m/s. The rocket continues to rise in unpowered flight, reaches maximum height, and falls back to the ground. The upward acceleration of the rocket during the burn phase is closest to:

   A) 38 m/s^2 B) 37 m/s^2 C) 36 m/s^2 D) 35 m/s^2 E) 34 m/s^2

   Answer: A
   Var: 50+

22) A toy rocket is launched vertically from ground level (y = 0 m), at time t = 0.0 s. The rocket engine provides constant upward acceleration during the burn phase. At the instant of engine burnout, the rocket has risen to 68 m and acquired a velocity of 90 m/s. The rocket continues to rise in unpowered flight, reaches maximum height, and falls back to the ground. The maximum height reached by the rocket is closest to:

   A) 481 m   B) 457 m   C) 433 m   D) 505 m   E) 529 m

   Answer: A
   Var: 50+

23) A toy rocket is launched vertically from ground level (y = 0 m), at time t = 0.0 s. The rocket engine provides constant upward acceleration during the burn phase. At the instant of engine burnout, the rocket has risen to 49 m and acquired a velocity of 90 m/s. The rocket continues to rise in unpowered flight, reaches maximum height, and falls back to the ground. The time interval, during which the rocket is in unpowered flight, is closest to:

   A) 19 s   B) 17 s   C) 16 s   D) 15 s   E) 14 s

   Answer: A
   Var: 50+

24) A toy rocket is launched vertically from ground level (y = 0 m), at time t = 0.0 s. The rocket engine provides constant upward acceleration during the burn phase. At the instant of engine burnout, the rocket has risen to 58 m and acquired a velocity of 60 m/s. The rocket continues to rise in unpowered flight, reaches maximum height, and falls back to the ground. The speed of the rocket upon impact on the ground is closest to:

   A) 69 m/s   B) 63 m/s   C) 56 m/s   D) 77 m/s   E) 84 m/s

   Answer: A
   Var: 50+

Situation 2.1

A rock is projected upward from the surface of the moon, at time t = 0.0 s, with a velocity of 30 m/s. The acceleration due to gravity at the surface of the moon is 1.62 m/s².

25) In Situation 2.1, the time when the rock is ascending at a height of 180 m is closest to:

A) 8 s   B) 12 s   C) 17 s   D) 23 s   E) 30 s

Answer: A
Var: 1

26) In Situation 2.1, the height of the rock when it is descending with a velocity of 20 m/s is closest to:

A) 115 m   B) 125 m   C) 135 m   D) 145 m   E) 155 m

Answer: E
Var: 1

27) In Situation 2.1, the average velocity of the rock during the first 22.0 s of flight is closest to:

A) 10 m/s   B) 12 m/s   C) 14 m/s   D) 16 m/s   E) 18 m/s

Answer: B
Var: 1

Figure 2.2

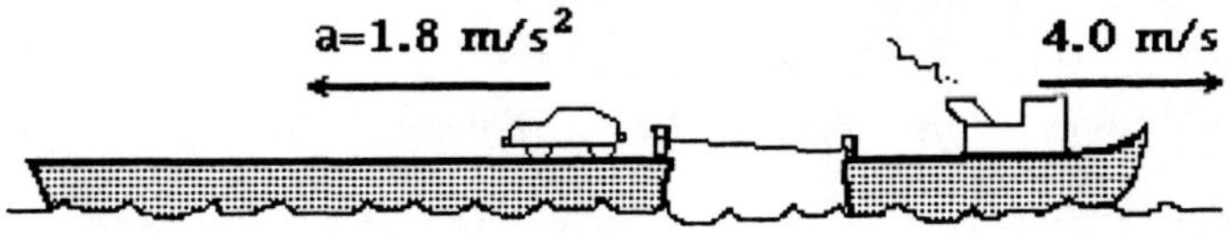

A flat–topped barge is being towed by a tugboat at a constant velocity of 4.0 m/s. A car, on the barge at the front end, starts from rest at time t = 0 s and moves towards the rear of the barge with a constant acceleration of 1.8 m/s². Consider all velocities in the direction of the towing as positive.

28) In Figure 2.2, the velocity of the car, relative to land, when it has moved 22 m on the barge is closest to:

A) +5 m/s   B) +9 m/s   C) –5 m/s   D) –9 m/s   E) –13 m/s

Answer: C
Var: 1

29) In Figure 2.2, at a certain instant, the velocity of the car relative to land is zero. The time at which this occurs is closest to:

A) 2.0 s   B) 2.2 s   C) 2.4 s   D) 2.6 s   E) 2.8 s

Answer: B
Var: 1

30) Two people are walking side by side at a speed of 1.2 m/s in an airport. They come to a moving sidewalk 120 m long, moving in their direction at 1.0 m/s. One person steps on the moving sidewalk and keeps walking at her normal speed, while her friend continues walking along the stationary walkway. How much sooner does the person on the moving sidewalk reach the end of the moving sidewalk than does her companion who is walking without this aid?

A) 44.6 s   B) 62.2 s   C) 55.6 s   D) 47.5 s   E) 45.5 s

Answer: E
Var: 1

Short Answer Questions

1) A soccer ball is released from rest at the top of a grassy incline. After 6.2 seconds, the ball travels 47 meters. One second later, the ball reaches the bottom of the incline.
a) What was the ball's acceleration? (Assume that the acceleration was constant.)
b) How long was the incline?

Answer: a) $2.4 \, m/s^2$
            b) 63 m
Var: 50+

2) A rock is thrown directly upward from the edge of the roof of a building that is 34.6 meters tall. The rock misses the building on its way down, and is observed to strike the ground 4.00 seconds after being thrown. Take the acceleration due to gravity to have magnitude $9.80 \, m/s^2$ and neglect any effects of air resistance. With what speed was the rock thrown?

Answer: 11.0 m/s
Var: 50+

3) The position of an object as a function of time is given by $x(t) = at^3 - bt^2 + ct - d$, where $a = 2.9 \, m/s^3$, $b = 5.6 \, m/s^2$, $c = 6.0 \, m/s$ and $d = 7.0 \, m$.
(a) Find the instantaneous acceleration at $t = 2.9 \, s$.
(b) Find the average acceleration over the first 2.9 seconds.

Answer: (a) $39 \, m/s^2$
            (b) $14 \, m/s^2$
Var: 50+

4) A helicopter is approaching the deck of a ship on which the pilot wishes to land. The ship is moving at 2.4 m/s west with respect to the water, which is flowing 5.6 m/s east. The helicopter is moving at 14 m/s west with respect to the air, and the wind is blowing 15 m/s east with respect to the ground. What is the speed and direction of the ship's motion relative to the helicopter?

Answer: 2.2 m/s east
Var: 50+

5) The acceleration of a rocket ship obeys the equation $a(t) = (3.4 \, \text{m}/\text{s}^3)t + 1.0 \, \text{m}/\text{s}^2$. Find the speed of the ship at $t = 5.9$ s if it is at rest at $t = 0$.

Answer: 65 m/s
Var: 50+

Chapter 3   Motion in Two or Three Dimensions

Multiple Choice Questions

1) Shown here are the velocity and acceleration vectors for an object in several different types of motion. In which case is the object slowing down and turning to the right?

A)

B)

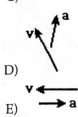

C)

D)

E)

Answer: B
Var: 1

2) Which of the following ideas is helpful in understanding projectile motion?

A) $v_x^2 + v_y^2$ = constant.

B) Acceleration is +g when the object is rising and –g when falling.

C) The velocity of the object is zero at the point of maximum elevation.

D) In the absence of friction the trajectory will depend on the object's mass as well as its initial velocity and launch angle.

E) The horizontal motion is independent of the vertical motion.

Answer: E
Var: 1

3) The x- and y-coordinates of a particle in motion, as functions of time t, are given by:
$$x = 7t^2 - 4t + 6 \qquad y = 3t^3 - 3t^2 - 12t - 5$$
The x- and y-components of the average velocity, in the interval from t = 0.0 s to t = 5.5 s, are closest to:

A) $v_x = 34.5$ m/s, $v_y = 62.25$ m/s

B) $v_x = 73$ m/s, $v_y = 232.75$ m/s

C) $v_x = 36$ m/s, $v_y = 61$ m/s

D) $v_x = -34.5$ m/s, $v_y = 62.25$ m/s

E) $v_x = -73$ m/s, $v_y = 227.25$ m/s

Answer: A
Var: 50+

4) The x- and y-coordinates of a particle in motion, as functions of time t, are given by:
$$x = 6t^2 - 5t + 6 \qquad y = 5t^3 - 3t^2 - 12t - 9$$
The y-component of the average acceleration in the interval from t = 0.0 s to t = 4.8 s is closest to:

A) 66 m/s^2 B) 138 m/s^2 C) 64 m/s^2 D) -138 m/s^2 E) -64 m/s^2

Answer: A
Var: 50+

5) The x- and y-coordinates of a particle in motion, as functions of time t, are given by:
$$x = 4t^2 - 3t + 6 \qquad y = 2t^3 - 3t^2 - 12t - 8$$
At the instant the x-component of velocity is equal to zero, the y-component of the acceleration is closest to:

A) -1.5 m/s^2 B) 3.0 m/s^2 C) -3.7 m/s^2 D) -10 m/s^2 E) -15 m/s^2

Answer: A
Var: 50+

6) The x- and y-coordinates of a particle in motion, as functions of time t, are given by:
$$x = 5t^2 - 3t + 6 \qquad y = 3t^3 - 3t^2 - 12t - 3$$
The smallest magnitude of the acceleration is closest to:

A) 10 m/s^2 B) 5 m/s^2 C) 12 m/s^2 D) 13 m/s^2 E) 15 m/s^2

Answer: A
Var: 50+

7) A girl shoots an arrow from the top of a cliff. The arrow is initially at a point 19 meters above the level field below. The arrow is shot at an angle of $30°$ above horizontal with a speed of 15.4 m/s. How far out from the base of the cliff will the arrow land?

A) 38.8 m   B) 17.8 m   C) 28.3 m   D) 27.8 m   E) 21.0 m

Answer: A
Var: 50+

Figure 3.1

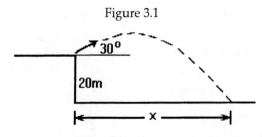

8) A projectile is fired from the origin (at y = 0 m) as shown in the figure. The initial velocity components are $V_{0x} = 940$ m/s and $V_{0y} = 96$ m/s. The projectile reaches maximum height at point P, then it falls and strikes the ground at point Q. In Figure 3.1, the y–coordinate of point P is closest to:

   A) 470 m   B) 45,550 m   C) 45,080 m   D) 940 m   E) 90,160 m

Answer: A
Var: 50+

9) A projectile is fired from the origin (at y = 0 m) as shown in the figure. The initial velocity components are $V_{0x} = 140$ m/s and $V_{0y} = 84$ m/s. The projectile reaches maximum height at point P, then it falls and strikes the ground at point Q. In Figure 3.1, the x–component of the velocity of the shell at point P is closest to:

   A) 140 m/s   B) 35 m/s   C) 70 m/s   D) 105 m/s   E) zero

Answer: A
Var: 50+

10) A projectile is fired from the origin (at y = 0 m) as shown in the figure. The initial velocity components are $V_{0x} = 670$ m/s and $V_{0y} = 20$ m/s. The projectile reaches maximum height at point P, then it falls and strikes the ground at point Q. In Figure 3.1, the y–component of the velocity of the shell of point P is closest to:

   A) zero   B) +20 m/s   C) +40 m/s   D) –20 m/s   E) –40 m/s

Answer: A
Var: 50+

11) A projectile is fired from the origin (at y = 0 m) as shown in the figure. The initial velocity components are $V_{0x} = 450$ m/s and $V_{0y} = 68$ m/s. The projectile reaches maximum height at point P, then it falls and strikes the ground at point Q. In Figure 3.1, the y–component of the acceleration of the shell at point P is closest to:

   A) zero   B) +5 m/s^2 C) +10 m/s^2 D) –5 m/s^2 E) –10 m/s^2

Answer: E
Var: 50+

Figure 3.2

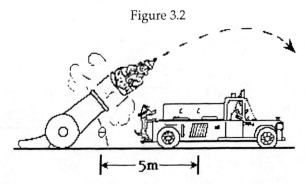

|←——5m——→|

12) In Figure 3.2, suppose the situation sketched. Once in a circus in Germany, I saw a stunt in which clown fired out of a cannon landed in a speeding toy fire engine which was racing away from him. The clown, of mass 60 kg, is fired with speed v_O at the same instant the fire engine starts to move directly away from him. The fire engine moves forward with a constant acceleration of $g/4$. The fire engine is 5 meters ahead of the clown when they start. Assume the clown lands at the same elevation from which he is fired. The cannon makes an angle Θ with horizontal, where $\sin\Theta = 4/5$ and $\cos\Theta = 3/5$. With what speed must the clown leave the cannon in order to land in the truck?

    A) 8.75 m/s   B) 6.50 m/s   C) 2.15 m/s   D) 4.43 m/s   E) 4.85 m/s

Answer: A
Var: 1

Figure 3.3

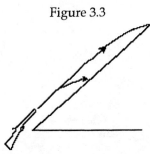

13) In Figure 3.3, two bullets are fired simultaneously uphill parallel to an inclined plane. The bullets have different masses and different initial velocities. Which will strike the plane first?

    A) The fastest one.

    B) The slowest one.

    C) The heaviest one.

    D) The lightest one.

    E) They strike the plane at the same time.

Answer: E
Var: 1

Figure 3.4

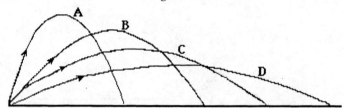

14) Shown in Figure 3.4 are the trajectories of four artillery shells. Each was fired with the same speed. Which was in the air the longest time?

A) A

B) B

C) C

D) D

E) All were in the air for the same time.

Answer: A
Var: 1

15) A projectile is fired at time t = 0.0s, from point 0 at the edge of a cliff, with initial velocity components of v_{ox} = 80 m/s and v_{oy} = 600 m/s. The projectile rises, then falls into the sea at point P. The time of flight of the projectile is 150.0 s.

Figure 3.5a

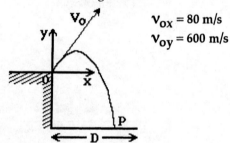

v_{ox} = 80 m/s
v_{oy} = 600 m/s

In Figure 3.5a, the magnitude of the velocity at time t = 15.0 s is closest to:

A) 460 m/s   B) 453 m/s   C) 455 m/s   D) 751 m/s   E) 747 m/s

Answer: A
Var: 50+

16) A projectile is fired at time t = 0.0s, from point 0 at the edge of a cliff, with initial velocity components of $v_{ox} = 40$ m/s and $v_{oy} = 800$ m/s. The projectile rises, then falls into the sea at point P. The time of flight of the projectile is 200.0 s.

Figure 3.5b

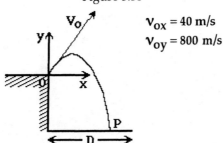

In Figure 3.5b, the x-coordinate of the projectile when its y-component of velocity equals 640 m/s is closest to:

A) 650 m   B) 620 m   C) 590 m   D) 560 m   E) 690 m

Answer: A
Var: 50+

17) A projectile is fired at time t = 0.0s, from point 0 at the edge of a cliff, with initial velocity components of $v_{ox} = 10$ m/s and $v_{oy} = 500$ m/s. The projectile rises, then falls into the sea at point P. The time of flight of the projectile is 125.0 s.

Figure 3.5c

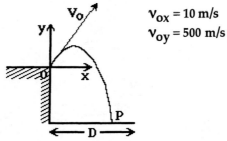

In Figure 3.5c, the height H of the cliff is closest to:

A) 14,060 m   B) 12,550 m   C) 15,550 m   D) 17,050 m   E) 18,550 m

Answer: A
Var: 50+

23

18) A projectile is fired at time t = 0.0s, from point 0 at the edge of a cliff, with initial velocity components of $v_{ox} = 80$ m/s and $v_{oy} = 300$ m/s. The projectile rises, then falls into the sea at point P. The time of flight of the projectile is 75.0 s.

Figure 3.5d

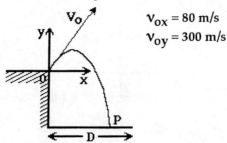

In Figure 3.5d, the horizontal distance D is closest to:

   A) 6000 m   B) 6720 m   C) 7440 m   D) 8160 m   E) 8880 m

Answer: A
Var: 50+

19) A projectile is fired at time t = 0.0s, from point 0 at the edge of a cliff, with initial velocity components of $v_{ox} = 70$ m/s and $v_{oy} = 500$ m/s. The projectile rises, then falls into the sea at point P. The time of flight of the projectile is 125.0 s.

Figure 3.5e

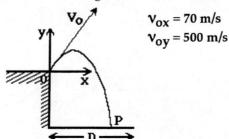

In Figure 3.5e, the y–coordinate of the projectile when its x–coordinate is 3500 m is closest to:

   A) +12,750 m   B) 430 m   C) –430 m   D) +7750 m   E) +3750 m

Answer: A
Var: 50+

20) A geosynchronous satellite travels around the earth once every 24 hours (thereby always staying above the same point on the earth's surface). Such satellites are at a distance of 4.23×10^7 m from the center of the earth. How fast is such a satellite moving with respect to the earth?

   A) 2.40×10^3 m/s

   B) 5.67×10^4 m/s

   C) 3.08×10^3 m/s

   D) 5.55×10^2 m/s

   E) 7.17×10^5 m/s

Answer: C
Var: 1

21) Which of the following is an accurate statement?

A) All points on a rotating disk experience the same radial acceleration.

B) All points on a rotating disk have the same angular velocity.

C) All points on a car tire have zero acceleration if the car is moving with constant linear velocity.

D) The vector sum of the tangential acceleration and the centripetal acceleration can be zero for a point on a rotating disk.

E) All points on a rotating disk have the same linear speed.

Answer: B
Var: 1

22) A long distance swimmer is able to swim through still water at 4 km/h. She wishes to try to swim from Port Angeles, WA due north to Victoria, B.C., a distance of 50 km. An ocean current flows through the Strait of Juan de Fuca from west to east at 3 km/h. In what direction should she swim to make the crossing along a straight line between the two cities?

A) $37°$ west of north

B) $37°$ east of north

C) $41°$ west of north

D) $41°$ east of north

E) $49°$ west of north

Answer: A
Var: 1

Figure 3.6

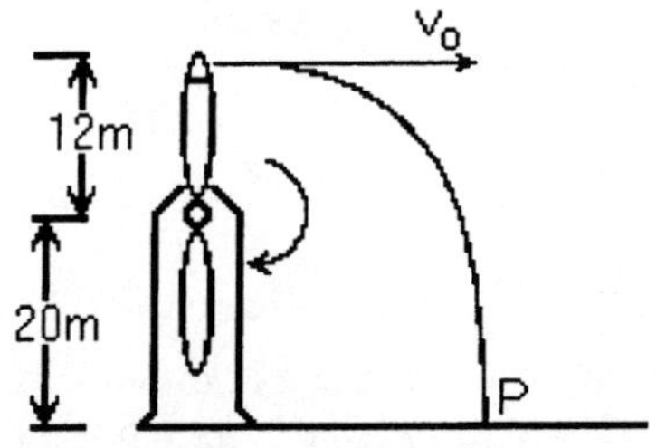

A wind farm generator uses a two-bladed propeller mounted on a pylon at a height of 20 m. The length of each propeller blade is 12 m. A tip of the propeller breaks off when the propeller is vertical. At that instant, the period of the motion of the propeller is 1.2 s. The fragment flies off horizontally, falls, and strikes the ground at P.

23) In Figure 3.6, the distance from the base of the pylon to the point where the fragment strikes the ground is closest to:

A) 120 m   B) 130 m   C) 140 m   D) 150 m   E) 160 m

Answer: E
Var: 1

24) In Figure 3.6, the angle with respect to the vertical at which the fragment strikes the ground is closest to:

A) $58°$ B) $63°$ C) $68°$ D) $73°$ E) $78°$

Answer: C
Var: 1

25) Two particles, A and B, are in uniform circular motion about a common center with the same radial acceleration. Particle A moves in a circle of 2.6 m radius with a periods of 6.7 s. Particle B moves with a speed of 7.5 m/s. The period of the motion of particle B is closest to:

A) 21 s B) 19 s C) 18 s D) 22 s E) 23 s

Answer: A
Var: 50+

26) Two particles, A and B, are in uniform circular motion about a common center. The acceleration of particle A is 4.0 times that of particle B. The period of particle B is 2.3 times the period of particle A. The ratio of the radius of the motion of particle A to that of particle B is closest to:

A) 0.76 B) 1.7 C) 3.0 D) 0.58 E) 9

Answer: A
Var: 50+

Short Answer Questions

1) The second hand of a clock is 16.0 cm long (from the center of the clock face to the tip of the second hand). What is the magnitude of the average velocity (not speed) of the tip of the second hand during a time interval of 27 seconds?

Answer: 1.17 cm/s
Var: 1

2) The horizontal coordinates of a Frisbee in a strong wind are given by
$x = -12t + 4t^2$, $y = 10t - 3t^2$, where x and y are in meters, and t is measured in seconds. (a) What is the acceleration of the Frisbee? Give a magnitude and a direction, measuring angles from the positive x–direction. (b) What is the magnitude of the velocity at $t = 2$, to the nearest m/s?

Answer: (a) $10 \, \text{m/s}^2$, $323°$
       (b) 4 m/s
Var: 1

3) A projectile returns to its original height after 4.08 seconds, during which time it travels 76.2 meters horizontally. If air resistance can be neglected, what was the projectile's initial speed? (Use $g = 9.80 \, \text{m/s}^2$)

Answer: 27.4 m/s
Var: 1

4) A rock is thrown from the roof of a building, with an initial velocity of 10.0 m/s at an angle of 30.0° above the horizontal. The rock is observed to strike the ground 43.0 m from the base of the building. What is the height of the building?

Answer: 96.0 meters
Var: 1

5) A child sits on a merry-go-round, 1.5 meters from the center. The merry-go-round is turning at a constant rate, and the child is observed to have a radial acceleration of 2.3 m/s². How long does it take for the merry-go-round to make one revolution?

Answer: 5.1 seconds
Var: 1

6) The compass of an aircraft indicates that it is headed due east, and its airspeed indicator shows that it is moving through the air at 150 km/hr. After flying for 2 hours the aircraft is 350 km east and 74 km south of its starting point. What is the magnitude and direction of the wind velocity?

Answer: magnitude: 45 km/hr
              direction: 56° south of east
Var: 1

Chapter 4   Newton's Laws of Motion

Multiple Choice Questions

1) A force of 1 Newton will cause a mass of 1 kg to have an acceleration of 1 m/s². Thus it follows that a force of 7 Newtons applied to a mass of 7 kg will cause it to acquire an acceleration of

    A) 1 m/s²   B) 0.14 m/s²   C) 8 m/s²   D) 7 m/s²   E) 49 m/s²

Answer: A
Var: 8

2) A plastic ball in a liquid is acted upon by its weight and by a buoyant force. The weight of the ball is 2.7 N. The buoyant force has a magnitude of 7.1 N and acts vertically upward. An external force acting on the ball maintains it in a state of rest. The external force, including direction, is closest to:

    A) 4.4 N, downward

    B) 2.7 N, upward

    C) 7.1 N, upward

    D) 4.4 N, upward

    E) 7.1 N, downward

Answer: A
Var: 50+

3) A plastic ball in a liquid is acted upon by its weight and by a buoyant force. The weight of the ball is 3.2 N. The buoyant force has a magnitude of 5.0 N and acts vertically upward. At a given instant, the ball is released from rest. The acceleration of the ball at that instant, including direction, is closest to:

    A) 5.5 m/s², upward

    B) 2.8 m/s², upward

    C) zero

    D) 2.8 m/s², downward

    E) 5.5 m/s², downward

Answer: A
Var: 50+

4) A plastic ball in a liquid is acted upon by its weight and by a buoyant force. The weight of the ball is 2.2 N. The buoyant force has a magnitude of 5.8 N and acts vertically upward. At a given instant, the ball has zero velocity. At that instant, an external force acting on the ball imparts an acceleration of 3.0 m/s^2 in the downward direction of the ball. The external force, including direction, is closest to:

A) 4.3 N, downward

B) 3.6 N, upward

C) 3.6 N, downward

D) 10 N, upward

E) 10 N, downward

Answer: A
Var: 50+

5) A plastic ball in a liquid is acted upon by its weight and by a buoyant force. The weight of the ball is 6.4 N. The buoyant force has a magnitude of 7.1 N and acts vertically upward. After release from rest, the velocity of the ball increases and eventually reaches constant velocity. In addition to the weight and buoyant force, a drag force is present when the ball moves through the liquid. When constant velocity has been achieved, the drag force, including direction, is closest to:

A) 0.70 N, downward

B) 6.4 N, upward

C) 7.1 N, upward

D) 0.70 N, upward

E) 7.1 N, downward

Answer: A
Var: 50+

6) Consider what happens when you jump up in the air. Which of the following is the most accurate statement?

A) It is the upward force exerted by the ground that pushes you up, but this force can never exceed your weight.

B) You are able to spring up because the earth exerts a force upward on you which is stronger than the downward force you exert on the earth.

C) Since the ground is stationary, it cannot exert the upward force necessary to propel you into the air. Instead, it is the internal forces of your muscles acting on your body itself which propels the body into the air.

D) When you push down on the earth with a force greater than your weight, the earth will push back with the same magnitude force and thus propel you into the air.

E) When you jump up the earth exerts a force F_1 on you and you exert a force F_2 on the earth. You go up because $F_1 > F_2$, and this is so because F_1 is to F_2 as the earth's mass is to your mass.

Answer: D
Var: 1

29

Figure 4.1

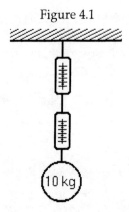

7) In Figure 4.1, a 10 kg mass is suspended from two spring scales, each of which has negligible weight. Thus

A) Each scale will read 5 kg.

B) The top scale will read zero, the lower scale will read 10 kg.

C) The lower scale will read zero, the top scale will read 10 kg.

D) Each scale will show a reading between one and 10 kg, such that the sum of the two is 10 kg. However, exact readings cannot be determined without more information.

E) None of these is true.

Answer: E
Var: 1

8) If you were to move into outer space far from any stellar objects,

A) your mass would change, but your weight would not change.

B) your weight would change, but your mass would not change.

C) both your weight and mass would change.

D) neither your weight nor your mass would change.

E) None of these is true.

Answer: B
Var: 1

9) Two football teams, the Raiders and the Jets, are engaged in a tug-of-war. The Raiders are pulling with a force of 5,000 N. Which of the following is an accurate statement?

A) The tension in the rope depends on whether or not the teams are in equilibrium.

B) The Jets are pulling with a force of more than 5,000 N if they are winning, i.e. pulling the Raiders in the direction toward the Jets.

C) The Jets are pulling with a force of 5,000 N.

D) The tension in the rope is 10,000 N.

E) None of these statements is true.

Answer: C
Var: 1

10) A block is on a frictionless table, on earth. The block accelerates at 5.3 m/s^2 when a 80 N horizontal force is applied to it. The block and table are set up on the moon. The acceleration due to gravity at the surface of the moon is 1.62 m/s^2. The weight of the block on the moon is closest to:

A) 24 N   B) 21 N   C) 18 N   D) 15 N   E) 12 N

Answer: A
Var: 50+

11) A block is on a frictionless table, on earth. The block accelerates at 8.4 m/s^2 when a 90 N horizontal force is applied to it. The block and table are set up on the moon. The acceleration due to gravity at the surface of the moon is 1.62 m/s^2. A horizontal force of 45 N is applied to the block when it is on the moon. The acceleration imparted to the block is closest to:

A) 4.2 m/s^2 B) 3.8 m/s^2 C) 4.6 m/s^2 D) 5.0 m/s^2 E) 5.5 m/s^2

Answer: A
Var: 50+

12) A block is on a frictionless table, on earth. The block accelerates at 3.0 m/s^2 when a 90 N horizontal force is applied to it. The block and table are set up on the moon. The acceleration due to gravity at the surface of the moon is 1.62 m/s^2. A horizontal force, equal in magnitude to the weight of the block on earth, is applied to the block when it is on the moon. The acceleration imparted to the block is closest to:

A) 10 m/s^2 B) 4 m/s^2 C) 6 m/s^2 D) 8 m/s^2 E) 2 m/s^2

Answer: A
Var: 50+

Figure 4.2

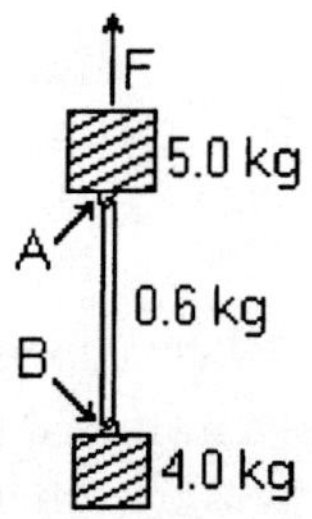

A 5.0 kg block and a 4.0 kg block are connected by a 0.6 kg rod. The links between the blocks and the rod are denoted by A and B. A force F is applied to the upper block.

13) In Figure 4.2, the blocks and rod assembly moves downward at constant velocity. The applied force F is closest to:

A) 88 N   B) 90 N   C) 92 N   D) 94 N   E) 96 N

Answer: D
Var: 1

14) In Figure 4.2, the blocks and rod assembly moves upward at constant velocity. The force in link A is closest to:

A) 39 N   B) 41 N   C) 43 N   D) 45 N   E) 47 N

Answer: D
Var: 1

15) In Figure 4.2, the applied force F equals 150 N. The force in link B is closest to:

A) 54 N   B) 56 N   C) 58 N   D) 60 N   E) 62 N

Answer: E
Var: 1

16) In Figure 4.2, the force in link B is 40 N. The acceleration of the blocks and rod assembly, including direction, is closest to:

A) zero

B) 1.2 m/s^2, upward

C) 2.4 m/s^2, upward

D) 1.2 m/s^2, downward

E) 2.4 m/s^2, downward

Answer: A
Var: 1

17) In Figure 4.2, the blocks and rod assembly accelerates upward at 2.0 m/s^2. The force in link A exceeds the force in link B by an amount that is closest to:

A) 6 N   B) 7 N   C) 8 N   D) 9 N   E) 10 N

Answer: B
Var: 1

18) A man pushes against a rigid, immovable wall. Which of the following is the most accurate statement concerning this situation?

A) The man can never exert a force on the wall which exceeds his weight.

B) If the man pushes on the wall with a force of 200 N, we can be sure that the wall is pushing back with a force of exactly 200 N on him.

C) Since the wall cannot move, it cannot exert any force on the man.

D) The man cannot be in equilibrium since he is exerting a net force on the wall.

E) The friction force on the man's feet is directed to the left.

Answer: B
Var: 1

19) Some baseball players are said to be able to throw a fast ball at 91 mph. How high would such a ball rise if thrown straight up in the absence of air friction?

A) 84 m   B) 422 m   C) 99 m   D) 116 m   E) 66 m

Answer: A
Var: 20

Figure 4.3

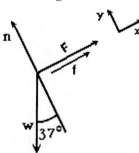

20) A box with weight w = 770 N is on a rough surface, inclined at an angle of 37 degrees. The box is kept from sliding down (in equilibrium) by means of an external force F. The other forces acting on the box are the normal and friction forces, denoted by n and f. A force diagram, showing the four forces which act on the box, is shown in Figure 4.3. The magnitude of f is 140 N. The magnitude of the normal force N is closest to:

A) 615 N   B) 578 N   C) 539 N   D) 500 N   E) 462 N

Answer: A
Var: 50+

21) A box with weight w = 930 N is on a rough surface, inclined at an angle of 37 degrees. The box is kept from sliding down (in equilibrium) by means of an external force F. The other forces acting on the box are the normal and friction forces, denoted by n and f. A force diagram, showing the four forces which act on the box, is shown in Figure 4.3. The magnitude of f is 190 N. The magnitude of the external force F is closest to:

A) 368 N   B) 414 N   C) 461 N   D) 508 N   E) 554 N

Answer: A
Var: 50+

22) A box with weight w = 610 N is on a rough surface, inclined at an angle of 37 degrees. The box is kept from sliding down (in equilibrium) by means of an external force F. The other forces acting on the box are the normal and friction forces, denoted by n and f. A force diagram, showing the four forces which act on the box, is shown in Figure 4.3. The magnitude of f is 210 N. The external force F is removed and the box accelerates. The magnitudes of the other forces are unchanged. The acceleration of the box is closest to:

A) 2.5 m/s^2 B) 3.5 m/s^2 C) 4.5 m/s^2 D) 1.5 m/s^2 E) 0.94 m/s^2

Answer: A
Var: 50+

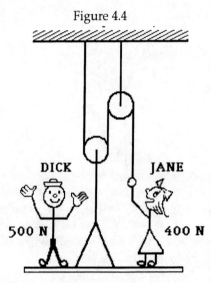

Figure 4.4

23) Dick and Jane stand on a platform of negligible weight, as shown in Figure 4.4. Dick weighs 500 N and Jane weighs 400 N. Jane is supporting some of her weight on the end of the rope she is holding. What is the downward force she is exerting on the platform?

    A) 0   B) 50 N   C) 100 N   D) 240 N   E) 300 N

Answer: C
Var: 1

24) Bumpers on cars are not of much use in a collision. To see why, calculate the average force a bumper would have to exert if it brought a 1200 kg car (a so-called "compact" model) to a rest in 15 cm when the car had an initial speed of 2 m/s (about 4.5 mph). Bumpers are built with springs which compress to provide a stopping force without (hopefully) denting the metal.

    A) 1.8×10^4 N

    B) 1.6×10^4 N

    C) 5.4×10^4 N

    D) 6.5×10^5 N

    E) 3.2×10^4 N

Answer: B
Var: 1

Figure 4.5

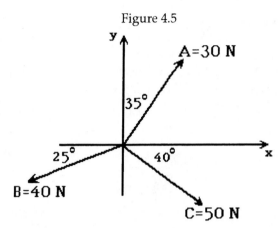

Three forces A, B, and C act on a body as shown. A fourth force F is required to keep the body in equilibrium.

25) In Figure 4.5, the x–component of force F is closest to:

    A) +19 N   B) +28 N   C) +32 N   D) –28 N   E) –32 N

Answer: C
Var: 1

26) In Figure 4.5, the y–component of force F is closest to:

    A) +24 N   B) +28 N   C) +32 N   D) –28 N   E) –32 N

Answer: A
Var: 1

Figure 4.6

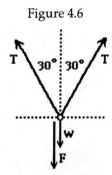

27) A 9.7 kg box is held at rest by two ropes that form $30°$ angles with the vertical. An external force F acts vertically downward on the box. The force exerted by each of the two ropes is denoted by T. A force diagram, showing the four forces that act on the box in equilibrium, is shown in Figure 4.6. The magnitude of force F is 550 N. The magnitude of force T is closest to:

    A) 373 N   B) 324 N   C) 259 N   D) 518 N   E) 647 N

Answer: A
Var: 50+

28) A 4.2 kg box is held at rest by two ropes that form $30°$ angles with the vertical. An external force F acts vertically downward on the box. The force exerted by each of the two ropes is denoted by T. A force diagram, showing the four forces that act on the box in equilibrium, is shown in Figure 4.6. The force F is adjusted so that the magnitude of force T is equal to the weight w. The magnitude of force F, for which this occurs, is closest to:

   A) 30 N   B) 32 N   C) 33 N   D) 34 N   E) 35 N

Answer: A
Var: 50+

Figure 4.7

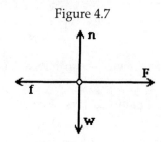

29) A box with weight 67 N is on a rough horizontal surface. An external force F is applied horizontally to the box. A normal force and a friction force are also present, denoted by n and f. A force diagram, showing the four forces that act on the box, is shown in Figure 4.7. When force F equals 3.0 N, the box is in motion at constant velocity. When force F equals 3.9 N, the acceleration of the box is closest to:

   A) 0.13 m/s^2 B) 0.16 m/s^2 C) 0.18 m/s^2 D) 0.20 m/s^2 E) 0.22 m/s^2

Answer: A
Var: 50+

30) A box with weight 23 N is on a rough horizontal surface. An external force F is applied horizontally to the box. A normal force and a friction force are also present, denoted by n and f. A force diagram, showing the four forces that act on the box, is shown in Figure 4.7. When force F equals 2.3 N, the box is in motion at constant velocity. The box decelerates when force F is removed. The magnitude of the acceleration of the box is closest to:

   A) 0.98 m/s^2 B) 0.75 m/s^2 C) 0.50 m/s^2 D) 0.25 m/s^2 E) zero

Answer: A
Var: 50+

Short Answer Questions

Figure 4.8

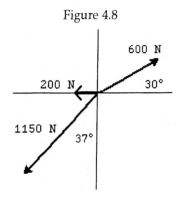

1) In Figure 4.8, the three forces shown on the diagram act on an object at the origin. Find the magnitude and direction of the resultant of these forces. Express the direction by giving the angle that the resultant force makes with the positive x–axis, and take counterclockwise angles to be positive.

Answer: magnitude: R = 720 N
direction: $\Phi = 239°$

Var: 1

Figure 4.9

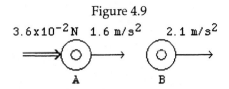

2) In Figure 4.9, two small objects (magnets, for instance) of the same mass exert forces on each other of the magnitude F. When an object A is subjected to an external force of 2.1×10^{-2} N, A accelerates at 1.6 m/s^2 and B accelerates 2.1 m/s^2, as shown. Find F. Neglect other forces, and assume that the accelerations are parallel.

Answer: 2.0×10^{-2} N
Var: 1

3) A box of mass 38 kg is at rest on a horizontal frictionless surface. A constant horizontal force F then acts on the box, and accelerates it to the right. It is observed that it takes the box 2.7 seconds to travel 39 meters. What is the magnitude of the force?

Answer: 410 N
Var: 50+

4) A locomotive is pulling 19 freight cars, each of which is loaded with roughly the same weight. The mass of each can be taken to be 37,000 kg. If the train is accelerating at 0.37 m/s^2 on a level track, what is the tension in the coupling between the second and third cars? The car nearest the locomotive is counted as the first.

Answer: 230,000 N
Var: 50+

37

Figure 4.10

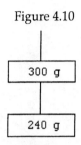

5) In Figure 4.10, two blocks are connected by a string, as shown, and the upper block is pulled upward by a different string. The masses of the upper and lower blocks are 300 grams and 240 grams respectively. The string between the blocks will break if its tension exceeds 3.6 newtons, and the string which pulls the combination upward will break if its tension exceeds 7.8 newtons.

a) What is the largest upward acceleration that the blocks can be given without either string breaking? (Take $g = 9.8 \text{ m/s}^2$.)

b) If the upward acceleration is slightly higher than this, which string breaks?

Answer: a) 4.6m/S^2

b) upper string.

Var: 1

Chapter 5   Applying Newton's Laws

Multiple Choice Questions

Figure 5.1

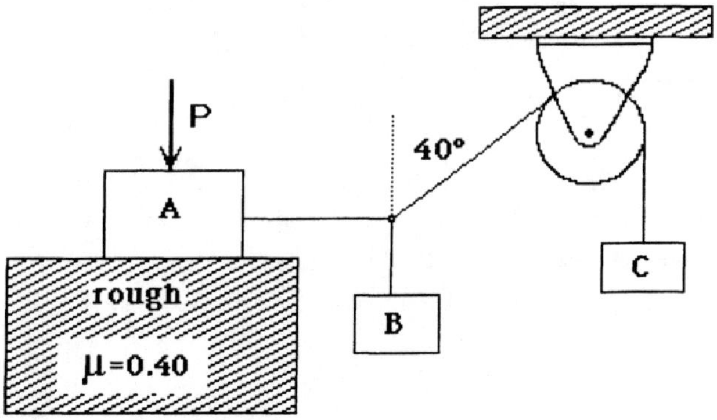

1) A system of blocks and a frictionless pulley is shown in Figure 5.1. Block A has a mass of 8.0 kg and is on a rough surface ($\mu = 0.40$). Block C has a mass of 5.0 kg. An external force P = 14.0 N, applied vertically to block A, maintains the system in static equilibrium as shown in Figure 5.1. The mass of block B is closest to:

   A) 3.8 kg   B) 3.5 kg   C) 3.2 kg   D) 2.9 kg   E) 2.6 kg

Answer: A
Var: 50+

2) A system of blocks and a frictionless pulley is shown in Figure 5.1. Block A has a mass of 8.0 kg and is on a rough surface ($\mu = 0.40$). Block C has a mass of 6.0 kg. An external force P = 25.0 N, applied vertically to block A, maintains the system in static equilibrium as shown in Figure 5.1. The frictional force on block A is closest to:

   A) 38 N   B) 41 N   C) 45 N   D) 34 N   E) 31 N

Answer: A
Var: 50+

3) A system of blocks and a frictionless pulley is shown in Figure 5.1. Block A has a mass of 7.0 kg and is on a rough surface ($\mu = 0.40$). Block C has a mass of 2.0 kg. An external force P = 1.0 N, applied vertically to block A, maintains the system in static equilibrium as shown in Figure 5.1. The external 1.0 N is removed. The masses of blocks B and C are adjusted, so that the system remains at rest as shown, but is on the verge of moving. The mass of block A is unchanged. The tensions in the two vertical ropes are closest to:

   A) 33 N and 43 N

   B) 23 N and 36 N

   C) 33 N and 36 N

   D) 36 N and 43 N

   E) 36 N and 46 N

Answer: A
Var: 50+

Figure 5.2

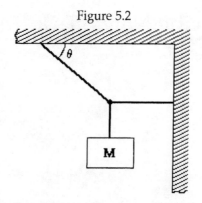

4) In Figure 5.2, a block of mass M hangs in equilibrium. The rope which is fastened to the wall is horizontal and has a tension of 27 N. The rope which is fastened to the ceiling has a tension of 83 N, and makes an angle Θ with the ceiling. The angle Θ is

    A) 71°   B) 19°   C) 18°   D) 55°   E) 45°

Answer: A
Var: 50+

Figure 5.3

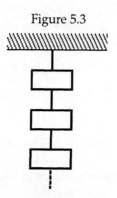

5) In Figure 5.3, a certain type of string will break if the tension in the string exceeds 500 N. A number of 3–kg weights are hung one below the other from a hook in the ceiling using this string. The number of weights which causes the string to break and the string segment which will break are as follows:

    A) When the 18th weight is added, the top string segment will break.

    B) Each segment has a tension of 29.4 N, and there is no limit to the number of weights which can be suspended.

    C) When the 18th weight is added, the bottom string segment will break.

    D) When the 18th weight is added, all string segments will break.

    E) When the 167th weight is added, all string segments will break.

Answer: A
Var: 23

Figure 5.4

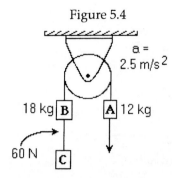

Three blocks, connecting ropes, and a light frictionless pulley comprise a system, as shown. An external force P is applied downward on block A. The system accelerates at the rate of 2.5 m/s². The tension in the rope connecting block B and block C equals 60 N.

6) In Figure 5.4, the external force P is closest to:

   A) 170 N   B) 190 N   C) 210 N   D) 230 N   E) 250 N

Answer: B
Var: 1

7) In Figure 5.4, the tension in the rope connecting block A and block B is closest to:

   A) 240 N   B) 260 N   C) 280 N   D) 300 N   E) 320 N

Answer: C
Var: 1

8) In Figure 5.4, the mass of block C is closest to:

   A) 5 kg   B) 7 kg   C) 9 kg   D) 11 kg   E) 13 kg

Answer: A
Var: 1

Figure 5.5

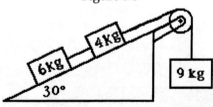

A system comprising blocks, a light frictionless pulley, a frictionless incline, and connecting ropes is shown. The 9 kg block accelerates downward when the system is released from rest.

9) In Figure 5.5, the acceleration of the system is closest to:

   A) 1.5 m/s²   B) 1.7 m/s²   C) 1.9 m/s²   D) 2.1 m/s²   E) 2.3 m/s²

Answer: D
Var: 1

10) In Figure 5.5, the tension in the rope connecting the 6 kg block and the 4 kg block is closest to:

   A) 30 N   B) 33 N   C) 36 N   D) 39 N   E) 42 N

Answer: E
Var: 1

Figure 5.6

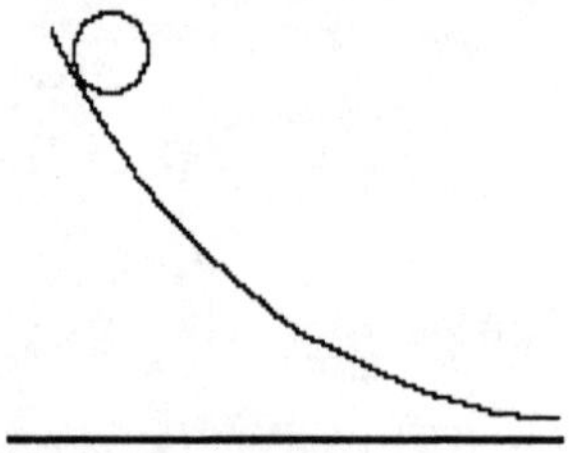

11) In Figure 5.6, as the ball shown rolls down the hill,

    A) its speed increases and its acceleration decreases.

    B) its speed decreases and its acceleration increases.

    C) both its speed and its acceleration increase.

    D) both speed and acceleration remain constant.

    E) both speed and acceleration decrease.

Answer: A
Var: 1

12) A bunch of bananas hangs from the end of a rope that passes over a light, frictionless pulley. A monkey of mass equal to the mass of the bananas hangs from the other end of the rope. The monkey and the bananas are initially balanced and at rest. Now the monkey starts to climb up the rope, moving away from the ground with speed v. What happens to the bananas?

    A) They move downward at speed v.

    B) They remain stationary.

    C) They move up at speed 1/2 v.

    D) They move up at speed v.

    E) They move up at speed 2 v.

Answer: D
Var: 1

Figure 5.7

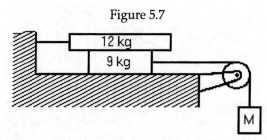

A system comprising blocks, a light frictionless pulley, and connecting ropes is shown. The 9 kg block is on a smooth horizontal table ($\mu = 0$). The surfaces of the 12 kg block are rough, with $\mu = 0.30$.

13) In Figure 5.7, the mass M is set so that it descends at constant velocity when released. The mass M is closest to:

    A) 2.4 kg   B) 2.7 kg   C) 3.0 kg   D) 3.3 kg   E) 3.6 kg

Answer: E
Var: 1

14) In Figure 5.7, mass M is set at 5.0 kg. It accelerates downward when it is released. The acceleration of mass M is closest to:

   A) 1.0 m/s^2 B) 1.2 m/s^2 C) 1.4 m/s^2 D) 1.6 m/s^2 E) 1.8 m/s^2

   Answer: A
   Var: 1

Figure 5.8

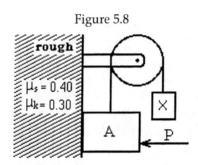

15) Block A of mass 6 kg and block X are attached to a rope which passes over a pulley. A 50 N force is applied horizontally to block A, keeping it in contact with a rough vertical face. The coefficients of static and kinetic friction are $\mu_s = 0.40$ and $\mu_k = 0.30$. The pulley is light and frictionless. In Figure 5.8, the mass of block X is set so that block A is on the verge of slipping upward. The mass of block X is closest to:

   A) 8.0 kg   B) 8.5 kg   C) 7.6 kg   D) 7.2 kg   E) 6.8 kg

   Answer: A
   Var: 50+

16) Block A of mass 3 kg and block X are attached to a rope which passes over a pulley. A 50 N force is applied horizontally to block A, keeping it in contact with a rough vertical face. The coefficients of static and kinetic friction are $\mu_s = 0.40$ and $\mu_k = 0.30$. The pulley is light and frictionless. In Figure 5.8, the mass of block X is set at 6.9 kg. The system is at rest. The friction force, including direction, on the 5 kg block is closest to:

   A) 38 N, downward

   B) 38 N, upward

   C) 19 N, downward

   D) 19 N, upward

   E) zero

   Answer: A
   Var: 50+

17) Block A of mass 3 kg and block X are attached to a rope which passes over a pulley. A 20 N force is applied horizontally to block A, keeping it in contact with a rough vertical face. The coefficients of static and kinetic friction are $\mu_s = 0.40$ and $\mu_k = 0.30$. The pulley is light and frictionless. In Figure 5.8, the mass of block X is set so that block A descends at constant velocity when it is set into motion. The mass of block X is closest to:

   A) 2.4 kg   B) 2.7 kg   C) 3.0 kg   D) 3.3 kg   E) 3.6 kg

   Answer: A
   Var: 50+

18) Block A of mass 1 kg and block X are attached to a rope which passes over a pulley. A 50 N force is applied horizontally to block A, keeping it in contact with a rough vertical face. The coefficients of static and kinetic friction are $\mu_s = 0.40$ and $\mu_k = 0.30$. The pulley is light and frictionless. In Figure 5.8, the mass of block X is set so that block A moves upward with an acceleration of 1.6 m/s^2. The mass of block X is closest to:

A) 3.2 kg   B) 3.0 kg   C) 2.8 kg   D) 2.6 kg   E) 2.4 kg

Answer: A
Var: 50+

19) Block A of mass 1 kg and block X are attached to a rope which passes over a pulley. A 60 N force is applied horizontally to block A, keeping it in contact with a rough vertical face. The coefficients of static and kinetic friction are $\mu_s = 0.40$ and $\mu_k = 0.30$. The pulley is light and frictionless. In Figure 5.8, the mass of block X is set at 0.80 kg. An external force pulls down on block X so that it descends with an acceleration of 2.0 m/s^2. The external force is closest to:

A) 24 N   B) 26 N   C) 22 N   D) 19 N   E) 17 N

Answer: A
Var: 50+

Figure 5.9

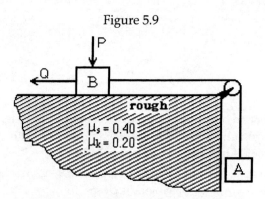

20) Blocks A and B of masses 13 kg, and 14 kg, respectively, are connected by a rope, which passes over a light frictionless pulley, as shown. The horizontal surface is rough. The coefficients of static and kinetic friction are 0.40 and 0.20, respectively. External forces P and Q act on block B, as shown. In Figure 5.9, force P equals 56 N. The maximum value of force Q, for which the system remains at rest is closest to:

A) 200 N   B) 170 N   C) 140 N   D) 160 N   E) 180 N

Answer: A
Var: 50+

21) Blocks A and B of masses 16 kg, and 13 kg, respectively, are connected by a rope, which passes over a light frictionless pulley, as shown. The horizontal surface is rough. The coefficients of static and kinetic friction are 0.40 and 0.20, respectively. External forces P and Q act on block B, as shown. In Figure 5.9, force P equals 52 N. The force for which the block descends at constant speed is closest to:

A) 120 N   B) 130 N   C) 140 N   D) 160 N   E) 85 N

Answer: A
Var: 50+

44

22) Blocks A and B of masses 10 kg, and 19 kg, respectively, are connected by a rope, which passes over a light frictionless pulley, as shown. The horizontal surface is rough. The coefficients of static and kinetic friction are 0.40 and 0.20, respectively. External forces P and Q act on block B, as shown. In Figure 5.9, force P equals 76 N. The force Q, for which the frictional force on block B equals zero, is closest to:

    A) 98 N   B) 39 N   C) 20 N   D) 190 N   E) 140 N

Answer: A
Var: 50+

23) Blocks A and B of masses 17 kg, and 10 kg, respectively, are connected by a rope, which passes over a light frictionless pulley, as shown. The horizontal surface is rough. The coefficients of static and kinetic friction are 0.40 and 0.20, respectively. External forces P and Q act on block B, as shown. In Figure 5.9, force Q equals zero. The force P, for which block B is on the verge of moving, is closest to:

    A) 320 N   B) 740 N   C) 460 N   D) 1600 N   E) 570 N

Answer: A
Var: 50+

24) Blocks A and B of masses 0 kg, and 16 kg, respectively, are connected by a rope, which passes over a light frictionless pulley, as shown. The horizontal surface is rough. The coefficients of static and kinetic friction are 0.40 and 0.20, respectively. External forces P and Q act on block B, as shown. In Figure 5.9, the system accelerates when forces P and Q are both equal to zero. The frictional force on block B is closest to:

    A) 31 N   B) 63 N   C) 94 N   D) 130 N   E) 160 N

Answer: A
Var: 15

25) An object of weight W falls from rest subject to a frictional drag force bv^2. What maximum ("terminal") velocity will it approach if $W = 4$ N and $b = 3$ N$\cdot$s^2/m?

    A) 1.78 m/s   B) 3.42 m/s   C) 1.15 m/s   D) 2.25 m/s   E) 0.75 m/s

Answer: C
Var: 1

26) A person is dragging a packing crate of mass 100 kg across a rough floor where the coefficient of friction is 0.40. He exerts a force F sufficient to give the crate a positive acceleration. At what angle above horizontal should his pulling force be directed in order to achieve the maximum acceleration?

    A) 21.8°   B) 27.7°   C) 30°   D) 34.5°   E) 45°

Answer: A
Var: 1

Figure 5.10

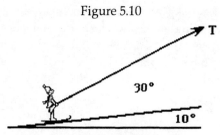

27) In Figure 5.10, a T-bar ski tow pulls a skier up a hill inclined at $10°$ above horizontal. The skier starts from rest and is pulled by a cable which exerts a tension T at an angle of $30°$ above the surface of the hill. The mass of the skier is 60 kg and the effective coefficient of friction between the skis and the snow is 0.10. What is the maximum tension in the cable if the starting acceleration is not to exceed 0.4 g?

    A) 246 N   B) 366 N   C) 431 N   D) 187 N   E) 535 N

Answer: C
Var: 1

28) A packing crate rests on a horizontal surface. It is acted on by three horizontal forces: 600 N to the left, 200 N to the right, and friction. The weight of the crate is 400 N. If the 600 N force is removed, the resultant force acting on the block is

    A) 200 N to the right.

    B) zero.

    C) 200 N to the left.

    D) 400 N to the left.

    E) impossible to determine from the information given.

Answer: B
Var: 1

Figure 5.11

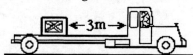

29) In Figure 5.11, a flatbed truck of mass 2000 kg traveling 20 m/s (about 45 MPH) carries a load of mass 500 kg positioned 3 meters behind the cab. The load is kept on the truck by friction, and the coefficient of friction between the load and the bed of the truck is 0.5. What is the shortest distance in which the truck can stop without having the load slide forward enough to hit the cab? (Note that the load can slide forward 3 meters before it hits the cab.)

    A) 48.7 m   B) 42.0 m   C) 17.5 m   D) 37.8 m   E) 26.2 m

Answer: D
Var: 1

30) A roadway is designed for traffic moving at a speed of 27 m/s. A curved section of the roadway is a circular arc of 610 m radius. The roadway is banked--so that a vehicle can go around the curve--with the lateral friction forces equal to zero. The angle at which the roadway is banked is closest to:

A) 7°　　　　　　B) 9°　　　　　　C) 5°　　　　　　D) 3°　　　　　　E) 1°

Answer: A
Var: 50+

31) A roadway is designed for traffic moving at a speed of 12 m/s. A curved section of the roadway is a circular arc of 440 m radius. The curved section is temporarily replaced with an unbanked roadway of the same radius. The coefficient of friction of this roadway is 0.40. The maximum safe driving speed for this unbanked, curved section is closest to:

A) 42 m/s　　　B) 40 m/s　　　C) 38 m/s　　　D) 36 m/s　　　E) 34 m/s

Answer: A
Var: 50+

32) A 50 kg crate is on a rough surface, inclined at 30 degrees from the horizontal. The coefficient of friction is 0.25. A horizontal force of 1000 N is applied to the crate, pushing it up the incline. The acceleration of the crate is closest to:

A) 7.8 m/s^2　　　B) 9.4 m/s^2　　　C) 11 m/s^2　　　D) 12 m/s^2　　　E) 4.1 m/s^2

Answer: A
Var: 50+

33) A ball of mass 4.0 kg is suspended by two wires from a horizontal arm, which is attached to a vertical shaft, as shown in Figure 5.12. The shaft is in uniform rotation about its axis such that the linear speed of the ball equals 2.7 m/s. The tension in wire 1 is closest to:

A) 12 N　　　　B) 15 N　　　　C) 9.0 N　　　　D) 6.0 N　　　　E) 3.0 N

Answer: A
Var: 50+

Figure 5.12

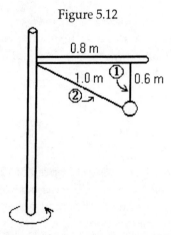

0.8 m

1.0 m ① 0.6 m

② ↗

34) A ball of mass 8.0 kg is suspended by two wires from a horizontal arm, which is attached to a vertical shaft, as shown in Figure 5.12. The shaft is in uniform rotation about its axis such that the linear speed of the ball equals 2.3 m/s. The tension in wire 2 is closest to:

A) 66 N   B) 55 N   C) 77 N   D) 88 N   E) 99 N

Answer: A
Var: 50+

35) A ball of mass 7.0 kg is suspended by two wires from a horizontal arm, which is attached to a vertical shaft, as shown in Figure 5.12. The shaft is in uniform rotation about its axis such that the linear speed of the ball equals 2.0 m/s. The rate of rotation is adjusted so that the tensions in the two wires are equal. The radial acceleration of the ball is closest to:

A) 5 m/s^2 B) 6 m/s^2 C) 7 m/s^2 D) 8 m/s^2 E) 10 m/s^2

Answer: A
Var: 50+

36) A ball of mass 3.0 kg is suspended by two wires from a horizontal arm, which is attached to a vertical shaft, as shown in Figure 5.12. The shaft is in uniform rotation about its axis such that the linear speed of the ball equals 2.2 m/s. The rotation is halted and the system is at rest. The tensions T_1 and T_2 in wires 1 and 2 are closest to:

A) T_1 = 29 N, T_2 = 0

B) T_1 = 0, T_2 = 37 N

C) T_1 = 0, T_2 = 29 N

D) T_1 = 29 N, T_2 = 18 N

E) T_1 = 29 N, T_2 = 50 N

Answer: A
Var: 50+

Figure 5.13

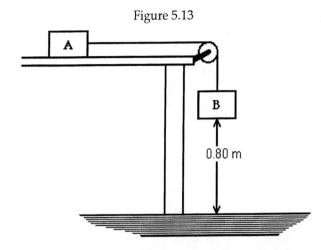

37) In Figure 5.13, two wooden blocks of 0.30 kg mass each are connected by a string which passes over a pulley. One block slides on a horizontal table, while the other hangs suspended by the string, as shown in the sketch. At t = 0, the suspended block is 0.80 m over the floor, and the blocks are released from rest. After 2.5 s, the suspended block reaches the floor. What is the coefficient of kinetic friction between the table and the sliding block?

A) 0.35   B) 0.52   C) 0.84   D) 0.65   E) 0.95

Answer: E
Var: 1

38) The reason a space station designed for human habitation is rotated is

A) to provide artificial gravity.

B) to conserve energy.

C) to provide propulsion.

D) to provide a steady input of sunlight.

E) to generate electricity.

Answer: A
Var: 1

39) A bunch of bananas hangs from a rope that passes over a light, frictionless pulley. On the other end of the rope hangs a monkey whose mass is the same as that of the bananas. Initially both the monkey and the bananas are at rest. The monkey starts to climb up the rope and in so doing causes himself at the same time to swing like a pendulum. What will happen?

A) The monkey and the bananas will both move up away from the ground at the same speed.

B) Whether or not the monkey is swinging like a pendulum will have no effect on the rate at which the bananas or the monkey move up or down with respect to the ground.

C) The bananas will move upward faster than the monkey does.

D) A situation in which the bananas move up and the monkey moves down toward the ground is not possible.

E) The monkey will move up faster than the bananas do, depending on how vigorously he is swinging.

Answer: C
Var: 1

Short Answer Questions

1) Jack is using a sled to haul firewood up a snowy hill to his cabin. The slope of the hill is $6°$ from the horizontal, the sled has a mass of 16 kg, the coefficient of kinetic friction between the sled runners and the snow is 0.13, and Jack can exert a force of 1400 newtons parallel to the ground. What is the largest load (in kilograms) that Jack can take in one trip? (Use $g = 9.8 \text{ m/s}^2$.)

Answer: 590 kg
Var: 1

Figure 5.14

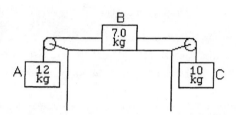

2) In Figure 5.14, a block of mass 7.0 kg on a tabletop is attached by strings to vertically hanging masses, 12 kg and 10 kg, as shown. The strings and pulleys are massless, the pulleys are frictionless, but the coefficient of friction between the block and the tabletop is 0.10. Describe the motion of the block, including the magnitude and direction of the acceleration.
(Use $g = 9.8 \text{ m/s}^2$.)

Answer: acceleration = 0.44 m/s^2; the block accelerates to the left.
Var: 1

3) A tobogganer coasts down a hill and then goes over a slight rise with speed 2.7 m/s. The top of this rise can be taken to be a circle of radius 4.1 m. The toboggan and occupant have a combined mass of 110 kg. If the coefficient of kinetic friction between the snow and the toboggan is 0.10, what frictional force is exerted on the toboggan by the snow as the toboggan goes over the top of the rise? (Use $g = 9.8 \text{ m/s}^2$.)

Answer: 88 N
Var: 1

4) A Ferris wheel has radius 5.0 m and makes one revolution in 8.0 seconds. A person weighing 670 N is sitting on one of the benches attached at the rim of the wheel. What is the apparent weight (the the normal force exerted on her by the bench) of the person as she passes through the highest point of her motion?

Answer: 460 N
Var: 1

5) A pickup truck is moving at 25 m/s when suddenly the brakes are applied and the truck comes to a stop in 4.7 s. A tool box of mass m rests on the bed of the truck 2.5 m from the cab. If the coefficient of kinetic friction between the tool box and the bed of the truck is 0.28, how much time elapses before the tool box strikes the cab?

Answer: 1.4 sec
Var: 1

Chapter 6   Work and Kinetic Energy

Multiple Choice Questions

Figure 6.1

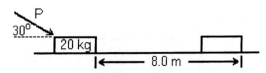

1) In Figure 6.1, a constant external force P = 170 N is applied to a 20 kg box, which is on a rough horizontal surface. The force pushes the box a distance of 8.0 m, in a time interval of 6.0 s, and the speed changes from $v_1 = 0.3$ m/s to $v_2 = 2.5$ m/s. The work done by the external force P is closest to:

   A) 1180 J   B) 1060 J   C) 940 J   D) 810 J   E) 680 J

   Answer: A
   Var: 50+

2) In Figure 6.1, a constant external force P = 130 N is applied to a 20 kg box, which is on a rough horizontal surface. The force pushes the box a distance of 8.0 m, in a time interval of 7.0 s, and the speed changes from $v_1 = 0.3$ m/s to $v_2 = 2.3$ m/s. The work done by friction is closest to:

   A) –850 J   B) +900 J   C) +950 J   D) +850 J   E) –950 J

   Answer: A
   Var: 50+

3) In Figure 6.1, a constant external force P = 170 N is applied to a 20 kg box, which is on a rough horizontal surface. The force pushes the box a distance of 8.0 m, in a time interval of 8.0 s, and the speed changes from $v_1 = 0.8$ m/s to $v_2 = 2.7$ m/s. The average rate of change of the kinetic energy of the box, in the 8.0 s time interval, is closest to:

   A) 8.3 W   B) 17 W   C) 160 W   D) 140 W   E) 150 W

   Answer: A
   Var: 50+

Figure 6.2

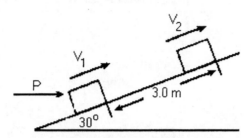

4) In Figure 6.2, a 300 kg crate is on a rough surface inclined at 30°. A constant external force P = 2400 N is applied horizontally to the crate. The force pushes the crate a distance of 3.0 m up the incline, in a time interval of 9.0 s, and the velocity changes from $v_1 = 0.7$ m/s to $v_2 = 2.9$ m/s. The work done by the weight is closest to:

A) –4400 J   B) –1400 J   C) +4400 J   D) +1400 J   E) zero

Answer: A
Var: 50+

5) In Figure 6.2, a 900 kg crate is on a rough surface inclined at 30°. A constant external force P = 7200 N is applied horizontally to the crate. The force pushes the crate a distance of 3.0 m up the incline, in a time interval of 6.5 s, and the velocity changes from $v_1 = 1.2$ m/s to $v_2 = 2.1$ m/s. The work done by the friction force is closest to:

A) –4100 J   B) –6800 J   C) +4100 J   D) +6800 J   E) zero

Answer: A
Var: 50+

6) In Figure 6.2, a 900 kg crate is on a rough surface inclined at 30°. A constant external force P = 7200 N is applied horizontally to the crate. The force pushes the crate a distance of 3.0 m up the incline, in a time interval of 9.0 s, and the velocity changes from $v_1 = 1.4$ m/s to $v_2 = 2.0$ m/s. The work done by the normal force is closest to:

A) zero   B) +6400 J   C) +4600 J   D) +9000 J   E) +13,500 J

Answer: A
Var: 50+

7) In Figure 6.2, a 700 kg crate is on a rough surface inclined at 30°. A constant external force P = 5600 N is applied horizontally to the crate. The force pushes the crate a distance of 3.0 m up the incline, in a time interval of 3.0 s, and the velocity changes from $v_1 = 0.8$ m/s to $v_2 = 2.6$ m/s. The average power delivered by the external force P during the 3.0 s time interval is closest to:

A) 4850 W   B) 2800W   C) 5600 W   D) 3380 W   E) 3970 W

Answer: A
Var: 50+

8) A girl throws a stone from a bridge. Consider the following ways she might throw the stone. The speed of the stone as it leaves her hand is the same in each case.
Case A: Thrown straight up.
Case B: Thrown straight down.
Case C: Thrown out at an angle of $45°$ above horizontal.
Case D: Thrown straight out horizontally.
In which case will the speed of the stone be greatest when it hits the water below?

   A) Case A

   B) Case B

   C) Case C

   D) Case D

   E) The speed will be the same in all cases.

   Answer: E
   Var: 1

9) In order to do work on an object,

   A) it is necessary that friction be present.

   B) it is necessary that friction not be present.

   C) the object must move.

   D) the force doing the work must be directed perpendicular to the motion of the object.

   E) the applied force must be greater than the reaction force of the object.

   Answer: C
   Var: 1

Figure 6.3

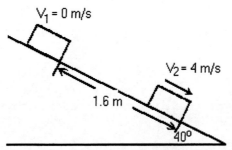

An 8.0 kg block is released from rest, $v_1 = 0$ m/s, on a rough incline. The block moves a distance of 1.6 m down the incline, in a time interval of 0.80 s, and acquires a velocity of $v_2 = 4.0$ m/s.

   10) In Figure 6.3, the work done by the weight is closest to:
   A) +80 J   B) +100 J   C) +120 J   D) –80 J   E) –100 J

   Answer: A
   Var: 1

11) In Figure 6.3, the average rate at which the friction force does work during the 0.80 s time interval is closest to:

A) zero   B) +20 W   C) +40 W   D) –20 W   E) –40 W

Answer: D
Var: 1

12) In Figure 6.3, the average rate at which the normal force does work during the 0.80 s time interval is closest to:

A) zero   B) +100 W   C) +120 W   D) –100 W   E) –120 W

Answer: A
Var: 1

13) In Figure 6.3, the average rate at which the block gains kinetic energy during the 0.80 s time interval is closest to:

A) 77 W   B) 80 W   C) 83 W   D) 86 W   E) 89 W

Answer: B
Var: 1

14) A 60 kg person drops from rest a distance of 1.20 m to a platform of negligible mass supported by a stiff spring. The platform drops 6 cms before the person comes to rest. What is the spring constant of the spring?

A) 2.56×10^5 N/m

B) 3.92×10^5 N/m

C) 5.45×10^4 N/m

D) 4.12×10^5 N/m

E) 8.83×10^4 N/m

Answer: D
Var: 1

15) An object is subject to a restoring force $F = 4x^3$, where x is the displacement of the object from its equilibrium position. How much work must be done to move the object from x = 0 to x = 0.27 m?

A) 5.31×10^{-3} J

B) 2.13×10^{-2} J

C) 1.97×10^{-2} J

D) 7.87×10^{-2} J

E) 2.36×10^{-1} J

Answer: A
Var: 50+

Figure 6.4

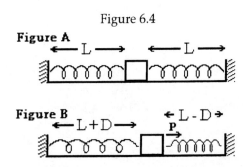

Figure A

L → ← L →

Figure B

L+D → ← L - D →
P

16) In Figure 6.4, two identical springs have unstretched lengths of 0.25 m and force constants of 500 N/m. The springs are attached to a small cube and stretched to a length L of 0.31 m as in Figure A. An external force P pulls the cube a distance D = 0.02 m to the right and holds it there. (See Figure B). The work required to assemble the springs and cube in Figure A is closest to:

   A) 1.80 J   B) 0.90 J   C) 16.80 J   D) 78.40 J   E) 156.80 J

   Answer: A
   Var: 50+

17) In Figure 6.4, two identical springs have unstretched lengths of 0.25 m and force constants of 400 N/m. The springs are attached to a small cube and stretched to a length L of 0.36 m as in Figure A. An external force P pulls the cube a distance D = 0.02 m to the right and holds it there. (See Figure B). The external force P, that holds the cube in place in Figure B, is closest to:

   A) 16 N   B) 14 N   C) 12 N   D) 10 N   E) 8.0 N

   Answer: A
   Var: 50+

18) In Figure 6.4, two identical springs have unstretched lengths of 0.25 m and force constants of 600 N/m. The springs are attached to a small cube and stretched to a length L of 0.38 m as in Figure A. An external force P pulls the cube a distance D = 0.02 m to the right and holds it there. (See Figure B). The work done by the external force P in pulling the cube 0.02 m is closest to:

   A) 9.1 J   B) 6.8 J   C) 4.6 J   D) 11 J   E) 14 J

   Answer: A
   Var: 50+

Figure 6.5

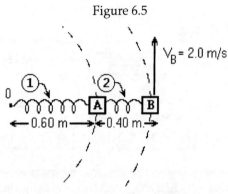

Block A (0.40 kg) and block B (0.30 kg) are on a frictionless table. Spring 1 connects block A to a frictionless peg at 0 and spring 2 connects block A and block B. The blocks are in uniform circular motion about 0, and the springs have lengths of 0.60 m and 0.40 m, as shown. The linear speed of block B is 2.0 m/s.

19) In Figure 6.5, the amount of stretch of spring 2 is 0.06 m. The force constant of spring 2 is closest to:

A) 18 N/m   B) 20 N/m   C) 22 N/m   D) 24 N/m   E) 26 N/m

Answer: B
Var: 1

20) In Figure 6.5, the force constant of spring 1 is equal to 30 N/m. The unstretched length of spring 1 is closest to:

A) 0.51 m   B) 0.52 m   C) 0.53 m   D) 0.54 m   E) 0.55 m

Answer: C
Var: 1

Figure 6.6

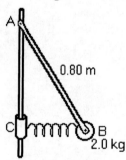

21) In Figure 6.6, a 0.80 m light rod is loosely pinned to a vertical shaft at a. A 2.0 kg disk is attached to the rod at b. A spring is attached to the rod at B and to a sleeve on the shaft at c. The sleeve is frictionless, allowing it to move freely up or down, so that the spring is always horizontal when stretched. The unstretched length of the spring is 0.554 m and the force constant is 330 N/m. The shaft is in rotation and the spring has a stretched length of 0.609 m. The radial acceleration of the disk is closest to:

A) 20.7 m/s^2 B) 21.3 m/s^2 C) 20.0 m/s^2 D) 19.4 m/s^2 E) 18.8 m/s^2

Answer: A
Var: 50+

22) In Figure 6.6, a 0.80 m light rod is loosely pinned to a vertical shaft at a. A 2.0 kg disk is attached to the rod at b. A spring is attached to the rod at B and to a sleeve on the shaft at c. The sleeve is frictionless, allowing it to move freely up or down, so that the spring is always horizontal when stretched. The unstretched length of the spring is 0.380 m and the force constant is 190 N/m. The shaft is in rotation and the rod forms a 40° angle with the shaft. The spring is stretched and horizontal. The radial acceleration of the disk is closest to:

A) $21.0 \, \text{m/s}^2$ B) $20.2 \, \text{m/s}^2$ C) $19.7 \, \text{m/s}^2$ D) $19.2 \, \text{m/s}^2$ E) $18.7 \, \text{m/s}^2$

Answer: A
Var: 50+

23) In Figure 6.6, a 0.80 m light rod is loosely pinned to a vertical shaft at a. A 2.0 kg disk is attached to the rod at b. A spring is attached to the rod at B and to a sleeve on the shaft at c. The sleeve is frictionless, allowing it to move freely up or down, so that the spring is always horizontal when stretched. The unstretched length of the spring is 0.544 m and the force constant is 270 N/m. The shaft is in rotation and the spring has a length of 0.544 m and is barely slack. The radial acceleration of the disk is closest to:

A) $9.1 \, \text{m/s}^2$ B) $11 \, \text{m/s}^2$ C) $7.2 \, \text{m/s}^2$ D) $6.7 \, \text{m/s}^2$ E) $9.8 \, \text{m/s}^2$

Answer: A
Var: 50+

24) A certain car traveling 33.0 mph skids to a stop in 39 meters from the point where the brakes were applied. In approximately what distance would the car stop had it been going 66.0 mph?

A) 156 meters

B) 110 meters

C) 78 meters

D) 55 meters

E) 39 meters

Answer: A
Var: 50+

25) A sand mover at a quarry lifts 2,000 kg of sand per minute a vertical distance of 12 meters. The sand is initially at rest and is discharged at the top of the sand mover with speed 5 m/s into a loading chute. At what minimum rate must power be supplied to this machine?

A) 524 w   B) 3.92 kw   C) 6.65 kw   D) 4.34 kw   E) 1.13 kw

Answer: D
Var: 1

Short Answer Questions

1) An object of mass 2 kg is repelled from the origin by a force in the +x-direction whose magnitude varies with x according to $F = (7 \text{N} \cdot \text{m}^2) x^{-2}$. How much work is done by this force when the object moves from $x = 2$ m to $x = 3$ m? (Be sure to say whether this work is positive or negative.)

Answer: 1.17 J
Var: 1

2) A 7.0-kg rock is subject to a variable force given by the equation

$$F(x) = 6.0\,N - (2.0\,N/m)x + (6.0N/m^2)x^2.$$

If the rock initially is at rest at the origin, find its speed when it has moved 9.0 m.

Answer: 20 m/s
Var: 1

Figure 6.7

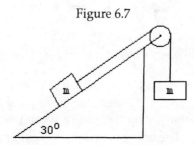

3) In Figure 6.7, two masses, each 24 kg, are at rest and connected as shown. The coefficient of kinetic friction between the inclined surface and the mass is 0.31. Find the speed of the masses after they have moved 1.6 m.

Answer: 1.9 m/s
Var: 1

Figure 6.8

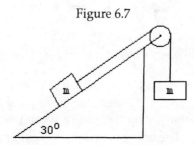

4) In Figure 6.8, a 5.00-kg block is moving at 5.00 m/s along a horizontal frictionless surface toward an ideal spring that is attached to a wall. After the block collides with the spring, the spring is compressed a maximum distance of 0.68 m. What is the speed of the block when the spring is compressed to only one-half of the maximum distance?

Answer: 4.3 m/s
Var: 1

5) An engine is being used to raise a 89 kg crate vertically upward. If the power output of the engine is 1620 W, how long does it take the engine to lift the crate a vertical distance of 18.7 m? Friction in the system is negligible.

Answer: 10 seconds
Var: 1

58

Chapter 7   Potential Energy and Energy Conservation

Multiple Choice Questions

1)

Figure 7.1a

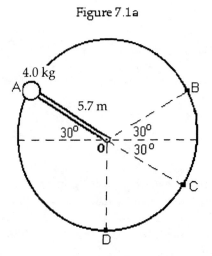

A 5.7 m massless rod is loosely pinned to a frictionless pivot at 0. A 4.0 kg ball is attached to the other end of the rod. The ball is held at A, where the rod makes a 30° angle above the horizontal, and is released. The ball–rod assembly then swings freely in a vertical circle between A and B. In Figure 7.1a, the ball passes through C, where the rod makes an angle of 30° below the horizontal. The speed of the ball as it passes through C is closest to:

  A) 10.6 m/s   B) 9.5 m/s   C) 8.4 m/s   D) 11.9 m/s   E) 13.9 m/s

Answer: A
Var: 50+

2)

Figure 7.1b

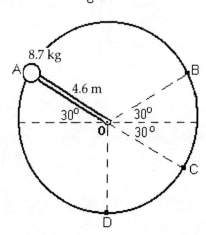

A 4.6 m massless rod is loosely pinned to a frictionless pivot at 0. A 8.7 kg ball is attached to the other end of the rod. The ball is held at A, where the rod makes a 30° angle above the horizontal, and is released. The ball–rod assembly then swings freely in a vertical circle between A and B. In Figure 7.1b, the tension in the rod when the ball passes through the lowest point at D is closest to:

A) 348 N   B) 435 N   C) 261 N   D) 174 N   E) 87 N

Answer: A
Var: 50+

3) A ball of mass m is suspended from a rope of length R. The ball is set into freely–swinging circular motion in a vertical plane. The centripetal acceleration of the ball at the top of the circle is 8 g. The centripetal acceleration of the ball at the bottom of the circle is closest to:

A) 12 g   B) 11 g   C) 10 g   D) 13 g   E) 14 g

Answer: A
Var: 14

Figure 7.2

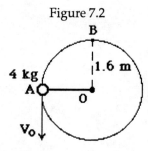

4) In Figure 7.2, a 4.0 kg ball is on the end of a 1.6 m rope which is fixed at 0. The ball is held at A, with the rope horizontal, and is given an initial downward velocity. The ball moves through three quarters of a circle and arrives at B, with the rope barely under tension. The initial velocity of the ball, at A, is closest to:

A) 4.0 m/s   B) 5.6 m/s   C) 6.3 m/s   D) 6.9 m/s   E) 7.9 m/s

Answer: D
Var: 1

5) When we speak of a conservative force, what is it that is being "conserved"?

    A) Linear momentum

    B) Force

    C) Kinetic energy

    D) Potential energy

    E) Total mechanical energy

Answer: E
Var: 1

Figure 7.3

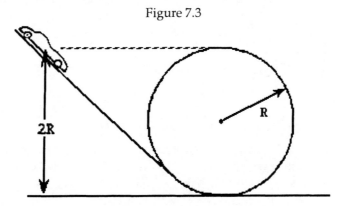

6) In Figure 7.3, a toy race car of mas m is released from rest on the loop-the-loop track. If it is released at a height 2R above the floor, how high is it above the floor when it leaves the track, neglecting friction?

    A) 1.67 R   B) 2.00 R   C) 1.50 R   D) 1.33 R   E) 1.25 R

Answer: A
Var: 1

7) Two objects, one of mass m and the other of mass 2 m, are dropped from the top of a building. When they hit the ground:

    A) both will have the same kinetic energy.

    B) the heavier one will have twice the kinetic energy of the lighter one.

    C) the heavier one will have four times the kinetic energy of the lighter one.

    D) the heavier one will have half the kinetic energy of the lighter one.

    E) the heavier one will have one-fourth the kinetic energy of the lighter one.

Answer: B
Var: 1

8) A 2.0 kg ball is attached to a light rod that is 1.2 m long. The other end of the rod is loosely pinned at a frictionless pivot. The rod is raised until it is inverted, with the ball above the pivot. The rod is released and the ball moves in a vertical circle. The tension in the rod as the ball moves through the bottom of the circle is closest to:

    A) 20 N   B) 40 N   C) 60 N   D) 80 N   E) 100 N

Answer: E
Var: 1

9) The force constant of a spring is 800 N/m and the unstretched length is 0.55 m. A 1.7 kg block is suspended from the spring. An external force slowly pulls the block down, until the spring has been stretched to a length of 0.66 m. The external force is then removed, and the block rises. In this situation, the external force on the block before it is removed is closest to:

A) 71 N B) 181 N C) 291 N D) 401 N E) 511 N

Answer: A
Var: 50+

10) The force constant of a spring is 300 N/m and the unstretched length is 0.78 m. A 2.1 kg block is suspended from the spring. An external force slowly pulls the block down, until the spring has been stretched to a length of 0.94 m. The external force is then removed, and the block rises. In this situation, when the spring has contracted to a length of 0.78 m, the upward velocity of the block is closest to:

A) 0.65 m/s B) 4.8 m/s C) 7.0 m/s D) 8.5 m/s E) 9.2 m/s

Answer: A
Var: 50+

11) The force constant of a spring is 400 N/m and the unstretched length is 0.65 m. A 2.0 kg block is suspended from the spring. An external force slowly pulls the block down, until the spring has been stretched to a length of 0.78 m. The external force is then removed, and the block rises. In this situation, when the spring has contracted to a length of 0.66 m, the acceleration of the block, including direction, is closest to:

A) 7.8 m/s^2, downward
B) 12 m/s^2, downward
C) 12 m/s^2, upward
D) 120 m/s^2, downward
E) 120 m/s^2, upward

Answer: A
Var: 50+

12)

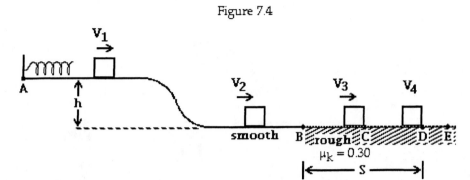

Figure 7.4

A 1.82 kg block is held in place against the spring by a 83 N horizontal external force. The external force is removed, and the block is projected with a velocity $v_1 = 1.2$ m/s upon separation from the spring. The block descends a ramp and has a velocity $v_2 = 1.8$ m/s at the bottom. The track is frictionless between points A and B. The track is frictionless between points A and B. The block enters a rough section at B, extending to E. The coefficient of kinetic friction is 0.32. The velocity of the block is $v_3 = 1.4$ m/s at C. The block moves on to D, where it stops. In Figure 7.4, the force constant of the spring is closest to:μ

A) 2630 N/m   B) 2100 N/m   C) 1310 N/m   D) 1170 N/m   E) 760 N/m

Answer: A
Var: 50+

13)

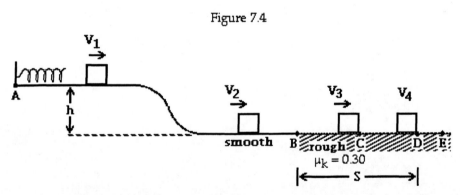

Figure 7.4

A 0.43 kg block is held in place against the spring by a 20 N horizontal external force. The external force is removed, and the block is projected with a velocity $v_1 = 1.2$ m/s upon separation from the spring. The block descends a ramp and has a velocity $v_2 = 2.1$ m/s at the bottom. The track is frictionless between points A and B. The track is frictionless between points A and B. The block enters a rough section at B, extending to E. The coefficient of kinetic friction is 0.36. The velocity of the block is $v_3 = 1.4$ m/s at C. The block moves on to D, where it stops. In Figure 7.4, the initial compression of the spring, in cm, is closest to:

A) 3.1   B) 1.7   C) 6.4   D) 6.2   E) 9.5

Answer: A
Var: 50+

63

14)

Figure 7.4

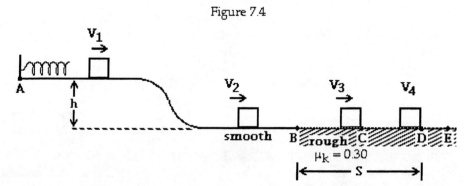

A 1.07 kg block is held in place against the spring by a 31 N horizontal external force. The external force is removed, and the block is projected with a velocity $v_1 = 1.2$ m/s upon separation from the spring. The block descends a ramp and has a velocity $v_2 = 1.6$ m/s at the bottom. The track is frictionless between points A and B. The track is frictionless between points A and B. The block enters a rough section at B, extending to E. The coefficient of kinetic friction is 0.34. The velocity of the block is $v_3 = 1.4$ m/s at C. The block moves on to D, where it stops. In Figure 7.4, the height of the ramp h, in cm, is closest to:

A) 5.7   B) 7.3   C) 9.4   D) 11   E) 13

Answer: A
Var: 50+

15)

Figure 7.4

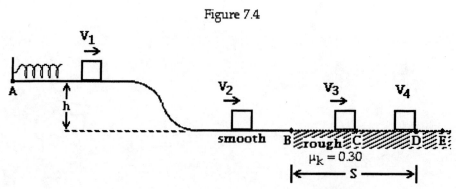

A 1.79 kg block is held in place against the spring by a 31 N horizontal external force. The external force is removed, and the block is projected with a velocity $v_1 = 1.2$ m/s upon separation from the spring. The block descends a ramp and has a velocity $v_2 = 1.8$ m/s at the bottom. The track is frictionless between points A and B. The track is frictionless between points A and B. The block enters a rough section at B, extending to E. The coefficient of kinetic friction is 0.30. The velocity of the block is $v_3 = 1.4$ m/s at C. The block moves on to D, where it stops. In Figure 7.4, the work done by friction between points B and C is closest to:

A) –1.1 J   B) –2.3 J   C) –18 J   D) –5.8 J   E) –6.4 J

Answer: A
Var: 50+

16)

Figure 7.4

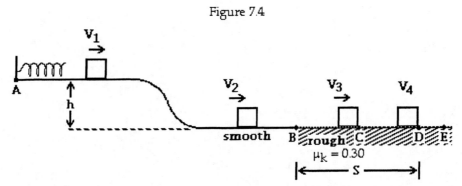

A 1.25 kg block is held in place against the spring by a 85 N horizontal external force. The external force is removed, and the block is projected with a velocity $v_1 = 1.2$ m/s upon separation from the spring. The block descends a ramp and has a velocity $v_2 = 1.7$ m/s at the bottom. The track is frictionless between points A and B. The track is frictionless between points A and B. The block enters a rough section at B, extending to E. The coefficient of kinetic friction is 0.31. The velocity of the block is $v_3 = 1.4$ m/s at C. The block moves on to D, where it stops. In Figure 7.4, the distance s that the block travels between points B and D is closest to:

A) 0.48 m   B) 0.15 m   C) 0.32 m   D) 0.63 m   E) 0.95 m

Answer: A
Var: 50+

65

Figure 7.5

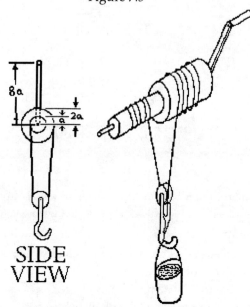

SIDE
VIEW

17) Shown in Figure 7.5 is a windlass of a type used to lift molten ore in ancient times. The radii of the two spools are a and 2a, and the length of the crank handle is 8a. What is the maximum weight that could be lifted by applying a force of 200 N to the crank handle? Assume negligible friction.

   A) 1500 N   B) 2000 N   C) 3200 N   D) 4000 N   E) 6400 N

Answer: C
Var: 1

18) A particle of mass m is released from rest at the top of a spherical dome of radius R. How far below the starting point will the particle leave the surface of the dome?

   A) 0.25 R   B) 0.17 R   C) 0.33 R   D) 0.42 R   E) 0.37 R

Answer: B
Var: 1

Figure 7.6

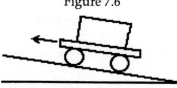

19) In Figure 7.6, some loggers try to pull a heavy generator up an incline by placing logs as rollers under it. Suppose the incline is $5°$ and each of the two logs has weight W. The generator has weight 2W. What minimum force would they have to exert to move the generator at a steady speed up the slope?

   A) 0.55 W   B) 0.26 W   C) 1.12 W   D) 0.33 W   E) 0.65 W

Answer: B
Var: 1

20)   Figure 7.7

The force constant of a spring is 400 N/m and its unstretched length is 20 cm. The spring is placed inside a smooth tube that is 20 cm tall (Figure a). A 0.36 kg disk is lowered onto the spring (Figure b). An external force P pushes the disk down further, until the spring is 8.0 cm long (Figure c). The external force is removed, the disk is projected upward and it emerges from the tube (Figure d).

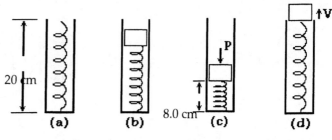

In Figure 7.7, the compression of the spring in Figure B, in cm, is closest to:

   A) 0.88   B) 0.99   C) 1.1   D) 1.2   E) 1.3

Answer: A
Var: 50+

21)   Figure 7.7.1

The force constant of a spring is 300 N/m and its unstretched length is 17 cm. The spring is placed inside a smooth tube that is 17 cm tall (Figure a). A 0.50 kg disk is lowered onto the spring (Figure b). An external force P pushes the disk down further, until the spring is 6.8 cm long (Figure c). The external force is removed, the disk is projected upward and it emerges from the tube (Figure d).

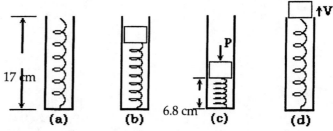

In Figure 7.7.1, the external force P in Figure C is closest to:

   A) 26 N   B) 16 N   C) 36 N   D) 46 N   E) 56 N

Answer: A
Var: 50+

22)

Figure 7.7.2

The force constant of a spring is 800 N/m and its unstretched length is 17 cm. The spring is placed inside a smooth tube that is 17 cm tall (Figure a). A 0.39 kg disk is lowered onto the spring (Figure b). An external force P pushes the disk down further, until the spring is 6.8 cm long (Figure c). The external force is removed, the disk is projected upward and it emerges from the tube (Figure d).

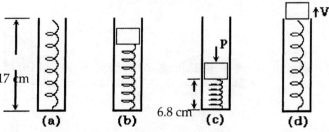

In Figure 7.7.2, the elastic potential energy of the spring in Figure C is closest to:

A) 4.2 J   B) 3.2 J   C) 2.8 J   D) 2.3 J   E) 1.4 J

Answer: A
Var: 50+

23)

Figure 7.7.3

The force constant of a spring is 400 N/m and its unstretched length is 19 cm. The spring is placed inside a smooth tube that is 19 cm tall (Figure a). A 0.46 kg disk is lowered onto the spring (Figure b). An external force P pushes the disk down further, until the spring is 7.6 cm long (Figure c). The external force is removed, the disk is projected upward and it emerges from the tube (Figure d).

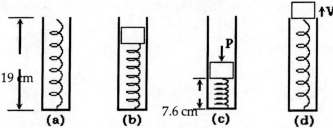

In Figure 7.7.3, the initial acceleration of the disk when the external force P is removed is closest to:

A) 89 m/s^2

B) 56 m/s^2

C) 160 m/s^2

D) 9900 m/s^2

E) 6600 m/s^2

Answer: A
Var: 50+

24)   Figure 7.7.4

The force constant of a spring is 300 N/m and its unstretched length is 18 cm. The spring is placed inside a smooth tube that is 18 cm tall (Figure a). A 0.62 kg disk is lowered onto the spring (Figure b). An external force P pushes the disk down further, until the spring is 7.2 cm long (Figure c). The external force is removed, the disk is projected upward and it emerges from the tube (Figure d).

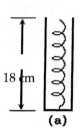
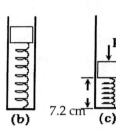
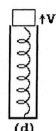

In Figure 7.7.4, the velocity V of the disk as it emerges from the tube in Figure D is closest to:

A) 1.9 m/s   B) 1.0 m/s   C) 2.8 m/s   D) 400 m/s   E) 240 m/s

Answer: A
Var: 50+

25) An object is attached to a hanging unstretched spring and slowly lowered to its equilibrium position, a distance of 4.8 cms below the starting point. If instead of having been lowered slowly the object was dropped from rest, how far then would the spring stretch?

A) 9.6 cms   B) 6.8 cms   C) 4.8 cms   D) 14 cms   E) 19 cms

Answer: A
Var: 50+

26) A spring with a spring constant of 600 N/m is compressed 4 cms. How much energy does it store?

A) 0.48 J   B) 4800 J   C) 0.96 J   D) 24 J   E) 0.24 J

Answer: A
Var: 50+

27) In the following, K = kinetic energy, U = potential energy, and W = work. In using the expression $K_2 + U_2 = K_1 + U_1 + W_{other}$ we recognize that

A) we are assuming no friction is present.

B) Gravitational and elastic potential energies would be included in U_1 and U_2.

C) Gravitational and elastic potential energies would be included in W_{other}.

D) K and U can be either positive or negative, depending on the reference point chosen.

E) W_{other} is always positive.

Answer: B
Var: 1

28) Which, if any, of the following statements concerning the work done by a conservative force is *not* true?

A) It is reversible.

B) It can always be expressed as the difference between the initial and final values of a potential energy function.

C) It is independent of the path of the body and depends only on the starting and ending points.

D) When the starting and ending points are the same, the total work is zero.

E) All of the above statements are true.

Answer: E
Var: 1

Figure 7.8

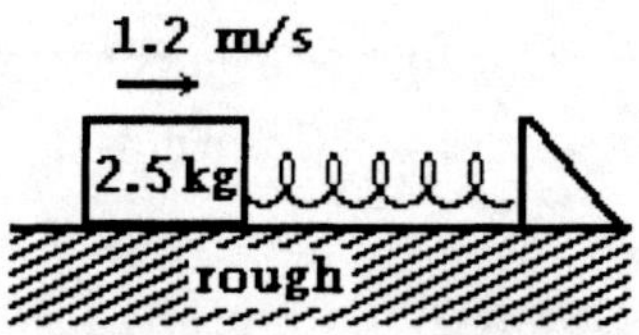

1.2 m/s

A 2.5 kg, sliding on a rough surface, has a speed of 1.2 m/s when it makes contact with a spring. The block comes to a momentary halt when the compression of the spring is 5.0 cm. The work done by the friction, from the instant the block makes contact with the spring until is comes to a momentary halt, is –0.50 J.

29) In Figure 7.8, the force constant of the spring is closest to:

A) 840 N/m   B) 890 N/m   C) 940 N/m   D) 990 N/m   E) 1040 N/m

Answer: E
Var: 1

30) In Figure 7.8, the coefficient of friction is closest to:

A) 0.33   B) 0.35   C) 0.37   D) 0.39   E) 0.41

Answer: E
Var: 1

31) In Figure 7.8, after compressing the spring, the block moves away from it. The speed of the block, upon separation from the spring, is closest to:

A) 0.75 m/s   B) 0.80 m/s   C) 0.85 m/s   D) 0.90 m/s   E) 0.95 m/s

Answer: B
Var: 1

32) The potential energy function of a particle moving in one dimension is

$$U = kx^2 \, e^{-x^2/a^2}$$

where $a = 7.80$ nm

At what value of x is a point of stable equilibrium located?

A) 7.80 nm   B) 12.62 nm   C) 11.03 nm   D) 6.81 nm   E) 11.10 nm

Answer: A
Var: 50+

Figure 7.9

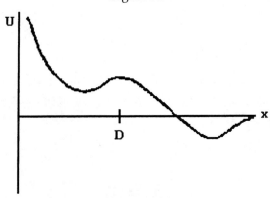

33) In Figure 7.9, a graph of potential energy versus position for a particle moving in a straight line. From this curve, for the region shown, we deduce that

A) this could not represent an actual physical situation, since the drawing shows the potential energy going negative, which is not physically realizable.

B) there are three positions of stable equilibrium.

C) the force on the particle would be strongest when the particle is near the origin.

D) the force on the particle would be greatest when the particle is near point D.

E) for a given value of x, the particle can have a total energy that lies either above or below the value given by the curve at that point.

Answer: C
Var: 1

34) Which of the following is an accurate statement?

A) Kinetic energy is always positive.

B) Potential energy is always positive.

C) Total energy is always positive.

D) None of these is true.

E) More than one of these is true.

Answer: A
Var: 1

Short Answer Questions

1) A roller coaster descends 35 meters in its initial drop and then rises 23 meters before going over the first hill. If a passenger at the top of the hill feels an apparent weight which is one half of her normal weight, what is the radius of curvature of the first hill? Assume no frictional losses, and neglect the initial speed of the roller coaster.

Answer: 48 m
Var: 1

Figure 7.10

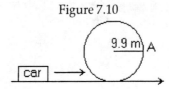

2) In Figure 7.10, a stunt car driver negotiates the frictionless track shown in such a way that the car is barely on the track at the top of the loop. The radius of the track is 9.9 m and the mass of the car is 1800 kg. Find the force of the car on the track when the car is at point A.

Answer: 53,000 N
Var: 1

Figure 7.11

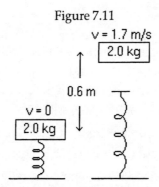

3) In Figure 7.11, a block of mass 2.0 kg is placed on a compressed vertical spring that is compressed 0.050 m. (The spring and the block are not attached.) The spring is released, and it propels the block vertically upward. When the block has risen 0.60 m above its initial position, its velocity is 1.7 m/s. How much potential energy was originally stored in the spring?

Answer: 15 J
Var: 1

Figure 7.12

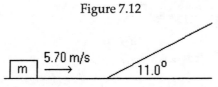

4) In Figure 7.12, a block of mass m is moving along the horizontal frictionless surface with a speed of 5.70 m/s. If the slope is 11.0° and the coefficient of kinetic friction between the block and the incline is 0.260, how far does the block travel up the incline?

Answer: 3.72 m
Var: 1

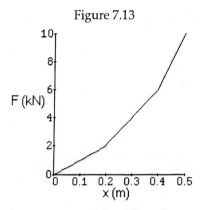

Figure 7.13

5) In Figure 7.13, a large spring will exert an upward force on an object; this force depends on the distance x the spring is compressed. The force F as a function of compression is shown in the graph. How much will the spring be compressed when it supports a mass of 800 kg? Since the graph is only approximate, you are justified in using $g = 10 \text{ m/s}^2$.

Answer: 0.45 m
Var: 1

Chapter 8   Momentum, Impulse, and Collisions

Multiple Choice Questions

Figure 8.1

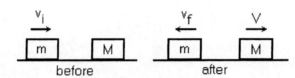

1) A block of mass m = 8.5 kg, moving on as frictionless surface with a speed v_i = 6.6 m/s, makes a perfectly elastic collision with a block of mass M at rest. After the collision, the 8.5 block recoils with a speed of v_f = 0.5 m/s. In Figure 8.1, the mass M is closest to:

A) 9.9 kg   B) 7.1 kg   C) 9.1 kg   D) 120 kg   E) 8.5 kg

Answer: A
Var: 50+

2) A block of mass m = 4.3 kg, moving on as frictionless surface with a speed v_i = 4.8 m/s, makes a perfectly elastic collision with a block of mass M at rest. After the collision, the 4.3 block recoils with a speed of v_f = 1.0 m/s. In Figure 8.1, the speed of the block of mass M after the collision is closest to:

A) 3.8 m/s   B) 4.3 m/s   C) 4.8 m/s   D) 5.3 m/s   E) 5.8 m/s

Answer: A
Var: 50+

3) A block of mass m = 7.8 kg, moving on as frictionless surface with a speed v_i = 7.8 m/s, makes a perfectly elastic collision with a block of mass M at rest. After the collision, the 7.8 block recoils with a speed of v_f = 0.8 m/s. In Figure 8.1, the blocks are in contact for 0.20 s. The average force on the 7.8 kg block, while the two blocks are in contact, is closest to:

A) 335 N   B) 320 N   C) 304 N   D) 58 N   E) 273 N

Answer: A
Var: 50+

Figure 8.2

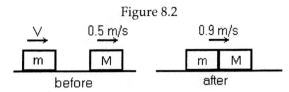

4) A block of mass m = 25 kg has a speed V and is behind a block of mass M = 82 kg that has a speed of 0.5 m/s. The surface is frictionless. The blocks collide and couple. After the collision, the blocks have a common speed of 0.9 m/s. In Figure 8.2, the loss of kinetic energy of the blocks due to the collision is closest to:

A) 28 J   B) 7.7 J   C) 13 J   D) 33 J   E) 94 J

Answer: A
Var: 50+

5) A block of mass m = 37 kg has a speed V and is behind a block of mass M = 77 kg that has a speed of 0.5 m/s. The surface is frictionless. The blocks collide and couple. After the collision, the blocks have a common speed of 0.9 m/s. In Figure 8.2, the impulse on the 12 kg block due to the collision is closest to:

A) 31 N • s   B) 15 N • s   C) 39 N • s   D) 54 N • s   E) 69 N • s

Answer: A
Var: 50+

6) A 49 g steel ball is released from rest and falls vertically onto a steel plate. The ball strikes the plate and is in contact with it for 0.5 ms. The ball rebounds elastically, and returns to its original height. The time interval for a round trip is 7.00 s. In this situation, the average force exerted on the ball during contact with the plate is closest to:

A) 6720 N   B) 3360 N   C) 5590 N   D) 4490 N   E) 7850 N

Answer: A
Var: 50+

7) A 30 g steel ball is released from rest and falls vertically onto a steel plate. The ball strikes the plate and is in contact with it for 0.5 ms. The ball rebounds elastically, and returns to its original height. The time interval for a round trip is 9.00 s. In this situation, assume the plate does not deform during contact. The maximum elastic energy stored by the ball is closest to:

A) 29 J   B) 44 J   C) 58 J   D) 87 J   E) 120 J

Answer: A
Var: 50+

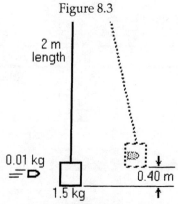

Figure 8.3

2 m length

0.01 kg

1.5 kg

0.40 m

8) In Figure 8.3, a bullet of mass 0.01 kg moving horizontally strikes a block of wood of mass 1.5 kg which is suspended as a pendulum. The bullet lodges in the wood, and together they swing upward a distance of 0.40 m. What was the velocity of the bullet just before it struck the wooden block? The length of the string is 2 meters.

A) 66.7 m/s   B) 250 m/s   C) 366 m/s   D) 423 m/s   E) 646 m/s

Answer: A
Var: 1

9) Consider two less-than-desirable options. In the first you are driving 30 mph and crash head-on into an identical car also going 30 mph. In the second option you are driving 30 mph and crash head-on into a stationary brick wall. In neither case does your car bounce off the thing it hits, and the collision time is the same in both cases. Which of these two situations would result in the greatest impact force?

A) Hitting the other car.

B) Hitting the brick wall.

C) The force would be the same in both cases.

D) We cannot answer this question without more information.

E) None of these is true.

Answer: C
Var: 1

76

Figure 8.4

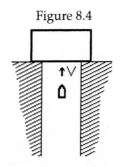

10) A 18 g bullet is shot vertically into an 10 kg block. The block lifts upward 9 mm. The bullet penetrates the block in a time interval of 0.001 s. Assume the force on the bullet is constant during penetration. In Figure 8.4, the initial kinetic energy of the bullet is closest to:

   A) 490 J   B) 330 J   C) 250 J   D) 0.0016 J   E) 0.88 J

Answer: A
Var: 50+

11) A 22 g bullet is shot vertically into an 7 kg block. The block lifts upward 5 mm. The bullet penetrates the block in a time interval of 0.001 s. Assume the force on the bullet is constant during penetration. In Figure 8.4, the impulse on the block due to capture of the bullet is closest to:

   A) 2.2 N · s   B) 1.6 N · s   C) 10 N · s   D) 33 N · s   E) 69 N · s

Answer: A
Var: 50+

12) A 22 g bullet is shot vertically into an 6 kg block. The block lifts upward 5 mm. The bullet penetrates the block in a time interval of 0.001 s. Assume the force on the bullet is constant during penetration. In Figure 8.4, the penetration of the bullet into the block, in cm, is closest to:

   A) 4.3   B) 3.7   C) 3.0   D) 2.4   E) 4.9

Answer: A
Var: 50+

Figure 8.5

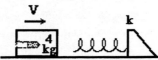

13) An 8 g bullet is shot into a 4.0 kg block, at rest on a frictionless horizontal surface. The bullet remains lodged in the block. The block moves into a spring and compresses it by 5.1 cm. The force constant of the spring is 1900 N/m. In Figure 8.5, the initial velocity of the bullet is closest to:

   A) 560 m/s   B) 530 m/s   C) 580 m/s   D) 600 m/s   E) 620 m/s

Answer: A
Var: 50+

14) An 8 g bullet is shot into a 4.0 kg block, at rest on a frictionless horizontal surface. The bullet remains lodged in the block. The block moves into a spring and compresses it by 6.9 cm. The force constant of the spring is 2400 N/m. In Figure 8.5, the impulse of the block (including the bullet), due to the spring, during the entire time interval in which block and spring are in contact is closest to:

A) 14 N · s   B) 12 N · s   C) 10 N · s   D) 8.5 N · s   E) 6.8 N · s

Answer: A
Var: 50+

15) In an impressive lecture demonstration a small steel ball bearing of mass m is held on top of a Superball of mass M (a Superball is a rubber ball of very high coefficient of restitution, i.e. it bounces high!). The combination is then dropped from rest together. When the Superball strikes the floor it immediately rebounds nearly elastically, striking the ball bearing which is still moving downward. This collision is also fairly elastic, and as a result the ball bearing is knocked backwards and shoots straight up to a height H. If h is the height from which the objects were dropped, and M >> m, then the small ball bearing will rise to a height

A) 4 h   B) 16 h   C) 6.67 h   D) 5 h   E) 9 h

Answer: E
Var: 1

16) A girl of mass 57 kg throws a ball of mass 0.7 kg against a wall. The ball strikes the wall horizontally with a speed of 29 m/s, and it bounces back with this same speed. The ball is in contact with the wall 0.05 s. What is the average force exerted on the wall by the ball?

A) 810 N   B) 410 N   C) 66,120 N   D) 33,060 N   E) 16,530 N

Answer: A
Var: 50+

17) Iraq was reportedly developing a "supergun" with a barrel some 70 meters long, which was to be able to launch huge artillery shells several hundred miles. During World War I, Germany used a "Big Bertha" cannon to hurl shells into Paris 30 miles away. This gun also had a long barrel. What is the reason for using a long barrel in these guns?

A) To provide a more favorable ratio of kinetic energy to potential energy.

B) To reduce frictional losses.

C) To allow the force of the expanding gases from the gunpowder to act for a longer time.

D) To increase the force exerted on the bullet due to the expanding gases from the gunpowder.

E) To reduce the force exerted on the bullet due to the expanding gases from the gunpowder.

Answer: C
Var: 1

Figure 8.6

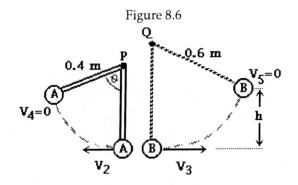

18) Ball A, of mass 3.0 kg, is attached to a 0.4 m light rod, freely pivoted at P. Ball B is suspended from Q by a 0.6 m rope and is at rest. Ball A is raised to a certain level and is released. Ball A descends, and has a speed $V_1 = 3.6$ m/s at the bottom, prior to striking ball B. The speed of balls A and B after the collision are $V_2 = 1.4$ m/s and $V_3 = 2.1$ m/s, as shown. In Figure 8.6, the mass of ball B is closest to:

   A) 7.1 kg   B) 6.3 kg   C) 5.4 kg   D) 4.5 kg   E) 3.6 kg

   Answer: A
   Var: 50+

19) Ball A, of mass 3.0 kg, is attached to a 0.4 m light rod, freely pivoted at P. Ball B is suspended from Q by a 0.6 m rope and is at rest. Ball A is raised to a certain level and is released. Ball A descends, and has a speed $V_1 = 3.6$ m/s at the bottom, prior to striking ball B. The speed of balls A and B after the collision are $V_2 = 1.8$ m/s and $V_3 = 2.3$ m/s, as shown. In Figure 8.6, the magnitude of the impulse on ball A is closest to:

   A) 16.2 N · s   B) 5.4 N · s   C) 9.0 N · s   D) 7.2 N · s   E) 18.0 N · s

   Answer: A
   Var: 50+

20) Ball A, of mass 3.0 kg, is attached to a 0.4 m light rod, freely pivoted at P. Ball B is suspended from Q by a 0.6 m rope and is at rest. Ball A is raised to a certain level and is released. Ball A descends, and has a speed $V_1 = 3.6$ m/s at the bottom, prior to striking ball B. The speed of balls A and B after the collision are $V_2 = 1.4$ m/s and $V_3 = 2.1$ m/s, as shown. In Figure 8.6, ball A rebounds and swings through an angle θ, where the speed of v_4 is zero. The rebound angle θ is closest to:

   A) 41°   B) 39°   C) 37°   D) 43°   E) 45°

   Answer: A
   Var: 50+

79

21) Ball A, of mass 3.0 kg, is attached to a 0.4 m light rod, freely pivoted at P. Ball B is suspended from Q by a 0.6 m rope and is at rest. Ball A is raised to a certain level and is released. Ball A descends, and has a speed $V_1 = 3.6$ m/s at the bottom, prior to striking ball B. The speed of balls A and B after the collision are $V_2 = 1.7$ m/s and $V_3 = 2.1$ m/s, as shown. In Figure 8.6, ball B rises through a height h, where the speed v_5 is zero. The height h is closest to:

A) 0.22 m   B) 0.18 m   C) 0.27 m   D) 0.31 m   E) 0.36 m

Answer: A
Var: 50+

Figure 8.7

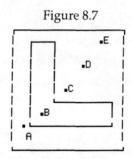

22) In Figure 8.7, an L-shaped piece is cut from a uniform sheet of metal. Which of the points indicated is closest to the center of mass of the object?

A) A   B) B   C) C   D) D   E) E

Answer: C
Var: 1

Figure 8.8

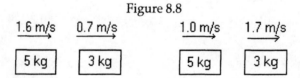

23) In Figure 8.8, determine the character of the collision. The masses of the blocks, and the velocities before and after are given. The collision is:

A) perfectly elastic

B) partially inelastic

C) completely inelastic

D) characterized by an increase in kinetic energy

E) not possible because momentum is not conserved.

Answer: B
Var: 1

80

Figure 8.9

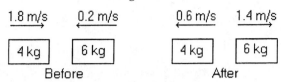

1.8 m/s   0.2 m/s   0.6 m/s   1.4 m/s

| 4 kg | 6 kg | | 4 kg | 6 kg |

Before   After

24) In Figure 8.9, determine the character of the collision. The masses of the blocks, and the velocities before and after are given. The collision is:

A) perfectly elastic

B) partially inelastic

C) completely inelastic

D) characterized by an increase in kinetic energy

E) not possible because momentum is not conserved.

Answer: A
Var: 1

Figure 8.10

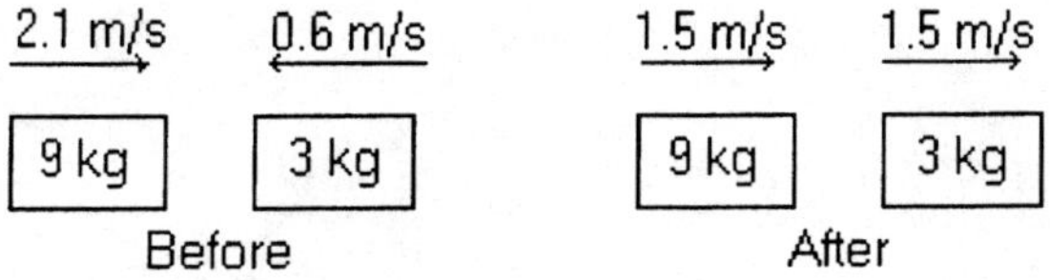

2.1 m/s   0.6 m/s   1.5 m/s   1.5 m/s

| 9 kg | 3 kg | | 9 kg | 3 kg |

Before   After

25) In Figure 8.10, determine the character of the collision. The masses of the blocks, and the velocities before and after are given. The collision is:

A) perfectly elastic

B) partially inelastic

C) completely inelastic

D) characterized by an increase in kinetic energy

E) not possible because momentum is not conserved.

Answer: E
Var: 1

Figure 8.11

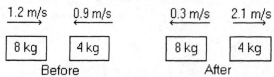

Before   After

26) In Figure 8.11, determine the character of the collision. The masses of the blocks, and the velocities before and after are given. The collision is:

A) perfectly elastic

B) partially inelastic

C) completely inelastic

D) characterized by an increase in kinetic energy

E) not possible because momentum is not conserved.

Answer: D
Var: 1

Figure 8.12

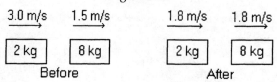

Before   After

27) In Figure 8.12, determine the character of the collision. The masses of the blocks, and the velocities before and after are given. The collision is:

A) perfectly elastic

B) partially inelastic

C) completely inelastic

D) characterized by an increase in kinetic energy

E) not possible because momentum is not conserved.

Answer: C
Var: 1

Figure 8.13

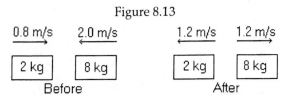

0.8 m/s   2.0 m/s   1.2 m/s   1.2 m/s

2 kg   8 kg   2 kg   8 kg

Before   After

28) In Figure 8.13, determine the character of the collision. The masses of the blocks, and the velocities before and after are given. The collision is:

A) perfectly elastic

B) partially inelastic

C) completely inelastic

D) characterized by an increase in kinetic energy

E) not possible because momentum is not conserved.

Answer: B
Var: 1

Figure 8.14

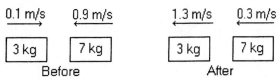

0.1 m/s   0.9 m/s   1.3 m/s   0.3 m/s

3 kg   7 kg   3 kg   7 kg

Before   After

29) In Figure 8.14, determine the character of the collision. The masses of the blocks, and the velocities before and after are given. The collision is:

A) perfectly elastic

B) partially inelastic

C) completely inelastic

D) characterized by an increase in kinetic energy

E) not possible because momentum is not conserved.

Answer: B
Var: 1

Figure 8.15

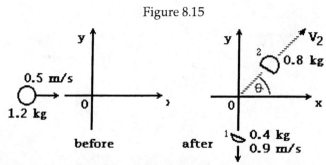

before   after

A 1.2 kg spring-activated toy bomb slides on a smooth surface along the x-axis with a speed of 0.50 m/s. At the origin 0, the bomb explodes into two fragments. Fragment 1 has a mass of 0.4 kg and a speed of 0.9 m/s along the negative y-axis.

30) In Figure 8.15, the x-component of the impulse on fragment 2, due to the explosion, is closest to:

A) 0.2 N • s   B) 0.4 N • s   C) 0.6 N • s   D) 0.8 N • s   E) 1.0 N • s

Answer: A
Var: 1

31) In Figure 8.15, the angle q, made by the velocity vector of fragment 2 and the x-axis, is closest to:

A) 31°   B) 37°   C) 38°   D) 53°   E) 59°

Answer: A
Var: 1

32) In Figure 8.15, the energy released by the explosion is closest to:

A) 0.20 J   B) 0.24 J   C) 0.28 J   D) 0.32 J   E) 0.36 J

Answer: D
Var: 1

Figure 8.16

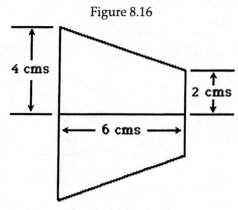

33) In Figure 8.16, a truncated homogeneous metal cone has a circular base of radius 4 cms and circular flat top of radius 2 cms. Its height is 6 cms. How far from the large diameter end is the center of mass located?

A) 2.56 cms   B) 1.80 cms   C) 2.88 cms   D) 2.25 cms   E) 2.36 cms

Answer: E
Var: 1

Figure 8.17

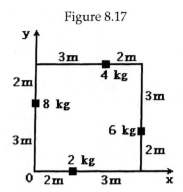

34) In Figure 8.17, four point masses are placed as shown. The x- and y-coordinates of the center of mass are closest to:

A) (2.2, 2.6)   B) (2.2, 2.7)   C) (2.3, 2.6)   D) (2.3, 2.7)   E) (2.3, 2.8)

Answer: E
Var: 1

Figure 8.18

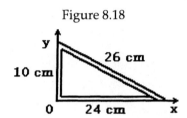

35) In Figure 8.18, a 60 cm length of uniform wire, of 60 g mass, is bent into a right triangle. The x- and y-coordinates of the center of mass, in cm, are closest to:

A) (8, 3)   B) (8, 5)   C) (9, 4)   D) (10, 3)   E) (10, 5)

Answer: D
Var: 1

Short Answer Questions

1) A particle of mass 5.25×10^{-27} kg, moving at 2.83×10^5 m/s, strikes an identical particle which is initially at rest. After the interaction, the particles (which can't be distinguished) are observed moving at angles 58.4° and 31.6°, both angles being measured with respect to the original direction of motion. What are the final speeds of the particles?

Answer: 2.41×10^5 m/s at 31.6°, 1.48×10^5 m/s at 58.4°
Var: 50+

2) A high school pitcher is employing a ballistic pendulum to determine the speed of his fastball. A 5.6-kg lump of clay is suspended from a cord 2.0 m long. When the pitcher throws his fastball aimed at the clay, the ball becomes embedded in the clay and the two swing up to a maximum height of 0.15 m. If the mass of the baseball is 0.21 kg, find the speed of the pitch.

Answer: 47 m/s
Var: 50+

85

Figure 8.19

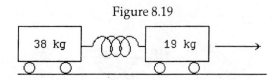

3) In Figure 8.19, a 19-kg cart is connected by means of a coiled spring to a 38-kg cart. The two carts are moving to the right at a speed of 68 m/s when the spring suddenly becomes uncoiled and propels the 19-kg cart forward with a speed of 76 m/s. Find the speed of the second cart with respect to the center of the mass of the system.

Answer: 4.0 m/s
Var: 50+

4) A force of 5.3 N is needed to hold on to an umbrella in a strong wind. If the air molecules each have a mass of 4.7×10^{-26} kg, and each strikes the umbrella (without rebounding) with a speed of 2.0 m/s in the same direction, how many atoms strike the umbrella each second? Assume that the wind blows horizontally so that the gravity can be neglected.

Answer: 5.6×10^{25} per second
Var: 1

5) A rocket is to be launched from deep space where there is no gravitational field. 81% of the initial mass of the rocket is fuel and this fuel is ejected with a relative velocity of 2300 m/s. Assuming that all of the fuel is used, find the final speed of the last portion of the ejected fuel relative to a stationary observer.

Answer: 1500 m/s
Var: 1

Chapter 9   Rotation of Rigid Bodies

Multiple Choice Questions

1) At time t = 0 s, a wheel has an angular displacement of zero radians and an angular velocity of +28 rad/s. The wheel has a constant acceleration of –0.55 rad/s^2. In this situation, the time t, at which the wheel comes to a mandatory halt, is closest to:

   A) 51 s   B) 42 s   C) 34 s   D) 25 s   E) 59 s

   Answer: A
   Var: 50+

2) At time t = 0 s, a wheel has an angular displacement of zero radians and an angular velocity of +26 rad/s. The wheel has a constant acceleration of –0.43 rad/s^2. In this situation, the time t (after t = 0 s), at which the kinetic energy of the wheel is twice the initial value, is closest to:

   A) 150 s   B) 130 s   C) 110 s   D) 85 s   E) 60 s

   Answer: A
   Var: 50+

3) At time t = 0 s, a wheel has an angular displacement of zero radians and an angular velocity of +21 rad/s. The wheel has a constant acceleration of –0.55 rad/s^2. In this situation, the maximum value of the angular displacement, in rad, is closest to:

   A) +401   B) +501   C) +601   D) +702   E) +802

   Answer: A
   Var: 50+

4) At time t = 0 s, a wheel has an angular displacement of zero radians and an angular velocity of +11 rad/s. The wheel has a constant acceleration of –0.56 rad/s^2. In this situation, the time at which the angular displacement is +86 rad and decreasing is closest to:

   A) 29 s   B) 20 s   C) 11 s   D) 7 s   E) 46 s

   Answer: A
   Var: 50+

5) At time t = 0 s, a wheel has an angular displacement of zero radians and an angular velocity of +16 rad/s. The wheel has a constant acceleration of –0.47 rad/s^2. In this situation, the average angular velocity in the interval from t = 0 s to t = 20 s is closest to:

   A) 11 rad/s   B) 8 rad/s   C) 7 rad/s   D) 14 rad/s   E) 2 rad/s

   Answer: A
   Var: 50+

6) A machinist turns the power on to a grinding wheel, at rest, at time t = 0 s. The wheel accelerates uniformly for 10 s and reaches the operating angular velocity of 52 rad/s. The wheel is run at that angular velocity for 37 s and then power is shut off. The wheel decelerates uniformly at 1.2 rad/s^2 until the wheel stops. In this situation, the operating speed of the wheel, in rpm, is closest to:

A) 500   B) 480   C) 460   D) 430   E) 410

Answer: A
Var: 50+

7) A machinist turns the power on to a grinding wheel, at rest, at time t = 0 s. The wheel accelerates uniformly for 10 s and reaches the operating angular velocity of 58 rad/s. The wheel is run at that angular velocity for 25 s and then power is shut off. The wheel decelerates uniformly at 1.4 rad/s^2 until the wheel stops. In this situation, the angular acceleration of the wheel between t = 0 s and t = 10 s is closest to:

A) 5.8 rad/s^2 B) 7.0 rad/s^2 C) 8.1 rad/s^2 D) 9.3 rad/s^2 E) 10 rad/s^2

Answer: A
Var: 50+

8) A machinist turns the power on to a grinding wheel, at rest, at time t = 0 s. The wheel accelerates uniformly for 10 s and reaches the operating angular velocity of 75 rad/s. The wheel is run at that angular velocity for 35 s and then power is shut off. The wheel decelerates uniformly at 2.6 rad/s^2 until the wheel stops. In this situation, the total number of revolutions made by the wheel is closest to:

A) 650   B) 420   C) 480   D) 590   E) 880

Answer: A
Var: 50+

9) A machinist turns the power on to a grinding wheel, at rest, at time t = 0 s. The wheel accelerates uniformly for 10 s and reaches the operating angular velocity of 38 rad/s. The wheel is run at that angular velocity for 34 s and then power is shut off. The wheel decelerates uniformly at 2.1 rad/s^2 until the wheel stops. In this situation, the time interval of deceleration is closest to:

A) 18 s   B) 16 s   C) 20 s   D) 22 s   E) 24 s

Answer: A
Var: 50+

10) A machinist turns the power on to a grinding wheel, at rest, at time t = 0 s. The wheel accelerates uniformly for 10 s and reaches the operating angular velocity of 87 rad/s. The wheel is run at that angular velocity for 23 s and then power is shut off. The wheel decelerates uniformly at 1.6 rad/s^2 until the wheel stops. In this situation, the average angular velocity in the time interval from t = 0 s to t = 25 s is closest to:

A) 52 rad/s   B) 46 rad/s   C) 39 rad/s   D) 33 rad/s   E) 26 rad/s

Answer: A
Var: 50+

11) A machinist turns the power on to a grinding wheel, at rest, at time t = 0 s. The wheel accelerates uniformly for 10 s and reaches the operating angular velocity of 42 rad/s. The wheel is run at that angular velocity for 39 s and then power is shut off. The wheel decelerates uniformly at 2.0 rad/s^2 until the wheel stops. In this situation, the average angular acceleration in the time interval from t = 0 s to t = 25 s is closest to:

A) 1.7 rad/s^2 B) 1.3 rad/s^2 C) 2.1 rad/s^2 D) 2.5 rad/s^2 E) 2.9 rad/s^2

Answer: A
Var: 50+

12) A small mass is placed on a record turntable that is rotating at 45 rpm. The acceleration of the mass is

A) directed perpendicular to the line joining the mass and the center of rotation.

B) independent (in magnitude) of the position of the mass on the turntable.

C) greater the closer the mass is to the center.

D) greater the farther the mass is from the center.

E) zero.

Answer: D
Var: 1

13) A turbine blade rotates with angular velocity ω(t) = 6 – 0.6t^2. What is the angular acceleration of the blade at t = 9.50 s?

A) –11.4 rad/s^2

B) –5.70 rad/s^2

C) –24.1 rad/s^2

D) –5.40 rad/s^2

E) –48.1 rad/s^2

Answer: A
Var: 50+

14) A boy riding on the outer edge of a merry-go-round throws a gold ring to his friend standing on the ground near the merry-go-round. The diameter of the merry-go-round is 16 m and it rotates at 6 rpm. The boy throws the ring with speed 12 m/s (relative to himself). The friend is positioned 10 m radially out from the boy when he throws the ring. How long does it take the ring to reach the friend?

A) 1.22 s   B) 1.13 s   C) 0.769 s   D) 0.918 s   E) 0.833 s

Answer: D
Var: 1

Figure 9.1

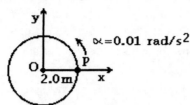

Point P is on the rim of a wheel of radius 2.0 m. At time t = 0, the wheel is at rest, and P is on the x-axis. The wheel undergoes a uniform angular acceleration of 0.01 rad/s^2 about the center O.

15) In Figure 9.1, the tangential acceleration of P at time t = 0 s is closest to:

A) zero

B) 0.005 m/s^2

C) 0.010 m/s^2

D) 0.015 m/s^2

E) 0.020 m/s^2

Answer: E
Var: 1

16) In Figure 9.1, the linear speed of P, when it reaches the y-axis, is closest to:

A) 0.18 m/s   B) 0.24 m/s   C) 0.35 m/s   D) 0.49 m/s   E) 0.71 m/s

Answer: C
Var: 1

17) In Figure 9.1, the magnitude of the acceleration of P, when it reaches the y-axis, is closest to:

A) 0.063 m/s^2

B) 0.066 m/s^2

C) 0.069 m/s^2

D) 0.072 m/s^2

E) 0.075 m/s^2

Answer: B
Var: 1

18) In Figure 9.1, the angle formed between the acceleration vector of P and the y-axis, when P reaches the y-axis, is closest to:

A) zero   B) 18°   C) 36°   D) 72°   E) 90°

Answer: B
Var: 1

19) In Figure 9.1, the time t, when P returns to the original position on the x-axis, is closest to:

A) 13 s   B) 18 s   C) 25 s   D) 35 s   E) 50 s

Answer: D
Var: 1

20) A slender rod 100.00 cm long is used as a meter stick. Two parallel axes which are perpendicular to the rod are considered. The first axis passes through the 50 cm mark and the second axis passes through the 30 cm mark. The ratio of the moment of inertia through the second axis to that of the first axis is closest to:

A) 1.5 B) 1.7 C) 1.9 D) 2.1 E) 2.3

Answer: A
Var: 1

Table 9.1

mass (kg)	x	y
40	0	7
60	5	2
100	7	10

21) In Table 9.1, the masses and the coordinates x and y of a set of three point masses in the x–y plane. The masses are interconnected by light struts, forming a rigid body. The moment of inertia of the rigid body, through the center of mass and perpendicular to the x–y plane, is closest to:

A) 3000 kg $\cdot$ m^2

B) 3200 kg $\cdot$ m^2

C) 3400 kg $\cdot$ m^2

D) 3600 kg $\cdot$ m^2

E) 3800 kg $\cdot$ m^2

Answer: E
Var: 1

22) A cylinder is observed to be rolling freely at constant speed on a horizontal surface. Which of the following statements is true?

A) It is possible that the cylinder is both rolling and sliding at the same time, i.e. that v, the speed of the centerpoint, is not equal to rw.

B) Even if the surface has friction, the cylinder cannot roll without slipping.

C) If the cylinder is rolling without slipping, there must be a non–zero friction force exerted by the surface.

D) It is not possible for the cylinder to roll unless friction is present.

E) If friction is present it is not possible for the motion to occur without loss of energy.

Answer: A
Var: 1

23) To drive a typical car at 40 mph on a level road for one hour requires about 3.2×10^7 J of energy. Suppose one tried to store this much energy in a spinning flywheel which was then coupled to the wheels of the car. A large flywheel cannot be spun too fast or it will fracture. If one used a flywheel of radius 0.60 m and mass 400 kg, what frequency of revolution would be required to store 2×10^7 J? Incidentally, 2500 rpm is about the maximum feasible rate of revolution with present materials technology for such a flywheel.

   A) 227 Hz   B) 455 Hz   C) 119 Hz   D) 66.7 Hz   E) 688 Hz

   Answer: C
   Var: 1

Figure 9.2

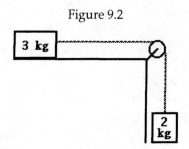

24) In Figure 9.2, two blocks, of masses 2 kg and 3 kg, are connected by a light string which passes over a pulley of moment of inertia 0.004 kg $\cdot$ m^2 and radius 5 cms. The coefficient of friction for the table top is 0.30. The blocks are released from rest. Using energy methods, one can deduce that after the upper block has moved 0.6 m, its speed is:

   A) 1.22 m/s   B) 5.44 m/s   C) 3.19 m/s   D) 1.95 m/s   E) 1.40 m/s

   Answer: E
   Var: 1

25) In rotational dynamics, moment of inertia plays a role analogous to one of the quantities encountered in linear motion, namely

   A) momentum.

   B) mass.

   C) a "couple" or "moment" of a force.

   D) translational kinetic energy.

   E) impulse.

   Answer: B
   Var: 1

Figure 9.3

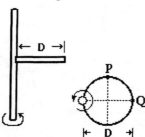

26) A uniform disk is attached at the rim to a vertical shaft and is used as a cam. Two views of the disk and shaft are shown. The disk has a diameter of 38 cm. The moment of inertia of the disk about the axis of the shaft is 7.5×10^{-3} kg • m^2. The shaft rotates uniformly about its axis at 70 rpm. In Figure 9.3, the mass of the disk is closest to:

   A) 0.14 kg   B) 0.12 kg   C) 0.092 kg   D) 0.16 kg   E) 0.18 kg

Answer: A
Var: 50+

27) A uniform disk is attached at the rim to a vertical shaft and is used as a cam. Two views of the disk and shaft are shown. The disk has a diameter of 89 cm. The moment of inertia of the disk about the axis of the shaft is 5.9×10^{-3} kg • m^2. The shaft rotates uniformly about its axis at 28 rpm. In Figure 9.3, the kinetic energy of the disk, in mJ, is closest to:

   A) 25   B) 15   C) 7.6   D) 43   E) 74

Answer: A
Var: 50+

28) A uniform disk is attached at the rim to a vertical shaft and is used as a cam. Two views of the disk and shaft are shown. The disk has a diameter of 49 cm. The moment of inertia of the disk about the axis of the shaft is 4.4×10^{-3} kg • m^2. The shaft rotates uniformly about its axis at 38 rpm. In Figure 9.3, the linear velocity of point P is closest to:

   A) 1.4 m/s   B) 0.91 m/s   C) 1.1 m/s   D) 1.6 m/s   E) 1.8 m/s

Answer: A
Var: 50+

29) A uniform disk is attached at the rim to a vertical shaft and is used as a cam. Two views of the disk and shaft are shown. The disk has a diameter of 84 cm. The moment of inertia of the disk about the axis of the shaft is 7.8×10^{-3} kg • m^2. The shaft rotates uniformly about its axis at 75 rpm. In Figure 9.3, the magnitude of the acceleration of point Q is closest to:

   A) 52 m/s^2

   B) 38 m/s^2

   C) 24 m/s^2

   D) 470,000 m/s^2

   E) 240,000 m/s^2

Answer: A
Var: 50+

Figure 9.4

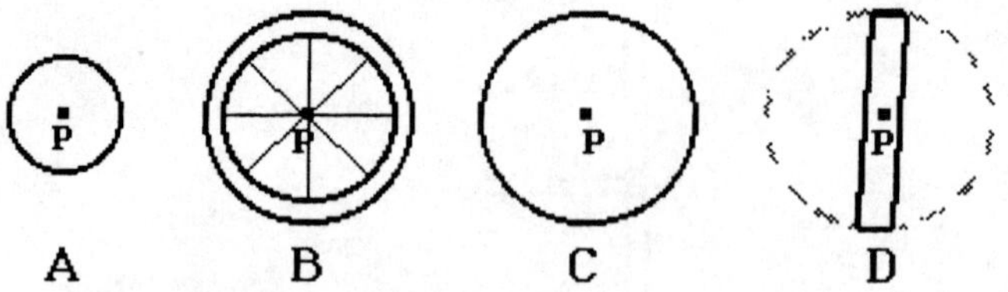

A   B   C   D

30) In Figure 9.4 are scale drawings of four objects, each of the same mass and uniform thickness. Which has the greatest moment of inertia when rotated about an axis perpendicular to the plane of the drawing? In each case the axis passes through point P.

A) A

B) B

C) C

D) D

E) The moment of inertia is the same for all of these objects.

Answer: B
Var: 1

31) A cylinder is placed on a plane inclined at 30° above horizontal. The axis of the cylinder is horizontal. What is the minimum value of the coefficient of friction if the cylinder is to roll down without slipping?

A) 0.25   B) 0.19   C) 0.37   D) 0.12   E) 0.31

Answer: B
Var: 1

Short Answer Questions

1) A bicycle wheel has an initial angular velocity of 6.8 rad/s. After turning through one–half of a revolution, the angular velocity is reduced to 3.1 rad/s. If the angular acceleration of the wheel is constant during the motion, how long will it take the wheel to make the one–half revolution?

Answer: 0.63 seconds
Var: 50+

Figure 9.5

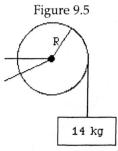

14 kg

2) In Figure 9.5, a rope is wrapped around a wheel of radius R = 2.0 meters. The wheel is mounted with frictionless bearings on an axle through its center. A block of mass 14 kg is suspended from the end of the rope. When the system is released from rest it is observed that the block descends 10 meters in 2.0 seconds. What is the moment of inertia of the wheel?

Answer: 54 kg • m^2
Var: 1

3) A futuristic design for a car is to have a large disk–like flywheel within the car storing kinetic energy. The flywheel has mass 370 kg with a radius of 0.50 m and can rotate up to 420 rev/s. Assuming all of this stored kinetic energy could be transferred to the linear velocity of the 2100–kg car, find the maximum attainable speed of the car.

Answer: 391 m/s
Var: 50+

Figure 9.6

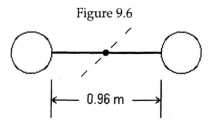

|← 0.96 m →|

4) In Figure 9.6, a weightlifter's barbell consists of two identical spherical masses each with radius 0.17 m and mass of 50 kg. The weights are connected by a 0.96 m steel rod with mass of 12 kg. Find the moment of inertia of the barbell through the axis at the center.

Answer: 44 kg • m^2
Var: 1

5) A disk is rotating at 6.0 rev/s. At t = 0, a torque is applied to the disk so that an acceleration is produced obeying the relation $\alpha(t) = \gamma - \beta t$ where γ = 9.0 rev/s^2 and β = 4.0 rev/s^3. How many revolutions does the disk make in coming to rest?

Answer: 59 rev
Var: 1

Chapter 10   Dynamics of Rotational Motion

Multiple Choice Questions

Figure 10.1

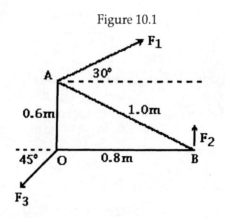

1) A light triangular plate OAB is in a horizontal plane. Three forces, F_1=4 N, F_2 = 9 N, and F_3 = 7 N, act on the plate, which is pivoted about a vertical axes through point O. In Figure 10.1, the moment arm of force F_1 about the axis through point O is closest to:

A) 2.1 N • m   B) 1.2 N • m   C) 1.5 N • m   D) 1.8 N • m   E) 2.4 N • m

Answer: A
Var: 50+

2) A light triangular plate OAB is in a horizontal plane. Three forces, F_1=7 N, F_2 = 3 N, and F_3 = 8 N, act on the plate, which is pivoted about a vertical axes through point O. In Figure 10.1, consider the counterclockwise sense as positive. The sum of the torques about the vertical axis through point O, acting on the plate due to forces F_1, F_2, and F_3, is closest to:

A) –1.2 N • m

B) 0.30 N • m

C) 1.2 N • m

D) –0.30 N • m

E) zero

Answer: A
Var: 50+

3) A light triangular plate OAB is in a horizontal plane. Three forces, F_1=1 N, F_2 = 7 N, and F_3 = 8 N, act on the plate, which is pivoted about a vertical axes through point O. In Figure 10.1, the plate is not moving. The magnitude of the force exerted on the plate by the pivot is closest to:

A) 5.1 N   B) 5.6 N   C) 7.2 N   D) 15 N   E) 16 N

Answer: A
Var: 50+

4) A drum has a radius of 0.40 m and a moment of inertia of 6.5 kg • m^2. The frictional torque of the drum bearings is 3.0 N • m. A ring at one end of a rope is slipped on a short peg on the rim of the drum, and a 39 m length of rope is wound upon it. The drum is initially at rest. A constant force is applied to the free end of the rope until the rope is completely unwound and slips off the peg. At that instant, the angular velocity of the drum is 25 rad/s. The drum then decelerates and comes to a halt. In this situation, the constant force applied to the rope is closest to:

A) 60 N   B) 47 N   C) 34 N   D) 21 N   E) 7.5 N

Answer: A
Var: 50+

5) A drum has a radius of 0.40 m and a moment of inertia of 6.5 kg • m^2. The frictional torque of the drum bearings is 3.0 N • m. A ring at one end of a rope is slipped on a short peg on the rim of the drum, and a 44 m length of rope is wound upon it. The drum is initially at rest. A constant force is applied to the free end of the rope until the rope is completely unwound and slips off the peg. At that instant, the angular velocity of the drum is 14 rad/s. The drum then decelerates and comes to a halt. In this situation, the angular momentum of the drum at the instant the rope slips off the peg is closest to:

A) 91 kg • m^2/s
B) 82 kg • m^2/s
C) 68 kg • m^2/s
D) 55 kg • m^2/s
E) 109 kg • m^2/s

Answer: A
Var: 50+

6) A drum has a radius of 0.40 m and a moment of inertia of 2.4 kg • m^2. The frictional torque of the drum bearings is 3.0 N • m. A ring at one end of a rope is slipped on a short peg on the rim of the drum, and a 18 m length of rope is wound upon it. The drum is initially at rest. A constant force is applied to the free end of the rope until the rope is completely unwound and slips off the peg. At that instant, the angular velocity of the drum is 17 rad/s. The drum then decelerates and comes to a halt. In this situation, the total amount of negative work done by friction is closest to:

A) 482 J   B) 135 J   C) 274 J   D) 378 J   E) 829 J

Answer: A
Var: 50+

7) A drum has a radius of 0.40 m and a moment of inertia of 2.1 kg • m^2. The frictional torque of the drum bearings is 3.0 N • m. A ring at one end of a rope is slipped on a short peg on the rim of the drum, and a 24 m length of rope is wound upon it. The drum is initially at rest. A constant force is applied to the free end of the rope until the rope is completely unwound and slips off the peg. At that instant, the angular velocity of the drum is 13 rad/s. The drum then decelerates and comes to a halt. In this situation, the total time interval in which the drum is in motion is closest to:

   A) 18 s B) 9.2 s C) 14 s D) 23 s E) 27 s

Answer: A
Var: 50+

Figure 10.2

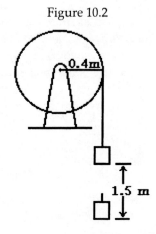

A wheel has a radius of 0.40 m and is mounted on frictionless bearings. A block is suspended from a rope which is wound on the wheel and attached to it. The wheel is released from rest and the block descends 1.5 m in 2.00 s. The tension in the rope during the descent of the block is 20 N.

8) In Figure 10.2, the mass of the block is closest to:

   A) 1.9 kg B) 2.0 kg C) 2.1 kg D) 2.2 kg E) 2.3 kg

Answer: D
Var: 1

9) In Figure 10.2 the moment of inertia of the wheel is closest to:

   A) 3.5 kg • m^2
   B) 3.7 kg • m^2
   C) 3.9 kg • m^2
   D) 4.1 kg • m^2
   E) 4.3 kg • m^2

Answer: E
Var: 1

Figure 10.3

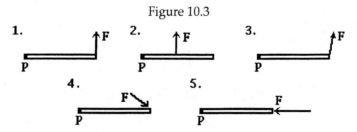

10) In Figure 10.3, a given force F is applied to a rod in several different ways. In which case is the torque due to F about the pivot P greatest?

    A) 1   B) 2   C) 3   D) 4   E) 5

Answer: A
Var: 1

Figure 10.4

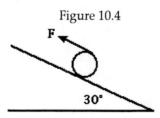

11) In Figure 10.4, a solid cylinder of 5 cms radius is positioned on a frictionless plane inclined at $30°$ above horizontal. A force F is exerted by a string wrapped around the spool. When F has a certain critical value the center of mass of the spool does not move. When this is the case, what is the angular acceleration of the spool?

    A) 196 rad/s^2

    B) 340 rad/s^2

    C) 260 rad/s^2

    D) 392 rad/s^2

    E) 98 rad/s^2

Answer: A
Var: 50+

Figure 10.5

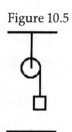

12) In Figure 10.5, a mass of 40.98 kg is attached to a light string which is wrapped around a cylindrical spool of radius 10 cm and moment of inertia 4.00 kg • m². The spool is suspended from the ceiling, and the mass is then released from rest a distance 5.70 m above the floor. How long does it take to reach the floor?

A) 3.54 s   B) 3.37 s   C) 1.13 s   D) 4.98 s   E) 7.02 s

Answer: A
Var: 50+

Figure 10.6

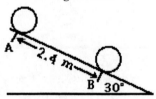

The radius of a 3.0 kg wheel is 6.0 cm. The wheel is released from rest at point A on a 30° incline. The wheel rolls without slipping and moves 2.4 m to point B in 1.20s.

13) In Figure 10.6, the moment of inertia of the wheel is closest to:

A) 0.0048 kg • m²

B) 0.0051 kg • m²

C) 0.0054 kg • m²

D) 0.0057 kg • m²

E) 0.0060 kg • m²

Answer: B
Var: 1

14) In Figure 10.6, the angular acceleration of the wheel is closest to:

A) 48 rad/s²   B) 56 rad/s²   C) 65 rad/s²   D) 73 rad/s²   E) 82 rad/s²

Answer: B
Var: 1

15) A hoop is released from rest at the top of a plane inclined at 24° above horizontal. How long does it take the hoop to roll 24.0 m down the plane?

A) 4.91 s   B) 4.48 s   C) 3.27 s   D) 3.13 s   E) 7.70 s

Answer: A
Var: 50+

Figure 10.7

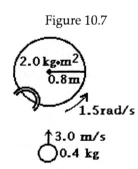

A turntable as a radius of 8.0 m and a moment of inertia of 2.0 kg • m^2. The turntable is rotating with an angular velocity of 1.5 rad/s about a vertical axis though its center on frictionless bearings. A 0.40 kg ball is projected horizontally toward the turntable axis with a velocity of 3.0 m/s. The ball is caught by a cup-shaped mechanism on the rim of the turntable.

16) In Figure 10.7, the initial angular momentum of the ball about the turntable axis is closest to:

A) zero

B) 0.3 kg • m^2/s

C) 0.5 kg • m^2/s

D) 0.8 kg • m^2/s

E) 1.0 kg • m^2/s

Answer: A
Var: 1

17) In Figure 10.7, the fraction of the initial kinetic energy of the system, which is lost during the capture of the ball, is closest to:

A) 0.45   B) 0.50   C) 0.55   D) 0.60   E) 0.65

Answer: B
Var: 1

Figure 10.8

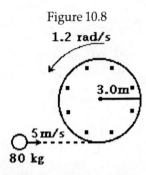

18) In Figure 10.8, a carousel has a radius of 3.0 m and a moment of inertia of 8000 kg • m². The carousel is rotating unpowered and without friction with an angular velocity of 1.2 rad/s. An 80 kg man runs with a velocity of 5.0 m/s, on a line tangent to the rim of the carousel, overtaking it. The man runs onto the carousel and grabs hold of a pole on the rim. The change in the angular velocity of the carousel is closest to:

A) +0.04 rad/s

B) +0.06 rad/s

C) +0.08 rad/s

D) –0.05 rad/s

E) –0.07 rad/s

Answer: A
Var: 1

19) A disk and a sphere are released simultaneously at the top of an inclined plane. They roll down without slipping. Which will reach the bottom first?

A) The one of smallest diameter.

B) The one of greatest mass.

C) The hoop.

D) The sphere.

E) They will reach the bottom at the same time.

Answer: D
Var: 1

20) A spinning ice skater is able to control the rate at which she rotates by pulling in her arms. We can best understand this effect by observing that in this process:

A) her angular momentum remains constant.

B) her moment of inertia remains constant.

C) her kinetic energy remains constant.

D) her total velocity remains constant.

E) she is subject to a constant non-zero torque.

Answer: A
Var: 1

21) Which of the following is an accurate statement?

    A) the angular momentum of a moving particle depends on the specific origin with respect to which the angular momentum is calculated.

    B) A particle moving in a straight line with constant speed necessarily has zero angular momentum.

    C) If the torque acting on a particle is zero about an arbitrary origin, then the angular momentum of the particle is also zero about that origin.

    D) Consider a planet moving in a circular orbit about a star. Even if the planet is spinning it is not possible for its total angular momentum to be zero.

    E) If the speed of a particle is constant, then the angular momentum of the particle about any specific origin must also be constant.

Answer: A
Var: 1

22) A uniform disk has a mass of 3.7 kg and a radius of 0.38 m. The disk is mounted on frictionless bearings and is used as a turntable. The turntable is initially rotating at 20 rpm. A thin-walled hollow cylinder has the same mass and radius as the disk. It is released from rest, just above the turntable, and on the same vertical axis. The hollow cylinder slips on the turntable for 0.20 s until it acquires the same final angular velocity as the turntable. The final angular momentum of the system is closest to:

    A) 0.56 kg • m^2/s

    B) 0.68 kg • m^2/s

    C) 0.80 kg • m^2/s

    D) 0.96 kg • m^2/s

    E) 1.1 kg • m^2/s

Answer: A
Var: 50+

23) A uniform disk has a mass of 3.4 kg and a radius of 0.53 m. The disk is mounted on frictionless bearings and is used as a turntable. The turntable is initially rotating at 50 rpm. A thin-walled hollow cylinder has the same mass and radius as the disk. It is released from rest, just above the turntable, and on the same vertical axis. The hollow cylinder slips on the turntable for 0.20 s until it acquires the same final angular velocity as the turntable. The average torque exerted on the hollow cylinder during the 0.20 s time interval in which slipping occurs is closest to:

    A) 8.3 N • m   B) 6.3 N • m   C) 13 N • m   D) 16 N • m   E) 17 N • m

Answer: A
Var: 50+

24) A uniform disk has a mass of 2.3 kg and a radius of 0.54 m. The disk is mounted on frictionless bearings and is used as a turntable. The turntable is initially rotating at 50 rpm. A thin–walled hollow cylinder has the same mass and radius as the disk. It is released from rest, just above the turntable, and on the same vertical axis. The hollow cylinder slips on the turntable for 0.20 s until it acquires the same final angular velocity as the turntable. The loss of kinetic energy of the system is closest to:

A) 3.1 J   B) 2.6 J   C) 3.6 J   D) 2.1 J   E) 1.6 J

Answer: A
Var: 50+

25)   Figure 10.9

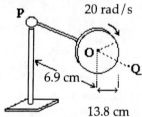

In Figure 10.9, the rotor of a gyroscope is a uniform disk which has a radius of 13.8 cm and a moment of inertia about its axis of 4.0×10^{-3} kg • m^2. The length of the rotor shaft is 6.9 cm. The ball pivot at P is frictionless. At a given instant, the rotor shaft is horizontal and the rotor is rotating with an angular velocity of 20 rad/s about its axis OP, as shown. The rotor is viewed from point Q on the axis. The precessional linear velocity of point O, including the direction seen from point Q, is closest to:

A) 0.25 rad/s, leftward

B) 0.25 rad/s, upward

C) 0.25 rad/s, rightward

D) 0.49 rad/s, downward

E) 0.49 rad/s, rightward

Answer: A
Var: 50+

26) In an interesting lecture demonstration a student sits in a swivel chair holding a spinning bicycle wheel oriented with its axis vertical. Initially the chair is motionless. Now the student rotates the axis of the spinning wheel by 180°, so that it is again vertical, but now the wheel is spinning in the opposite sense with respect to the room. When this is done the student and chair begin to rotate also. Which of the following is an accurate statement concerning this process?

    A) In the final state the chair will be rotating in the opposite sense of the wheel, but at a much higher frequency.

    B) In the final state the chair will be rotating in the same sense as the wheel, but at a much lower frequency.

    C) Assuming the swivel bearing of the chair is frictionless, angular kinetic energy is conserved in this process.

    D) Angular momentum, but not angular kinetic energy, is conserved in this process, independent of whether or not friction is present.

    E) Angular velocity is conserved in this process.

Answer: D
Var: 1

27) When is the angular momentum of a system constant?

    A) When the total kinetic energy is constant.

    B) When no net external force acts on the system.

    C) When the linear momentum and the energy are constant.

    D) When no torque acts on the system.

    E) When the moment of inertia is constant.

Answer: D
Var: 1

28) A bicycle wheel of radius 0.32 m and mass 2.60 kg is set spinning at 4.00 Hz. A bolt is attached to extend the axle in length, and a string is attached to the axle at a distance of 0.13 m from the wheel. Initially the axle of the spinning wheel is horizontal, and the wheel is suspended only from the string. At what rate will the wheel process about the vertical?

    A) 4.7 rpm   B) 3.1 rpm   C) 30 rpm   D) 0.50 rpm   E) 1.3 rpm

Answer: A
Var: 50+

Figure 10.10

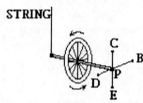

29) In Figure 10.10, a rapidly spinning bicycle wheel is suspended from a string attached to the axle, as shown here. Initially the axis is held fixed in the position shown. When the axle is released, point P on the axle will:

A) remain where it is.

B) move toward point B.

C) move toward point C.

D) move toward point D.

E) move toward point E.

Answer: B
Var: 1

Short Answer Questions

Figure 10.11

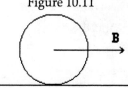

1) In Figure 10.11, a lawn roller in the form of a solid cylinder ($I = 1/2\ mR^2$) is being pulled horizontally by a horizontal force B applied to an axle through the center of the roller, as shown in the sketch. The roller has radius 0.83 meters and mass 53 kg. What magnitude B of the force is required to produce an acceleration a = 9.2 m/s² of the center of mass of the roller? (Assume that the lawn roller rolls without slipping.)

Answer: 730 N
Var: 50+

2) A 31.1-kg child is standing on the outer edge of a merry-go-round which has moment of inertia 895 kg • m² and radius 2.40 m. The entire system is initially rotating at 0.180 rev/s. Find the angular velocity if the child moves to a final position 1.10 m from the center of the merry-go-round.

Answer: 0.207 rev/s
Var: 50+

3) A bicycle wheel is rotating with an angular velocity of 3.1 rev/s. The brakes coefficient of kinetic friction between the wheel and the brakes is 0.87, find the number of revolutions the wheel makes in coming to rest. The moment of inertia of the wheel is 0.24 kg • m and its radius is 0.32 m.

Answer: 2.8 rev
Var: 1

Figure 10.12

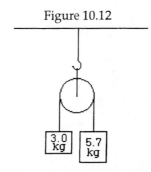

4) Figure 10.12 represents an Atwood's machine. There is no slipping between the cord and the surface of the wheel. The blocks have mass of 3.0 kg and 5.7 kg and the wheel has a radius of 0.12 m and mass of 10.3 kg. If the 5.7 kg mass falls 1.5 m, find the speed of each block. (Assume the wheel is in the shape of a disk.)

Answer: 2.4 m/s
Var: 1

5) A 58 kg runner is standing on the outer edge of a horizontal turntable mounted on a frictionless axis through its center. The turntable has a radius of 2.9 m and moment of inertia 500.0 kg • m^2 and is currently at rest. The runner starts his run along the outer edge and is observed to run with a speed, relative to the earth, of 5.6 m/s. If he runs for 60 s, how many revolutions does the turntable make?

Answer: 18 rev
Var: 1

Chapter 11   Equilibrium and Elasticity

Multiple Choice Questions

Figure 11.1

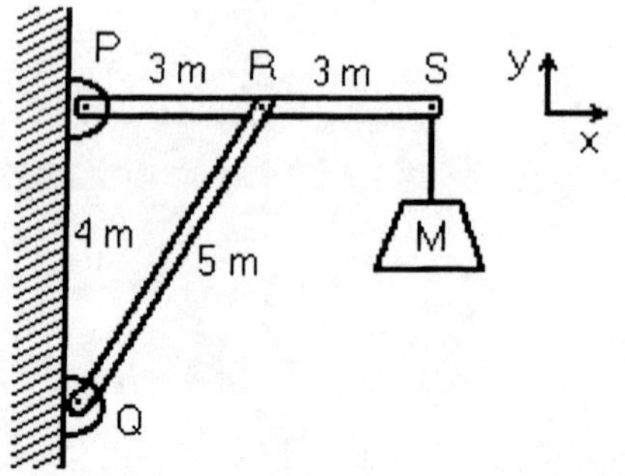

1) A uniform 200 kg beam, 6 m long, is freely pivoted at P. The beam is supported in a horizontal position by a light strut, 5 m long, which is freely pivoted at Q and is loosely pinned to the beam at R. A load of mass is suspended from the end of the beam at S. A maximum compression of 23,000 N in the strut is permitted, due to safety. In Figure 11.1, the maximum mass M of the load is closest to:

   A) 838 kg   B) 604 kg   C) 1073 kg   D) 1038 kg   E) 1273 kg

Answer: A
Var: 50+

2) A uniform 800 kg beam, 6 m long, is freely pivoted at P. The beam is supported in a horizontal position by a light strut, 5 m long, which is freely pivoted at Q and is loosely pinned to the beam at R. A load of mass is suspended from the end of the beam at S. A maximum compression of 11,000 N in the strut is permitted, due to safety. In Figure 11.1, under maximum load, the x–component of the force exerted on the beam by the pivot at P is closest to:

   A) 6600 N   B) 8800 N   C) 7700 N   D) 9900 N   E) 11,000 N

Answer: A
Var: 50+

3) A uniform 500 kg beam, 6 m long, is freely pivoted at P. The beam is supported in a horizontal position by a light strut, 5 m long, which is freely pivoted at Q and is loosely pinned to the beam at R. A load of mass is suspended from the end of the beam at S. A maximum compression of 17,000 N in the strut is permitted, due to safety. In Figure 11.1, under maximum load the y–component of the force exerted on the beam by the pivot at P is closest to:

   A) 4350 N   B) 2650 N   C) 6050 N   D) 6800 N   E) zero

Answer: A
Var: 50+

4) Suppose that a heavy person and a light person are balanced on a teeter-totter made of a plank of wood. Each person now moves in toward the fulcrum a distance of 25 cms. What effect will this have on the balance of the teeter-totter?

    A) The teeter-totter will remain in balance.

    B) The heavy person's end will go down.

    C) The light person's end will go down.

    D) One cannot tell whether either end will rise or fall without knowing the relative mass of the plank.

    E) Only if the plank has significant mass will the light person's end go down.

Answer: C
Var: 1

Figure 11.2

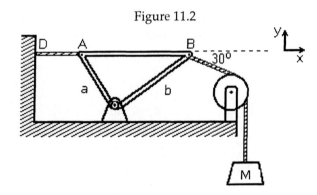

5) A right triangular frame ABC, made of light struts, is freely pivoted at point C. Strut AB is maintained in a horizontal position by a horizontal rope between points A and D. Strut AC has length a = 0.4 m and strut BC has length b = 0.3 m. A block of mass M = 4 kg is suspended from a rope which is attached at B and which passes over a frictionless pulley. The rope at B forms a 30° angle with the horizontal, as shown. In Figure 11.2, the tension in the horizontal rope AD is closest to:

    A) 49 N   B) 34 N   C) 20 N   D) 45 N   E) 60 N

Answer: A
Var: 50+

6) A right triangular frame ABC, made of light struts, is freely pivoted at point C. Strut AB is maintained in a horizontal position by a horizontal rope between points A and D. Strut AC has length a = 0.6 m and strut BC has length b = 0.5 m. A block of mass M = 9 kg is suspended from a rope which is attached at B and which passes over a frictionless pulley. The rope at B forms a 30° angle with the horizontal, as shown. In Figure 11.2, the x-component of the force exerted on the triangular frame by the pivot at point C is closest to:

    A) 37 N   B) 44 N   C) 53 N   D) 64 N   E) 77 N

Answer: A
Var: 50+

109

7) A right triangular frame ABC, made of light struts, is freely pivoted at point C. Strut AB is maintained in a horizontal position by a horizontal rope between points A and D. Strut AC has length a = 0.7 m and strut BC has length b = 0.5 m. A block of mass M = 3 kg is suspended from a rope which is attached at B and which passes over a frictionless pulley. The rope at B forms a 30° angle with the horizontal, as shown. In Figure 11.2, the y–component of the force exerted on the triangular frame by the pivot at point C is closest to:

A) 15 N   B) 11 N   C) 21 N   D) 29 N   E) 26 N

Answer: A
Var: 50+

8) Rectangular sheets of plywood, each of mass 7 kg and thickness 2 cms, are to be stacked in a rectangular box of mass 4900 kg. The center of mass of the box is 6 meters above the bottom. How many sheets of plywood should be stacked in the box in order to provide maximum stability? By maximum stability I mean the following: Place the box on an inclined plane. Maximum stability means maximum angle of incline, assuming no slipping.

A) 254   B) 203   C) 127   D) 51   E) 300

Answer: A
Var: 50+

Figure 11.3

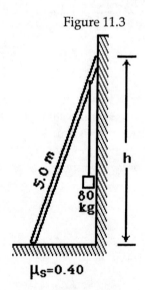

$\mu_s=0.40$

9) A 10 kg uniform ladder, 5.0 m long, is placed against a smooth wall at a height of 4.5 m. The base of the ladder rests on a rough horizontal surface whose coefficient of static friction is 0.40. An 80 kg block is suspended from the top rung of the ladder, close to the wall. In Figure 11.3, the force exerted on the wall by the ladder is closest to:

A) 400 N   B) 1700 N   C) 830 N   D) 490 N   E) 580 N

Answer: A
Var: 50+

110

10) A 70 kg uniform ladder, 5.0 m long, is placed against a smooth wall at a height of 4.5 m. The base of the ladder rests on a rough horizontal surface whose coefficient of static friction is 0.40. An 80 kg block is suspended from the top rung of the ladder, close to the wall. In Figure 11.3, the magnitude of the force exerted on the base of the ladder, due to contact with the rough horizontal surface is closest to:

A) 1570   B) 1550   C) 1540   D) 1580   E) 1600

Answer: A
Var: 50+

Figure 11.4

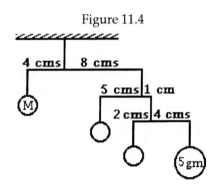

11) In Figure 11.4, what mass M is required to balance the mobile?

A) 18 gms   B) 30 gms   C) 36 gms   D) 60 gms   E) 90 gms

Answer: C
Var: 1

12) An interesting (and perplexing) demonstration is carried out as follows: A student supports a meter stick on the index finger of each hand. The meter stick is held horizontal. Now the student moves her hands together. First the stick slides on one hand and then on the other, alternating back and forth until finally her fingers come together right under the midpoint of the stick, no matter where her hands were positioned when she started. Suppose, for example, she started with her right hand finger under the 90 cm mark and her left hand under the 30 cm mark. As she moves her hands together the stick slides over the right hand until the right hand is under the 60 cm mark. Now the stick stops sliding over the right hand and begins to slide over the left hand, continuing until the left hand is under the 55 cm mark, at which time the stick switches back to sliding over the right hand. From this data determine the ratio of the coefficient of static friction to the coefficient of sliding friction for the stick resting on a person's hand. The result is:

A) 1.8   B) 2.5   C) 3.0   D) 1.5   E) 2.0

Answer: E
Var: 1

Figure 11.5

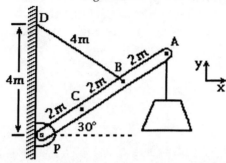

13) A 100 kg nonuniform beam, 6.0 m long, is loosely pinned at the pivot at P. A 400 kg block is suspended from the end of the boom at A. The boom forms a 30° angle with the horizontal, and is supported by a cable, 4.0 m long, between points D and B. Point B is 4.0 m from P, and point D is 4.0 m above P. The center of mass of the boom is at point C, which is 2.0 m from P. In Figure 11.5, the tension in the cable is closest to:

A) 6400 N   B) 5800 N   C) 5600 N   D) 5300 N   E) 4900 N

Answer: A
Var: 7

14) A 400 kg nonuniform beam, 6.0 m long, is loosely pinned at the pivot at P. A 900 kg block is suspended from the end of the boom at A. The boom forms a 30° angle with the horizontal, and is supported by a cable, 4.0 m long, between points D and B. Point B is 4.0 m from P, and point D is 4.0 m above P. The center of mass of the boom is at point C, which is 2.0 m from P. In Figure 11.5, the x–component of the pivot force on the boom is closest to:

A) 13,000 N   B) 5500 N   C) 21,000 N   D) 7600 N   E) 3200 N

Answer: A
Var: 35

15) A 200 kg nonuniform beam, 6.0 m long, is loosely pinned at the pivot at P. A 600 kg block is suspended from the end of the boom at A. The boom forms a 30° angle with the horizontal, and is supported by a cable, 4.0 m long, between points D and B. Point B is 4.0 m from P, and point D is 4.0 m above P. The center of mass of the boom is at point C, which is 2.0 m from P. In Figure 11.5, the y–component of the pivot force on the boom is closest to:

A) 2900 N   B) 4400 N   C) 6400 N   D) 7800 N   E) 8300 N

Answer: A
Var: 34

Figure 11.6

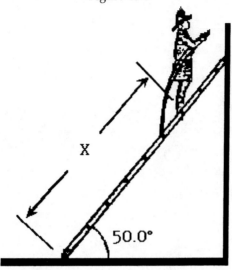

16) In Figure 11.6, a ladder of weight 200 N and length 10 meters leans against a smooth wall (no friction on wall). A firefighter of weight 600 N climbs a distance x up the ladder. The coefficient of friction between the ladder and the floor is 0.5. What is the maximum value of x if the ladder is not to slip?

A) 3.93 m   B) 5.00 m   C) 6.04 m   D) 6.28 m   E) 8.44 m

Answer: D
Var: 1

Figure 11.7

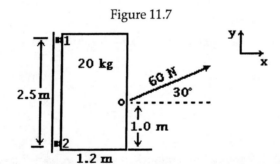

A 20 kg uniform door has a width of 1.2 m and a height of 2.5 m. The door is mounted on a post by a pair of hinges, marked 1 and 2, at the top and bottom of the door. An external force of 60 N, at an angle of 30° above the horizontal, is applied to the doorknob, as shown. The doorknob is 1.0 m above the bottom of the door.

17) In Figure 11.7, the x-component of the force, erected on the door at the top by hinge 1, is closest to:

A) zero   B) +55 N   C) +80 N   D) –55 N   E) –80 N

Answer: D
Var: 1

18) In Figure 11.7, the x-component of the force, exerted on the door at the bottom by hinge 2, is closest to:

A) zero   B) +29 N   C) +65 N   D) –29 N   E) –65 N

Answer: A
Var: 1

113

19) In Figure 11.7, the sum of the y-components of the forces, exerted on the door by hinges 1 and 2, is closest to:

A) 145 N   B) 165 N   C) 195 N   D) 225 N   E) 250 N

Answer: B
Var: 1

Situation 11.1

A steel wire, 3.2 m long, has a diameter of 1.2 mm. The wire stretches 1.6 m when it bears a load. Young's modulus for steel is 2.0×10^{11} Pa and the Poisson ratio is 0.19.

20) In Situation 11.1, the mass of the load is closest to:

A) 12 kg   B) 16 kg   C) 20 kg   D) 24 kg   E) 28 kg

Answer: A
Var: 1

21) In Situation 11.1, the ratio of the reduction in the diameter of the wire to the initial unstressed diameter is closest to:

A) 1×10^{-5} B) 2×10^{-5} C) 5×10^{-5} D) 1×10^{-4} E) 2.5×10^{-4}

Answer: D
Var: 1

Situation 11.2

The base of an aluminum block, which is fixed in place, measures 90 cm by 90 cm. The height of the block is 60 cm. A force, applied to the upper force and parallel to it, produces a shear strain of 0.0060. The shear modulus of aluminum is 3.0×10^{10} Pa.

22) In Situation 11.2, the displacement of the upper force, in the direction of the applied force, in mm, is closest to:

A) 3.0   B) 3.6   C) 4.2   D) 4.8   E) 5.4

Answer: B
Var: 1

23) In Situation 11.2, the shear stress on the block, in MPa, is closest to:

A) 180   B) 360   C) 600   D) 720   E) 900

Answer: A
Var: 1

Figure 11.8

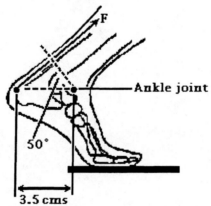

24) In Figure 11.8, the Achilles tendon exerts a force F = 720 N. What is the torque it exerts about the ankle joint?

   A) 12.2 N • m   B) 16.2 N • m   C) 21.2 N • m   D) 25.9 N • m   E) 36.0 N • m

Answer: B
Var: 1

25) A sample of tendon 3 cms long and 4 mm in diameter is found to break under a minimum force of 128 N. If the sample had been 1.5 cms long it would have broken under a minimum force of

   A) 32 N   B) 64 N   C) 128 N   D) 256 N   E) 512 N

Answer: C
Var: 1

26) Which of the following is an accurate statement?

   A) The ratio stress/strain is called the elastic modulus.

   B) "Strain" has a meaning very close to "force".

   C) "Stress" has a meaning very close to "stretch".

   D) Tensile stress is measured in Newtons.

   E) Tensile strain is measured in meters.

Answer: A
Var: 1

Situation 11.3

A 12 liter volume of oil is subjected to pressure which produces a volume strain of -3.0×10^{-4}. The bulk modulus of the oil is 6.0×10^9 Pa and is independent of the pressure.

27) In Situation 11.3, the reduction in the volume of the oil, in ml, is closest to:

   A) 2.0   B) 2.4   C) 2.8   D) 3.2   E) 3.6

Answer: E
Var: 1

28) In Situation 11.3, the compressibility of the oil, is SI units, is closest to:

   A) 5.4×10^{-11}

   B) 1.7×10^{-10}

   C) 5.4×10^{-10}

   D) 1.7×10^{-9}

   E) 5.4×10^{-9}

Answer: B
Var: 1

29) In Situation 11.3, the change in the pressure of the oil, in atm, is closest to:

   A) 12   B) 14   C) 16   D) 18   E) 20

Answer: D
Var: 1

Short Answer Questions

1)

Figure 11.9

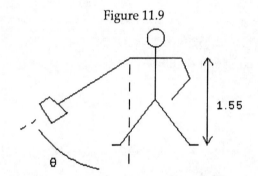

In Figure 11.9, a lumberjack (with mass 92 kg and center of gravity 1.15 meters above his boots when standing) grabs the handle of a double-bladed axe of mass 16 kg. On a bet, he lifts the axe in a circle of radius 1.55 meters (the height of his shoulder), keeping his arm and the axe handle locked as a rigid object. If he can hold the axe steady at an angle of $\theta = 76°$ from the vertical, what are the coordinates of the center of gravity of the lumberjack–axe combination? (Make the reasonable assumptions that the mass of the axe is concentrated at the blade, and that the mass of the lumberjack's arm itself does not affect the calculation significantly.) Measure the center of gravity position from the point on the ground between the lumberjack's boots. The pivot point of his shoulder is 25 cm from his vertical axis.

Answer: 1.15 m vertical, 26 cm horizontal
Var: 50+

2)

Figure 11.10

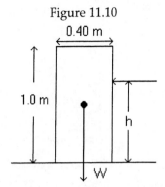

In Figure 11.10, a rectangular crate 0.40 m wide and 1.0 m tall sits on a horizontal surface. The crate weighs 960 N, and its center of gravity is at its geometric center. A horizontal force F is applied at a distance h above the floor. If h = 0.56 m, what minimum value of F is required to make the crate start to tip over? (Assume that μ is large enough that the crate does not start to slide.)

Answer: 343 N
Var: 50+

3)

Figure 11.11

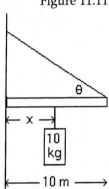

In Figure 11.11, a 10.0 m long bar is attached by a frictionless hinge to a wall and held horizontal by a rope that makes an angle θ of 35° with the bar. The bar is uniform and weighs 59.2 N. How far from the hinge should a 10.0 kg mass be suspended for the tension T in the rope to be 177 N?

Answer: 7.3 meters from the hinge
Var: 50+

4)

Figure 11.12

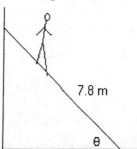

7.8 m

θ

In Figure 11.2, a uniform ladder 12 meters long rests against a vertical friction– less wall. The ladder weighs 400.0 N and makes an angle θ of 49° with the floor. A man weighing 693 N climbs slowly up the ladder, the ladder starts to slip. What is μ_s, the coefficient of static friction between the floor and the ladder?

Answer: 0.52
Var: 50+

5) An aluminum wire and a steel wire, each of length 2 m, are hung from the ceiling. A 5.0 kg mass is suspended from the lower end of each wire. The aluminum wire has a diameter of 2.2 mm. What must be the diameter of the steel wire if it is to stretch the same distance as the aluminum wire, so that the two wires maintain equal lengths after the masses are attached? The Young's modulus for aluminum is 0.70×10^{11} Pa and for steel it is 2.0×10^{11} Pa.

Answer: 1.3 mm
Var: 1

6) When the pressure applied to an unknown liquid is increased from 1.0×10^7 Pa to 5.5×10^7 Pa, the volume of the liquid decreases by 0.70%. Calculate the bulk modulus of the liquid.

Answer: 6.4×10^9 Pa
Var: 1

118

Chapter 12 Gravitation

Multiple Choice Questions

1) The gravitational acceleration at the surface of planet X is 12.0 m/s², and the radius of the planet is 48,900 km. The altitude above the surface of planet X, at which the weight of a body is equal to that on the surface of the earth, in km, is closest to:

   A) 5200   B) 6300   C) 7300   D) 8300   E) 9400

   Answer: A
   Var: 50+

2) At a given point above the surface of the earth, the gravitational acceleration is equal to 5.4 m/s². The altitude of this point, above the surface of the earth, in km, is closest to:

   A) 2200   B) 2800   C) 4200   D) 5700   E) 6900

   Answer: A
   Var: 39

3) At a given point below the surface of the earth, the gravitational acceleration is equal to 8.9 m/s². Assume the earth is of uniform density. The depth of this point, below the surface of the earth, in km, is closest to:

   A) 590   B) 850   C) 1100   D) 440   E) 300

   Answer: A
   Var: 40

4) What is the gravitational force acting on a person due to another person standing 8 meters away? Assume each individual has 58 kg mass.

   A) 3.5×10^{-9} N

   B) 5.2×10^{2} N

   C) 2.8×10^{-8} N

   D) 6.0×10^{-11} N

   E) 4.8×10^{-10} N

   Answer: A
   Var: 50+

5) Consider an object that drops a distance h in a time of 66 s on the surface of the earth (neglecting air effects). How long would it take the same object to drop the same distance on the surface of Pluto? The mass of Pluto is 1.1×10^{22} kg and its radius is 4.0×10^{5} m.

   A) 96 s   B) 66 s   C) 54 s   D) 120 s   E) 34 s

   Answer: A
   Var: 50+

6) A meteor of mass about 3.4×10^{12} kg (a chunk of ice about a mile in diameter) is heading straight for Jupiter. When it hits there will be a huge release of energy, visible here on earth. Assuming it has fallen from far away, how much energy will be released when it hits Jupiter? The radius of Jupiter is about 7×10^7 m and its mass is 1.9×10^{27} kg.

A) 6.1×10^{21} J

B) 3.4×10^{19} J

C) 6.8×10^{19} J

D) 5.4×10^{22} J

E) 5.8×10^{18} J

Answer: A
Var: 50+

7) A 520 kg object is released from rest at an altitude of 800 km above the north pole of the earth. Ignore atmospheric friction. The speed of the object as it strikes the surface of the earth, in km/s, is closest to:

A) 3.7   B) 1.9   C) 2.3   D) 2.7   E) 4.0

Answer: A
Var: 50+

8) An object is projected vertically upward from the surface of a nonrotating planet of radius R, with an initial velocity equal to 48% of the escape velocity for the planet. The maximum distance from the center of the planet attained by the object is closest to:

A) 1.3 R   B) 1.2 R   C) 1.4 R   D) 1.6 R   E) 1.7 R

Answer: A
Var: 48

9) An object is projected vertically from the surface of a nonrotating planet, with an initial velocity equal to 2.3 times the escape velocity for the planet. The ratio of the velocity of the object, at a very large distance from the planet, to the escape velocity for the planet is closest to:

A) 2.1   B) 1.9   C) 1.7   D) 2.3   E) 2.5

Answer: A
Var: 50+

10) An object, projected vertically from the surface of a nonrotating planet, arrives at infinity with a velocity equal to 50% of the escape velocity for the planet. The ratio of the initial velocity of the object to the escape velocity for the planet is closest to:

A) 1.1   B) 1.2   C) 1.3   D) 1.5   E) 1.6

Answer: A
Var: 50

11) Suppose that a person can jump straight up a distance of 22 cms on the surface of the earth. How small would a planet have to be so that the person could jump completely off (i.e. jump up and not come down)? Assume the earth's radius is 6380 km and that the small planet has the same density as the earth.

A) 1.19 km   B) 741 km   C) 37.5 km   D) 0.0159 km   E) 0.457 km

Answer: A
Var: 50+

12) A newspaper article discussing the space program noted that it is easier to launch a satellite into an eastward orbit then into a westward one. Is this true?

A) Yes, this is true because the rotation of the earth toward the east gives the satellite added speed, thereby reducing the speed required with respect to earth if orbital velocity is to be attained.

B) Yes, this is true because launching to the east reduces wind resistance.

C) No, this is not true because the kinetic energy of the launch vehicle is independent of the direction in which it is launched.

D) No, this is not true because launching toward the east means an even greater launch speed is needed to attain orbiting speed due to the earth's rotation.

E) No, this is not true because it is the upward component of velocity that is important in reaching an orbit, not the horizontal component east and west.

Answer: A
Var: 1

13) A theoretical physicist consulting for NASA pointed out early in the space program that the effect of friction on an orbiting satellite would result in its speeding up. Is this true?

A) No, this is not true because friction is inherently a dissipative force which reduces the kinetic energy and hence, speed of an object.

B) No, this is not true because satellites orbit in a perfect vacuum where there is no friction.

C) No, this is not true because conservation of angular momentum requires that a satellite maintain a constant speed in a circular orbit whether or not friction acts.

D) Yes, this is true. The force of friction reduces the total energy of the satellite, but as the satellite spirals in toward the earth the kinetic energy increases 1 Joule for every 2 Joule decrease in potential energy, so kinetic energy increases while total energy decreases.

E) Yes, this is true because for a satellite friction acts in the forward direction, unlike the situation in an inertial frame of reference where friction acts to oppose motion.

Answer: D
Var: 1

14) A satellite is in circular orbit at an altitude of 1300 km above the surface of a nonrotating planet with an orbital speed of 1.6 km/s. The escape velocity for the planet is 8.1 km/s. In this situation, the orbital period of the satellite, in minutes, is closest to:

A) 92   B) 83   C) 75   D) 66   E) 57

Answer: A
Var: 50+

15) A satellite is in circular orbit at an altitude of 1800 km above the surface of a nonrotating planet with an orbital speed of 1.8 km/s. The escape velocity for the planet is 10.9 km/s. In this situation, the mass of the planet is closest to:

A) 9.2×10^{22} kg

B) 4.6×10^{22} kg

C) 6.9×10^{22} kg

D) 1.4×10^{23} kg

E) 1.9×10^{23} kg

Answer: A
Var: 50+

Situation 12.1

	radius	gravitational acceleration at the surface	orbital radius	orbital period
Moon I			5×10^7 m	
Moon II			9×10^7 m	3×10^5 s
Moon III	2×10^5 m	0.20 m/s^2		2×10^6 s

An Earth station receives data transmitted back in time from a future intergalactic expedition. The table summarizes the data for the moons of a planet that will be discovered in a distant galaxy.

16) In Situation 12.1, the mass of the planet is closest to:

A) 1.2×10^{24} kg

B) 1.7×10^{24} kg

C) 2.4×10^{24} kg

D) 3.4×10^{24} kg

E) 4.8×10^{24} kg

Answer: E
Var: 1

17) In Situation 12.1, the mass of Moon III is closest to:

A) 2.4×10^{19} kg

B) 4.8×10^{19} kg

C) 1.2×10^{20} kg

D) 2.4×10^{20} kg

E) 4.8×10^{20} kg

Answer: C
Var: 1

18) In Situation 12.1, the centripetal acceleration of Moon II due to orbital motion is closest to:

A) $0.02 \ m/s^2$ B) $0.04 \ m/s^2$ C) $0.06 \ m/s^2$ D) $0.08 \ m/s^2$ E) $0.10 \ m/s^2$

Answer: B
Var: 1

19) In Situation 12.1, the orbital period of Moon I is closest to:

A) $1.2 \times 10^5 \ s$ B) $1.4 \times 10^5 \ s$ C) $1.7 \times 10^5 \ s$ D) $2.0 \times 10^5 \ s$ E) $2.3 \times 10^5 \ s$

Answer: A
Var: 1

20) In Situation 12.1, the orbital radius of Moon III is closest to:

A) $2.6 \times 10^8 \ m$

B) $3.2 \times 10^8 \ m$

C) $4.0 \times 10^8 \ m$

D) $5.0 \times 10^8 \ m$

E) $6.0 \times 10^8 \ m$

Answer: B
Var: 1

21) With a single firing of a rocket from the earth's surface, is it possible to launch a vehicle into a stable orbit around the earth?

A) Yes, but the orbit would be elliptical.

B) Yes, but only if the right direction of launch is chosen.

C) Yes, provided the launch is made at the right time of year with respect to the sun.

D) No, because the vehicle would crash back into the earth before it made one complete cycle.

E) No, because the energy required would be too great.

Answer: D
Var: 1

22) Which of the following is a true statement?

A) It is possible to place a satellite in a circular orbit above the earth's equator, but it is not possible to place a satellite in a circular "polar" orbit, i.e. and orbit that takes the satellite over both the north and south poles of the earth.

B) The fact that planet X in the solar system is farther from the sun than is planet Y does not mean that the orbital period of X is greater than for Y.

C) The earth is in free fall under the action of the net gravitational force of the sun and the planets.

D) The force of the moon on the earth is greater than the force of the sun on the earth.

E) It is possible to place communication satellites in stationary orbits such that they always remain directly above (i.e. radially out from) any desired point on earth.

Answer: C
Var: 1

23) Halley's comet orbits the sun in an elliptical orbit. Its distance from the sun ranges from 8.75 x 10^{10} m to 5.26 x 10^{12} m. Its minimum speed is 908 m/s. What is its maximum speed?

A) 2.33 x 10^3 m/s

B) 5.46 x 10^4 m/s

C) 6.55 x 10^4 m/s

D) 3.12 x 10^5 m/s

E) 7.06 x 10^5 m/s

Answer: B
Var: 1

Table 12.1

	Mass	Radius	orbital radius	orbital period
Moon A	4×10^{20} kg		2×10^8 m	4×10^6 s
Moon B	1.5×10^{20} kg	2×10^5 m	3×10^8 m	

Ekapluto is an unknown planet that has two moons in circular orbits. The table summarizes the hypothetical data about the moons.

24) In Table 12.1, the mass of Ekapluto is closest to:

A) 1 x 10^{22} kg

B) 3 x 10^{22} kg

C) 1 x 10^{23} kg

D) 3 x 10^{23} kg

E) 1 x 10^{24} kg

Answer: D
Var: 1

25) In Table 12.1, the orbital period of Moon B is closest to:

A) 5.6 x 10^6 s   B) 6.0 x 10^6 s   C) 6.4 x 10^6 s   D) 6.9 x 10^6 s   E) 7.4 x 10^6 s

Answer: E
Var: 1

26) In Table 12.1, the maximum gravitational force between the two moons is closest to:

A) 1.6 x 10^{13} N

B) 4.4 x 10^{13} N

C) 1.0 x 10^{14} N

D) 2.0 x 10^{14} N

E) 4.0 x 10^{14} N

Answer: E
Var: 1

124

27) In Table 12.1, a meteoroidal fragment is in circular orbit around Moon B, at a small altitude above the surface. The speed of this body is closest to:

A) 220 m/s   B) 320 m/s   C) 440 m/s   D) 640 m/s   E) 880 m/s

Answer: A
Var: 1

28) In Table 12.1, the gravitational acceleration at the surface of Moon B is closest to:

A) 0.10 m/s^2 B) 0.15 m/s^2 C) 0.20 m/s^2 D) 0.25 m/s^2 E) 0.30 m/s^2

Answer: D
Var: 1

29) The reason an astronaut in an earth satellite feels weightless is that

A) the astronaut is beyond the range of the earth's gravity.

B) the astronaut is falling.

C) the astronaut is at a point in space where the effects of the moon's gravity and the earth's gravity cancel.

D) this is a psychological effect associated with rapid motion.

E) the astronaut's acceleration is zero.

Answer: B
Var: 1

Short Answer Questions

1) What is the difference in the weight of a 132 kg person as measured at sea level and at the top of the Vinson Massif, the highest peak in Antarctica? The product
$GM_{Earth} = 3.99 \times 10^{14}$ N $\cdot$ m^2 $\cdot$ kg^{-1}, the radius of the Earth is 6.38×10^6 m, and the height above sea level of the Vinson Massif is 5.14×10^3 m. Neglect the flattening of the Earth at the poles.

Answer: 2.08 N
Var: 50+

2) A man–made satellite of mass 2465 kg is in orbit around the earth, making one revolution in 423 minutes. What is the magnitude of the gravitational force exerted on the satellite by the earth? (The mass of the earth is 6.0×10^{24} kg.)

Answer: 2.8×10^3 N
Var: 50+

3) An astronaut is standing on the surface of the moon which has a radius $R = 1.74 \times 10^6$ m and a mass $m = 7.35 \times 10^{22}$ kg. An experiment is planned where a projectile needs to be launched straight up from the surface. What does the initial speed of the projectile need to be for it to reach a height of 2.55×10^6 m above the moon's surface?

Answer: 1.83 km/s
Var: 1

4) A satellite is in orbit around a planet with orbital speed determined to be 8680 m/s. Find the escape velocity from the planet from this position of its orbit.

Answer: 12,300 m/s
Var: 50+

5) A geostationary satellite in orbit around the Earth has a period identical to that of the Earth's daily rotation; the radius of such an orbit is 4.23×10^4 kilometers. A system of satellites is proposed such that 9 satellites are in orbit at the same radius and each passes over a point fixed on the Earth 8 times per day (the times will be evenly spaced). What will be the orbital radius of each satellite? There will be two such radii; only the smaller will be practical.

Answer: 9.78×10^3 km
Var: 12

Chapter 13   Periodic Motion

Multiple Choice Questions

1) A 5.7 kg block attached to a spring executes simple harmonic motion on a frictionless horizontal surface. At time t = 0 s, the block has a displacement of –0.20 m, a velocity of –0.80 m/s, and an acceleration of +4.1 m/s². The force constant of the spring is closest to:

A) 120 N/m   B) 110 N/m   C) 98 N/m   D) 91 N/m   E) 82 N/m

Answer: A
Var: 50+

2) A 5.8 kg block attached to a spring executes simple harmonic motion on a frictionless horizontal surface. At time t = 0 s, the block has a displacement of –0.10 m, a velocity of –0.80 m/s, and an acceleration of +5.8 m/s². The amplitude of the motion is closest to:

A) 0.15 m   B) 5.8 m   C) 0.21 m   D) 0.25 m   E) 0.28 m

Answer: A
Var: 50+

3) A 0.077 kg block on a horizontal frictionless surface is attached to a spring whose force constant is 150 N/m. The block is pulled from its equilibrium position at x = 0 m to a displacement x = +0.080 m and is released from rest. The block then executes simple harmonic motion along the x–axis (horizontal). The displacement of the block at time t = 0.40 s is closest to:

A) 0.03 m   B) –0.03 m   C) –0.08 m   D) 0.08 m   E) 0.3 m

Answer: A
Var: 50+

4) A 1.6 kg block on a horizontal frictionless surface is attached to a spring whose force constant is 420 N/m. The block is pulled from its equilibrium position at x = 0 m to a displacement x = +0.080 m and is released from rest. The block then executes simple harmonic motion along the x–axis (horizontal). The velocity of the block at time t = 0.40 s is closest to:

A) –0.1 m/s   B) 0.1 m/s   C) –1 m/s   D) 1 m/s   E) zero

Answer: A
Var: 50+

5) A 0.019 kg block on a horizontal frictionless surface is attached to a spring whose force constant is 120 N/m. The block is pulled from its equilibrium position at x = 0 m to a displacement x = +0.080 m and is released from rest. The block then executes simple harmonic motion along the x–axis (horizontal). When the displacement is x = 0.051 m, the kinetic energy of the block is closest to:

A) 0.23 J   B) 0.21 J   C) 0.24 J   D) 0.26 J   E) 0.27 J

Answer: A
Var: 50+

6) A 0.030 kg block on a horizontal frictionless surface is attached to a spring whose force constant is 290 N/m. The block is pulled from its equilibrium position at x = 0 m to a displacement x = +0.080 m and is released from rest. The block then executes simple harmonic motion along the x-axis (horizontal). When the displacement is x = – 0.046 m, the acceleration of the block is closest to:

   A) 450 m/s^2 B) 230 m/s^2 C) 340 m/s^2 D) 1200 m/s^2 E) 1600 m/s^2

Answer: A
Var: 50+

7) A 0.34 kg block on a horizontal frictionless surface is attached to a spring whose force constant is 470 N/m. The block is pulled from its equilibrium position at x = 0 m to a displacement x = +0.080 m and is released from rest. The block then executes simple harmonic motion along the x-axis (horizontal). The maximum elastic potential energy of the system is closest to:

   A) 1.5 J   B) 1.4 J   C) 1.6 J   D) 1.8 J   E) 1.9 J

Answer: A
Var: 50+

Figure 13.1

8) In Figure 13.1, two masses, M = 5 kg and m = 4 kg, are attached to a spring of spring constant 100 N/m. The system is set into oscillation with an amplitude of 74 cm. At the instant when the acceleration is a maximum the 5 kg mass separates from the 4 kg mass which then remains attached to the spring and continues to oscillate. The amplitude of oscillation of the 4 kg mass will be

   A) 74 cm   B) 59 cm   C) 33 cm   D) 93 cm   E) 170 cm

Answer: A
Var: 50+

9) For an object undergoing simple harmonic motion,

   A) the acceleration is greatest when the speed is greatest.

   B) the displacement is greatest when the speed is greatest.

   C) the acceleration is greatest when the displacement is greatest.

   D) the maximum potential energy is larger than the maximum kinetic energy.

   E) the total energy oscillates at frequency $f = \dfrac{1}{2\pi}\sqrt{\dfrac{k}{m}}$

Answer: C
Var: 1

10) A particle is in simple harmonic motion along the x-axis with a period of 6.3 s and an amplitude of 0.35 m. The equilibrium position of the particle is at x = 0. At time t = 0, the particle is at x = +0.28 m and it is moving in the negative x-direction. The magnitude of the velocity of the particle, at time t = 0 s is closest to:

A) 0.21 m/s   B) 0.45 m/s   C) 0.35 m/s   D) 0.53 m/s   E) 0.66 m/s

Answer: A
Var: 50+

11) A particle is in simple harmonic motion along the x-axis with a period of 1.9 s and an amplitude of 0.91 m. The equilibrium position of the particle is at x = 0. At time t = 0, the particle is at x = +0.64 m and it is moving in the negative x-direction. The x-component of the acceleration at time t = 0 is closest to:

A) –7.0   B) 7.0   C) –10.0   D) 10   E) zero

Answer: A
Var: 50+

12) A particle is in simple harmonic motion along the x-axis with a period of 2.8 s and an amplitude of 0.68 m. The equilibrium position of the particle is at x = 0. At time t = 0, the particle is at x = +0.20 m and it is moving in the negative x-direction. The time interval required for the particle to reach x = – 0.68 m from its initial position at t = 0 s is closest to:

A) 0.84 s   B) 1.0 s   C) 1.3 s   D) 1.5 s   E) 1.7 s

Answer: A
Var: 50+

13) A particle is in simple harmonic motion along the x-axis with a period of 4.2 s and an amplitude of 0.23 m. The equilibrium position of the particle is at x = 0. At time t = 0, the particle is at x = +0.14 m and it is moving in the negative x-direction. At time t = 0, the ratio of the potential energy to the total mechanical energy is closest to:

A) 0.36   B) 0.48   C) 0.60   D) 0.78   E) 0.96

Answer: A
Var: 50+

Situation 13.1
A 0.90 kg solid disk has a radius of 10 cm and a thickness of 1.0 cm. The disk is used as a balance wheel in a mechanism and the torsion constant is 0.020 N • m/rad.

14) In Situation 13.1, the period of oscillation of the wheel is closest to:

A) 1.1 s   B) 1.5 s   C) 2.1 s   D) 3.0 s   E) 4.2 s

Answer: B
Var: 1

15) In Situation 13.1, the torque required to hold the wheel at a 90° angular displacement from equilibrium is closest to:

A) 0.01 N • m   B) 0.02 N • m   C) 0.03 N • m   D) 0.04 N • m   E) 0.05 N • m

Answer: C
Var: 1

Figure 13.2

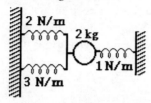

16) In Figure 13.2, a mass of 2 kg is attached to three springs of spring constants 1 N/m, 2 N/m, and 3 N/m. When the mass is at rest the springs are unstretched. For this system

A) $\omega^2 = 1/2$ rad/s^2

B) $\omega^2 = 1$ rad/s^2

C) $\omega^2 = 3/2$ rad/s^2

D) $\omega^2 = 2$ rad/s^2

E) $\omega^2 = 3$ rad/s^2

Answer: E
Var: 1

17) It has been suggested that a possible transportation system to connect two cities such as Boston and Washington, D.C. might function like this: Drill a tunnel straight from Boston to Washington. A car released in Boston would fall under the influence of gravity, gaining speed, and then finally coasting back to the surface at Washington. The only expenditure of energy required would be that to overcome friction, and this could be reduced by using an evacuated tunnel or magnetic levitation of the train or other possible techniques. Assuming the density of the earth is constant (it isn't), and using only the value of the acceleration of gravity at the earth's surface (9.8 m/s^2) and the radius of the earth (6380 km) determine how long it would take to travel between any two cities via a straight tunnel. The result, rather surprisingly, is about

A) 42 minutes

B) 1 hour 23 minutes

C) 2 hours 54 minutes

D) 58 minutes

E) 6 hours 33 minutes

Answer: A
Var: 1

Situation 13.2

A balance wheel is in oscillation with an angular amplitude of 120° and a frequency of 1.5 Hz. At time t = 0, the angular displacement is a maximum.

18) In Situation 13.2, the angular displacement in radians at time t = 1.2 s is closest to:

A) –1.6   B) –0.8   C) –0.2   D) +0.6   E) +1.4

Answer: D
Var: 1

19) In Situation 13.2, the angular velocity of the wheel at time $t = 1.2$ s is closest to:

    A) zero

    B) $+9.4$ rad/s^2

    C) $+18.8$ rad/s^2

    D) -9.4 rad/s^2

    E) -18.8 rad/s^2

Answer: C
Var: 1

20) In Situation 13.2, the maximum angular acceleration of the wheel is closest to:

    A) 150 rad/s^2

    B) 170 rad/s^2

    C) 190 rad/s^2

    D) 210 rad/s^2

    E) 230 rad/s^2

Answer: C
Var: 1

Situation 13.3

A 4.0 kg body is freely pivoted about a point 0.15 m from the center of mass. The period of small amplitude oscillations of this physical pendulum is 1.2 s.

21) In Situation 13.3, the centroidal moment of inertia of the body is closest to:

    A) 0.09 kg $\cdot$ m^2

    B) 0.12 kg $\cdot$ m^2

    C) 0.15 kg $\cdot$ m^2

    D) 0.18 kg $\cdot$ m^2

    E) 0.21 kg $\cdot$ m^2

Answer: B
Var: 1

22) In Situation 13.3, the length of a simple pendulum that has the same frequency of oscillation and the same amplitude as the physical pendulum is closest to:

    A) 0.32 m   B) 0.34 m   C) 0.36 m   D) 0.38 m   E) 0.40 m

Answer: C
Var: 1

23) A meter stick is freely pivoted about the 20 cm mark. The frequency of small amplitude oscillations is closest to:

    A) 0.5 Hz   B) 0.7 Hz   C) 0.9 Hz   D) 1.2 Hz   E) 1.5 Hz

Answer: B
Var: 1

24) A coin is placed on a platform attached to a spring that oscillates vertically in simple harmonic motion. The amplitude of the displacement is 1.20 cm. What is the maximum frequency for which the coin will always remain in contact with the platform?

A) 2.25 Hz
B) 6.89 Hz
C) 12.2 Hz
D) 4.55 Hz
E) 8.75 Hz

Answer: D
Var: 1

25) If both the mass of a simple pendulum and its length are doubled, the period will

A) be unchanged.

B) increase by a factor of 2.

C) increase by a factor of 4.

D) increase by a factor of 1.4

E) increase by a factor of 0.71.

Answer: D
Var: 1

26) What happens when a periodic driving force is applied to a vibrating system?

A) The system will stop vibrating and finally come to a stop.

B) The system will exhibit chaotic motion.

C) The system will vibrate at the frequency of the driving force.

D) The system will vibrate at its natural frequency.

E) It will vibrate at some multiple of the driving frequency (call a harmonic or "overtone").

Answer: C
Var: 1

Situation 13.4

A 5.0 kg block is attached to a spring whose force constant is 125 N/m. The block is pulled from its equilibrium position at $x = 0$ m to a position at $x = +0.687$ m and is released from rest. The block then executes damped oscillation along the x-axis. The damping force is proportional to the velocity. When the block first returns to $x = 0$ m, its x-component of velocity is -2.0 m/s and its x-component of acceleration is +5.6 m/s^2.

27) In Situation 13.4, the magnitude of the acceleration of the block upon release at $x = +0.687$ m is closest to:

A) 16.4 m/s^2
B) 17.2 m/s^2
C) 18.0 m/s^2
D) 18.8 m/s^2
E) 19.6 m/s^2

Answer: B
Var: 1

28) In Situation 13.4, the damping coefficient b is closest to:

A) 14 kg/s^2
B) 16 kg/s^2
C) 18 kg/s^2
D) 20 kg/s^2
E) 22 kg/s^2

Answer: A
Var: 1

29) In Situation 13.4, the work done by the damping force during the travel of the block from $x = +0.687$ m to $x = 0$ m is closest to:

A) –10 J   B) –15 J   C) –20 J   D) –25 J   E) –30 J

Answer: C
Var: 1

Short Answer Questions

1) An object of mass 6.8 kg is attached to a spring of force constant 1500 N/m. The object is set into simple harmonic motion, with an initial velocity of $v_0 = 4.6$ m/s and an initial displacement of $x_0 = 0.23$ m. Calculate the maximum velocity the object has during its motion.

Answer: 5.7 m/s
Var: 50+

2) An object is undergoing simple harmonic motion with frequency $f = 2.9$ Hz and amplitude $A = 0.12$ m. At $t = 0$ the object is at $x = 0$. How long does it take the object to go from $x = 0$ to $x = 0.048$ m?

Answer: 0.023 seconds
Var: 50+

3) A pendulum is adjusted to have a period of precisely 2 seconds, and is set in motion. After 13 minutes, its amplitude has decreased to 1/5 of its initial value.

a) If the motion of the pendulum can be represented by $\Theta = \Theta_0 e^{-\gamma t} \cos(2\pi f t)$, what is γ? Recall that $1/5 = \exp(-1.609)$.

b) Find the ratio $\dfrac{2\pi f}{\gamma}$

Answer: a) 2.1×10^{-3} s^{-1}
            b) 1.5×10^3

Var: 50+

4) A large stick is pivoted about one end and allowed to swing back and forth as a physical pendulum. The mass of the stick is 8.30 kg and its center of gravity (found by finding its balance point) is 2.80 m from the pivot. If the period of the swinging stick is 4.00 seconds, what is its moment of inertia, about an axis through the pivot?

Answer: 92.2 kg $\cdot$ m^2
Var: 50+

5)

Figure 13.3

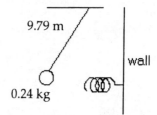

9.79 m

wall

0.24 kg

In Figure 13.3, a 0.24-kg ball is suspended from a string 9.79 m long and is pulled slightly to the left. As the ball swings through the lowest part of its motion it encounters a spring attached to the wall. The spring pushes against the ball and eventually the ball is returned to its original starting position. Find the time for one complete cycle of this motion if the spring constant is 21 N/m. (Assume that once the pendulum ball hits the spring there is no effect due to the vertical movement of the ball.)

Answer: 3.5 s
Var: 50+

Chapter 14   Fluid Mechanics

Multiple Choice Questions

Figure 14.1

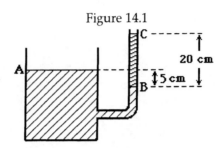

1) A container has a vertical tube, whose inner radius is 18.00 mm, connected to it at its side. An unknown liquid reaches level A in the container and level B in the tube--level A being 5.0 cm higher than level B. The liquid supports a 20.0 cm high column of oil, between levels B and C, whose density is 590 kg/m^3. In Figure 14.1, the mass of the oil, in grams, is closest to:

   A) 120   B) 240   C) 360   D) 480   E) 600

   Answer: A
   Var: 50+

2) A container has a vertical tube, whose inner radius is 13.00 mm, connected to it at its side. An unknown liquid reaches level A in the container and level B in the tube--level A being 5.0 cm higher than level B. The liquid supports a 20.0 cm high column of oil, between levels B and C, whose density is 500 kg/m^3. In Figure 14.1, the gauge pressure at level B is closest to:

   A) 980 Pa   B) 490 Pa   C) 740 Pa   D) 1200 Pa   E) 1500 Pa

   Answer: A
   Var: 50+

3) A container has a vertical tube, whose inner radius is 18.00 mm, connected to it at its side. An unknown liquid reaches level A in the container and level B in the tube--level A being 5.0 cm higher than level B. The liquid supports a 20.0 cm high column of oil, between levels B and C, whose density is 460 kg/m^3. In Figure 14.1, the density of the unknown liquid is closest to:

   A) 1800 kg/m^3

   B) 2000 kg/m^3

   C) 1400 kg/m^3

   D) 1600 kg/m^3

   E) 1700 kg/m^3

   Answer: A
   Var: 50+

4) A 7.1 kg solid sphere, made of metal whose density is 4100 kg/m³, is suspended by a cord. The density of water is 1000 kg/m³. When the sphere is immersed in water, the tension in the cord is closest to:

    A) 53 N   B) 61 N   C) 70 N   D) 78 N   E) 87 N

Answer: A
Var: 50+

5) A 8.2 kg solid sphere, made of metal whose density is 2300 kg/m³, is suspended by a cord. When the sphere is immersed in a liquid of unknown density, the tension in the cord is 23 N. The density of the liquid is closest to:

    A) 1600 kg/m³

    B) 1500 kg/m³

    C) 1400 kg/m³

    D) 1300 kg/m³

    E) 1200 kg/m³

Answer: A
Var: 50+

6) A 9.6 kg solid sphere, made of metal whose density is 2300 kg/m³, is suspended by a cord. The sphere floats when placed in a liquid of density 3500 kg/m³. The fraction of the volume of the sphere that is submerged is closest to:

    A) 0.66   B) 0.68   C) 0.70   D) 0.64   E) 0.62

Answer: A
Var: 50+

Figure 14.2

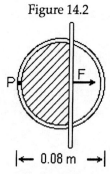

|← 0.08 m →|

7) A circular wire, 0.08 m in diameter, with a slider wire on it, is in a horizontal plane. A liquid film is formed, bounded by the wires, on the left side of the slider, as shown. The surface tension of the liquid is 99 mN/m. An applied force F, perpendicular to the slider, maintains the film in equilibrium. Ignore the sag in the film. In Figure 14.2, when the slider is 0.06 m from point P, the applied force F, in mN, is closest to:

    A) 14   B) 10   C) 6.9   D) 3.4   E) 17

Answer: A
Var: 50+

8) A circular wire, 0.08 m in diameter, with a slider wire on it, is in a horizontal plane. A liquid film is formed, bounded by the wires, on the left side of the slider, as shown. The surface tension of the liquid is 31 mN/m. An applied force F, perpendicular to the slider, maintains the film in equilibrium. Ignore the sag in the film. In Figure 14.2, when the equilibrium force F is 3.7 mN, the distance of the slider from the center of the circle, in mm, is closest to:

    A) 27   B) 23   C) 20   D) 17   E) 13

Answer: A
Var: 50+

9) A circular wire, 0.08 m in diameter, with a slider wire on it, is in a horizontal plane. A liquid film is formed, bounded by the wires, on the left side of the slider, as shown. The surface tension of the liquid is 12 mN/m. An applied force F, perpendicular to the slider, maintains the film in equilibrium. Ignore the sag in the film. In Figure 14.2, the maximum value of the equilibrium force F, in mN, is closest to:

    A) 1.9   B) 0.96   C) 1.4   D) 2.4   E) 2.9

Answer: A
Var: 50+

10) How many grams of ethanol (specific gravity 0.80) should be added to 5 grams of chloroform (specific gravity 1.50) if the resulting mixture is to have a specific gravity of 1.20?

    A) 2.0 gms   B) 2.4 gms   C) 1.8 gms   D) 4.4 gms   E) 1.6 gms

Answer: A
Var: 1

11) Consider a brick that is totally immersed in water. The long edge of the brick is vertical. The pressure on the brick is

    A) the same on all surfaces of the brick.

    B) greatest on the face with largest area.

    C) greatest on the top of the brick.

    D) greatest on the sides of the brick.

    E) greatest on the bottom of the brick.

Answer: E
Var: 1

12) What force does the water exert (in addition to that due to atmospheric pressure) on a submarine window of radius 77 cms at a depth of 7100 meters in sea water (density 1025 kg/m^3)?

A) 1.33 x 10^8 N

B) 1.33 x 10^{12} N

C) 6.64 x 10^{11} N

D) 4.23 x 10^7 N

E) 6.64 x 10^7 N

Answer: A
Var: 50+

Figure 14.3

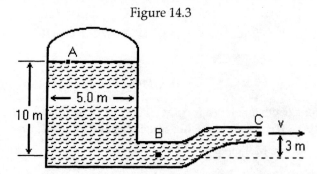

13) A pressurized cylindrical tank, 5.0 m in diameter, contains water which emerges from the pipe at point C, with a velocity of 29 m/s. Point A is 10 m above point B and point C is 3 m above point B. The area of the pipe at point B is 0.08 m^2 and the pipe narrows to an area of 0.04 m^2 at point C. Assume the water is an ideal fluid in laminar flow. The density of water is 1000 kg/m^3. In Figure 14.3, the mass flow rate in the pipe is closest to:

A) 1200 Kg/s   B) 1000 Kg/s   C) 930 Kg/s   D) 810 Kg/s   E) 700 Kg/s

Answer: A
Var: 50+

14) A pressurized cylindrical tank, 5.0 m in diameter, contains water which emerges from the pipe at point C, with a velocity of 95 m/s. Point A is 10 m above point B and point C is 3 m above point B. The area of the pipe at point B is 0.09 m^2 and the pipe narrows to an area of 0.03 m^2 at point C. Assume the water is an ideal fluid in laminar flow. The density of water is 1000 kg/m^3. In Figure 14.3, the rate at which the water level is falling in the tank, in mm/s, is closest to:

A) 150   B) 170   C) 120   D) 100   E) 77

Answer: A
Var: 50+

15) A pressurized cylindrical tank, 5.0 m in diameter, contains water which emerges from the pipe at point C, with a velocity of 22 m/s. Point A is 10 m above point B and point C is 3 m above point B. The area of the pipe at point B is 0.05 m^2 and the pipe narrows to an area of 0.04 m^2 at point C. Assume the water is an ideal fluid in laminar flow. The density of water is 1000 kg/m^3. In Figure 14.3, the gauge pressure in the pipe at point B, in kPa, is closest to:

A) 120　　　　　B) 87　　　　　C) 150　　　　　D) 180　　　　　E) 200

Answer: A
Var: 50+

16) A pressurized cylindrical tank, 5.0 m in diameter, contains water which emerges from the pipe at point C, with a velocity of 25 m/s. Point A is 10 m above point B and point C is 3 m above point B. The area of the pipe at point B is 0.08 m^2 and the pipe narrows to an area of 0.06 m^2 at point C. Assume the water is an ideal fluid in laminar flow. The density of water is 1000 kg/m^3. In Figure 14.3, the air pressure (absolute) in the tank above the water, in atmospheres, is closest to:

A) 3.4　　　　　B) 2.8　　　　　C) 4.1　　　　　D) 4.8　　　　　E) 5.1

Answer: A
Var: 50+

Figure 14.4

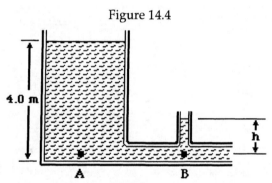

A vented tank of large cross-sectional area has a horizontal pipe 0.12 m in diameter at the bottom. The tank holds a liquid whose density is 1500 kg/m^3 to a height of 4.0 m. The velocity of the liquid in the pipe at point B holds a column of liquid to a height h. Assume the liquid is an ideal fluid in laminar flow.

17) In Figure 14.4, the volume flow rate out of the tank is closest to:

A) 0.03 m^3/s　　　B) 0.05 m^3/s　　　C) 0.07 m^3/s　　　D) 0.09 m^3/s　　　E) 0.11 m^3/s

Answer: D
Var: 1

18) In Figure 14.4, the height h of the liquid in the vertical tube is closest to:

A) 0.5 m　　　　　B) 0.7 m　　　　　C) 0.9 m　　　　　D) 1.1 m　　　　　E) 1.3 m

Answer: B
Var: 1

19) In Figure 14.4, the pressure difference, $P_a - P_b$, in kPa, is closest to:

    A) 11   B) 23   C) 36   D) 48   E) 59

Answer: D
Var: 1

20) If you have ever had to wade across a rocky creek while hiking in the mountains, you have probably noticed that by the time you get to the deep water in the center of the creek the rocks don't seem to hurt your bare feet so much. What is the reason for this?

    A) The greater pressure on one's feet in deep water means the rocks cannot dig in so much.

    B) The velocity of the water is less in deep regions than in shallow regions.

    C) One tends to stand on tiptoe in deep water, thereby reducing the area of the foot in contact with the rocks.

    D) Deeper water is colder, and hence more dense, than shallow water.

    E) One experiences a greater buoyant force in deeper water.

Answer: E
Var: 1

Figure 14.5

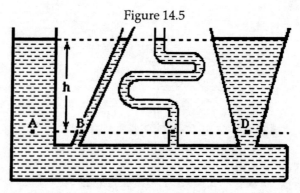

21) In Figure 14.5, fluid fills the container shown here. At which of the indicated points is the pressure greatest?

    A) A

    B) B

    C) C

    D) D

    E) The pressure is the same at each of the labeled points.

Answer: E
Var: 1

Figure 14.6

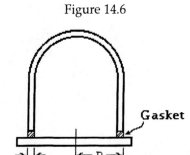

22) In Figure 14.6, in laboratory work a convenient vacuum chamber is often made using a glass bell jar placed on a metal plate. Between the bell jar and the base plate is a rubber gasket of thickness t, width w and outer radius R, where R >> w >> t. What is the pressure bearing down on the gasket in terms of atmospheric pressure P_a if R = 18 cm, w = 1.2 cm?

A) $13\,P_a$ B) $7.5\,P_a$ C) $6.0\,P_a$ D) $12\,P_a$ E) $?\,P_a$

Answer: B
Var: 1

23) A viscous fluid, having a viscosity of 80 poise, is between parallel plates that are 4.0 cm apart. Both plates are in motion, in opposite directions, with velocities of 3.0 cm/s, and the liquid between them is in laminar flow. The shear stress applied to the liquid, in SI units, is closest to:

A) 6   B) 12   C) 30   D) 60   E) 120

Answer: B
Var: 1

Situation 14.1

Water is in laminar flow, in a horizontal cylindrical pipe, 2.5 cm in radius. The pressure drop in a 20 m section of pipe is 3000 Pa. The viscosity of the water is 1.2×10^{-3} N · s/m^2.

24) In Situation 14.1, the volume flow rate of the water is closest to:

A) 0.008 m^3/s

B) 0.012 m^3/s

C) 0.02 m^3/s

D) 0.03 m^3/s

E) 0.05 m^3/s

Answer: C
Var: 1

25) In Situation 14.1, the velocity of the water along the axis of the pipe is closest to:

A) 5 m/s   B) 7 m/s   C) 10 m/s   D) 14 m/s   E) 20 m/s

Answer: E
Var: 1

26) In England in the Middle Ages an extensive system of canals was used for transportation. Some of these canals crossed over canyons by flowing over bridges (viaducts). Suppose that a heavily loaded barge crossed over such a waterway bridge.

A) The force downward on the bridge would increase because of the added weight of the barge.

B) The force on the bridge would not change when the barge passed over.

C) The force on the barge would become less because some water would be squeezed off of the bridge.

D) The force on the bridge would become less because of the buoyancy effect of the water on the barge.

E) Whether or not the force on the bridge would increase or decrease would depend on whether the water was flowing or stationary.

Answer: B
Var: 1

27) A barge loaded with lumber and iron ore floats in a lock by a dam (a closed pool of water like a big swimming pool). If some of the cargo is thrown overboard, the level of water in the lock will

A) rise.

B) drop.

C) stay the same.

D) rise, provided it is lumber that is thrown overboard.

E) rise, provided it is iron ore that is thrown overboard.

Answer: C
Var: 1

28) Two soap bubbles, of radii a and b, coalesce to form a single bubble of radius c. The external atmospheric pressure is P_O. In terms of these parameters the surface tension of the soap film is

A) $P_O = \dfrac{ab + ac + bc}{a + b + c}$

B) $P_O = \dfrac{c^3 - a^3 - b^3}{4(a^2 + b^2 - c^2)}$

C) $P_O = \dfrac{a^3 + b^3 + c^3}{4(a^2 + b^2 + c^2)}$

D) $P_O = \dfrac{a^2 + b^2 - c^2}{a + b - c}$

E) $P_O = \dfrac{abc}{a^2 + b^2 + c^2}$

Answer: B
Var: 1

Situation 14.2

A metal sphere has a mass of 7.5×10^{-3} kg and a radius of 8.0×10^{-3} m. A viscous liquid has a density of 2.4×10^3 kg/m^3 and a viscosity of 0.8 N • s/m^2. The sphere is released from rest in the liquid.

29) In Situation 14.2, the initial acceleration of the sphere upon release is closest to:

A) 2.0 m/s^2 B) 2.5 m/s^2 C) 3.0 m/s^2 D) 3.5 m/s^2 E) 4.0 m/s^2

Answer: C
Var: 1

30) In Situation 14.2, the viscous force on the sphere, when the velocity is 0.05 m/s, in mN, is closest to:

A) 5.5   B) 6.0   C) 6.5   D) 7.0   E) 7.5

Answer: B
Var: 1

31) In Situation 14.2, the terminal velocity of the sphere is closest to:

A) 0.19 m/s   B) 0.27 m/s   C) 0.37 m/s   D) 0.61 m/s   E) 0.75 m/s

Answer: A
Var: 1

32) Surface tension tends to keep a falling stream of water together. Suppose that water comes out of a faucet with velocity 2 m/s at a rate of 4 liters/min. It falls 50 cms. What then will be the radius of the stream?

   A) 3.26 mm   B) 1.67 mm   C) 4.25 mm   D) 3.56 mm   E) 2.39 mm

   Answer: E
   Var: 1

33) The Bernoulli effect is described by the equation
   $$P_1 + 1/2\rho v^2_1 + \rho g h_1 = P_2 + 1/2 r^2_2 + \rho g h_2$$
   The origin of this relation is that it is a statement of

   A) the conservation of linear momentum.

   B) Newton's Third Law, i.e equal action and reaction.

   C) the conservation of energy for a moving fluid.

   D) the continuity principle for fluids.

   E) F = ma as applied to a fluid.

   Answer: C
   Var: 1

34) The Bernoulli effect is responsible for the lift force on an airplane wing. Wings must therefore be designed so as to insure that

   A) air molecules will be deflected downward when they hit the wing.

   B) air molecules will be deflected upward when they hit the wing.

   C) air molecules move more rapidly past the upper surface of the wing than past the lower surface.

   D) air molecules move more rapidly past the lower surface of the wing than past the upper surface.

   E) wings are thick enough to create a significant pressure difference between the top and bottom surfaces of the wings because of the different heights of these surfaces.

   Answer: C
   Var: 1

Short Answer Questions

1)

Figure 14.7

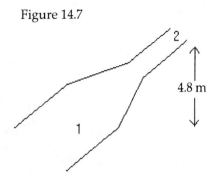

In Figure 14.7, water (density 1000 kg/m^3) is flowing in a pipeline. At point 1 the water velocity is 2.3 m/s. Point 2 is 4.8 m above point 1. The cross sectional area of the pipe is 0.06m^2 at point 1 and 0.020 m^2 at point 2. What is the pressure difference $P_1 - P_2$ between points 1 and 2?

Answer: 6.82 x 10^4 Pa
Var: 50+

Figure 14.8

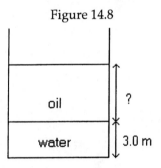

2) In Figure 14.8, an open tank contains a layer of oil floating on top of a layer of water (density 1000 kg/m^3) that is 3.0 m thick, as shown in the sketch. What must be the thickness of the oil layer if the gauge pressure at the bottom of the tank is to be 3.9 x 10^4 Pa?

The density of the oil is 670 kg/m^3.

Answer: 1.5 meters
Var: 50+

3) A wooden raft has a mass of 97 kg. When empty it floats in water (density 1000 kg/m^3) with 41% of its volume submerged. What mass of sand can be put on the raft without it sinking?

Answer: 140 kg
Var: 50+

145

4) Water is being pumped through a horizontal pipe that is 20.7 m long and 12.0 cm in diameter. A pump maintains a gauge pressure of 216 Pa at a large open tank at one end of the pipe. The other end of the pipe is open to the air. If this pipe is replaced by a second one of length 9 m and diameter 5.0 cm, what gauge pressure must the pump provide to give the same volume flow rate as for the first pipe?

Answer: 3.1×10^3 Pa
Var: 50+

5) Heated crude oil with a viscosity of 2.50 centipoise is flowing at a speed of 8.50 m/s through the center of a cylindrical pipe with a radius of 35.0 cm. At what point from the walls of the pipe is the speed 17.0% of the maximum speed at the center?

Answer: 3.11 cm
Var: 1

Chapter 15   Mechanical Waves

Multiple Choice Questions

1) A transverse wave is propagated in a string stretched along the x-axis. The equation of the wave, in SI units, is given by: $y = 0.002 \cos \pi(53t - 11x)$. The amplitude of the wave, in SI units, is closest to:

   A) 0.002

   B) 0.002π

   C) 0.002×11

   D) $0.002 \times 11\pi$

   E) $0.002\pi/11$

Answer: A
Var: 50+

2) A transverse wave is propagated in a string stretched along the x-axis. The equation of the wave, in SI units, is given by: $y = 0.009 \cos \pi(32t - 16x)$. The frequency of the wave, in SI units, is closest to:

   A) 16   B) 32   C) 48   D) 72   E) 96

Answer: A
Var: 50+

3) A transverse wave is propagated in a string stretched along the x-axis. The equation of the wave, in SI units, is given by: $y = 0.009 \cos \pi(87t - 16x)$. The wave speed, including the sense of direction along the x-axis, in SI units, is closest to:

   A) 5.4   B) –5.4   C) 0.18   D) –0.18   E) zero

Answer: A
Var: 50+

4) A transverse wave is propagated in a string stretched along the x-axis. The equation of the wave, in SI units, is given by: $y = 0.006 \cos \pi(58t - 12x)$. The propagation constant of the wave, in SI units, is closest to:

   A) 38   B) 58   C) 24   D) 6.0   E) 12

Answer: A
Var: 50+

5) A transverse wave is propagated in a string stretched along the x-axis. The equation of the wave, in SI units, is given by: $y = 0.006 \cos \pi(29t - 18x)$. The maximum velocity of a particle on the string, in SI units, is closest to:

   A) 0.55   B) 0.72   C) 0.89   D) 1.1   E) 1.2

Answer: A
Var: 50+

6) A string, 50 cm long and having a mass of 23 g, is attached to a 390 Hz vibrator at one end. The other end of the string is fixed and the string is kept under tension. The vibrator produces a transverse wave in the string, whose amplitude is 1.0 mm, and which propagates with a velocity of 59 m/s. The energy of the wave is absorbed at the fixed end. In this situation, the propagation constant of the wave, in SI units, is closest to:

A) 42   B) 6.6   C) 21   D) 13   E) 33

Answer: A
Var: 50+

7) A string, 10 cm long and having a mass of 34 g, is attached to a 260 Hz vibrator at one end. The other end of the string is fixed and the string is kept under tension. The vibrator produces a transverse wave in the string, whose amplitude is 1.0 mm, and which propagates with a velocity of 39 m/s. The energy of the wave is absorbed at the fixed end. In this situation, the tension in the string, in SI units, is closest to:

A) 520   B) 500   C) 540   D) 560   E) 580

Answer: A
Var: 50+

8) A string, 70 cm long and having a mass of 27 g, is attached to a 470 Hz vibrator at one end. The other end of the string is fixed and the string is kept under tension. The vibrator produces a transverse wave in the string, whose amplitude is 9.0 mm, and which propagates with a velocity of 75 m/s. The energy of the wave is absorbed at the fixed end. In this situation, the maximum transverse velocity, of a point on the string, in SI units, is closest to:

A) 27   B) 25   C) 23   D) 28   E) 30

Answer: A
Var: 50+

9) A string, 90 cm long and having a mass of 31 g, is attached to a 780 Hz vibrator at one end. The other end of the string is fixed and the string is kept under tension. The vibrator produces a transverse wave in the string, whose amplitude is 2.0 mm, and which propagates with a velocity of 50 m/s. The energy of the wave is absorbed at the fixed end. In this situation, the average power transmitted by the wave, in SI units, is closest to:

A) 83   B) 130   C) 170   D) 210   E) 250

Answer: A
Var: 50+

10) Which of the following is a FALSE statement?

   A) In a transverse wave the particle motion is perpendicular to the velocity vector of the wave.

   B) Not all waves are mechanical in nature.

   C) The speed of a wave and the speed of the vibrating particles that constitute the wave are different entities.

   D) Waves transport energy and matter from one region to another.

   E) A wave in which particles move back and forth in the same direction as the wave is moving is called a longitudinal wave.

   Answer: D
   Var: 1

11) The expression y = 2 sin (28t + 400x) represents

   A) a wave traveling along the x-axis toward the positive direction.

   B) a longitudinal wave.

   C) a wave of frequency 176 Hz.

   D) a wave of period 63.7 s.

   E) a wave of amplitude 4 units.

   Answer: A
   Var: 1

12) A wire, 2.0 m long, with a mass of 40 g, is under tension. A transverse wave is propagated on the wire, for which the frequency is 330 Hz, the wavelength is 0.50 m, and the amplitude is 2.9 mm. The time, for a crest of the transverse wave to travel the length of the wire, in ms, is closest to:

   A) 12   B) 11   C) 14   D) 15   E) 16

   Answer: A
   Var: 50+

13) A wire, 5.0 m long, with a mass of 60 g, is under tension. A transverse wave is propagated on the wire, for which the frequency is 360 Hz, the wavelength is 0.90 m, and the amplitude is 2.7 mm. The tension in the line, in SI units, is closest to:

   A) 1300   B) 1400   C) 1600   D) 1800   E) 2000

   Answer: A
   Var: 50+

14) A wire, 7.0 m long, with a mass of 50 g, is under tension. A transverse wave is propagated on the wire, for which the frequency is 160 Hz, the wavelength is 0.60 m, and the amplitude is 2.1 mm. The maximum transverse acceleration, of a point on a wire, in SI units, is closest to:

   A) 2100   B) 1900   C) 1600   D) 1300   E) 2400

   Answer: A
   Var: 50+

15) A wave on a stretched string is described by
$$y = 0.004 \sin (300t - 15x).$$
What is the maximum velocity of a particle on the string?

   A) 0.060 m/s

   B) 1.20 m/s

   C) 20.0 m/s

   D) 8.37×10^{-5} m/s

   E) 5.56 m/s

Answer: B
Var: 1

Figure 15.1

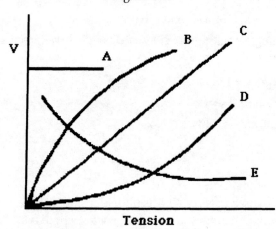

16) In Figure 15.1, which of the curves best represents the variation of wave speed as a function of tension for transverse waves on a stretched string?

   A) A   B) B   C) C   D) D   E) E

Answer: B
Var: 1

17) A crane lifts a 2500 kg mass using a steel cable whose mass per unit length is 0.65 kg/m. What is the speed of transverse waves on this cable?

   A) 225 m/s   B) 578 m/s   C) 1220 m/s   D) 1880 m/s   E) 194 m/s

Answer: E
Var: 1

18) Consider the transverse vibrational wave on a stretched string. The energy transported by such a wave is

A) zero.

B) proportional to the amplitude of the wave.

C) proportional to the square of the amplitude of the wave.

D) independent of the frequency of the wave.

E) independent of the tension in the string.

Answer: C
Var: 1

19) A wire of mass 5.00 grams and length 1.20 m is stretched with a tension of 36.0 N. Waves of frequency 50.0 Hz and amplitude 1.6 mm are traveling along the wire. What is the average power carried by the waves?

A) 1.68×10^{-4} W

B) 9.66×10^{-3} W

C) 4.34×10^{-4} W

D) 1.96×10^{-5} W

E) 6.57×10^{-3} W

Answer: D
Var: 1

20) A 5.0 g string, 0.92 m long, is under tension. The string produces a 400 Hz tone when it vibrates in the third harmonic. The speed of sound in air is 344 m/s. In this situation, the wavelength of the standing wave in the string, in SI units, is closest to:

A) 0.61   B) 0.92   C) 1.4   D) 1.8   E) 2.3

Answer: A
Var: 50+

21) A 4.0 g string, 0.33 m long, is under tension. The string produces a 100 Hz tone when it vibrates in the third harmonic. The speed of sound in air is 344 m/s. The wavelength of the tone in air, in SI units, is closest to:

A) 3.4   B) 2.4   C) 1.4   D) 0.33   E) 0.22

Answer: A
Var: 50+

22) A 4.0 g string, 0.67 m long, is under tension. The string produces a 300 Hz tone when it vibrates in the third harmonic. The speed of sound in air is 344 m/s. The tension in the string, in SI units, is closest to:

A) 110   B) 88   C) 69   D) 130   E) 150

Answer: A
Var: 50+

23) A string, 0.24 m long, vibrating in the n = 6 harmonic, excites an open pipe, 0.96 m long, into second overtone resonance. The speed of sound in air is 345 m/s. The number of antinodes in the standing wave pattern of the pipe is:

    A) 8   B) 6   C) 7   D) 9   E) 10

Answer: A
Var: 50+

24) A string, 0.20 m long, vibrating in the n = 2 harmonic, excites an open pipe, 0.94 m long, into second overtone resonance. The speed of sound in air is 345 m/s. The number of antinodes in the standing wave pattern of the string is:

    A) 2   B) 3   C) 4   D) 5   E) 6

Answer: A
Var: 50+

25) A string, 0.14 m long, vibrating in the n = 6 harmonic, excites an open pipe, 0.85 m long, into second overtone resonance. The speed of sound in air is 345 m/s. The distance between a node and an adjacent antinode, in the string, in mm, is closest to:

    A) 12   B) 5.8   C) 18   D) 23   E) 140

Answer: A
Var: 50+

26) A string, 0.21 m long, vibrating in the n = 2 harmonic, excites an open pipe, 0.93 m long, into second overtone resonance. The speed of sound in air is 345 m/s. The common resonant frequency of the string and the pipe, in SI units, is closest to:

    A) 560   B) 370   C) 460   D) 650   E) 720

Answer: A
Var: 50+

27) A string, 0.19 m long, vibrating in the n = 2 harmonic, excites an open pipe, 0.93 m long, into second overtone resonance. The speed of sound in air is 345 m/s. The velocity of transverse waves in the string, in SI units, is closest to:

    A) 110   B) 100   C) 94   D) 88   E) 82

Answer: A
Var: 50+

28) At one instant of time two transverse waves are traveling in the same direction along a stretched string. They are described by

    $y_1 = 0.03 \cos 2x$ and $y_2 = 0.03 \sin 2x$

How far from the origin is the nearest crest of the composite wave?

    A) 0.39 m   B) 0.79 m   C) 1.6 m   D) 0.25 m   E) 0.50 m

Answer: A
Var: 50+

29) An ocean wave directed straight in strikes a sea wall perpendicularly to its path and is reflected. The incoming wave travels 0.79 m/s and has a period of 4.8 s. The wave has an antinode at the wall. How far from the wall is the nearest node in the standing wave setup?

  A) 0.95 m   B) 0.47 m   C) 0.71 m   D) 1.4 m   E) 0.76 m

Answer: A
Var: 50+

30) What is the period of the wave described by
  $y = 8.2 \sin(166 t - 77x)$?

  A) 37.8 ms   B) 81.6 ms   C) 13.0 ms   D) 0.492 ms   E) 6.02 ms

Answer: A
Var: 50+

31) In a piano, very long strings sometimes have small lead weights attached to them. What is the purpose of these weights?

  A) To reduce the wave velocity for transverse waves on the string.

  B) To reduce the amplitude of vibration of the string.

  C) To damp out higher frequency overtones.

  D) To generate low frequency overtones corresponding to standing waves between two lead weights.

  E) To increase the tension in the string.

Answer: A
Var: 1

32) The reason weighted strings are used on pianos is

  A) to provide a greater range in sound intensity.

  B) to provide for higher frequencies.

  C) to provide for lower frequencies.

  D) to increase wave velocity in the string.

  E) None of these.

Answer: C
Var: 1

33) The standing waves which occur when a guitar string is strummed

  A) are sound waves.

  B) are not themselves sound waves, but they cause the sounding board of the instrument to emit sound waves.

  C) have a wavelength, but no frequency.

  D) have a frequency, but no wavelength.

  E) None of the above is true.

Answer: B
Var: 1

34) When a guitar is tuned, what is it that is changed?

    A) The wavelength of the fundamental.

    B) The frequency of the fundamental.

    C) The amplitude of the fundamental.

    D) The phase of the fundamental.

    E) More than one of the above.

Answer: B
Var: 1

35) What is the frequency of the fundamental mode of vibration of a steel piano wire stretched to a tension of 440 N? The wire is 0.600 m long and has a mass of 5.60 grams.

    A) 517 Hz   B) 234 Hz   C) 295 Hz   D) 312 Hz   E) 366 Hz

Answer: C
Var: 1

36) Two violinists are trying to tune their instruments in an orchestra. One is producing the desired frequency, 440 Hz. The other is producing a frequency of 448.4 Hz. By what percentage should the out of tune musician change the tension in his string to bring his instrument into tune at 440 Hz?

    A) 2.0%   B) 1.0%   C) 0.5%   D) 4.0%   E) 0.6%

Answer: A
Var: 1

37) Which of the following is an accurate statement?

    A) A system like a vibrating string has only one resonant frequency.

    B) In order for a singer to break a wine glass by singing, she must adjust the amplitude of the sound she makes so that it is exactly equal to the amplitude of vibration of the wine glass.

    C) The resonant frequency of a system is the name given to the lowest possible frequency at which the system will naturally vibrate.

    D) An organ pipe has an infinite number of resonant frequencies.

    E) When an oscillatory system is driven by a sinusoidal force, the response amplitude of the system will be the same as the amplitude of the driving force.

Answer: D
Var: 1

Short Answer Questions

1) The equation of a certain traveling transverse wave is
$$y(x,t) = 6.00 \sin(46.00\pi t - 2.860\pi x),$$
where t is in seconds and x and y are in centimeters. Find the speed of propagation, the period, and wavelength for these waves. (Express your answer in SI units.)

Answer: speed = 0.161 m/s period = 0.0435 s wavelength = 0.00699 m
Var: 50+

2) In a given situation transverse waves on a string carry an average power of 36 watts. What does the average power carried by the waves become if (a) the amplitude of the waves is increased from 5.0 cm to 38 cm while the frequency and wave speed are held fixed, or (b) the tension with which the string is stretched is increased from 5.0 N to 27 N while the frequency and amplitude of the waves is held fixed?

Answer: (a) 2100 watts (b) 84 watts
Var: 50+

3) Standing waves of frequency 21 Hz are produced on a string that has mass per unit length 0.0160 kg/m. With what tension must the string be stretched between two supports if adjacent nodes in the standing wave are to be 0.73 meters apart?

Answer: 15 N
Var: 50+

4) The proverbial bird on the wire is resting on a high tension line separating two telephone poles very far apart. The bird starts at t = 0 to bounce periodically, first up and then down, exactly 5 times every 10.0 s with an amplitude of 3.40 cm. If the wave velocity is 20.0 m/s, find the vertical position of the point 3.00 m away from the bird at time t = 0.356 s.

Answer: 2.05 cm
Var: 50+

5) A thin steel wire with Young's modulus of 2.00×10^{11} Pa and density 7.80×10^3 kg/m^3 is stretched between two supports with tension 373.0 N. If the radius of the wire is 2.60×10^{-3} m, find the ratio of the speed of longitudinal waves to the speed of transverse waves in the wire.

Answer: 107
Var: 1

Chapter 16   Sound and Hearing

Multiple Choice Questions

1) A 120 Hz tone has an intensity level of 22 dB. The velocity of sound in air is 345 m/s. The bulk modulus of air is 142 kPa. The pressure amplitude of the sound waves, in SI units, is closest to:

   A) 3.6×10^{-4} B) 3.6×10^{-5} C) 7.2×10^{-5} D) 7.2×10^{-4} E) 1.8×10^{-4}

   Answer: A
   Var: 50+

2) A 200 Hz tone has an intensity level of 84 dB. The velocity of sound in air is 345 m/s. The bulk modulus of air is 142 kPa. The displacement amplitude of the sound waves, in SI units, is closest to:

   A) 8.8×10^{-7} B) 1.8×10^{-6} C) 4.4×10^{-6} D) 8.8×10^{-6} E) 1.8×10^{-5}

   Answer: A
   Var: 50+

3) A 130 Hz tone has an intensity level of 55 dB. The velocity of sound in air is 345 m/s. The bulk modulus of air is 142 kPa. A 165 Hz tone has the same displacement amplitude as does the 130 Hz tone. The difference in the intensity level of the 165 Hz tone relative to that of the 130 Hz tone, in dB, is closest to:

   A) 2.1   B) 1.0   C) –1.0   D) –2.1   E) zero

   Answer: A
   Var: 50+

4) A 530 Hz tone has an intensity level of 66 dB. The velocity of sound in air is 345 m/s. The bulk modulus of air is 142 kPa. An 694 Hz tone has the same pressure amplitude as does the 530 Hz tone. The difference in the intensity level, of the 694 Hz tone relative to that of the 530 Hz tone, in dB, is closest to:

   A) zero   B) 2.3   C) –2.3   D) –1.2   E) 1.2

   Answer: A
   Var: 50+

5) The howler monkey is the loudest land animal and can be heard up to a distance of 9.0 km. Assume the acoustic output of a howler to be uniform in all directions. The acoustic power emitted by the howler, in mW, is closest to:

   A) 1.0   B) 0.34   C) 3.4   D) 10   E) 34

   Answer: A
   Var: 50+

6) The howler monkey is the loudest land animal and can be heard up to a distance of 1.4 km. Assume the acoustic output of a howler to be uniform in all directions. The distance at which the intensity level of a howler's call is 49 dB, in SI units, is closest to:

A) 5.0   B) 6.0   C) 7.5   D) 8.4   E) 9.9

Answer: A
Var: 50+

7) The howler monkey is the loudest land animal and can be heard up to a distance of 7.1 km. Assume the acoustic output of a howler to be uniform in all directions. A chorus of five howlers call at the same time. The largest distance at which the chorus can be heard, in km, is closest to:

A) 16   B) 11   C) 22   D) 29   E) 36

Answer: A
Var: 50+

8) The howler monkey is the loudest land animal and can be heard up to a distance of 8.6 km. Assume the acoustic output of a howler to be uniform in all directions. A juvenile howler monkey has an acoustic output of 12 μW. The ratio, of the acoustic intensity produced by the juvenile howler, to the reference intensity I_0, at a distance of 350 m, is closest to:

A) 7.8   B) 16   C) 5.2   D) 12   E) 21

Answer: A
Var: 50+

9) An enclosed chamber with sound absorbing walls has a 2.0 m x 1.0 m opening for an outside window. A loudspeaker is located outdoors, 22 m away and facing the window. The intensity level of the sound entering the window space from the loudspeaker is 82 dB. Assume the acoustic output of the loudspeaker is uniform in all directions and that acoustic energy incident upon the ground is completely absorbed. The acoustic power, entering through the window space, in μW, is closest to:

A) 320   B) 160   C) 630   D) 1600   E) 3200

Answer: A
Var: 50+

10) An enclosed chamber with sound absorbing walls has a 2.0 m x 1.0 m opening for an outside window. A loudspeaker is located outdoors, 42 m away and facing the window. The intensity level of the sound entering the window space from the loudspeaker is 78 dB. Assume the acoustic output of the loudspeaker is uniform in all directions and that acoustic energy incident upon the ground is completely absorbed. The sound intensity at a point midway between the loudspeaker and the window, in SI units, is closest to:

A) 2.5×10^{-4} B) 1.3×10^{-4} C) 6.3×10^{-5} D) 3.2×10^{-5} E) 1.6×10^{-5}

Answer: A
Var: 50+

11) An enclosed chamber with sound absorbing walls has a 2.0 m x 1.0 m opening for an outside window. A loudspeaker is located outdoors, 30 m away and facing the window. The intensity level of the sound entering the window space from the loudspeaker is 51 dB. Assume the acoustic output of the loudspeaker is uniform in all directions and that acoustic energy incident upon the ground is completely absorbed. The acoustic output of the loudspeaker, in SI units, is closest to:

A) 0.0014   B) 0.0028   C) 0.0071   D) 0.014   E) 0.028

Answer: A
Var: 50+

12) A glass window is installed in the window space and the intensity level of the sound entering through the window is reduced from 82 dB to 55 dB. The factor, by which the acoustic power entering the chamber is reduced by the glass window, is closest to:

A) 2.0×10^{-3} B) 1.6×10^{-2} C) 4.5×10^{-2} D) 8.3×10^{-2} E) 1.3×10^{-1}

Answer: A
Var: 50+

13) Consider the waves on a vibrating guitar string and the sound waves the guitar produces in the surrounding air. The string waves and the sound waves have the same

A) wavelength.

B) velocity.

C) frequency.

D) amplitude.

E) More than one of the above is true.

Answer: C
Var: 1

14) A sound wave is

A) a longitudinal pressure wave.

B) a transverse pressure wave.

C) a kind of electromagnetic wave.

D) the same as a string wave.

E) the name given to any wave in the auditory response frequency range (approximately 50–20,000 Hz).

Answer: A
Var: 1

15) Which of the following increases when a sound becomes louder?

   A) Frequency

   B) Wavelength

   C) Amplitude

   D) Period

   E) Velocity

Answer: C
Var: 1

16) What is the intensity level in decibels of a sound whose intensity is 10^{-7} W/m^2?

   A) 20 dB   B) 30 dB   C) 40 dB   D) 50 dB   E) 60 dB

Answer: D
Var: 1

17) An open pipe, 0.35 m long, vibrates in the second overtone with a frequency of 1550 Hz. In this situation, the distance from the center of the pipe to the nearest antinode, in cm, is closest to:

   A) 5.8   B) 2.9   C) 8.8   D) 12   E) zero

Answer: A
Var: 50+

18) An open pipe, 0.30 m long, vibrates in the second overtone with a frequency of 1760 Hz. In this situation, the speed of sound in air, in SI units, is closest to:

   A) 351   B) 346   C) 349   D) 344   E) 353

Answer: A
Var: 50+

19) An open pipe, 0.82 m long, vibrates in the second overtone with a frequency of 677 Hz. In this situation, the fundamental frequency of the pipe, in SI units, is closest to:

   A) 171   B) 226   C) 338   D) 451   E) 541

Answer: A
Var: 50+

20) An open pipe, 0.90 m long, vibrates in the second overtone with a frequency of 602 Hz. In this situation, the length of the shortest stopped pipe, that has the same resonant frequency as the open pipe in the second overtone, in cm, is closest to:

   A) 15   B) 7.5   C) 18   D) 30   E) 45

Answer: A
Var: 50+

Situation 16.1

A standing wave of the third overtone is induced in a stopped pipe, 1.2 m long. The speed of sound is 340 m/s.

21) In Situation 16.1, the number of antinodes in the standing wave pattern is:

    A) 3   B) 4   C) 5   D) 6   E) 7

Answer: B
Var: 1

22) In Situation 16.1, the frequency of the sound produced by the pipe, in SI units, is closest to:

    A) 210   B) 280   C) 350   D) 430   E) 500

Answer: E
Var: 1

23) Three tuning forks are available. One fork marked "A" produces a 440 Hz tone. The other forks are marked "X" and "Y". The frequency of fork Y is less than the frequency of fork X. When forks A and X are sounded together, a beat frequency of 4 Hz is heard. For forks A and Y, the beat frequency is 7 Hz. For forks X and Y, the beat frequency is 3 Hz. The frequencies of forks X and Y, respectively, in SI units, are closest to:

    A) 436 and 433

    B) 436 and 447

    C) 444 and 433

    D) 444 and 447

    E) 447 and 444

Answer: E
Var: 1

Situation 16.2

A stopped wire, 0.90 m long, resonates with a tone whose wavelength is 0.72 m.

24) In Situation 16.2, the number of the harmonic, for this resonant wavelength is:

    A) 2   B) 3   C) 4   D) 5   E) 6

Answer: D
Var: 1

25) In Situation 16.2, the distance between a node and an adjacent antinode, in the standing wave pattern in the pipe, in SI units, is closest to:

    A) 0.18   B) 0.22   C) 0.27   D) 0.36   E) 0.45

Answer: A
Var: 1

26) In Situation 16.2, the wavelength of the next higher overtone in this pipe, in SI units, is closest to:

    A) 0.36   B) 0.40   C) 0.45   D) 0.51   E) 0.58

Answer: D
Var: 1

27) In Situation 16.2, the overtone number of this normal mode is:

A) 2   B) 3   C) 4   D) 5   E) 6

Answer: A
Var: 1

28) In Situation 16.2, the frequency of this normal mode, in SI units, is closest to:

A) 160   B) 220   C) 270   D) 330   E) 380

Answer: C
Var: 1

29) Two loudspeakers placed 6.0 m apart are driven in phase by an audio oscillator, whose frequency range is 1032 Hz to 1396 Hz. A point P is located 5.3 m from one loudspeaker and 3.6 m from the other. The speed of sound is 344 m/s. The frequency produced by the oscillator, for which constructive interference of sound occurs at point P, in SI units, is closest to:

A) 1214   B) 1366   C) 1164   D) 1315   E) 1265

Answer: A
Var: 50+

30) Two loudspeakers placed 6.0 m apart are driven in phase by an audio oscillator, whose frequency range is 425 Hz to 789 Hz. A point P is located 5.3 m from one loudspeaker and 3.6 m from the other. The speed of sound is 344 m/s. The frequency produced by the oscillator, for which destructive interference occurs at point P, in SI units, is closest to:

A) 708   B) 769   C) 749   D) 728   E) 688

Answer: A
Var: 50+

31) Which of the following is an accurate statement?

A) The fundamental frequency of an organ pipe is determined primarily by the pipe diameter.

B) Standing sound waves can be set up in a pipe open on one end, but not on one open on both ends.

C) Standing waves can be set up in a pipe closed on both ends, but not in one with one end open and one end closed.

D) Displacement nodes and pressure nodes occur at the same place in an organ pipe.

E) The open end of a pipe is a pressure node for standing waves.

Answer: E
Var: 1

32) An organ pipe open at both ends has two successive harmonics with frequencies of 210 Hz and 240 Hz. What is the length of the pipe? The speed of sound is 345 m/s in air.

A) 5.25 m   B) 5.75 m   C) 2.76 m   D) 4.90 m   E) 3.62 m

Answer: B
Var: 1

Situation 16.3

Two loudspeakers S1 and S2, placed 5.0 m apart, are driven in phase by an audio oscillator. A boy stands at point P, which is 12.0 m from S1 and 13.0 m from S2. A right triangle is formed by S1, S2, and P. The wave from S2 arrives at point P 2.00 periods later than the wave from S1. The speed of sound is 350 m/s.

33) In Situation 16.3, the frequency of the oscillator, in SI units, is closest to:

    A) 350   B) 500   C) 700   D) 1000   E) 1400

Answer: C
Var: 1

34) In Situation 16.3, the boy walks directly away from S1, along the line through P, until destructive interference occurs. At that point, the wave from S2 arrives 1.50 periods later than the wave from S1. The distance of this point from S1, in SI units, is closest to:

    A) 14.3   B) 14.8   C) 15.3   D) 15.8   E) 16.3

Answer: E
Var: 1

Situation 16.4

A train is approaching a signal tower at a speed of 40 m/s. The train engineer sounds the 1000 Hz whistle and a switchman in the tower responds by sounding the 1200 Hz siren. The air is still and the speed of sound is 340 m/s.

35) In Situation 16.4, the wavelength of the train whistle tone reaching the switchman, in SI units, is given by:

    A) 0.30   B) 0.32   C) 0.34   D) 0.36   E) 0.38

Answer: A
Var: 1

36) In Situation 16.4, the frequency of the train whistle tone, heard by the switchman, in SI units, is given by:

    A) 1000

    B) 300/340 x 1000

    C) 340/300 x 1000

    D) 340/380 x 1000

    E) 380/340 x 1000

Answer: C
Var: 1

37) In Situation 16.4, the frequency of the train whistle tone, heard by a passenger on the train, in SI units, is given by:

   A) 1000

   B) 300/340 x 1000

   C) 340/300 x 1000

   D) 340/380 x 1000

   E) 380/340 x 1000

Answer: A
Var: 1

38) In Situation 16.4, the wavelength of the tower siren tone, reaching the engineer, in SI units, is closest to:

   A) 0.18   B) 0.22   C) 0.25   D) 0.28   E) 0.32

Answer: D
Var: 1

39) In Situation 16.4, the frequency of the tower siren tone, heard by the engineer, in SI units, is closest to:

   A) 1200

   B) 300/340 x 1200

   C) 340/300 x 1200

   D) 340/380 x 1200

   E) 380/340 x 1200

Answer: E
Var: 1

Situation 16.5

A carousel, 5.0 m in radius, has a pair of 600 Hz sirens, mounted on posts at opposite ends of a diameter. The carousel rotates with an angular velocity of 0.80 rad/s. A stationary listener is located at a distance from the carousel. The speed of sound is 350 m/s.

40) In Situation 16.5, the longest wavelength reaching the listener from the sirens, in cm, is closest to:

   A) 57.0   B) 57.7   C) 58.3   D) 59.0   E) 59.6

Answer: D
Var: 1

41) In Situation 16.5, the highest siren frequency heard by the listener, in SI units, is closest to:

   A) 603   B) 605   C) 607   D) 609   E) 611

Answer: C
Var: 1

42) In Situation 16.5, the maximum beat frequency of the sirens at the position of the listener, in SI units, is closest to:

    A) 6   B) 8   C) 10   D) 12   E) 14

Answer: E
Var: 1

43) In Situation 16.5, the listener mounts a bicycle and rides directly away from the carousel with a speed of 4.5 m/s. The highest siren frequency heard by the listener, in SI units, is given by:

    A) 345.5/346.0 x 600

    B) 354.5/346.0 x 600

    C) 345.5/354.0 x 600

    D) 354.0/354.5 x 600

    E) 354.5/354.0 x 600

Answer: A
Var: 1

44) A jet aircraft, in level flight at constant speed, is observed directly over head. A sonic boom is heard 6.0 s later, at which time the line of sight to the aircraft forms a 60 degree angle with respect to the horizontal. The speed of sound is 325 m/s. The Mach number for the aircraft is closest to:

    A) 1.2   B) 2.0   C) 2.1   D) 2.3   E) 2.4

Answer: A
Var: 50+

45) A jet aircraft, in level flight at constant speed, is observed directly over head. A sonic boom is heard 16.0 s later, at which time the line of sight to the aircraft forms a 54 degree angle with respect to the horizontal. The speed of sound is 325 m/s. The altitude of the aircraft, in SI units, is closest to:

    A) 8800   B) 6400   C) 11,000   D) 3200   E) 18,000

Answer: A
Var: 50+

46) One may readily deduce how sound intensity varies with distance from a uniformly radiating sound by making use of

    A) the relation v = f λ

    B) Newton's Laws of Motion.

    C) the Law of Conservation of Energy.

    D) the Law of Conservation of Momentum.

    E) the fact that sound is a longitudinal wave.

Answer: C
Var: 1

47) The reason a decibel scale is used to measure sound intensity level is that

   A) the intensity levels usually encountered are too small to be expressed in the usual exponential notation.

   B) the intensity levels usually encountered are too large to be expressed in the usual exponential notation.

   C) the ear is sensitive over such a broad range of intensities.

   D) the energy in a sound wave varies exponentially with the amplitude of the wave.

   E) decibels are dimensionless.

Answer: C
Var: 1

Figure 16.1

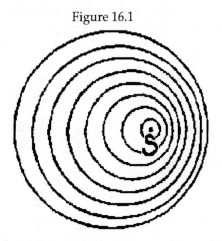

48) In Figure 16.1 are some wavefronts emitted by a source of sound S. This picture can help us to understand

   A) why the siren on a police car changes its pitch as it races past us.

   B) why a sound grows quieter as we move away from the source.

   C) how sonar works.

   D) the phenomenon of beats.

   E) why it is that our hearing is best near 3000 Hz.

Answer: A
Var: 1

Figure 16.2

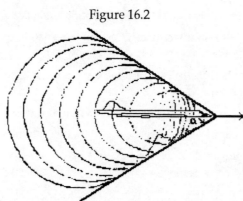

49) In Figure 16.2 are the shock waves produced by a fast moving aircraft. From this drawing one would estimate that the plan is moving at a speed of

A) Mach 0.56   B) Mach 1.75   C) Mach 2.2   D) Mach 1.44   E) Mach 1.20

Answer: B
Var: 1

50) The speed of sound in steel is 5000 m/s. What is the wavelength of a sound wave of frequency 890 Hz in steel?

A) 5.62 m   B) 1.79 m   C) 0.894 m   D) 1.12 m   E) 0.178 m

Answer: A
Var: 50+

51) The speed of sound in an alcohol, at a temperature of 20°C, is 1080 m/s. The density of the alcohol at that temperature is 700 kg/m^3. The bulk modulus of the alcohol, at a temperature of 20°C, in MPa, is closest to:

A) 816   B) 857   C) 898   D) 939   E) 980

Answer: A
Var: 50+

52) A pipe, 90 m long and 10.0 cm in diameter contains olive oil. The density of the olive oil is 843 kg/m^3 and the bulk modulus is 1.6 x 10^9 Pa. A 98.2 Hz longitudinal wave is transmitted in the oil. The time for the wave to travel the length of the pipe, in the oil, in ms, is closest to:

A) 65   B) 61   C) 57   D) 52   E) 48

Answer: A
Var: 50+

53) A pipe, 10 m long and 10.0 cm in diameter contains olive oil. The density of the olive oil is 880 kg/m^3 and the bulk modulus is 1.2 x 10^9 Pa. A 800 Hz longitudinal wave is transmitted in the oil. The wavelength of the longitudinal wave, in the oil, in SI units, is closest to:

A) 1.5   B) 1.6   C) 1.3   D) 1.2   E) 1.0

Answer: A
Var: 50+

166

54) A pipe, 90 m long and 10.0 cm in diameter contains olive oil. The density of the olive oil is 850 kg/m^3 and the bulk modulus is 1.9 x 10^9 Pa. A 820 Hz longitudinal wave of amplitude 3.0 mm is transmitted in the oil. The intensity of the wave, is closest to:

A) 1.5 x 10^8 B) 3.0 x 10^8 C) 7.6 x 10^7 D) 3.8 x 10^7 E) 1.9 x 10^7

Answer: A
Var: 50+

55) A metal bar 14.0 m long has a density of 5800 kg/m^3 and a diameter of 6 cms. Longitudinal sound waves take 3.00 x 10^{-3} s to travel the length of the bar. What is Young's modulus for this material?

A) 1.26 x 10^{11} Pa

B) 2.64 x 10^{11} Pa

C) 2.05 x 10^{11} Pa

D) 1.37 x 10^{11} Pa

E) 0.91 x 10^{11} Pa

Answer: A
Var: 1

Situation 16.6

A uniform bar of metal, 0.40 m long, with a diameter of 2.0 cm, has a mass of 1.1 kg. A 1.5 MHz longitudinal wave is propagated along the length of the bar. A wave compression traverses the length of the bar in 0.12 ms.

56) In Situation 16.6, the wavelength of the longitudinal wave in the metal, in mm, is closest to:

A) 2.2   B) 2.6   C) 3.0   D) 3.4   E) 3.8

Answer: A
Var: 1

57) In Situation 16.6, the value of Young's modulus for the metal, in GPa (G = giga = 10^9), is closest to:

A) 73   B) 79   C) 85   D) 91   E) 97

Answer: E
Var: 1

58) The molecular mass of helium is 4.00 x 10^{-3} kg/mol and the adiabatic constant is 1.67. The speed of sound in helium gas, taken as an ideal gas, at a temperature of 290 K and a pressure of 80 kPa, in SI units, is closest to:

A) 800   B) 900   C) 1000   D) 1100   E) 1200

Answer: C
Var: 1

Situation 16.7

The maximum angular frequency of sound, that can be transmitted in gold, is 1.40×10^{13} rad/s. Assume the lattice spacing for gold is the same as the interatomic distance which is 0.288 nm. The mass of a gold atom is 3.27×10^{-25} kg.

59) In Situation 16.7, the interatomic force constant of gold, in SI units, is closest to:

A) 11 B) 16 C) 23 D) 32 E) 45

Answer: B
Var: 1

60) In Situation 16.7, the propagation constant of a longitudinal wave in gold, for which the angular frequency is 1.0×10^{13} rad/s, in SI units, is closest to:

A) 4.5×10^9 B) 5.0×10^9 C) 5.5×10^9 D) 6.0×10^9 E) 6.5×10^9

Answer: C
Var: 1

61) In Situation 16.7, a longitudinal wave in gold has a wavelength of 1.8 nm. The ratio of the angular frequency of this wave to the maximum angular frequency of longitudinal waves in gold is closest to:

A) 0.44 B) 0.46 C) 0.48 D) 0.50 E) 0.52

Answer: C
Var: 1

62) In Situation 16.7, the phonon energy of a longitudinal wave in gold, whose wavelength is 1.8 nm, in SI units, is closest to:

A) 1.5×10^{-22}

B) 2.5×10^{-22}

C) 4.2×10^{-22}

D) 7.0×10^{-22}

E) 1.2×10^{-21}

Answer: D
Var: 1

63) The speed of sound in an ideal gas depends on

A) the specific heat ratio, C_p/C_v.

B) the temperature.

C) the molecular speed in the gas.

D) the molecular mass.

E) all of these.

Answer: E
Var: 1

64) Under certain conditions the speed of sound in air is 340 m/s. If the temperature were to rise by 1.00%, what would the speed of sound then be?

    A) 340 m/s   B) 341 m/s   C) 342 m/s   D) 339 m/s   E) 338 m/s

Answer: C
Var: 1

Short Answer Questions

1) A certain source of sound waves radiates uniformly in all directions. At a distance of 25 m from the source the intensity level is 73 db. What is the total acoustic power output of the source, in watts? (Note: The reference intensity I_O is 1×10^{-12} W/m^2.)

Answer: 1.6×10^{-1} watts
Var: 50+

2)

Figure 16.3

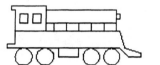

14 m/s

In Figure 16.3, a man is traveling on a bicycle at 14 m/s along a straight road that runs parallel to some railroad tracks. He hears the whistle of a train that is behind him, as shown in the sketch. The frequency emitted by the train is 800 Hz, but the frequency the man hears is 755 Hz. Take the velocity of sound to be 340 m/s.
a) What frequency is heard by a stationary observer located between the train and the bicycle?
b) What is the speed of the train, and is the train traveling away from or towards the bicycle?

Answer: a) 787 Hz
        b) 5.6 m/s, away from the bicycle
Var: 50+

3) Two violists are tuning their A–strings, for which the fundamental frequency is 440 Hz when properly tuned. When both play the A–note, 7.2 beats per second are heard. By what fractional amount must the player of the viola with the lower frequency increase the tension in his string to make its frequency identical to that of the other viola? Assume that the other viola is already properly tuned. Express your answer in percent (%).

Answer: 3.3 %
Var: 50+

4) What must be the length of an organ pipe that is open at one end and closed at the other if its fundamental frequency is to be 9 times that of a pipe that is 7.30 meters long and open at both ends?

Answer: 0.406 meters
Var: 50+

Figure 16.4

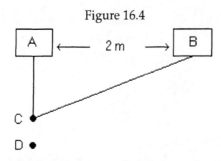

5) In Figure 16.4, two identical loudspeakers, A and B, driven by the same amplifier, are separated by 2.00 m and produce sound waves of the same frequency. A small microphone is placed at point C, 2.30 m from speaker A along the line perpendicular to the line connecting the two speakers. At this point destructive interference occurs. If the microphone is now moved along this line to point D, 5.10 m from speaker A, constructive interference occurs. Find the frequency of the sound waves. The speed of sound is 344 m/s. Assume that there are no other points between C and D where interference occurs.

Answer: 465 Hz
Var: 50+

6) On a day when the temperature is 21.0°C, a closed organ pipe produces sound with a fundamental frequency of 695 Hz. On a second day this same pipe produces sound with a fundamental frequency of 702 Hz. What is the temperature, in °C, on the second day?

Answer: 27.0°C
Var: 1

7) An organ pipe closed at one end has two successive harmonics with frequencies of 2170 Hz and 2790 Hz. What is the fundamental frequency of the pipe?

Answer: 310 Hz
Var: 1

8) A police siren produces a sound level of 78.0 dB with a pressure amplitude of 0.75 Pa. Find the new intensity level if the pressure amplitude changes to 2.70 Pa.

Answer: 89.1 dB
Var: 50+

9) Two police cars have identical sirens that produce a frequency of 570 Hz. A stationary listener is standing between two cars. One car is parked and the other is approaching the listener and both have their sirens on. The listener notices 2.6 beats per second. Find the speed of the approaching police car. (The speed of sound is 340 m/s.)

Answer: 1.5 m/s
Var: 50+

10) Find the ratio of the speed of sound in nitrogen gas to that of air at room temperature, $T = 20.0°C$. The molecular mass of nitrogen is 28.01 g/mol and γ is 1.40. The molecular mass of air is 28.8 g/mol and γ is 1.40.

Answer: 1.01 times as fast
Var: 1

Chapter 17   Temperature and Heat

Multiple Choice Questions

1) An aluminum rod is 30.0 cm long and a steel rod is 10.0 cm long when both rods are at a temperature of 15°C. Both rods have the same diameter. The rods are joined end-to-end to form a rod 60.0 cm long. The coefficients of linear expansion of aluminum and steel are 2.4×10^{-5} K^{-1} and 1.2×10^{-5} K^{-1}, respectively. The temperature is raised to 85°C. The increase in the length of the joined rod, in mm, is closest to:

   A) 0.59   B) 0.53   C) 0.47   D) 0.41   E) 0.65

   Answer: A
   Var: 50+

2)   Figure 17.1a

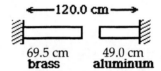

A brass rod is 69.5 cm long and an aluminum rod is 49.0 cm long when both rods are at an initial temperature of 0°C. The rods are placed in line with a gap of 1.5 cm between them. The distance between the far ends of the rods is maintained at 120.0 cm throughout. The temperature is raised until the two rods are barely in contact. The coefficients of linear expansion of brass and aluminum are 2.0×10^{-5} K^{-1} and 2.4×10^{-5} K^{-1}, respectively. In Figure 17.1a, the temperature at which contact of the rods barely occurs, in °C, is closest to:

   A) 585   B) 555   C) 526   D) 614   E) 643

   Answer: A
   Var: 50+

3)   Figure 17.1b

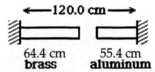

A brass rod is 64.4 cm long and an aluminum rod is 55.4 cm long when both rods are at an initial temperature of 0°C. The rods are placed in line with a gap of 0.2 cm between them. The distance between the far ends of the rods is maintained at 120.0 cm throughout. The temperature is raised until the two rods are barely in contact. The coefficients of linear expansion of brass and aluminum are 2.0×10^{-5} K^{-1} and 2.4×10^{-5} K^{-1}, respectively. In Figure 17.1b, the ratio of the increase in the length of the aluminum rod to that of the brass rod, is closest to:

   A) 1.03   B) 1.12   C) 1.20   D) 1.29   E) 1.38

   Answer: A
   Var: 50+

4) A glass flask has a volume of 200 ml at a temperature of $20°$ C. The flask contains 196 ml of mercury at an equilibrium temperature of $20°$C. The temperature is raised until the mercury reaches the 200 ml reference mark. The coefficients of volume expansion of mercury and glass are 18×10^{-5} K^{-1} and 2.0×10^{-5} K^{-1}, respectively. The temperature at which this occurs, in $°$C, is closest to:

A) 148   B) 138   C) 128   D) 133   E) 158

Answer: A
Var: 50+

Figure 17.2

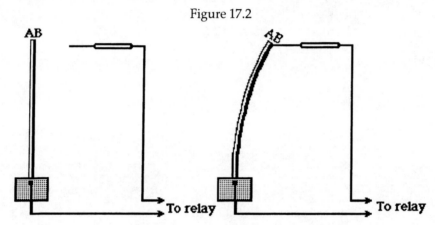

Shown here is a device that can be used to turn a furnace on or off, depending on the temperature sensed by the device.

5) In Figure 17.2, the principle underlying the operation of this device is that

A) different metals have different latent heats.

B) different metals have different thermal conductivities.

C) different metals have different thermal expansion coefficients.

D) heat always flows from hot to cold, never from cold to hot.

E) different metals have different heat capacities.

Answer: C
Var: 1

6) If you wanted to know how much the temperature of a particular piece of material would rise when a known amount of heat was added to it, which of the following would be most helpful to know?

A) Initial temperature

B) Specific heat

C) Density

D) Coefficient of linear expansion

E) Thermal conductivity

Answer: B
Var: 1

Table 17.1

	Coefficient of Linear Expansion	Young's Modulus
Brass	$2.0 \times 10^{-5} K^{-1}$	$0.9 \times 10^{11} Pa$
Steel	$1.2 \times 10^{-5} K^{-1}$	$2.0 \times 10^{11} Pa$

A brass bar and a steel bar are each 0.800 m long at a temperature of 20°C. Each bar is placed at that temperature between rigid walls 0.800 m apart. The cross-sectional areas for the brass and steel bars are 0.005 m2 and 0.003 m2, respectively. Thermal and elastic constants of the two materials are given in the table.

7) In Table 17.1, the temperature is raised until the combined force exerted by the two bars is 1.8 MN. The temperature at which this occurs, in °C, is closest to:

A) 100   B) 110   C) 120   D) 130   E) 140

Answer: D
Var: 1

8) In Table 15.3, the ratio of the stress in the steel bar to the stress in the brass bar, is closest to:

A) 0.76   B) 0.88   C) 1.14   D) 1.32   E) 1.45

Answer: D
Var: 1

9) A steel pipe 25.0 m long, installed when the temperature was 15°C, is used to transport superheated steam at a temperature of 155°C. Steel's coefficient of linear expansion is $1.2 \times 10^{-5} K^{-1}$, Young's modulus is 2.0×10^{11} Pa, and the breaking stress is 5.0×10^{8} Pa. The pipe is allowed to expand freely when the steam is transported. The increase in the length of the pipe, in mm, is closest to:

A) 42   B) 40   C) 38   D) 44   E) 47

Answer: A
Var: 50+

10) A steel pipe 35.0 m long, installed when the temperature was 15°C, is used to transport superheated steam at a temperature of 135°C. Steel's coefficient of linear expansion is $1.2 \times 10^{-5} K^{-1}$, Young's modulus is 2.0×10^{11} Pa, and the breaking stress is 5.0×10^{8} Pa. When the temperature of the pipe is 15°C, it is bolted to the masonry so that linear expansion is totally prevented. The ratio of the thermal stress in the pipe to the breaking stress of steel, when the steam is transported, is closest to:

A) 0.58   B) 0.54   C) 0.50   D) 0.47   E) 0.43

Answer: A
Var: 50+

11) A substance has a melting point of $20°$ C and a heat of fusion of 1.9×10^4 J/kg. The boiling point is $150°$ C and the heat of vaporization is 3.8×10^4 J/kg at a pressure of one atmosphere. The specific heats for the solid, liquid, and gaseous phases are 600, 1000, and 400 J/kg • K, respectively. The quantity of heat required to raise the temperature of 1.00 kg of the substance from $-5°$C to $129°$C, in kJ, is closest to:

A) 140   B) 120   C) 130   D) 34   E) 160

Answer: A
Var: 50+

12) A substance has a melting point of $20°$ C and a heat of fusion of 1.9×10^4 J/kg. The boiling point is $150°$ C and the heat of vaporization is 3.8×10^4 J/kg at a pressure of one atmosphere. The specific heats for the solid, liquid, and gaseous phases are 600, 1000, and 400 J/kg • K, respectively. The quantity of heat surrendered by 3.80 kg of the substance when it is cooled from $240°$C to $124°$C, at a pressure of one atmosphere, in kJ, is closest to:

A) 380   B) 240   C) 320   D) 590   E) 730

Answer: A
Var: 50+

13) A 220 g metal container, insulated on the outside, holds 110 g of water in thermal equilibrium at $22°$C. A 24 g ice cube, at the melting point, is dropped into the water, and when thermal equilibrium is reached the temperature is $15°$C. Assume there is no heat exchange with the surroundings. For water, the specific heat capacity is 4190 J/kg • K and the heat of fusion is 3.34×10^5 J/kg. The specific heat capacity for the metal is closest to:

A) 4090 J/kg • K

B) 2920 J/kg • K

C) 4690 J/kg • K

D) 5190 J/kg • K

E) 5690 J/kg • K

Answer: A
Var: 50+

Figure 17.3

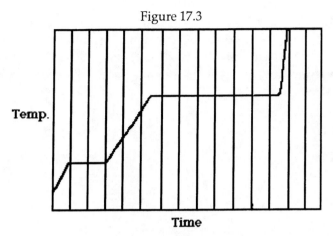

Temp.

Time

14) In Figure 17.3, heat is added to a pure substance in a closed container at a constant rate. A graph of the temperature of the substance as a function of time is shown here. If LF = latent heat of fusion and LV = latent heat of vaporization, what is the value of the ratio LV/LF for this substance?

A) 5.0   B) 4.5   C) 7.2   D) 3.5   E) 1.5

Answer: D
Var: 1

15) You may have noticed that when you get out of a swimming pool and stand dripping wet in a light breeze, you feel much colder than you feel after you dry off. Why is this?

A) The moisture on your skin has good thermal conductivity.

B) Water has a relatively large heat capacity.

C) This is a purely psychological effect resulting from the way in which sensory nerves in the skin are stimulated.

D) The water on your skin is colder than the surrounding air.

E) 540 calories of heat are required to evaporate each gram of water from your skin, and most of this heat flows out of your body.

Answer: E
Var: 1

16) How much heat must be added to a 3 kg block of ice at $-22°C$ to change it to water at $18°C$?

A) 330 kcal   B) 87 kcal   C) 120 kcal   D) 360 kcal   E) 300 kcal

Answer: A
Var: 50+

175

17) An 80 g aluminum calorimeter contains 350 g of water at an equilibrium temperature of 20° C. A 100 g piece of metal, initially at 347° C, is added to the calorimeter. The final temperature at equilibrium is 32° C. Assume there is no external heat exchange. The specific heat capacities of aluminum and water are 910 and 4190 J/kg • K, respectively. The specific heat capacity of the metal is closest to:

A) 590 J/kg • K

B) 540 J/kg • K

C) 440 J/kg • K

D) 390 J/kg • K

E) 640 J/kg • K

Answer: A
Var: 50+

18) An 90 g aluminum calorimeter contains 430 g of water at an equilibrium temperature of 20° C. A 140 g piece of metal, initially at 253° C, is added to the calorimeter. The final temperature at equilibrium is 32° C. Assume there is no external heat exchange. The specific heat capacities of aluminum and water are 910 and 4190 J/kg • K, respectively. The ratio of the quantity of heat gained by the aluminum to that of the water, is closest to:

A) 0.05   B) 0.09   C) 0.13   D) 0.17   E) 0.21

Answer: A
Var: 50+

Situation 17.1

Two experimental runs are performed to determine the calorimetric properties of an alcohol which has a melting point of -10° C. In the first run, a 200 g cube of frozen alcohol, at the melting point, is added to 300 g of water at 20° C in a styrofoam container. When thermal equilibrium is reached, the alcohol–water solution is at a temperature of 5° C. In the second run, an identical cube of alcohol is added to 500 g of water at 20° C and the temperature at thermal equilibrium is 10° C. The specific heat capacity of water is 4190 J/kg • K. Assume the styrofoam container and the surroundings do not partake in the heat exchange.

19) In Situation 17.1, the heat of fusion of the alcohol is closest to:

A) 5.5×10^4 J/kg

B) 6.3×10^4 J/kg

C) 7.1×10^4 J/kg

D) 7.9×10^4 J/kg

E) 8.7×10^4 J/kg

Answer: B
Var: 1

176

20) In Situation 15.4, the specific heat capacity of the alcohol is closest to:

  A) 1700 J/kg • K

  B) 1900 J/kg • K

  C) 2100 J/kg • K

  D) 2300 J/kg • K

  E) 2500 J/kg • K

Answer: C
Var: 1

21) A heat conducting rod, 1.10 m long, is made of an aluminum section, 0.20 m long, and a copper section, 0.90 m long. Both sections have a cross-sectional area of 0.0004 m². The aluminum end and the copper end are maintained at temperatures of 10° C and 250° C, respectively. The thermal conductivities of aluminum and copper are 205 and 385 W/m • K, respectively. The temperature of the aluminum–copper junction in the rod, in °C, is closest to:

  A) 81   B) 73   C) 66   D) 59   E) 54

Answer: A
Var: 50+

22) A heat conducting rod, 1.10 m long, is made of an aluminum section, 0.20 m long, and a copper section, 0.90 m long. Both sections have a cross-sectional area of 0.0004 m². The aluminum end and the copper end are maintained at temperatures of 30° C and 210° C, respectively. The thermal conductivities of aluminum and copper are 205 and 385 W/m • K, respectively. The heat current conducted in the rod is closest to:

  A) 22 W   B) 19 W   C) 24 W   D) 27 W   E) 30 W

Answer: A
Var: 50+

Figure 17.4

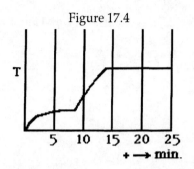

23) In Figure 17.4, a sample of a pure compound is contained in a closed, well–insulated container. Heat is added at a constant rate and the sample temperature is recorded. The resulting data is sketched below. Which of the following conclusions is justified from the data given?

A) The sample never boiled.

B) The heat of fusion is greater than the heat of vaporization.

C) After 5 minutes the sample was a mixture of solid and liquid.

D) The heat capacity of the solid phase was greater than that of the liquid phase.

E) After 20 minutes the solid was all liquid.

Answer: C
Var: 1

24) Some properties of glass are listed here.

Density	2300 kg/m^3
Specific heat	$840 \text{ J/kg} \cdot {}^{\circ}C$
Coefficient of linear thermal expansion	$8.5 \times 10^{-6} ({}^{\circ}C)^{-1}$
Thermal conductivity	$0.80 \text{ J/s} \cdot m \cdot {}^{\circ}C$

A glass window pane is 2.7 m high, 2.4 m wide and 9 mm thick. The temperature at the inner surface of the glass is 22°C and at the outer surface 4°C. How much heat is lost each hour through the window?

A) 3.7×10^7 J   B) 3.7×10^4 J   C) 1.0×10^4 J   D) 1.0×10^1 J   E) 3.7×10^5 J

Answer: A
Var: 50+

Situation 17.2

A heat-conducting rod is constructed with a 0.15 m length of alloy A and a 0.40 m length of alloy B, joined end-to-end. Both pieces have cross–section areas of 0.002 m^2. The thermal conductivity of alloy B is known to be 1.8 times as great as that for alloy A. The end of the rod in alloy A is maintained at a temperature of 10° C and the other end is maintained at an unknown temperature. The temperature at the junction of the alloys is 40° C. The heat current in the rod is 56 W.

25) In Situation 17.2, the temperature of the end of the rod in alloy B, in °C, is closest to:

A) 80   B) 84   C) 88   D) 92   E) 96

Answer: B
Var: 1

178

26) In Situation 17.2, the thermal conductivity of alloy A is closest to:

A) 120 W/m • K

B) 125 W/m • K

C) 130 W/m • K

D) 135 W/m • K

E) 140 W/m • K

Answer: E

Var: 1

Situation 17.3

A concrete wall of a cold storage room measures 3.0 m high, 5.0 m wide, and 20 cm thick. The room temperature is maintained at −10° C and the outside temperature is 20° C. The inside wall is to be covered by a layer of wood in order to reduce the heat current through the wall by 90 percent. The thermal conductivities of concrete and wood are 0.8 and 0.04 W/m • K, respectively.

27) In Situation 17.3, the temperature difference across the layer of wood, in °C, is closest to:

A) 24   B) 25   C) 26   D) 27   E) 28

Answer: D

Var: 1

28) In Situation 17.3, the thickness of the layer of wood required, in mm, is closest to:

A) 60   B) 70   C) 80   D) 90   E) 100

Answer: D

Var: 1

29) Which of the following is a true statement?

A) Several days after a snowstorm, the roof on Jones' house is uniformly covered with snow, whereas on Smith's house next door the snow has completely melted off. A likely reason for this is that Smith's house has better roof insulation than does Jones'.

B) When you get out of a swimming pool and stand dripping wet in a breeze you feel colder than you would if your skin were dry. This is a purely psychological effect, since measurement of your skin temperature would yield the same value in both cases, wet or dry.

C) In some regions the following sign is frequently seen as one approaches a bridge: "CAUTION: BRIDGE MAY BE ICY". One reason you might expect a bridge to be icier than the road leading up to it is that the bridge has both its top and bottom exposed to cold air, whereas only the top surface of the road is in contact with cold air.

D) When the metal cooling coils in a freezer become coated with ice this helps the freezer more effectively remove heat from warm foods placed in the freezer.

E) Thermos bottles have a vacuum between the inner and outer layers of glass in order to reduce heat transfer due to radiation, since radiation cannot travel through a vacuum.

Answer: C

Var: 1

Figure 17.5

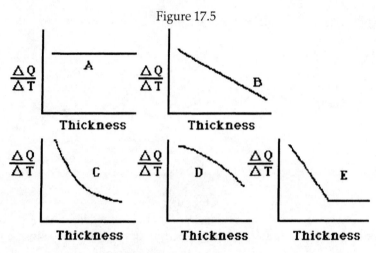

30) In Figure 17.5, an architect is interested in estimating the heat loss (in kcal/sec) through a sheet of insulating material as a function of the thickness of the sheet. Assuming fixed temperatures on the two faces of the sheet, which of the graphs best represents the heat transfer as a function of the thickness of the insulating sheet?

A) A   B) B   C) C   D) D   E) E

Answer: C
Var: 1

Situation 17.4

Two large parallel plates are separated by 0.5 m. A circle, of 1.5 m radius, is delineated on the left plate. A second circle, of the same radius, is delineated on the right plate and is opposite the first. The temperature of the left plate is 700 K and the emissivity is 1.00. The temperature of the right plate is 600 K and the emissivity is 0.80.

31) In Situation 17.4, the net heat current radiated, in the space between the two circles, in kW, is closest to:

A) 42   B) 55   C) 73   D) 96   E) 140

Answer: B
Var: 1

32) In Situation 17.4, the temperature of the left plate is maintained at 700 K. The temperature of the right plate is changed, such that there is now zero net heat current radiated, in the space between the circles. The temperature of the right plate, in SI units, is closest to:

A) 620   B) 660   C) 740   D) 780   E) 820

Answer: C
Var: 1

33) A sphere, 0.30 m in radius, has a surface emissivity of 0.48 and is at a temperature of 600 K. The sphere is surrounded by a concentric spherical shell whose inner surface has a radius of 0.90 m and an emissivity of 1.00. The temperature of the shell is 400 K. The net heat current radiated, including direction, in the space between the sphere and the shell, in kW, is closest to:

A) 4.0, outward

B) 8.3, outward

C) 18.8, outward

D) 6.5, inward

E) 10.8, inward

Answer: E
Var: 1

34) In years of heavy snow pack in the mountains it is sometimes desirable to induce early melting of the snow, rather than wait until it all melts suddenly and causes floods. It has been suggested that a way to accomplish this might be to have planes fly over the snow fields and sprinkle them with black soot. What do you think of this idea? Would it work?

A) Yes, it would probably work because the black surface would be a better absorber of sunlight than would the white snow.

B) Yes, it would work because the soot would raise the melting point of the snow.

C) Yes, it would work because the soot would decrease the specific heat capacity of the snow.

D) No, it would not work because it is infrared radiation and not visible radiation which melts the snow.

E) No, it would not work because sunlight has very little effect on how fast the snow melts.

Answer: A
Var: 1

Short Answer Questions

1) A rod, with sides insulated to prevent heat loss, has one end immersed in boiling water (T = 100°C) and the other end in a water–ice mixture. The rod has uniform cross–sectional area 4.44 cm^2 and length 17 cm. The heat conducted by the rod melts the ice at a rate of 1 gram every 26 seconds. What is the thermal conductivity of the rod? (Recall that the heat of fusion of water is 3.34 x 10^5 J/kg.)

Answer: 49 W/m • °C
Var: 50+

2) How many grams of ice at –19°C must be added to 566 grams of water that is initially at a temperature of 61°C to produce water at a final temperature of 6°C? Assume that no heat is lost to the surroundings and that the container has negligible mass. The specific heat of liquid water is 4190 J/kg • °C and of ice is 2000 J/kg • °C. For water the normal melting point is 0°C and the heat of fusion is 334 x 10^3 J/kg. The normal boiling point is 100° C and the heat of vaporization is 2.256 x 10^6 J/kg.

Answer: 330 g
Var: 50+

3) A radiating body has a Kelvin temperature T_O, and its surroundings are at 500K ($T_O > 500K$). If the Kelvin temperature of the radiating body is increased to $4T_O$, the net rate at which the body radiates increases by a factor of 631. What was the original temperature T_O?

Answer: 569 K
Var: 50+

4) A wire that is 5.8 m long and that has a radius of 1.6 mm is found to increase in length by 2.0 cm when it is heated from 0°C to 133°C. The wire is then stretched between rigid supports so that it is just taut (zero tension) when its temperature is 0°C. When the wire is cooled to –99°C the tension in the wire is found to be 4280 N. What is Young's modulus for this wire?

Answer: 2.1×10^{11} Pa
Var: 50+

5) A piece of iron of mass 0.12 kg is taken from an oven where its temperature is 336°C and quickly placed in an insulated copper can that contains 0.20 kg of water. The copper can has mass 0.50 kg, and it and the water in it are originally at a temperature of 20°C. Calculate the final temperature of the system, assuming no heat is lost to the surroundings. Use the following specific heats: water, c = 4190 J/kg • °C; iron, c = 470 J/kg • °C; and copper, c = 390 J/kg • °C.

Answer: 36°C
Var: 1

Chapter 18   Thermal Properties of Matter

Multiple Choice Questions

1) A sealed 54 m^3 tank is filled with 5000 moles of oxygen gas (diatomic) at an initial temperature of 270 K. The gas is heated to a final temperature of 490 K. The atomic mass of oxygen is 16.0 g/mol. The mass density of the oxygen gas, in SI units, is closest to:

   A) 3.0   B) 1.5   C) 2.2   D) 3.7   E) 5.9

   Answer: A
   Var: 50+

2) A sealed 76 m^3 tank is filled with 5000 moles of oxygen gas (diatomic) at an initial temperature of 270 K. The gas is heated to a final temperature of 440 K. The atomic mass of oxygen is 16.0 g/mol. The initial pressure of the gas, in MPa, is closest to:

   A) 0.15   B) 0.17   C) 0.19   D) 0.13   E) 0.11

   Answer: A
   Var: 50+

3) A sealed 31 m^3 tank is filled with 5000 moles of oxygen gas (diatomic) at an initial temperature of 270 K. The gas is heated to a final temperature of 360 K. The atomic mass of oxygen is 16.0 g/mol. The final pressure of the gas, in MPa, is closest to:

   A) 0.48   B) 0.51   C) 0.54   D) 0.56   E) 0.60

   Answer: A
   Var: 50+

4) A sealed 16 m^3 tank is filled with 2000 moles of oxygen gas (diatomic) at an initial temperature of 270 K. The gas is heated to a final temperature of 320 K. The atomic mass of oxygen is 16.0 g/mol. The heat transferred to the gas, in MJ, is closest to:

   A) 2.1   B) 2.5   C) 1.7   D) 1.2   E) 0.80

   Answer: A
   Var: 50+

5) A 7.4 L volume of neon gas (monatomic) is at a pressure of 4.6 atmospheres and a temperature of 360 K. The atomic mass of neon is 20.2 g/mol. The mass of the neon gas, in SI units, is closest to:

   A) 2.3×10^{-2} B) 1.4×10^{-2} C) 1.1×10^{1} D) 2.3×10^{1} E) 2.3×10^{3}

   Answer: A
   Var: 50+

6) A 2.5 L volume of neon gas (monatomic) is at a pressure of 4.8 atmospheres and a temperature of 390 K. The atomic mass of neon is 20.2 g/mol. The number of neon atoms in the gas is closest to:

A) 2.2×10^{24} B) 2.2×10^{22} C) 6.9×10^{23} D) 2.2×10^{25} E) 6.9×10^{22}

Answer: A
Var: 50+

7) A 1.8 L volume of neon gas (monatomic) is at a pressure of 4.0 atmospheres and a temperature of 440 K. The atomic mass of neon is 20.2 g/mol. In this situation, the temperature of the gas is increased to 540 and the volume is increased to 3.8 L. The final pressure of the gas, in atmospheres, is closest to:

A) 2.3   B) 2.1   C) 2.6   D) 2.8   E) 3.0

Answer: A
Var: 50+

Figure 18.1

8) In Figure 18.1, an ideal gas is contained between two pistons in a vertical cylinder. The upper piston has negligible mass and the lower piston has mass m. The lower piston rests on a long spring of spring constant 7000 N/m. The gas between the pistons is initially at atmospheric pressure (1×10^5 Pa) and the pistons are initially separated by 0.9 m. The area of each piston is 0.012 m². Atmospheric pressure acts on the outer surface of each piston. The system is in equilibrium.

Now a downward force is applied to the upper piston causing it to move slowly downward until equilibrium is once more established with a downward force of 920 N acting on the upper piston. This process takes place slowly, and no temperature change occurs in the gas trapped between the pistons. How far does the upper piston move in this process?

A) 0.52 m   B) 0.40 m   C) 0.33 m   D) 0.44 m   E) 0.64 m

Answer: A
Var: 50+

9) In the equation pV = nRT,

A) T is measured in degrees Celsius.

B) R is the resistance of the system.

C) R has different values for different gases.

D) V is the velocity of the flowing gas.

E) n is the number of moles of gas.

Answer: E
Var: 1

10) The van der Walls equation of state is

$$(p + \frac{an^2}{V^2})(V - nb) - nRT$$

A) the term an^2/V^2 is introduced to account for the fact that not all gas molecules are at the same pressure.

B) The term nb accounts for the fact that a molecule has a finite volume and is not a point particle.

C) It is applicable to solids, but not to liquids or gases.

D) The term an^2/V^2 is introduced to account for the fact that molecules tend to repel each other.

E) This equation of state is not as accurate as the ideal gas law equation of state, but it is useful as an approximation of the ideal gas law.

Answer: B
Var: 1

11) A 0.90 m^3 gas tank holds 4.0 moles of nitrogen gas (diatomic), at a temperature of 280 K. The atomic mass of nitrogen is 14.0 g/mol and the molecular radius is 3.0 x 10^{-10} m. The mass density of the gas, in SI units, is closest to:

A) 0.12   B) 0.062   C) 0.084   D) 0.15   E) 0.17

Answer: A
Var: 50+

12) A 0.10 m^3 gas tank holds 2.0 moles of nitrogen gas (diatomic), at a temperature of 400 K. The atomic mass of nitrogen is 14.0 g/mol and the molecular radius is 3.0 x 10^{-10} m. The pressure of the gas, in kPa, is closest to:

A) 67   B) 59   C) 51   D) 43   E) 35

Answer: A
Var: 50+

13) A 0.20 m^3 gas tank holds 5.0 moles of nitrogen gas (diatomic), at a temperature of 290 K. The atomic mass of nitrogen is 14.0 g/mol and the molecular radius is 3.0 x 10^{-10} m. The mean free path of the nitrogen molecules, in nm, is closest to:

   A) 42   B) 52   C) 62   D) 72   E) 82

   Answer: A
   Var: 50+

14) A 0.50 m^3 gas tank holds 5.0 moles of nitrogen gas (diatomic), at a temperature of 260 K. The atomic mass of nitrogen is 14.0 g/mol and the molecular radius is 3.0 x 10^{-10} m. The rms speed of the molecules, in SI units, is closest to:

   A) 480   B) 680   C) 340   D) 19   E) 83

   Answer: A
   Var: 50+

15) A 5.0 liter gas tank holds 1.9 moles of helium (monatomic) and 1.4 moles of oxygen (diatomic), at a temperature of 370 K. The atomic masses of helium and oxygen are 4.0 g/mol and 16.0 g/mol, respectively. The total mass of the gas in the tank, in grams, is closest to:

   A) 52   B) 30   C) 41   D) 64   E) 75

   Answer: A
   Var: 50+

16) A 5.0 liter gas tank holds 2.8 moles of helium (monatomic) and 0.7 moles of oxygen (diatomic), at a temperature of 360 K. The atomic masses of helium and oxygen are 4.0 g/mol and 16.0 g/mol, respectively. The total random translational kinetic energy of the gas in the tank, in kJ, is closest to:

   A) 160   B) 150   C) 170   D) 180   E) 190

   Answer: A
   Var: 50+

17) A 5.0 liter gas tank holds 2.0 moles of helium (monatomic) and 1.2 moles of oxygen (diatomic), at a temperature of 350 K. The atomic masses of helium and oxygen are 4.0 g/mol and 16.0 g/mol, respectively. The ratio of the rms speed of helium to that of oxygen, is closest to:

   A) 1.4   B) 2.0   C) 2.8   D) 4.0   E) 5.6

   Answer: C
   Var: 50+

Figure 18.2

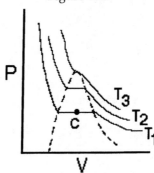

18) Figure 18.2 is a typical pV–diagram for a non–ideal gas. Which of the following is an accurate statement concerning this information?

A) These curves are called isobars.

B) T_3 is the boiling temperature of the material.

C) At point C the material is a mixture of liquid and vapor.

D) $T_1 > T_2 > T_3$

E) At temperature T_3 no phase changes occur.

Answer: C
Var: 1

19) A 24 liter tank contains helium gas at 27°C and a pressure of 22.0 Atm. How many moles of gas are in the tank?

A) 238 moles   B) 138 moles   C) 17.5 moles   D) 21.5 moles   E) 76.0 moles

Answer: D
Var: 1

20) A cylinder fitted with a movable piston contains gas at 27°C, pressure 0.50 x 10^5 Pa, and volume 1.25 m^3. What will be the final temperature if the gas is compressed to 0.80 m^3 and the pressure rises to 0.82 x 10^5 Pa?

A) 41.8°C   B) 67.7°C   C) 125°C   D) 246°C   E) 154°C

Answer: A
Var: 1

Situation 18.1

A sealed container holds 0.020 moles of nitrogen (N_2) gas, at a pressure of 1.5 atmospheres and a temperature of 290 K. The atomic mass of nitrogen is 14.0 g/mol.

21) In Situation 18.1, the number of molecules in the gas, is closest to:

A) 1.5 x 10^{21} B) 3.0 x 10^{21} C) 6.0 x 10^{21} D) 1.2 x 10^{22} E) 2.4 x 10^{22}

Answer: D
Var: 1

22) In Situation 18.1, the mass density of the gas, in SI units, is closest to:

    A) 0.9   B) 1.3   C) 1.8   D) 2.2   E) 2.6

Answer: C
Var: 1

23) In Situation 18.1, the average translational kinetic energy of a nitrogen molecule, in SI units, is closest to:

    A) 4×10^{21} B) 6×10^{21} C) 8×10^{21} D) 10×10^{21} E) 12×10^{21}

Answer: B
Var: 1

24) In Situation 18.1, the quantity of heat, transferred at constant volume, that raises the temperature of the gas to 300 K, in SI units, is closest to:

    A) 1.8   B) 2.5   C) 3.3   D) 4.2   E) 5.0

Answer: D
Var: 1

Situation 18.2

The mean free path of an oxygen molecule is 2.0×10^{-5} m, when the gas is at a pressure of 120 Pa and a temperature of 275 K. The atomic mass of oxygen is 16.0 g/mol.

25) In Situation 18.2, the radius of an oxygen molecule, in nm, is closest to:

    A) 0.22   B) 0.24   C) 0.26   D) 0.28   E) 0.30

Answer: E
Var: 1

26) In Situation 18.2, he average time interval between collisions of an oxygen molecule, in ns, is closest to:

    A) 20   B) 45   C) 95   D) 200   E) 420

Answer: B
Var: 1

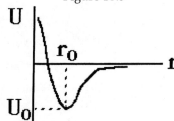
Figure 18.3

27) Figure 18.3 is a graph of potential energy versus separation of molecules for a typical substance. Which of the following is a FALSE statement concerning this data?

A) r_0 is the molecular separation one would expect of the substance is a gas.

B) The average kinetic energy of a molecule is larger than U_0 if the substance is a gas.

C) The intermolecular force is a maximum at $r = r_0$.

D) The force on a molecule changes from repulsive to attractive at $r = r_0$.

E) The curve shows that the intermolecular force becomes repulsive and very large for $r < r_0$.

Answer: B
Var: 1

28) Dust particles in a grain elevator frequently have masses of the order of 10^{-9} kg. What is the rms speed of such a particle in air at $27°C$?

A) 3.5×10^{-6} m/s

B) 5.6×10^{-5} m/s

C) 7.8×10^{-4} m/s

D) 5.2×10^{-3} m/s

E) 4.9×10^{-2} m/s

Answer: A
Var: 1

29) Using the kinetic–molecular model of an ideal gas, the way we go about determining the pressure exerted by a gas is to

A) calculate the kinetic energy and then use the principal of virtual work.

B) recognize that there is no heat flow out of an isolated system.

C) determine the acceleration of each molecule and then apply $F = ma$.

D) determine how many molecules strike a wall each second and what momentum change is associated with each, then apply $F = dp/dt$.

E) recognize that if the gas causes the wall to move a distance dx, the work done is $F_x dx$ and this is equal to the loss in kinetic energy of the gas molecules.

Answer: D
Var: 1

30) Which of the following is a FALSE statement?

   A) The average kinetic energy of a molecule moving in three dimensions is always $3kT/2$.

   B) A dumbbell molecule like O_2 is considered to have eight degrees of freedom.

   C) The average kinetic energy associated with each degree of freedom of a molecule is $1/2kT$.

   D) Vibrational motion, as well as translational motion, can contribute to the heat capacities of gases.

   E) Rotational motion, as well as translational motion, can contribute to the heat capacities of gases.

Answer: C
Var: 1

Situation 18.3

The temperature of a gas is increased by 110 K and, as a result, the rms translational velocity of the molecules increases from 400 m/s to 480 m/s.

31) In Situation 18.3, the molecular mass of the gas, in g/mol, is closest to:

   A) 39   B) 41   C) 43   D) 45   E) 47

Answer: A
Var: 1

32) In Situation 18.3, the final temperature of the gas, in SI units, is closest to:

   A) 300   B) 320   C) 340   D) 360   E) 380

Answer: D
Var: 1

33) A 500 g cube of copper is heated from $0°C$ at constant volume. The atomic mass of copper is 63.5 g/mol. Assume the rule of Dulong and Petit is applicable. The heat required for the temperature change, in kJ, is closest to:

   A) 10   B) 13   C) 17   D) 20   E) 23

Answer: D
Var: 1

34) Three quantities encountered in the kinetic theory of gases are the most probably speed, v_{mp}, the average speed, v_{av} and the root mean square speed, v_{rms}. For an ideal gas, which of these is largest, if any?

   A) v_{mp}

   B) v_{av}

   C) v_{rms}

   D) All three are equal for an ideal gas.

   E) The answer depends on whether a monatomic gas or a polyatomic gas is under consideration.

Answer: C
Var: 1

Short Answer Questions

1) If a certain sample of an ideal gas has a temperature of $113°C$ and exerts a pressure of 6.7×10^4 Pa on the walls of its container, how many gas molecules are present in each cm^3 of volume? Assume that the gas is ideal. The gas constant is R = 8.314 J/mol • K and Avagadro's number is $N_A = 6.022 \times 10^{23}$ molecules/mol.

Answer: 1.3×10^{19} molecules
Var: 50+

Figure 18.4

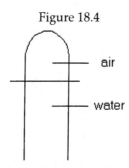

2) In Figure 18.4, an air pocket at the top of a vertical tube, closed at the upper end and open at the lower, occupies a volume of 470 cm^3 at the surface of a lake where the air pressure is 1.0×10^5 Pa and the temperature is $37°C$. What is the volume of the air in the pocket if the tube is taken to a depth of 76 meters, where the temperature is $7°C$? Assume that none of the air escapes from the tube. The density of the water in the lake is 1000 kg/m^3.

Answer: 50 cm^3
Var: 50+

3) A closed 8.00–L tank contains argon at $33.0°C$ and absolute pressure 8.00×10^5 Pa. How much energy is required to raise the temperature of the argon gas to $62.0°C$? Assume that argon is an ideal monatomic gas.

Answer: 919 J
Var: 50+

4) What is the total translational kinetic energy in a classroom filled with nitrogen at 9.30×10^5 Pa and $20.7°C$? The dimensions of the classroom are 4.60 m x 5.70 m x 8.80 m.

Answer: 3.22×10^8 J
Var: 50+

5) A flask contains a mixture of argon and neon gases. The root-mean- square speed of the argon gas is determined to be 1210 m/s. What is the root-mean- square speed of the neon gas? The atomic masses are argon, 39.95 g/mole; neon, 20.18 g/mole.

Answer: 1700 m/s
Var: 1

Chapter 19   The First Law of Thermodynamics

Multiple Choice Questions

1) The temperature of an ideal gas in a sealed $0.30 \, m^3$ container is reduced from 340 K to 270 K. The final pressure of the gas is 20 kPA. The molar heat capacity at constant volume of the gas is 28.0 J/mol • K. The heat absorbed by the gas, in kJ, is closest to:

    A) –5.2   B) –6.8   C) 5.2   D) 6.8   E) zero

Answer: A
Var: 50+

2) The temperature of an ideal gas in a sealed $0.70 \, m^3$ container is reduced from 450 K to 270 K. The final pressure of the gas is 60 kPA. The molar heat capacity at constant volume of the gas is 28.0 J/mol • K. The work done by the gas, in kJ, is closest to:

    A) zero   B) –94   C) –120   D) 94   E) 120

Answer: A
Var: 50+

3) A compression, at a constant pressure of 110 kPa, is performed on 4.0 moles of an ideal monatomic gas ($C_V = 3/2 \, R$). The compression reduces the volume of the gas from $0.25 \, m^3$ to $0.12 \, m^3$. The change in the internal energy of the gas, in kJ, is closest to:

    A) –21   B) –36   C) 21   D) 36   E) zero

Answer: A
Var: 50+

4) A compression, at a constant pressure of 40 kPa, is performed on 7.0 moles of an ideal monatomic gas ($C_V = 3/2 \, R$). The compression reduces the volume of the gas from $0.21 \, m^3$ to $0.12 \, m^3$. The work done by the gas, in kJ, is closest to:

    A) –3.6   B) 3.6   C) –9.0   D) 9.0   E) zero

Answer: A
Var: 50+

5) A monatomic ideal gas ($C_V = 3/2 \, R$) undergoes an isothermal expansion at 300 K, as the volume increased from $0.04 \, m^3$ to $0.32 \, m^3$. The final pressure is 80 kPa. The change in the internal energy of the gas, in kJ, is closest to:

    A) zero   B) 27   C) 53   D) –27   E) –53

Answer: A
Var: 50+

6) A monatomic ideal gas ($C_V = 3/2$ R) undergoes an isothermal expansion at 300 K, as the volume increased from 0.03 m^3 to 0.09 m^3. The final pressure is 130 kPa. The heat transfer to the gas, in kJ, is closest to:

A) 13   B) 6.4   C) –13   D) –6.4   E) zero

Answer: A
Var: 50+

7) An expansion process on a diatomic ideal gas ($C_V = 5/2$ R), has a linear path between the initial and final coordinates on a pV diagram. The coordinates of the initial state are: the pressure is 300 kPa, the volume is 0.02 m^3, and the temperature is 390 K. The final pressure is 120 kPa and the final temperature is 280 K. The work done by the gas, in SI units, is closest to:

A) 3300   B) 1700   C) 2500   D) 4200   E) 5000

Answer: A
Var: 50+

8) An expansion process on a diatomic ideal gas ($C_V = 5/2$ R), has a linear path between the initial and final coordinates on a pV diagram. The coordinates of the initial state are: the pressure is 300 kPa, the volume is 0.08 m^3, and the temperature is 390 K. The final pressure is 90 kPa and the final temperature is 320 K. The change in the internal energy of the gas, in SI units, is closest to:

A) –11,000   B) –6500   C) 11,000   D) 6500   E) zero

Answer: A
Var: 50+

Figure 19.1

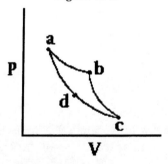

9) In Figure 19.1 is a cyclic process carried out in a gas. Which of the following is an accurate statement?

A) The work done in the process is equal to the area enclosed by the cyclic process.

B) The work done in the process is equal under the curve *abc*.

C) The work done in the process is equal to the area under the curve *adc*.

D) The work done in the process is equal to the area under ab minus the area under *dc*.

E) The work done in the process is zero.

Answer: A
Var: 1

Figure 19.2

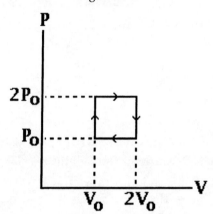

10) In Figure 19.2, an ideal gas is carried around the cyclic process. How much work is done in one cycle if $P_O = 8$ atm. and $V_O = 7.00$ liters?

A) 5660 J   B) 2260 J   C) 10,600 J   D) 11,300 J   E) 22,600 J

Answer: A
Var: 50+

11) Which of the following is a FALSE statement?

A) Heat is energy transferred into or out of a system as a result of a temperature difference between the system and its surroundings.

B) The heat added to an ideal gas during the transition from state 1 to state 2 depends only on the initial and final states, 1 and 2, and not on the path by which the gas went from one to the other.

C) When a gas goes from one state to another, the work done depends on the path followed.

D) It does not make sense to refer to "the amount of heat in a body".

E) When an ideal gas experiences a free expansion, its temperature doesn't change.

Answer: B
Var: 1

12) A cylinder contains 6 moles of an ideal gas at a temperature of 300 K. The gas is compressed at constant pressure until the final volume equals 0.84 times the initial volume. The molar heat capacity at constant volume of the gas is 24.0 J/mol • K. The heat absorbed by the gas, in kJ, is closest to:

A) –9.3   B) –6.9   C) 9.3   D) 6.9   E) –2.4

Answer: A
Var: 50+

13) A cylinder contains 9 moles of an ideal gas at a temperature of 300 K. The gas is compressed at constant pressure until the final volume equals 0.62 times the initial volume. The molar heat capacity at constant volume of the gas is 24.0 J/mol • K. The change in the the internal energy of the gas, in kJ, is closest to:

    A) –25   B) –33   C) 25   D) 33   E) –8.5

Answer: A
Var: 50+

14) A cylinder contains 6 moles of an ideal gas at a temperature of 300 K. The gas is compressed at constant pressure until the final volume equals 0.49 times the initial volume. The molar heat capacity at constant volume of the gas is 24.0 J/mol • K. The adiabatic constant for the gas is closest to:

    A) 1.35   B) 1.40   C) 1.47   D) 1.56   E) 1.67

Answer: A
Var: 50+

15) A sealed tank contains 11 moles of an ideal gas, at an initial temperature of 270 K. The pressure of the gas is increased until the final pressure equals 2.2 times the initial pressure. The heat capacity at constant pressure of the gas is 32.0 J/mol • K. The heat absorbed by the gas, in kJ, is closest to:

    A) 84   B) 110   C) 140   D) –55   E) –25

Answer: A
Var: 50+

16) A sealed tank contains 44 moles of an ideal gas, at an initial temperature of 270 K. The pressure of the gas is increased until the final pressure equals 1.9 times the initial pressure. The heat capacity at constant pressure of the gas is 27.0 J/mol • K. The change in the internal energy of the gas, in kJ, is closest to:

    A) 200   B) 290   C) 380   D) –110   E) –21

Answer: A
Var: 50+

17) A sealed tank contains 44 moles of an ideal gas, at an initial temperature of 270 K. The pressure of the gas is increased until the final pressure equals 1.9 times the initial pressure. The heat capacity at constant pressure of the gas is 27.0 J/mol • K. The adiabatic constant of the gas is closest to:

    A) 1.44   B) 1.31   C) 1.80   D) 1.24   E) 1.19

Answer: A
Var: 50+

18) Consider the equation $Q = \Delta U + W$. Which of the following statements is FALSE?

A) This is called the First Law of Thermodynamics.

B) This is called the law of conservation of energy.

C) Q can be positive or negative.

D) W is the work done by the system, and not on the system.

E) It follows that since Q and W are path dependent, then ΔU must also be path dependent.

Answer: E
Var: 1

19) Which of the following is FALSE?

A) An adiabatic process is one in which there is no heat transfer into or out of the system.

B) An isentropic process is one in which the internal energy of the system remains constant.

C) An isothermal process is one in which the temperature of the system stays constant.

D) An isochoric process is one in which the volume of the system stays constant.

E) An isobaric process is one in which the pressure stays constant.

Answer: B
Var: 1

20) An ideal gas is held in a container of volume V at pressure P. The average speed of a gas molecule under these conditions is v. If now the volume and pressure are changed to 2V and 2P, the average speed of a molecule will be

A) 1/2 v   B) v   C) 2v   D) 4v   E) v/4

Answer: C
Var: 1

Situation 19.1

Twenty moles of a monatomic ideal gas ($\gamma = 5/3$) undergo an adiabatic process. The initial pressure is 400 kPa and the initial temperature is 450 K. The final temperature of the gas is 320 K.

21) In Situation 19.1, the final volume of the gas, in SI units, is closest to:

A) 0.19   B) 0.23   C) 0.27   D) 0.31   E) 0.35

Answer: D
Var: 1

22) In Situation 19.1, the heat absorbed by the gas, in kJ, is closest to:

A) zero   B) +32   C) +54   D) –32   E) –54

Answer: A
Var: 1

23) In Situation 19.1, the change in the internal energy of the gas, in kJ, is closest to:

A) zero   B) +32   C) +54   D) –32   E) –54

Answer: D
Var: 1

Situation 19.2

An adiabatic process is performed on 15 moles of an ideal gas. The initial temperature is 320 K and the initial volume is 0.80 m³. The final volume is 0.40 m³. The adiabatic constant for the gas is 1.44.

24) In Situation 19.2, the final temperature of the gas, in SI units, is closest to:

   A) 435   B) 450   C) 465   D) 480   E) 495

   Answer: A
   Var: 1

25) In Situation 19.2, the heat absorbed by the gas, in kJ, is closest to:

   A) zero   B) +14   C) +32   D) –14   E) –32

   Answer: A
   Var: 1

26) In Situation 19.2, the work done by the gas, in kJ, is closest to:

   A) zero   B) +14   C) +32   D) –24   E) –32

   Answer: E
   Var: 1

27) In Situation 19.2, the heat capacity at constant pressure for the gas, in SI units, is closest to:

   A) 23   B) 25   C) 27   D) 29   E) 31

   Answer: C
   Var: 1

28) For an ideal gas the internal energy U depends only on

   A) volume.

   B) entropy.

   C) the amount of heat added to it.

   D) temperature.

   E) pressure.

   Answer: D
   Var: 1

29) The internal energy of an ideal gas

   A) does not depend on how many moles of gas are in the system.

   B) depends on the volume of the gas.

   C) depends on the pressure of the gas.

   D) depends only on the temperature of the gas, and not on pressure or volume.

   E) More than one of the above are true.

   Answer: D
   Var: 1

Situation 19.3

A substance has a density of 2000 kg/m^3 in the liquid state. At atmospheric pressure, the substance has a boiling point of 180°C and a heat of vaporization of 1.60 x 10^5 J/kg. The vapor has a density of 5.0 kg/m^3 at the boiling point and at atmospheric pressure.

30) In Situation 19.3, the work done by 1.0 kg of the substance, as it vaporizes at atmospheric pressure, in kJ, is closest to:

A) 20   B) 30   C) 40   D) 50   E) 60

Answer: A
Var: 1

31) In Situation 19.3, the change in the internal energy of 1.0 kg of the substance, as it vaporizes at atmospheric pressure, in kJ, is closest to:

A) 120   B) 140   C) 160   D) 180   E) 200

Answer: B
Var: 1

32) In Situation 19.3, assume the substance in the vapor state obeys the ideal gas law when the temperature is at the boiling point. The molecular mass of the substance, in g/mol, is closest to:

A) 130   B) 150   C) 170   D) 190   E) 210

Answer: D
Var: 1

33) An adiabatic compression is performed on an ideal gas. The final pressure is equal to 0.56 times the initial pressure and the final volume equals 1.50 times the initial volume. The adiabatic constant for the gas is closest to:

A) 1.43   B) 1.45   C) 1.48   D) 1.52   E) 1.57

Answer: A
Var: 1

34) When an ideal gas is expanded in volume at constant pressure, the average kinetic energy of the gas molecules

A) increases.

B) decreases.

C) does not change.

D) may either increase or decrease, depending on whether or not the process is carried out adiabatically.

E) may or may not change, but insufficient information is given at make such a determination.

Answer: A
Var: 1

35) An ideal gas with g = 1.67 is initially at $0°C$ in a volume of 10.0 liters at a pressure of 1.00 atm. It is expanded adiabatically to a volume of 10.4 liters. What then is the temperature?

A) $-7.10°C$ B) $2.53°C$ C) $-22.7°C$ D) $67.8°C$ E) $-19.5°C$

Answer: A
Var: 1

Short Answer Questions

Figure 19.3

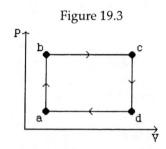

1) In Figure 19.3, in a certain process 1510 J of heat flows into a system, and at the same time the system expands against a constant external pressure of 7.00×10^4 Pa. If the volume of the system increases from 0.020 m^3 to 0.060 m^3, calculate the change in internal energy of the system. If the internal energy change is nonzero, be sure to indicate whether the internal energy change is positive or negative.

Answer: -1290 J
Var: 50+

Figure 19.4

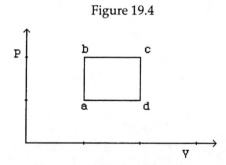

2) In Figure 19.4, consider the cycle shown, where state a is the initial state if the system. The internal energies of the states are: $U_a = 10$ J, $U_b = 35$ J, and $U_d = 39$ J. In process b → c, the work done by the gas is +91 J. Find the heat added to the system during the process b → c and the heat removed during process d → a.

Answer: b → c, 146 J; d → a, 50 J
Var: 1

3) A cylinder contains 3.7 moles of ideal gas, initially at a temperature of 108°C. The cylinder is provided with a frictionless piston, which maintains a constant pressure of 6.4×10^5 Pa on the gas. The gas is cooled until its temperature has decreased to 27°C. For the gas $C_V = 11.16$ J/mol • K. The gas constant R = 8.314 J/mol • K. Calculate:

(a) the work W done by gas
(b) the net change in the internal energy, ΔU, of the gas, and
(c) the heat transfer Q.

Answer: (a) W = –2500 J (b) ΔU = –3300 J (c) Q = –5800 J
Var: 50+

4) In the process represented below, 2.4 moles of an ideal monatomic gas start at state a, with pressure 1 atm (1.01×10^5 N/m^2) and volume 5.8×10^{-2} m^3. The pressure at states *b & c* is twice the original pressure, and the volume at states *c & d* is twice the original volume. Find

a) the heat added during the process a $\rightarrow$ b
b) the heat added during the process b $\rightarrow$ c
c) the net work done by the gas in one cycle, and
d) the thermal efficiency of the process.
For this gas $C_V = 12.471$ J/mol • K. The gas constant R = 8.314 J/mol • k.

Answer: a) 8800 J, b) 29,000 J, c) 5900 J, d) 15%
Var: 1

5) 2.5 moles of an ideal gas is at an initial temperature of 30°C and has an initial volume of 0.04 m^3. The gas expands adiabatically to a volume of 0.16 m^3. For the gas, $C_V = 12.47$ J/mol • K. The gas constant is R = 8.314 J/mol • K. Calculate the work done by the gas during this expansion.

Answer: 5600 J
Var: 50+

Chapter 20   The Second Law of Thermodynamics

Multiple Choice Questions

1) A Carnot engine is operated as an air conditioner to cool a house in the summer. The air conditioner removes 19 kJ of heat per second from the house, and maintains the inside temperature at 293 K, while the outside temperature is 375 K. The power required for the air conditioner under these operating conditions, in SI units, is closest to:

   A) 5300   B) 6400   C) 7400   D) 8500   E) 9600

   Answer: A
   Var: 50+

2) A Carnot engine is operated as a heat pump to heat a room in the winter. The heat pump delivers heat to the room at the rate of 39 kJ per second and maintains the room at a temperature of 293 K when the outside temperature is 261 K. The power requirement for the heat pump under these operating conditions, in SI units, is closest to:

   A) 4300   B) 3400   C) 9100   D) 7000   E) 4800

   Answer: A
   Var: 50+

3) Two Carnot heat engines operate in tandem as follows: engine A takes in 20.0 kJ per cycle from a heat reservoir at a temperature of 480 K. The heat rejected by engine A is received by engine B, which performs 4.3 kJ of net work per cycle. Engine B, in turn, rejects heat at a temperature of 330 K. The temperature at which engine A rejects heat to engine B, in SI units, is closest to:

   A) 433   B) 424   C) 414   D) 405   E) 382

   Answer: A
   Var: 50+

4) Two Carnot heat engines operate in tandem as follows: engine A takes in 19.0 kJ per cycle from a heat reservoir at a temperature of 410 K. The heat rejected by engine A is received by engine B, which performs 2.6 kJ of net work per cycle. Engine B, in turn, rejects heat at a temperature of 260 K. The work per cycle performed by engine A, in kJ, is closest to:

   A) 4.4   B) 6.3   C) 5.7   D) 5.0   E) 7.0

   Answer: A
   Var: 50+

5) A real (non–Carnot) heat engine, operating between heat reservoirs at temperatures of 670 K and 270 K, performs 3.1 kJ of net work, and rejects 9.2 kJ of heat, in a single cycle. The thermal efficiency of this heat engine is closest to:

   A) 0.25   B) 0.23   C) 0.20   D) 0.28   E) 0.30

   Answer: A
   Var: 50+

6) A real (non–Carnot) heat engine, operating between heat reservoirs at temperatures of 690 K and 270 K, performs 4.3 kJ of net work, and rejects 8.2 kJ of heat, in a single cycle. The thermal efficiency of a Carnot heat engine, operating between the same heat reservoirs, in percent, is closest to:

A) 61   B) 55   C) 49   D) 43   E) 37

Answer: A
Var: 50+

7) A 710 g quantity of an ideal gas undergoes a reversible isothermal compression at a temperature of 330 K. The compression reduces the volume of the gas from 0.40 m^3 initially, to 0.18 m^3 finally. The molecular mass of the gas is 45.0 g/mol. The entropy change for the gas, in SI units, is closest to:

A) –100   B) –59   C) 100   D) 59   E) zero

Answer: A
Var: 50+

8) A 160 g quantity of ethanol, in the liquid state at its melting point of –114.4°C, is frozen at atmospheric pressure. The heat of fusion of ethanol is 1.04×10^5 J/kg and the molecular mass is 46.1 g/mol. The change in the entropy of the ethanol as it freezes, in SI units, is closest to:

A) –110   B) –96   C) –120   D) 96   E) 110

Answer: A
Var: 50+

9) Which of the following is NOT an accurate statement?

A) The flow of heat from a cold body to a hot body would violate the first law of thermodynamics.

B) Reversible processes are equilibrium processes.

C) The free expansion of a gas is an example of an irreversible process.

D) Macroscopic kinetic energy is associated with organized, coordinated motion of molecules, whereas heat transfer involve changes in energy of random, disordered molecular motion.

E) All real processes are irreversible.

Answer: B
Var: 1

10)

Figure 20.1

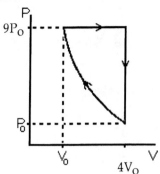

In Figure 20.1, an ideal gas with $C_p/C_v = 1.4$ is carried through the cycle illustrated here. The compression is adiabatic. What is the efficiency of an engine utilizing this cycle?

   A) 15%   B) 21%   C) 26%   D) 31%   E) 37%

Answer: A
Var: 44

11) Which of the following is an accurate statement?

   A) An important distinction between the Diesel cycle and the Otto cycle is that for the Diesel cycle high efficiencies may be obtained with low compression ratios.

   B) An important distinction between the Diesel cycle and the Otto cycle is that there is no fuel in the cylinder at the beginning of the compression stroke and no spark plug is used.

   C) The efficiency of the Otto cycle does not depend on the compression ratio.

   D) A typical gasoline engine has an efficiency of about 2%.

   E) Because a Diesel engine requires no fuel ignition system, Diesel engines tend to be lighter and easier to start than a comparable gasoline engine.

Answer: B
Var: 1

12) 36 moles of liquid helium are vaporized at its boiling point of 4.22 K, at atmospheric pressure. The heat of vaporization of helium, at atmospheric pressure, is 2.09×10^5. The change in the entropy of the helium, as it vaporizes, in SI units, is closest to:

   A) 7500   B) 11,000   C) 15,000   D) –7500   E) –11,000

Answer: A
Var: 50+

13)

Figure 20.2a

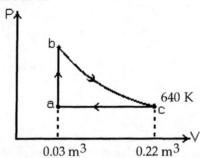

A heat engine takes 9.0 moles of an ideal gas through the reversible cycle *abca*, on the pV diagram, as shown. The path *bc* is an isothermal process. The temperature at *c* is 640 K, and the volumes at *a* and *c* are 0.03 m^3 and 0.22 m^3, respectively. The molar heat capacity at constant volume, of the gas, is 18 J/mol • K. In Figure 20.2a, for the path *ab*, the heat absorbed by the gas, in kJ, is closest to:

A) 90   B) 130   C) –90   D) –130   E) zero

Answer: A
Var: 50+

14)

Figure 20.2b

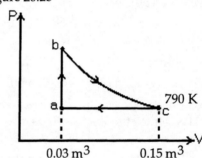

A heat engine takes 6.0 moles of an ideal gas through the reversible cycle *abca*, on the pV diagram, as shown. The path *bc* is an isothermal process. The temperature at *c* is 790 K, and the volumes at *a* and *c* are 0.03 m^3 and 0.15 m^3, respectively. The molar heat capacity at constant volume, of the gas, is 26 J/mol • K. In Figure 20.2b, for the path *bc*, the work done by the gas, in kJ, is closest to:

A) 63   B) 160   C) –63   D) –160   E) zero

Answer: A
Var: 50+

15)

Figure 20.2c

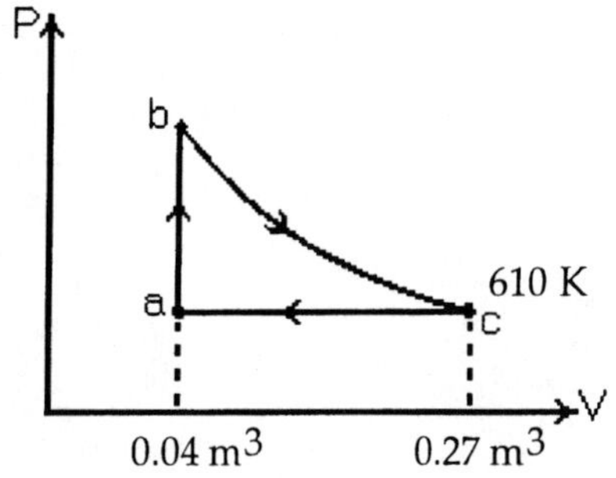

A heat engine takes 2.0 moles of an ideal gas through the reversible cycle *abca*, on the pV diagram, as shown. The path *bc* is an isothermal process. The temperature at *c* is 610 K, and the volumes at *a* and *c* are 0.04 m^3 and 0.27 m^3, respectively. The molar heat capacity at constant volume, of the gas, is 40 J/mol • K. In Figure 20.2c, for the path *ca*, the heat absorbed by the gas, in kJ, is closest to:

A) –50   B) 50   C) –42   D) 42   E) zero

Answer: A
Var: 50+

16)

Figure 20.2d

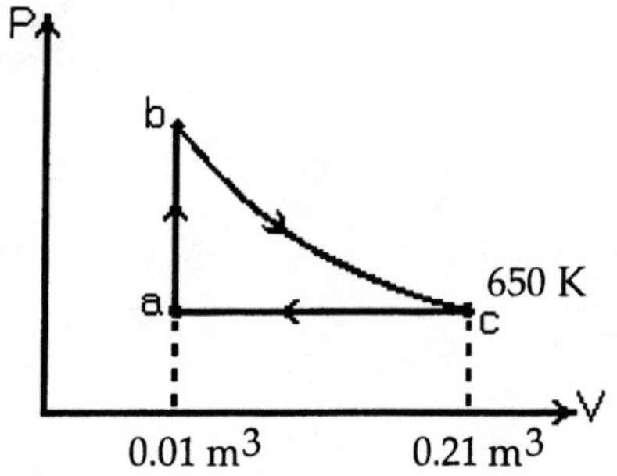

A heat engine takes 6.0 moles of an ideal gas through the reversible cycle *abca*, on the pV diagram, as shown. The path *bc* is an isothermal process. The temperature at *c* is 650 K, and the volumes at *a* and *c* are 0.01 m^3 and 0.21 m^3, respectively. The molar heat capacity at constant volume, of the gas, is 26 J/mol • K. In Figure 20.2d, for the path *ca*, the work done by the gas, in kJ, is closest to:

A) –31   B) 31   C) –650   D) 650   E) zero

Answer: A
Var: 50+

17)

Figure 20.2e

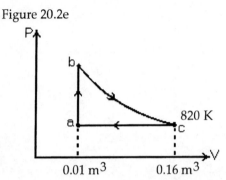

A heat engine takes 7.0 moles of an ideal gas through the reversible cycle *abca*, on the pV diagram, as shown. The path *bc* is an isothermal process. The temperature at *c* is 820 K, and the volumes at *a* and *c* are 0.01 m^3 and 0.16 m^3, respectively. The molar heat capacity at constant volume, of the gas, is 37 J/mol • K. In Figure 20.2e, the thermal efficiency of the engine, is closest to:

A) 0.26   B) 0.026   C) 0.33   D) 0.40   E) 0.53

Answer: A
Var: 50+

Figure 20.3

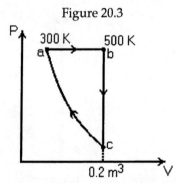

A heat engine performs the reversible cycle *abca* with 9.0 moles of an ideal gas. Path *ca* is an adiabatic process. The temperatures at points *a* and *b* are 300 K and 500 K, respectively. The volume at point c is 0.20 m^3. The adiabatic constant of the gas is 1.60.

18) In Figure 20.3, the heat absorbed by the gas in path *ab* , in kJ, is closest to:

A) zero   B) +25   C) +40   D) –25   E) –40

Answer: C
Var: 1

19) In Figure 20.3, the heat absorbed by the gas in path *ca*, in kJ, is closest to:

A) zero   B) +10   C) +16   D) –10   E) –16

Answer: A
Var: 1

20) In Figure 20.3, the work done by the gas in path *ab*, in kJ, is closest to:

A) zero   B) +15   C) +25   D) –15   E) –25

Answer: B
Var: 1

21) In Figure 20.3, the work done by the gas in path *ca*, in kJ, is closest to:

A) zero   B) +6   C) +10   D) –6   E) –10

Answer: E
Var: 1

22) In Figure 20.3, the thermal efficiency of the heat engine is closest to:

A) 0.07   B) 0.10   C) 0.13   D) 0.16   E) 0.19

Answer: C
Var: 1

Figure 20.4

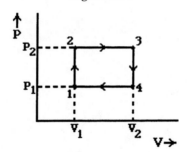

23) In Figure 20.4, a gas initially at P_1, V_1 is caused to change its volume and pressure reversibly such that it moves along the path sketched here. In one cycle the net work done by the gas is thus

A) P_1V_1

B) $P_2V_{•}2 - P_1V_1$

C) $V_2(P_2 - P_1)$

D) $(P_2 - P_1))(V_2 - V_1)$

E) $P_2(V_2 - V_1)$

Answer: D
Var: 1

24) Which of the following is a FALSE statement?

   A) A heat pump can deliver heat Q into a house while doing work W, where W can be less than Q.

   B) A refrigerator is a heat engine operating in reverse.

   C) The performance coefficient of a refrigerator ranges from 0 to 1.

   D) An air conditioner operates on the same principle as a refrigerator.

   E) The evaporator coils of a refrigerator are in contact with the cold reservoir and the condenser coils are in contact with the hot reservoir.

Answer: C
Var: 1

25) Which of the following is a TRUE statement?

   A) The second law of thermodynamics is a consequence of the first law of thermodynamics.

   B) It is possible for heat to flow spontaneously from a hot body to a cold one or from a cold one to a hot one, depending on whether or not the process is reversible or irreversible.

   C) It is not possible to convert work entirely into heat.

   D) It is impossible to transfer heat from a cooler to a hotter body.

   E) All of these statements are false.

Answer: E
Var: 1

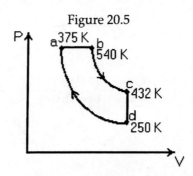

Figure 20.5

A diesel engine operates reversibly on the cycle *abcda*, using 9.0 moles of an ideal gas. Paths *bc* and *da* are adiabatic processes. The operating temperatures, of points *a, b, c,* and *d* of the cycle are 375 K, 450 K, 432 K, and 250 K, respectively. The adiabatic constant of the gas is 1.50.

26) In Figure 20.5, the heat intake during the isobaric expansion, in kJ, is closest to:

   A) 25   B) 29   C) 33   D) 37   E) 41

Answer: D
Var: 1

27) In Figure 20.5, the heat rejected in the isochoris process, in kJ, is closest to:

   A) 19   B) 21   C) 23   D) 25   E) 27

Answer: E
Var: 1

28) In Figure 20.5, the change in the internal energy of the gas, in the adiabatic compression, in kJ, is closest to:

A) zero   B) +16   C) +19   D) –16   E) –19

Answer: C
Var: 1

29) In Figure 20.5, the work performed by the engine, in the adiabatic expansion, in kJ, is closest to:

A) 13   B) 16   C) 19   D) 24   E) 29

Answer: B
Var: 1

30) In Figure 20.5, the thermal efficiency of the engine, in percent, is closest to:

A) 21   B) 23   C) 26   D) 30   E) 35

Answer: C
Var: 1

31) An important feature of the Carnot cycle is that

A) its efficiency can be 100%.

B) its efficiency depends only on the absolute temperature of the hot reservoir used.

C) its efficiency is determined by the temperatures of the hot and cold reservoirs between which it works and by the properties of the working substance used, and on nothing else.

D) it is an example of an irreversible process that can be analyzed exactly without approximations.

E) no engine can be more efficient than a Carnot engine operating between the same two temperatures.

Answer: E
Var: 1

32) Which of the following is a FALSE statement?

A) The difference in entropy between two states of a system is independent of the path between the two states.

B) Entropy is a quantitative measure of disorder.

C) The total entropy change in one cycle of a Carnot engine is zero.

D) The entropy of an isolated system is conserved, i.e. constant.

E) Entropy can be measured in units of J/K.

Answer: D
Var: 1

33) The efficiency of a Carnot engine operating between 323°C and 700°C is

A) 61.6%   B) 32.3%   C) 61.7%   D) 38.3%   E) 53.3%

Answer: D
Var: 1

34) A number of alternative energy conversion schemes are being studied world–wide because of the many problems associated with fossil fuels and nuclear energy sources. Which of the following is NOT one of the ideas being seriously pursued?

A) Solar energy.

B) Wind energy.

C) Ocean temperature gradient engines.

D) Gravity converters.

E) Biomass conversion.

Answer: D
Var: 1

Short Answer Questions

1) A Carnot heat engine operates between reservoirs at $T_H = 1935$ K and $T_C = 150$ K. In each cycle, 220 J of heat energy is rejected to the low temperature reservoir. In each cycle, how much mechanical work W is performed by the engine?

Answer: 2620 J
Var: 50+

2) A Carnot refrigerator takes heat from water at $0°$C and rejects heat to a room at $16°$C. Suppose that 59 grams of water at $0°$C are converted to ice at $0°$C by the refrigerator. Calculate the mechanical energy that must be supplied to the refrigerator. (Note: The heat of fusion of water is $L = 3.34 \times 10^5$ J/kg.)

Answer: 1200 J
Var: 50+

3) 36 g of water at $10°$C is mixed with 420 g of ice at $-10°$C. What mass of water freezes? What is the change in entropy of the system? (The heat capacity of water is 4190 J/kg • $°$C, that of ice is 2090 J/kg • $°$C, and the heat of fusion of water is 3.34×10^5 J/kg.)

Answer: a) 22 g   b) 7.2×10^{-1} J/k
Var: 50+

4) In an engine where the process is modeled by an Otto cycle, the working fluid is an ideal monatomic gas, with $\gamma = 1.5$. At the beginning of the power stroke, the temperature of the hot gas is $230°$C, and at the end of the power stroke (just before the exhaust stroke), the temperature of the cooler gas is $27°$C. What is the compression ratio of this engine? (The power stroke in an Otto–cycle engine is adiabatic, so PV^γ is constant during the power stroke.)

Answer: 2.8
Var: 50+

5) A Carnot engine is operated between a hot and a cold reservoir. The temperature difference between the two reservoirs is $234°$C. If the efficiency of this ideal engine is 29.0%, find the temperature of the cold reservoir in $°$C.

Answer: $300°$C
Var: 50+

Chapter 21   Electric Charge and Electric Field

Multiple Choice Questions

1)

Figure 21.1a

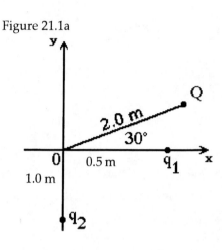

A point charge Q = –800 nC and two unknown point charges, q_1 and q_2, are placed as shown. The electric field at the origin O, due to charges Q, q_1 and q_2, is equal to zero. In Figure 21.1a, the number of excess electrons in charge Q, is closest to:

A) 5.0×10^{12} B) 6.2×10^{12} C) 7.5×10^{12} D) 8.7×10^{12} E) 1.0×10^{13}

Answer: A
Var: 50+

2)

Figure 21.1b

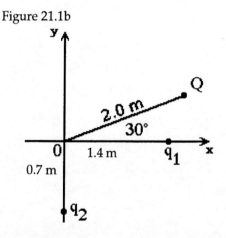

A point charge Q = –500 nC and two unknown point charges, q_1 and q_2, are placed as shown. The electric field at the origin O, due to charges Q, q_1 and q_2, is equal to zero. In Figure 21.1b, the charge q_1, in nC, is closest to:

A) 210   B) 120   C) 250   D) –120   E) –210

Answer: A
Var: 50+

3)

Figure 21.1c

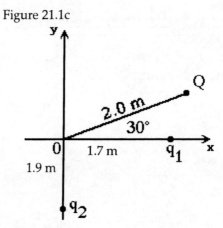

A point charge Q = –400 nC and two unknown point charges, q_1 and q_2, are placed as shown. The electric field at the origin O, due to charges Q, q_1 and q_2, is equal to zero. In Figure 21.1c, the charge q_2, in nC, is closest to:

A) –180   B) –310   C) 180   D) 310   E) 360

Answer: A
Var: 50+

4)

Figure 21.2a

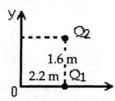

Two point charges, Q_1 = –2.0 μC and Q_2 = +5.0 μC, are placed as shown. In Figure 21.2a, the number of excess electrons in charge Q_1 is closest to:

A) 1.3×10^{13} B) 1.3×10^{14} C) 4.0×10^{11} D) 4.0×10^{12} E) 4.0×10^{13}

Answer: A
Var: 50+

5)   Figure 21.2b

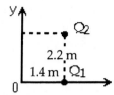

Two point charges, $Q_1 = -2.0\ \mu C$ and $Q_2 = +2.0\ \mu C$, are placed as shown. In Figure 21.2b, the x-component of the electric field, at the origin O, is closest to:

A) 7800 N/C

B) 11,000 N/C

C) -11,000 N/C

D) -7800 N/C

E) 2300 N/C

Answer: A
Var: 50+

6)   Figure 21.2c

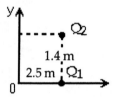

Two point charges, $Q_1 = -1.0\ \mu C$ and $Q_2 = +4.0\ \mu C$, are placed as shown. In Figure 21.2c, the y-component of the electric field, at the origin O, is closest to:

A) -2100 N/C

B) -13,000 N/C

C) 2100 N/C

D) 13,000 N/C

E) zero

Answer: A
Var: 50+

7)   Figure 21.2d

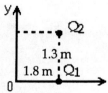

Two point charges, $Q_1 = -4.0\ \mu C$ and $Q_2 = +2.0\ \mu C$, are placed as shown. In Figure 21.2d, the magnitude of the electric force on either charge is closest to:

A) 0.043 N   B) 0.033 N   C) 0.052 N   D) 0.062 N   E) 0.071 N

Answer: A
Var: 50+

8)   Figure 21.2e

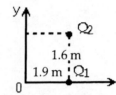

Two point charges, $Q_1 = -1.0 \ \mu C$ and $Q_2 = +2.0 \ \mu C$, are placed as shown. In Figure 21.2e, a proton is released at the midpoint between Q_1 and Q_2. The y–component of the acceleration of the proton is closest to:

A) $-4.0 \times 10^{12} \ m/s^2$

B) $1.3 \times 10^{12} \ m/s^2$

C) $-1.7 \times 10^{12} \ m/s^2$

D) $4.0 \times 10^{12} \ m/s^2$

E) $-1.3 \times 10^{12} \ m/s^2$

Answer: A
Var: 50+

Figure 21.3

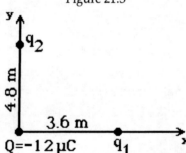

A point charge $Q = -12 \ \mu C$, and two other charges, q_1 and q_2, are placed as shown. The electric force components on charge Q are $F_x = +0.005 \ N$ and $F_y = -0.003 \ N$.

9) In Figure 21.3, the number of excess electrons in charge Q is closest to:

A) 5.5×10^{13} B) 6.5×10^{13} C) 7.5×10^{13} D) 8.5×10^{13} E) 9.5×10^{13}

Answer: C
Var: 1

10) In Figure 21.3, charge q_1, in nC, is closest to:

A) +200   B) +400   C) +600   D) –200   E) –400

Answer: C
Var: 1

11) In Figure 21.3, charge q_2, in nC, is closest to:

A) +320   B) +480   C) +640   D) –480   E) –640

Answer: E
Var: 1

12) In Figure 21.3, charge Q is moved to a new position, such that the resultant electric field at the origin, due to charges q_1, q_2, and Q, is equal to zero. The x– and y–coordinates of the new position of charge Q are closest to:

A) +9m, –13m

B) +13m, +9m

C) +13m, –9m

D) –9m, +13m

E) –13m, +9m

Answer: C
Var: 1

13) If you rub a balloon on your sweater and then press it to a wall, it will often stick there. Why does this happen?

A) Rubbing removes a surface layer of grease, allowing the rubber to come in sufficiently close contact with the wall so that air pressure holds it there.

B) Rubbing the balloon charges it electrostatically, and this charge on the balloon induces an opposite charge on the wall. The attraction between the induced charge and the charge on the balloon holds the balloon to the wall.

C) A wall typically has a net electric charge on it, and rubbing the balloon charges it electrostatically. If the wall happens to have opposite charge to that on the balloon, the balloon will stick.

D) Rubbing the balloon causes moisture to condense on it, and surface tension causes the balloon to stick to the wall.

E) Rubbing the balloon surface causes it to become slightly conducting. When the balloon is touched to the wall, electrons flow from the balloon to the wall. This sets up an electric field which bonds the balloon weakly to the wall.

Answer: B
Var: 1

14) Two uncharged metal spheres, #1 and #2, are mounted on insulating support rods. A third metal sphere, carrying a positive charge, is then placed near #2. Now a copper wire is momentarily connected between #1 and #2 and then removed. Finally, sphere #3 is removed. In this final state

A) spheres #1 and #2 are still uncharged.

B) sphere #1 carries positive charge and #2 carries negative charge.

C) sphere #1 carries negative charge and #2 carries positive charge.

D) spheres #1 and #2 both carry positive charge.

E) spheres #1 and #2 both carry negative charge.

Answer: B
Var: 1

Figure 21.4

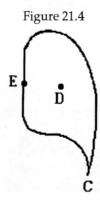

15) In Figure 21.4, charge is placed on the piece of copper. How will the charge be distributed on the object?

A) Uniformly throughout the volume.

B) Uniformly over the surface

C) With greatest density near point C on the surface.

D) With greatest density near point D in the interior.

E) With greatest density near point E on the flat surface.

Answer: C
Var: 1

Situation 21.1

Two identical small conducting spheres are separated by 0.60m. The spheres carry different amounts of charge and each sphere experiences an attractive electric force of 10.8N. The total charge on the two spheres is –24 μC.

16) In Situation 21.1, the positive charge on one of the spheres, in μC, is closest to:

A) 12   B) 18   C) 24   D) 30   E) 36

Answer: A
Var: 1

17) In Situation 21.1, the two spheres are connected by a slender conducting wire, which is then removed. The electric force on each sphere is closest to:

A) zero

B) 3.6 N, attractive

C) 5.4 N, attractive

D) 3.6 N, repulsive

E) 5.4 N, repulsive

Answer: D
Var: 1

Figure 21.5

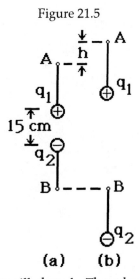

(a) (b)

Two small insulating spheres are attached to silk threads. The spheres have equal masses of 40 g, and have electric charges of q_1 = +2.0 μC and q_2 = -2.0 μC. The spheres are brought into the initial positions shown in Figure (a), with a vertical separation of 15 cm between them.

18) In Figure 21.5, the tension in the lower thread in Figure (a) is closest to:

A) 1.2 N B) 1.4 N C) 1.6 N D) 1.8 N E) 2.0 N

Answer: A
Var: 1

19) In Figure 21.5, the upper thread is slowly pulled upward, while point B is kept fixed. When point A has been raised through a height h, the lower sphere suddenly falls, as shown in Figure (b). The height h, is closest to:

A) 9 cm B) 11 cm C) 13 cm D) 15 cm E) 17 cm

Answer: D
Var: 1

Figure 21.6

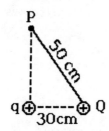

20) In Figure 21.6, a small 80 g insulating sphere is suspended from point P by a silk thread that is 50 cm long. The sphere bears an unknown electric charge Q. A positive point charge q = +2.0 µC is brought to a position directly below P, and the sphere is repelled to a new position, 30 cm to the right of q, as shown. The charge Q, in µC, is closest to:

    A) +1.5   B) +2.0   C) +2.5   D) +3.0   E) +3.5

Answer: D
Var: 1

Situation 21.2

A 50 g insulating sphere carries a charge Q = –60 µC and is suspended by a silk thread from a fixed point. An external electric field which is uniform and vertical is applied.

21) In Situation 21.2, the applied electric field has a magnitude of 3000 N/c and is directed downward. The tension in the thread is closest to:

    A) 0.2 N   B) 0.3 N   C) 0.4 N   D) 0.5 N   E) 0.7 N

Answer: B
Var: 1

22) In Situation 21.2, the applied electric field holds the sphere in place above the fixed point of suspension, and the tension in the thread is 0.35 N. The applied electric field, including direction, is closest to:

    A) 2000 N/C, upward

    B) 8000 N/C, upward

    C) 14,000 N/C, upward

    D) 8000 N/C, downward

    E) 14,000 N/C, downward

Answer: E
Var: 1

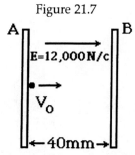

Figure 21.7

A pair of charges conducting plates produces a uniform field of 12,000 N/c, directed to the right, between the plates. The separation of the plates is 40 mm.

23) In Figure 21.7 , an electron is projected from plate A, directly towards plate B, with an initial velocity of $v_0 = 2.0 \times 10^7$ m/s. The velocity of the electron as it strikes plate B is closest to:

   A) 1.2×10^7 m/s

   B) 1.5×10^7 m/s

   C) 1.8×10^7 m/s

   D) 2.1×10^7 m/s

   E) 2.4×10^7 m/s

Answer: B
Var: 1

24) In Figure 21.7, an electron is projected from plate A, directly towards plate B, with an initial velocity $v_0 = 1.0 \times 10^7$ m/s. The closest approach of the electron to plate B is closest to:

   A) 16 mm   B) 18 mm   C) 20 mm   D) 22 mm   E) 24 mm

Answer: A
Var: 1

25)

Figure 21.8

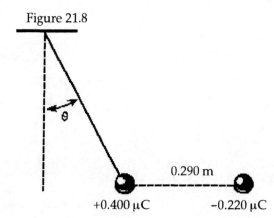

0.290 m

+0.400 μC   −0.220 μC

In Figure 21.8, a small spherical insulator of mass 6×10^{-2} kg and charge +0.400 μC is hung by a thin wire of negligible mass. A charge of −0.220 μC is held 0.290 m away from the sphere and directly to the right of it, so the wire makes an angle θ with the vertical (see drawing). What is the angle θ?

A) 0.919 °   B) 1.10 °   C) 1.30 °   D) 1.50°   E) 1.70 °

Answer: A
Var: 50+

Figure 21.9

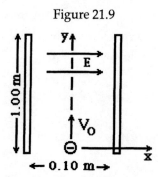

26) An electron is projected with an initial velocity $v_0 = 3.0 \times 10^7$ m/s along the y-axis, which is the center line between a pair of charged plates. The plates are 1.00 m long and are separated by 0.10 m. A uniform electric field E, in the positive x–direction, is presented between the plates. The magnitude of the acceleration of the electron is 4.3×10^{15} m/s^2. In Figure 21.9, the magnitude of the electric field between the plates is closest to:

A) 25,000 N/C

B) 22,000 N/C

C) 19,000 N/C

D) 17,000 N/C

E) 14,000 N/C

Answer: A
Var: 50+

27) An electron is projected with an initial velocity $v_0 = 2.9 \times 10^7$ m/s along the y-axis, which is the center line between a pair of charged plates. The plates are 1.00 m long and are separated by 0.10 m. A uniform electric field E, in the positive x-direction, is presented between the plates. The magnitude of the acceleration of the electron is 4.8×10^{15} m/s². In Figure 22.9, the x- and y-coordinates of the point at which the electron strikes one of the plates are closest to:

A) x = –50 mm, y = 130 mm

B) x = –50 mm, y = 94 mm

C) x = 50 mm, y = 94 mm

D) x = 50 mm, y = 130 mm

E) x = 50 mm, y = 190 mm

Answer: A
Var: 50+

28) An electron is projected with an initial velocity $v_0 = 4.1 \times 10^7$ m/s along the y-axis, which is the center line between a pair of charged plates. The plates are 1.00 m long and are separated by 0.10 m. A uniform electric field E, in the positive x-direction, is presented between the plates. The magnitude of the acceleration of the electron is 7.4×10^{15} m/s². In Figure 22.9, the magnitude of the electric field is changed so that an electron, projected with the same initial velocity, barely clears the far edge of one of the plates. The magnitude of this electric field is closest to:

A) 960 N/C   B) 840 N/C   C) 1000 N/C   D) 1200 N/C   E) 1300 N/C

Answer: A
Var: 50+

29)   Figure 21.10

In Figure 21.10, a conducting ring 0.29 m in radius carries a charge of +240 nC. A point charge Q is placed at the center of the ring. The electric field is equal to zero at field point P, which is on the axis of the ring, and 0.26 m from its center. The point charge Q, in nC, is closest to:

A) –71   B) –110   C) –160   D) 71   E) 110

Answer: A
Var: 50+

Figure 21.11

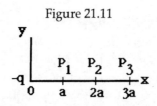

30) In Figure 21.11, a charge −q is placed at the origin and a second charge +Q is moved along the x-axis, starting at point P1. Note that point P_1 is at x = a, P_2 is at x = 2a, and P_3 is at x = 3a.

   A) The work done in moving Q from P_1 to P_2 is the same as that done in moving Q from P_2 to P_3.

   B) The work done in moving Q from P_1 to P_2 is the same as that done in moving Q from P_2 to P_3.

   C) The work done in moving Q from P_1 to P_2 is Fa, where F is the electric force which acts on Q.

   D) More than one of these is correct.

   E) None of these is correct.

Answer: E
Var: 1

31) An electron is accelerated through a potential difference V_1 and then directed into the region between two metal plates, with initial velocity parallel to the plates. A potential difference V_2 is applied between the plates, and this deflects the electron through an angle q. Which of the following changes will be most effective in increasing the angle of deflection?

   A) Increase V_1 and increase V_2.

   B) Increase V_1 and decrease V_2.

   C) Decrease V_1 and decrease V_2.

   D) Decrease V_1 and increase V_2.

   E) None of these will increase the angle of deflection.

Answer: D
Var: 1

32) Four charges of equal magnitudes but opposite signs are arranged at the corners of a square, as shown here. In which arrangement is the magnitude of the electric field at point P a maximum?

A)

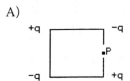

B)

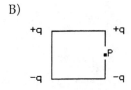

C)

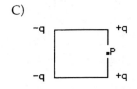

D)

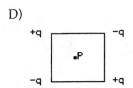

E) The maximum electric field occurs in more than one of these arrangements.

Answer: B
Var: 1

Figure 21.12

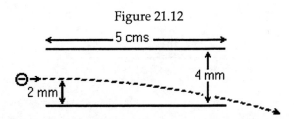

33) In Figure 21.12, an electron of speed 6.7×10^6 m/s is fired midway between two large parallel plates. The plates are maintained at a potential difference V_O and are separated by 4 mm. The length of the plates in the direction of electron motion is 5 cms. What is the maximum value of the potential difference V_O which will not result in the electron hitting the far edge of the lower plate?

A) 1.6V   B) 330V   C) 660V   D) 3300V   E) 6600V

Answer: A
Var: 50+

Figure 21.13

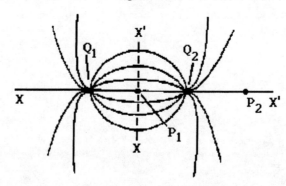

34) In Figure 21.13, the electric field lines arising from two charges Q_1 and Q_2 are shown. From this drawing we can see that

A) the electric field could be zero at P_1.

B) the electric field could be zero at P_2.

C) both Q_1 and Q_2 have the same sign.

D) $|Q_1| > |Q_2|$

E) None of these is true.

Answer: E
Var: 1

Short Answer Questions

Figure 21.14

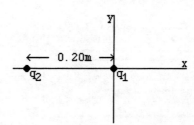

1) In Figure 21.14, charge $q_1 = 2.5 \times 10^{-6}$ C is placed at the origin and charge $q_2 = -6.5 \times 10^{-6}$ C is placed on the x-axis, at x = -0.20 m. Where along the x-axis can a third charge $Q = -8.3 \times 10^{-6}$ C be placed such that the resultant force on this third charge is zero?

Answer: 0.33 m
Var: 50+

2)

Figure 21.15

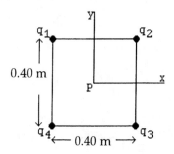

In Figure 21.15, calculate the x- and y-components of the electrical field produced at point P (at the center of the square) by the four charges placed at the corners of the square. The length of each side of the square is 0.40 m. The charges have the following values: $q_1 = 1.5 \times 10^{-6}$ C, $q_2 = -8.2 \times 10^{-6}$ C, $q_3 = -3.9 \times 10^{-6}$ C, and $q_4 = -8.0 \times 10^{-6}$ C. Be sure to indicate whether each component, if nonzero, is positive or negative for the coordinate system.

Answer: $E_x = 4.4 \times 10^5$ N/C ; $E_y = -4.1 \times 10^5$ N/C

Var: 50+

3)   Figure 21.16

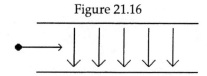

In Figure 21.16, a proton, mass 1.67×10^{-27} kg, is projected horizontally midway between two parallel plates that are separated by 0.50 cm, with an electrical field with magnitude 950,000 N/C between the plates. If the plates are 2.90 cm long, find minimum speed of the proton that just misses the lower plate as it emerges from the field.

Answer: 3.91×10^6 m/s

Var: 50+

4) Positive charge $Q = 4.3 \times 10^{-6}$ C is distributed uniformly along the positive y-axis from y = 0 to y = 0.40 m. A point charge $q = 4.8 \times 10^{-6}$ C is located on the negative y-axis at y = −0.80 m. Calculate the x and y components of the force exerted on q by the charge distribution. Be sure to indicate whether each component is positive or negative.

Answer: x-component: 0
           y-component: −0.19 N

Var: 50+

5) A block of a solid is known to contain many dipoles aligned in the same direction (such a material is known as an electret). In an electric field of magnitude 360 N/C, the block tends to orient itself so that the dipoles are aligned along the electric field lines. If 3.9 J are required to rotate the solid so that the dipole directions are reversed, and each dipole has dipole moment 2.8×10^{-30} C-m, how many dipoles are there in the block?

Answer: 1.9×10^{27}

Var: 50+

Chapter 22   Gauss' Law

Multiple Choice Questions

Figure 22.1

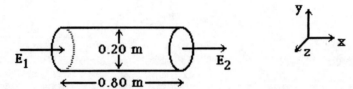

1) A nonuniform electric field is directed along the x–axis at all points in space. This magnitude of the field varies with x, but not with respect to y or z. The axis of a cylindrical surface, 0.80 m long and 0.20 m in diameter, is aligned parallel to the x–axis. The electric fields E_1 and E_2, at the ends of the cylindrical surface, have magnitudes of 3000 N/C and 7000 N/C respectively, and are directed as shown. In Figure 22.1, the electric flux entering the cylindrical surface at the left end is closest to:

A) 94 N • m^2/C

B) 30 N • m^2/C

C) 62 N • m^2/C

D) 126 N • m^2/C

E) 159 N • m^2/C

Answer: A
Var: 50+

2) A nonuniform electric field is directed along the x–axis at all points in space. This magnitude of the field varies with x, but not with respect to y or z. The axis of a cylindrical surface, 0.80 m long and 0.20 m in diameter, is aligned parallel to the x–axis. The electric fields E_1 and E_2, at the ends of the cylindrical surface, have magnitudes of 8000 N/C and 5000 N/C respectively, and are directed as shown. In Figure 23.1, the charge enclosed by the cylindrical surface is closest to:

A) –0.83 nC   B) 0.83 nC   C) –1.8 nC   D) –3.6 nC   E) 3.6 nC

Answer: A
Var: 50+

Figure 22.2

3) In Figure 22.2, three hollow, concentric spherical conductors are charged as follows:
The inner sphere carries charge Q
The middle sphere carries charge –2Q
The outer sphere carries charge –Q .
What is the charge on the outer surface of the middle sphere?

A) zero   B) –Q   C) +Q   D) +2Q   E) –2Q

Answer: B
Var: 1

Figure 22.3

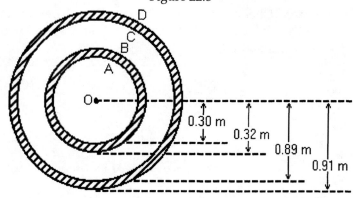

4) Two hollow conducting spheres have a common center O. The dimensions of the spheres are as shown. A charge of –250 nC is placed on the inner conductor and a charge of +40 nC is placed on the outer conductor. The inner and outer surfaces of the spheres are respectively denoted by A, B, C, and D, as shown. In Figure 22.3, the charges on surfaces A and B respectively, in nC, are closest to:

A) 0 and –250

B) 0 and –210

C) 0 and –40

D) –250 and –40

E) –40 and –250

Answer: A
Var: 50+

5) Two hollow conducting spheres have a common center O. The dimensions of the spheres are as shown. A charge of –260 nC is placed on the inner conductor and a charge of +10 nC is placed on the outer conductor. The inner and outer surfaces of the spheres are respectively denoted by A, B, C, and D, as shown. In Figure 23.3, the charges on surfaces C and D respectively, in nC, are closest to:

   A) +260 and –250

   B) +10 and 0

   C) +10 and –250

   D) +260 and +10

   E) 0 and +10

Answer: A
Var: 50+

6) Two hollow conducting spheres have a common center O. The dimensions of the spheres are as shown. A charge of –110 nC is placed on the inner conductor and a charge of +40 nC is placed on the outer conductor. The inner and outer surfaces of the spheres are respectively denoted by A, B, C, and D, as shown. In Figure 23.3, the radial component of the electric field, at a point which is 0.25 m from O, is closest to:

   A) zero

   B) +10,000 N/C

   C) +16,000 N/C

   D) –10,000 N/C

   E) –16,000 N/C

Answer: A
Var: 50+

7) Two hollow conducting spheres have a common center O. The dimensions of the spheres are as shown. A charge of –150 nC is placed on the inner conductor and a charge of +10 nC is placed on the outer conductor. The inner and outer surfaces of the spheres are respectively denoted by A, B, C, and D, as shown. In Figure 23.3, the radial component of the electric field, at a point which is 0.40 m from O, is closest to:

   A) –8400 N/C

   B) +8400 N/C

   C) +7900 N/C

   D) –7900 N/C

   E) zero

Answer: A
Var: 50+

8) Two hollow conducting spheres have a common center O. The dimensions of the spheres are as shown. A charge of –260 nC is placed on the inner conductor and a charge of +90 nC is placed on the outer conductor. The inner and outer surfaces of the spheres are respectively denoted by A, B, C, and D, as shown. In Figure 23.3, the radial component of the electric field, at a point which is 0.90 m from O, is closest to:

A) zero

B) +2900 N/C

C) –2900 N/C

D) +1900 N/C

E) –1900 N/C

Answer: A
Var: 50+

9) Two hollow conducting spheres have a common center O. The dimensions of the spheres are as shown. A charge of –200 nC is placed on the inner conductor and a charge of +10 nC is placed on the outer conductor. The inner and outer surfaces of the spheres are respectively denoted by A, B, C, and D, as shown. In Figure 23.3, the radial component of the electric field, at a point which is 0.95 m from O, is closest to:

A) –1900 N/C

B) +1900 N/C

C) –100 N/C

D) +100 N/C

E) zero

Answer: A
Var: 50+

Figure 22.4

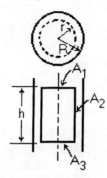

Consider an infinitely long cylindrical distribution of charge with constant density and radius R. In attempting to find the electric field at a point inside the cylinder (r < R) the calculation might go as sketched here:

$$\int_A \vec{E} \cdot d\vec{A} \;=\; \frac{1}{\varepsilon_0} \int_0^r \rho 2\pi r h\, dr \tag{1}$$

$$\int_A \vec{E} \cdot d\vec{A} \;=\; \int_{A_1} \vec{E} \cdot d\vec{A} \;+\; \int_{A_2} \vec{E} \cdot d\vec{A} \;+\; \int_{A_3} \vec{E} \cdot d\vec{A} \tag{2}$$

$$=\; \int_{A_2} \vec{E} \cdot d\vec{A} \tag{3}$$

$$=\; \vec{E} \int_{A_2} d\vec{A} \tag{4}$$

10) In Figure 22.4, we are able to go from equation (2) to equation (3) because

    A) there is no charge on surfaces A_1 or A_3.

    B) E is zero on A_1 and A_2.

    C) the contributions from the integrals over A_1 and A_3 have equal magnitude but opposite sign and thus cancel.

    D) E is perpendicular to $d\vec{A}$ over A_1 and A_3.

    E) E is constant over the surface.

Answer: D
Var: 1

11) In Figure 22.4, $\int_{A_2}$ da has the value A_2

A) $2\pi^2 + 2\pi rh$

B) $2\pi r^2$

C) $\pi r^2 h$

D) $\dfrac{\pi r^2 hp}{\varepsilon_0 E(r)}$

E) None of these is correct.

Answer: E
Var: 1

Figure 22.5

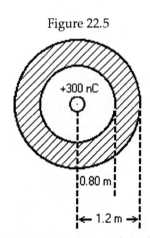

A hollow conducting sphere has radii of 0.80 m and 1.20 m. The sphere carries a charge of –500 nc. A point charge of +300 nC is present at the center.

12) In Figure 22.5, the surface charge density on the inner spherical surface is closest to:

A) zero

B) $+4 \times 10^{-8}$ C/m^2

C) $+6 \times 10^{-8}$ C/m^2

D) -4×10^{-8} C/m^2

E) -6×10^{-8} C/m^2

Answer: D
Var: 1

13) In Figure 22.5, the charge on the outer spherical surface, in nC, is closest to:

A) zero   B) –200   C) –300   D) –500   E) –800

Answer: B
Var: 1

14) In Figure 22.5, the radial component of the electric field at a point which is 0.60 m from the center is closest to:

   A) zero

   B) +5000 N/C

   C) +7500 N/C

   D) –5000 N/C

   E) –7500 N/C

   Answer: C
   Var: 1

15) In Figure 22.5, the radial component of the electric field at a point which is 0.90 m from the center is closest to:

   A) zero

   B) +2000 N/C

   C) +3000 N/C

   D) –2000 N/C

   E) –3000 N/C

   Answer: A
   Var: 1

16) In Figure 22.5, the radial component of the electric field at a point which is 1.50 m from the center is closest to:

   A) +1200 N/C

   B) +2000 N/C

   C) –800 N/C

   D) –1600 N/C

   E) –2000 N/C

   Answer: C
   Var: 1

Figure 22.6

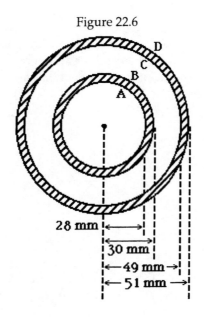

28 mm

30 mm

49 mm

51 mm

17) The cross section of a long coaxial cable is shown, with radii as given. The linear charge density on the inner conductor is –50 nC/m and the linear charge density on the outer conductor is –20 nC/m. The inner and outer cylindrical surfaces are respectively denoted by A, B, C, and D, as shown. In Figure 22.6, the linear charge densities on surfaces A and B, in nC/m, are closest to:

A) 0 and –50

B) 0 and –30

C) 0 and –20

D) –50 and +20

E) –50 and –20

Answer: A
Var: 50+

18) The cross section of a long coaxial cable is shown, with radii as given. The linear charge density on the inner conductor is –10 nC/m and the linear charge density on the outer conductor is –40 nC/m. The inner and outer cylindrical surfaces are respectively denoted by A, B, C, and D, as shown. In Figure 22.6, the linear charge densities on surfaces C and D, in nC/m, are closest to:

A) +10 and –50

B) +10 and –40

C) 0 and –40

D) –30 and –10

E) –10 and –30

Answer: A
Var: 50+

19) The cross section of a long coaxial cable is shown, with radii as given. The linear charge density on the inner conductor is -70 nC/m and the linear charge density on the outer conductor is -90 nC/m. The inner and outer cylindrical surfaces are respectively denoted by A, B, C, and D, as shown. In Figure 22.6, the radial component of the electric field at a point which is 34 mm from the axis is closest to:

A) -37,000 N/C

B) +37,000 N/C

C) -48,000 N/C

D) +48,000 N/C

E) zero

Answer: A
Var: 50+

20) The cross section of a long coaxial cable is shown, with radii as given. The linear charge density on the inner conductor is -30 nC/m and the linear charge density on the outer conductor is -60 nC/m. The inner and outer cylindrical surfaces are respectively denoted by A, B, C, and D, as shown. In Figure 22.6, the radial component of the electric field at a point which is 50 mm from the axis is closest to:

A) zero

B) +22,000 N/C

C) -22,000 N/C

D) +32,000 N/C

E) -32,000 N/C

Answer: A
Var: 50+

21) The cross section of a long coaxial cable is shown, with radii as given. The linear charge density on the inner conductor is -80 nC/m and the linear charge density on the outer conductor is -30 nC/m. The inner and outer cylindrical surfaces are respectively denoted by A, B, C, and D, as shown. In Figure 22.6, the magnitude of the electric field at a point which is 64 mm from the axis is closest to:

A) 31,000 N/C

B) 25,000 N/C

C) 20,000 N/C

D) 14,000 N/C

E) 8400 N/C

Answer: A
Var: 50+

Figure 22.7

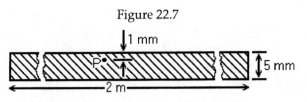

22) In Figure 22.7, an insulating slab 5 mm x 2 m x 2 m has a charge of 8 x 10^{-11} coulomb distributed uniformly throughout its volume. Determine the electric field at point P, which is located within the slab beneath its center, 1 mm from one of the faces.

   A) 0.68 V/m   B) 13.6 V/m   C) 22.6 V/m   D) 33.9 V/m   E) 56.5 V/m

Answer: A
Var: 1

Figure 22.8

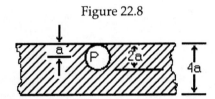

23) In Figure 22.8, charge is distributed uniformly with density throughout the volume of a large thin insulating slab of thickness 4 A. Suppose that some material is now removed, leaving a spherical cavity of radius a positioned as shown. What is the electric field, in units of P_a/ε_o, at point P?

   A) 0.33   B) 0.50   C) 0.67   D) 1.0   E) 1.05

Answer: E
Var: 1

24) When there is a net static charge present on a perfect conductor, and no other charges are present

   A) the charge will be uniformly distributed over the outside of the conductor (i.e., the surface charge density will be constant).

   B) every point throughout the entire conductor will be at zero potential.

   C) every point throughout the entire conductor will be at a constant potential, but not necessarily at zero potential.

   D) the electric field inside the conductor need not be zero if the conductor is hollow.

   E) the surface charge density will be greatest where the conductor is flat and smallest where there are sharp protuberances or points.

Answer: C
Var: 1

Situation 22.1

Electric charge is uniformly distributed inside a sphere of radius 0.30 m. The electric field at a point which is 0.50 m from the center of the sphere is 15,000 N/C, and is directed radially outward.

25) In Situation 22.1, the electric field vector is given, at a point which is within the sphere of charge. The distance of this point from the center of the sphere is closest to:

   A) 0.11 m   B) 0.13 m   C) 0.15 m   D) 0.17 m   E) 0.19 m

Answer: A
Var: 1

26) In Situation 22.1, the maximum magnitude of the electric field is closest to:

   A) 25,000 N/C

   B) 30,000 N/C

   C) 36,000 N/C

   D) 42,000 N/C

   E) 48,000 N/C

Answer: D
Var: 1

Short Answer Questions

Figure 22.9

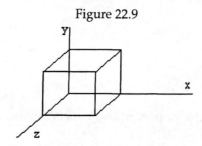

1) In Figure 22.9, a cube of insulating material has one corner at the origin. Each side of the cube has length 0.020 m, so the top face of the cube is parallel to the xz–plane and is at y = 0.02 m. It is observed that there is an electric field E = (7960 N/C • m)y j, that is in the +y direction and whose magnitude depends only on y. Use Gauss's Law to calculate the net charge enclosed by the cube.
(Note: $\varepsilon_0 = 8.854 \times 10^{-12}$ C^2/N • m2.)

Answer: 5.64×10^{-13} C
Var: 50+

236

Figure 22.10

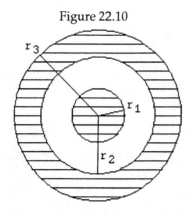

2) In Figure 22.10, a conducting sphere of radius r_1 = 0.050 m is placed at the center of a spherical conducting shell of inner radius r_2 = 0.100 m and outer radius r_3 = 0.140 m. The inner sphere carries a charge if -4.0×10^{-9} C. The outer spherical shell carries a net charge of 3.0×10^{-9} C. Calculate the magnitude of the electric field at the following distances from the center of the spheres:
(a) r = 0.075 m (in the air space between spheres),
(b) r = 0.120 m (in the metal of the spherical shell), and
(c) r = 0.200 m (outside the spherical shell).

Answer: (a) 6.4×10^3 N/C
        (b) 0
        (c) 2.3×10^2 N/C
Var: 1

Figure 22.11

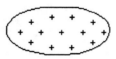

3) In Figure 22.11, a circular plate with radius 1.96 m contains 793 μC of a charge uniformly distributed. Find the magnitude of the electric field near the plate.

Answer: 3.72×10^6 N/C
Var: 50+

4) Positive charge is distributed uniformly throughout a large insulating cylinder of radius R = 0.500 m. The charge per unit length in the cylindrical volume is $\lambda = 6.00 \times 10^{-9}$ C/m. Calculate the magnitude of the electric field at a distance of 0.400 m from the axis of the cylinder. (Note: $\varepsilon_0 = 8.854 \times 10^{-12}$ $C^2/N^{-1} m^2$.)

Answer: 173 N/C
Var: 50+

5)

Figure 22.12

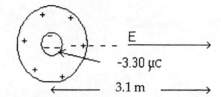

In Figure 22.13, two small concentric conducting spherical shells produce a radially outward electric field of magnitude 72,000 N/C a distance of 3.10 m from the center of the shells. If the inner shell contains a charge of –7.10 μC, find the amount of charge on the outer surface of the larger shell.

Answer: 76.8 μC
Var: 50+

238

Chapter 23   Electric Potential

Multiple Choice Questions

1)

Figure 23.1a

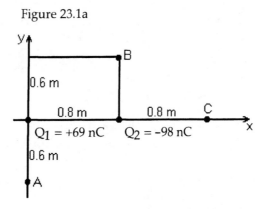

Point charges, Q_1 = +69 nC and Q_2 = –98 nC, are placed as shown. In Figure 23.1a, an external force transports an electron from point A to point B. The work done by the external force is closest to:

A) +1000 eV   B) +840 eV   C) +670 eV   D) –1000 eV   E) –670 eV

Answer: A
Var: 50+

2)

Figure 23.1b

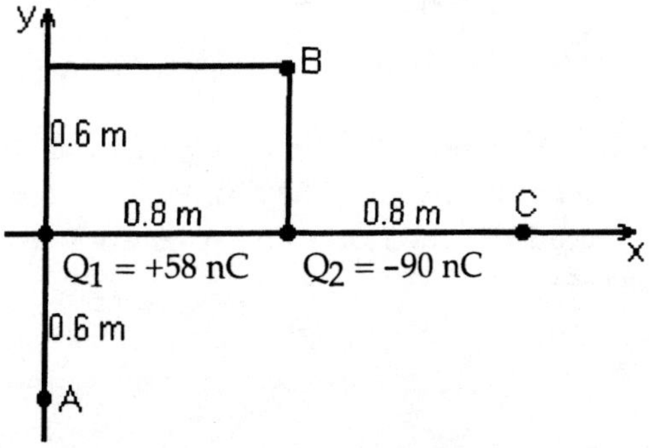

Point charges, Q_1 = +58 nC and Q_2 = –90 nC, are placed as shown. In Figure 23.1b, an electron is released from rest at point C. The speed of the electron as it arrives at infinity is closest to:

A) 1.6×10^7 B) 1.7×10^7 C) 1.9×10^7 D) 1.4×10^7 E) 1.2×10^7

Answer: A
Var: 50+

3)

Figure 23.1c

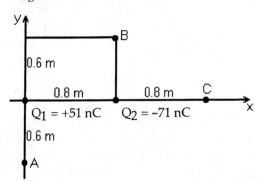

Point charges, $Q_1 = +51$ nC and $Q_2 = -71$ nC, are placed as shown. In Figure 23.1c, a point on the positive y-axis lies on the V = 0 equipotential surface. The y-coordinate of the point, in SI units, is closest to:

A) 0.83   B) 0.79   C) 0.86   D) 0.89   E) 0.92

Answer: A
Var: 50+

4)

Figure 23.2a

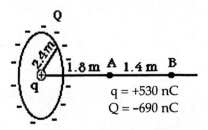

A charge Q = -690 nC is uniformly distributed on a ring of 2.4 m radius. A charge q = +530 nC is placed at the center of the ring. Points A and B are located on the axis of the ring, as shown. In Figure 23.2a, the work done by an external force that transports an electron from B to A is closest to:

A) -640 eV   B) -150 eV   C) 350 eV   D) 640 eV   E) 150 eV

Answer: A
Var: 50+

5)

Figure 23.2b

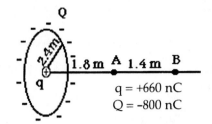

A charge Q = –800 nC is uniformly distributed on a ring of 2.4 m radius. A charge q = +660 nC is placed at the center of the ring. Points A and B are located on the axis of the ring, as shown. In Figure 23.2b, the electric potential is equal to zero at a point on the axis of the ring. The distance of this point from the center of the ring is closest to:

A) 3.5 m   B) 3.4 m   C) 3.2 m   D) 3.1 m   E) 3.6 m

Answer: A
Var: 50+

6)

Figure 23.2c

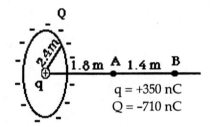

A charge Q = –710 nC is uniformly distributed on a ring of 2.4 m radius. A charge q = +350 nC is placed at the center of the ring. Points A and B are located on the axis of the ring, as shown. In Figure 23.2c, an electron is projected along the axis of the ring from infinity. The electron reaches and comes to a momentary halt at a point on the axis which is 5.0 m from the center of the ring. The initial speed of the electron at infinity is closest to:

A) 1.4×10^7 m/s

B) 9.1×10^6 m/s

C) 6.9×10^6 m/s

D) 4.6×10^6 m/s

E) 2.3×10^6 m/s

Answer: A
Var: 50+

241

7)

Figure 23.2d

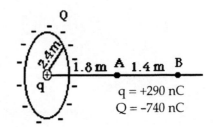

A charge Q = –740 nC is uniformly distributed on a ring of 2.4 m radius. A charge q = +290 nC is placed at the center of the ring. Points A and B are located on the axis of the ring, as shown. In Figure 23.2d, an external force removes the charge q from the center of the ring and transports it to infinity. The work done by this external force is closest to:

A) 8.0×10^{-4} J

B) 3.2×10^{-4} J

C) 2.1×10^{-3} J

D) -3.2×10^{-4} J

E) -2.1×10^{-3} J

Answer: A
Var: 50+

8)

Figure 23.3

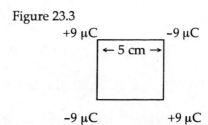

In Figure 23.3, four charges are placed at the corners of a square of side 5 cm. What is the electrostatic energy of this system?

A) –38 J   B) –29 J   C) –68 J   D) –75 J   E) –58 J

Answer: A
Var: 50+

9) A proton with a speed of 2.0×10^5 m/s falls through a potential difference V and thereby increases its speed to 7.0×10^5 m/s. Through what potential difference did the proton fall?

A) 2300 V   B) 210 V   C) 2600 V   D) 2800 V   E) 100 V

Answer: A
Var: 30

Figure 23.4

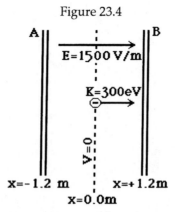

Two large conducting parallel plates A and B are separated by 2.4 m. A uniform field of 1500 V/m, in the positive x-direction, is produced by charges on the plates. The center plane at x = 0.0 m is an equipotential surface on which V = 0. An electron is projected from x= 0.0 m, with an initial kinetic energy K = 300 eV, in the positive x-direction, as shown.

10) In Figure 23.4, the initial velocity of the electron at x = 0.0 m is closest to:

    A) 6×10^6 m/s

    B) 7×10^6 m/s

    C) 9×10^6 m/s

    D) 1.0×10^7 m/s

    E) 1.2×10^7 m/s

Answer: D
Var: 1

11) In Figure 23.4, the electric potential difference V_A – V_B is closest to:

    A) +1200 V   B) +1800 V   C) +3600 V   D) –1800 V   E) –3600 V

Answer: C
Var: 1

12) In Figure 23.4, the x-coordinate, at which the electric potential is V = +600 V, is closest to:

    A) +0.2 m   B) +0.4 m   C) +0.6 m   D) –0.4 m   E) –0.6 m

Answer: D
Var: 1

13) In Figure 23.4, at a certain point the electron stops momentarily and it reverses its motion. The electric potential at that point is closest to:

    A) +300 V   B) +600 V   C) –300 V   D) –600 V   E) –900 V

Answer: C
Var: 1

14) In Figure 23.4, the kinetic energy of the electron as it reaches plate A is closest to:
   A) $+2.4 \times 10^{-16}$ J
   B) $+3.4 \times 10^{-16}$ J
   C) -2.4×10^{-16} J
   D) -2.9×10^{-16} J
   E) -3.4×10^{-16} J

Answer: B
Var: 1

15) Two conducting spherical shells are concentric, with radii of 0.70 m and 1.60 m. The electric potential of the inner shell, with the respect to the outer shell, is +1050 V. An electron is transported by an external force from the inner shell to the outer shell. The work done by the external force is closest to:
   A) 1.68×10^{-16} J
   B) 2.69×10^{-16} J
   C) 1.47×10^{-16} J
   D) 1.26×10^{-16} J
   E) 3.02×10^{-16} J

Answer: A
Var: 50+

16) Two conducting spherical shells are concentric, with radii of 0.80 m and 1.60 m. The electric potential of the inner shell, with the respect to the outer shell, is +1340 V. The maximum electric field magnitude between the shells is closest to:
   A) 3400 V/m   B) 1700 V/m   C) 840 V/m   D) 1100 V/m   E) 4700 V/m

Answer: A
Var: 50+

17) Two conducting spherical shells are concentric, with radii of 0.30 m and 2.40 m. The electric potential of the inner shell, with the respect to the outer shell, is +1390 V. The electric potential at a point between the shells is +480 V with respect to the outer shell. An electron is projected radially outward from this point with an initial kinetic energy of 200 eV. The kinetic energy of the electron, as it reaches either shell is closest to:
   A) 1110 eV   B) 910 eV   C) 1190 eV   D) 710 eV   E) 1670 eV

Answer: A
Var: 50+

Situation 23.1

Two long conducting cylindrical shells are coaxial and have radii of 20 mm and 80 mm. The electric potential of the inner conductor, with respect to the outer conductor, is +600 V.

18) In Situation 23.1, an electron is released from rest at the surface of the outer conductor. The speed of the electron as it reaches the inner conductor is closest to:

  A) 1.1×10^7 m/s

  B) 1.3×10^7 m/s

  C) 1.5×10^7 m/s

  D) 1.7×10^7 m/s

  E) 1.9×10^7 m/s

Answer: C
Var: 1

19) In Situation 23.1, the maximum electric field magnitude between the cylinders is closest to:

  A) 10,000 V/m

  B) 14,000 V/m

  C) 18,000 V/m

  D) 22,000 V/m

  E) 26,000 V/m

Answer: D
Var: 1

20) In Situation 23.1, an electron is in circular motion around the inner cylinder in an orbit of 30 mm radius. The speed of the electron is closest to:

  A) 5×10^6 m/s

  B) 6×10^6 m/s

  C) 7×10^6 m/s

  D) 5×10^6 m/s

  E) 5×10^6 m/s

Answer: E
Var: 1

21) In Situation 23.1, an electron is projected radially outward from a point between the shells at which the electric potential is +350 V with respect to the outer conductor. The initial kinetic energy of the electron is 150 eV. The kinetic energy of the electron, as it reaches either shell is closest to:

  A) +200 eV   B) +400 eV   C) +500 eV   D) –200 eV   E) –500 eV

Answer: B
Var: 1

22) A proton with speed 1.5×10^5 m/s falls through a potential difference of 100 volts, gaining speed. What is the speed reached?

   A) 4.56×10^5 m/s

   B) 2.04×10^5 m/s

   C) 3.55×10^5 m/s

   D) 8.80×10^5 m/s

   E) 1.55×10^6 m/s

Answer: B
Var: 1

23) A proton is projected toward a fixed nucleus of charge +Ze with velocity v_O. Initially the two particles are very far apart. When the proton is a distance R from the nucleus its velocity has decreased to $1/2 \, v_O$. How far from the nucleus will the proton be when its velocity has dropped to $1/4 \, v_O$?

   A) $1/16$ R

   B) $1/4$ R

   C) $1/2$ R

   D) $4/5$ R

   E) None of these.

Answer: D
Var: 1

24) An electron is released from rest at a distance of 9 cm from a proton. How fast will the electron be moving when it is 3 cm from the proton?

   A) 75 m/s

   B) 106 m/s

   C) 130 m/s

   D) 1.06×10^3 m/s

   E) 4.64×10^5 m/s

Answer: B
Var: 1

25) In a given region the electric field is constant and has the value 100 V/m. It points in the positive x-direction. If the potential at the point x = 4 cm on the x-axis is 6 volts, what would be the potential at the point x = 16 cm?

   A) –22 V   B) –18 V   C) –10 V   D) –6 V   E) +6 V

Answer: D
Var: 1

Figure 23.5

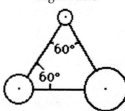

26) In Figure 23.5, three conducting spheres of radii 1 meter, 2 meters and 3 meters are connected by wires 50 meters long, as shown here. A charge of 4×10^{-4} coulombs is initially placed on the large sphere. Determine the charge on the large sphere in equilibrium.

A) Zero

B) 0.67×10^{-4} coulomb

C) 1.33×10^{-4} coulomb

D) 2.0×10^{-4} coulomb

E) 2.57×10^{-4} coulomb

Answer: D
Var: 1

27) Two conductors are joined by a long copper wire. Thus

A) each carries the same free charge.

B) each conductor must be at the same potential.

C) the electric field at the surface of each conductor is the same.

D) no free charge can be present on either conductor.

E) the potential on the wire is the average of the potential of each conductor.

Answer: B
Var: 1

28) Two isolated copper plates, each of area 0.4 m^2, carry opposite charges of magnitude 7.08×10^{-10} coulombs. They are placed opposite each other in parallel alignment, with a spacing of 2 mm. What will be the potential difference between the plates when their spacing is increased to 4 cm?

A) 0.4 V   B) 3.04 V   C) 3.2 V   D) 7.6 V   E) 8 V

Answer: E
Var: 1

Figure 23.6

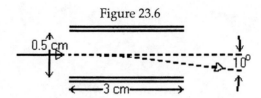

29) In Figure 23.6, a charged particle is accelerated through a potential of 15,000 volts, after which it passes between two deflecting plates. What voltage must be applied to these plates to deflect the particle through an angle of 10°?

A) 63 V   B) 112 V   C) 520 V   D) 642 V   E) 882 V

Answer: E
Var: 1

Short Answer Questions

1) Three point charges are placed at the following (x, y) coordinates: charge $+5.0 \times 10^{-6}$ C at (0, 0.7 m), charge $+7.0 \times 10^{-6}$ C at (0.9 m, 0), and charge -5.0×10^{-6} C at (0.9 m, 0.7 m). Calculate the electrical potential at the origin due to these three point charges. Take the zero of potential to be at infinity.

Answer: 95,000 volts
Var: 50+

2) A small metal sphere of mass 2.6 g and charge 9.4 μC is fired with an initial speed of 8.6 m/s directly toward the center of a second metal sphere carrying charge 8.3 μC. This second sphere is held fixed. If the spheres are initially a large distance apart, how close do they get to each other? Treat the spheres as point charges.

Answer: 7.3 meters
Var: 50+

Figure 23.7

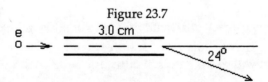

3) In Figure 23.7, a beam of electrons is traveling along the axis midway between two parallel plates at a speed of 1.3×10^{6} m/s. The plates are separated by 1.6 cm and are 3.0 cm long. What is the potential difference between the plates if the beam of electrons, upon leaving the region between the plates, is deflected 24° from the axis?

Answer: 2.3 V
Var: 50+

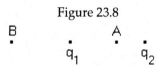

Figure 23.8

4) In Figure 23.8, two point charges, $q_1 = +24.0$ nC and $q_2 = -67.0$ nC, are separated by 0.500 m. A third charge of 26.0 nC is placed at the point A, 0.18 m to the left of q_2. Find the work needed to move the third charge to point B, 0.40 m to the left of q_1.

Answer: 6.6×10^{-5} J
Var: 50+

5) An oil droplet with 3 excess electrons is held stationary in a field of 4.24×10^4 N/C. What is the radius of the oil drop? (The density of the oil is 824 kg/m^3, e = 1.60×10^{-19} C.)

Answer: 8.45×10^{-7} m
Var: 50+

Chapter 24   Capacitance and Dielectrics

Multiple Choice Questions

1) Each plate of a parallel-plate air capacitor has an area of 0.0070 m^2, and the separation of the plates is 0.080 mm. An electric field of 7.3 x 10^6 V/m is present between the plates. The potential difference across the capacitor is closest to:

   A) 584 V   B) 389 V   C) 779 V   D) 973 V   E) 1168 V

   Answer: A
   Var: 50+

2) Each plate of a parallel-plate air capacitor has an area of 0.0050 m^2, and the separation of the plates is 0.030 mm. An electric field of 9.4 x 10^6 V/m is present between the plates. The energy density between the plates is closest to:

   A) 400 J/m^3 B) 270 J/m^3 C) 530 J/m^3 D) 660 J/m^3 E) 800 J/m^3

   Answer: A
   Var: 50+

3) Each plate of a parallel-plate air capacitor has an area of 0.0080 m^2, and the separation of the plates is 0.060 mm. An electric field of 3.5 x 10^6 V/m is present between the plates. The surface charge density on the plates, in $\mu C/m^2$, is closest to:

   A) 31   B) 66   C) 16   D) 47   E) 78

   Answer: A
   Var: 50+

4) Each plate of a parallel-plate air capacitor has an area of 0.0010 m^2, and the separation of the plates is 0.080 mm. An electric field of 4.7 x 10^6 V/m is present between the plates. The capacitance of the capacitor, in pF, is closest to:

   A) 110   B) 74   C) 190   D) 150   E) 220

   Answer: A
   Var: 50+

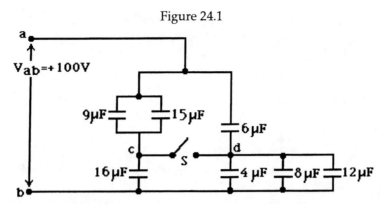

Figure 24.1

The capacitive network shown is assembled with initially uncharged capacitors. A potential difference, V_{ab} = +100 V, is applied across the network. The switch S in the network is kept open throughout.

5) In Figure 24.1, the total energy stored in the seven capacitors, in mJ, is closest to:

A) 48   B) 72   C) 96   D) 120   E) 144

Answer: B
Var: 1

6) In Figure 24.1, the potential difference V_{cd}, across the open switch S, in SI units, is closest to:

A) zero   B) +40   C) +60   D) –40   E) –60

Answer: B
Var: 1

7) In Figure 24.1, the charge on the 15 μF capacitor, in μC, is closest to:

A) 540   B) 600   C) 660   D) 720   E) 780

Answer: B
Var: 1

8) An air capacitor is formed from two long conducting cylindrical shells which are coaxial, and have radii of 11 mm and 104 mm. The electric potential of the inner conductor with respect to the outer conductor is –800 V. The energy stored in the capacitor, in a one meter section of length is closest to:

A) 8.0 μJ   B) 5.7 μJ   C) 11 μJ   D) 16 μJ   E) 22 μJ

Answer: A
Var: 50+

9) An air capacitor is formed from two long conducting cylindrical shells which are coaxial, and have radii of 12 mm and 89 mm. The electric potential of the inner conductor with respect to the outer conductor is –900 V. The maximum energy density of the capacitor in J/m^3 is closest to:

A) 6.2×10^{-3} B) 3.1×10^{-3} C) 1.6×10^{-3} D) 7.8×10^{-3} E) 3.9×10^{-4}

Answer: A
Var: 50+

10) The square plates of a 7000 pF capacitor measure 90 mm by 90 mm and are separated by a dielectric which is 0.15 mm thick. The voltage rating of the capacitor is 700 V. The maximum energy that can be stored in the capacitor, in mJ, is closest to:

A) 1.7 B) 2.1 C) 2.6 D) 3.0 E) 3.4

Answer: A
Var: 50+

11) The square plates of a 7000 pF capacitor measure 50 mm by 50 mm and are separated by a dielectric which is 0.25 mm thick. The voltage rating of the capacitor is 900 V. The dielectric constant of the dielectric is closest to:

A) 79 B) 72 C) 65 D) 58 E) 86

Answer: A
Var: 50+

12) The square plates of a 9000 pF capacitor measure 90 mm by 90 mm and are separated by a dielectric which is 0.29 mm thick. The voltage rating of the capacitor is 300 V. The dielectric strength of the dielectric, in kV/m, is closest to:

A) 1000 B) 930 C) 1100 D) 1200 E) 1300

Answer: A
Var: 50+

13) The capacitance of a capacitor depends on

    A) the charge on it.

    B) the potential difference across it.

    C) the energy stored in it.

    D) More than one of these.

    E) None of these.

Answer: E
Var: 1

14) Suppose you are building an electronic circuit and have three capacitors, each of different capacitance, available to use. What is the maximum number of different equivalent capacitances you can obtain by using the capacitors either singly or in combination?

A) 12 B) 17 C) 15 D) 14 E) 11

Answer: B
Var: 1

Figure 24.2

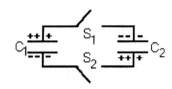

15) In Figure 24.2, two capacitors are separately charged by a 100 volt battery and then connected, with opposite polarity, by closing switches S_1 and S_2. What will be the potential difference across C_1 after the switches are closed?

$C_1 = 2\mu f$, $C_2 = 5\mu f$

    A) 28.6 V   B) 42.9 V   C) 71.4 V   D) 95.2 V   E) 100 V

Answer: B
Var: 1

Figure 24.3

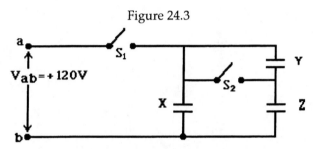

16) The network shown is assembled with uncharged capacitors X , Y, and Z, with $C_X= 5\ \mu F$, $C_Y= 2\ \mu F$ and $C_Z= 3\ \mu F$, and open switches, S_1 and S_2. A potential difference $V_{ab} = +120$ V is applied between points a and b. After the network is assembled, switch S_1 is closed, but switch S_2 is kept open. In Figure 24.3, the energy stored in capacitor X, in mJ, is closest to:

    A) 36   B) 0.60   C) 0.30   D) 72   E) 1.5

Answer: A
Var: 50+

17) The network shown is assembled with uncharged capacitors X , Y, and Z, with $C_X= 5\ \mu F$, $C_Y= 6\ \mu F$ and $C_Z= 8\ \mu F$, and open switches, S_1 and S_2. A potential difference $V_{ab} = +120$ V is applied between points a and b. After the network is assembled, switch S_1 is closed, but switch S_2 is kept open. In Figure 25.3, the charge on capacitor Y, in μC, is closest to:

    A) 410   B) 210   C) 310   D) 510   E) 620

Answer: A
Var: 50+

18) The network shown is assembled with uncharged capacitors X , Y, and Z, with $C_X = 7 \mu F$, $C_Y = 5 \mu F$ and $C_Z = 9 \mu F$, and open switches, S_1 and S_2. A potential difference $V_{ab} = +120$ V is applied between points a and b. After the network is assembled, switch S_1 is closed, but switch S_2 is kept open. In Figure 25.3, the voltage across capacitor Z, in SI units, is closest to:

A) 43   B) 67   C) 32   D) 25   E) 21

Answer: A
Var: 50+

19) The network shown is assembled with uncharged capacitors X , Y, and Z, with $C_X = 9 \mu F$, $C_Y = 4 \mu F$ and $C_Z = 8 \mu F$, and open switches, S_1 and S_2. A potential difference $V_{ab} = +120$ V is applied between points a and b. After the network is assembled, switch S_1 is closed, but switch S_2 is kept open. In Figure 25.3, switch S_1 is opened, and then switch S_2 is closed. The final voltage across capacitor X, in S_1 units, is closest to:

A) 82   B) 75   C) 69   D) 62   E) 55

Answer: A
Var: 50+

Figure 24.4

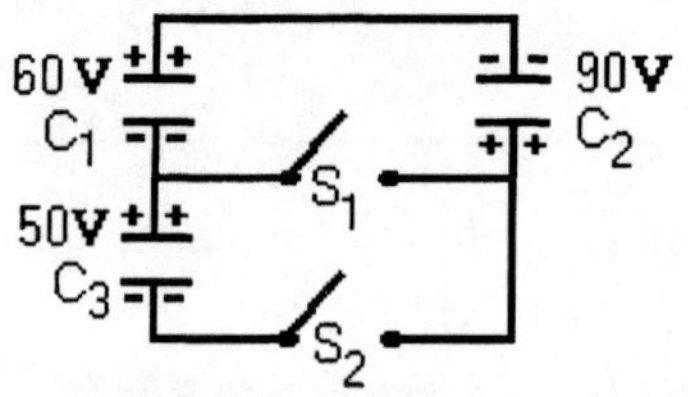

20) Three charged capacitors, $C_1 = 15\mu F$, $C_2 = 31\mu F$, and $C_3 = 48\mu F$, and two open switches, S_1 and S_2, are assembled into a network with initial voltages and polarities, as shown. Final status of the network is attained when the two switches, S_1 and S_2, are closed. In Figure 24.4, the initial total energy stored in the three capacitors, in mJ, is closest to:

A) 210   B) 170   C) 260   D) 300   E) 340

Answer: A
Var: 50+

21) Three charged capacitors, $C_1 = 17\mu F$, $C_2 = 34\mu F$, and $C_3 = 41\mu F$, and two open switches, S_1 and S_2, are assembled into a network with initial voltages and polarities, as shown. Final status of the network is attained when the two switches, S_1 and S_2, are closed. In Figure 25.4, the final charge on capacitor C_3, in mC, is closest to:

A) zero   B) 410   C) 1200   D) 2100   E) 3300

Answer: A
Var: 50+

254

Figure 24.5

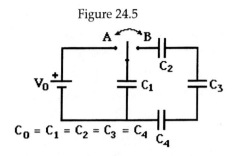

22) In Figure 24.5, the four identical capacitors in the circuit shown here are initially uncharged. The switch is thrown first to position A and then to position B. After this is done

A) $V_1 = V_2 = V_3 = V_4$

B) $V_1 = V_0$

C) $V_1 + V_2 + V_3 + V_4 = V_0$

D) $Q_1 = 3Q_2$

E) $Q_1 = Q_2$

Answer: D
Var: 1

Figure 24.6

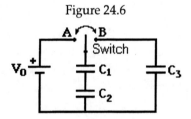

23) In the circuit shown in Figure 24.6 the capacitors are initially uncharged. The switch is first thrown to position A and then to position B. Let the charges on the capacitors be Q_1, Q_2, and Q_3 and the potential difference across them be V_1, V_2 and V_3. With the switch in position B

A) $V_1 = V_2 = V_3$

B) $V_1 + V_2 = V_3$

C) $V_3 = V_0$

D) $Q_1 = Q_2 = Q_3$

E) $Q_1 + Q_2 = Q_3$

Answer: B
Var: 1

255

24) An air filled parallel plate capacitor is connected to a battery and allowed to charge up. Now a slab of dielectric material is placed between the plates of the capacitor while the capacitor is still connected to the battery. After this is done one would find that

A) the energy stored in the capacitor had decreased.

B) the voltage across the capacitor had increased.

C) the charge on the capacitor had increased.

D) the charge on the capacitor had not changed.

E) None of these is true.

Answer: C
Var: 1

25) Which of the following explanations best explains how a dielectric affects the capacitance of a capacitor?

A) The dielectric effectively reduces the spacing of the capacitor plates, thus increasing the capacitance.

B) Charge is able to flow from the dielectric onto the capacitor plates, thus increasing the charge on the capacitor for a given potential difference and thereby increasing the capacitance.

C) Induced charge on the surface of the dielectric sets up an electric field which reinforces the field due to the free charge on the plates, thereby increasing the potential difference and the capacitance.

D) The electric field acting on the dielectric sets up mechanical stresses which result in greater stored energy for a given potential difference between the plates. Since the stored energy is $1/2CV^2$, this means that the capacitance is increased.

E) Induced charge on the surface of the dielectric sets up an electric field which partially cancels the field due to the free charge on the plates. This means that for a given free charge on the plates, the field and hence the potential difference is decreased, resulting in increased capacitance.

Answer: E
Var: 1

Short Answer Questions

1) A parallel-plate air capacitor is made from two plates 0.070 m square, spaced 6.0 mm apart. What must the potential difference between the plates be to produce an energy density of $0.088 \, J/m^3$?

Answer: 840 volts
Var: 50+

2) An isolated parallel–plate capacitor (not connected to a battery) has a charge of $Q = 1.4 \times 10^{-5}$ C. The separation between the plates initially is $d = 1.2$ mm, and for this separation the capacitance is 3.1×10^{-11} F. Calculate the work that must be done to pull the plates apart until their separation becomes 4.5 mm, if the charge on the plates remains constant. The capacitor plates are in a vacuum.

Answer: 8.7 J
Var: 50+

3) A parallel–plate capacitor, with air between the plates, is connected to a battery. The battery establishes a potential difference between the plates by placing charge of magnitude 3.12×10^{-6} C on each plate. The space between the plates is then filled with a dielectric material, with dielectric constant $K = 8.53$. What must the magnitude of the charge on each capacitor plate now be, to produce the same potential difference between the plates as before?

Answer: 2.66×10^{-5} C
Var: 50+

Figure 24.7

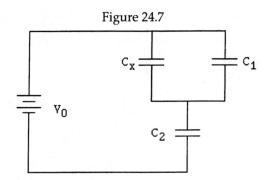

4) In the circuit sketched in Figure 24.7, $C_1 = 3.4 \times 10^{-6}$ F and $C_2 = 6.7 \times 10^{-6}$ F. What must be the capacitance C_x if the ratio V_0/V_1 is to be 5? (V_1 is the voltage across capacitor C_1.)

Answer: 2.3×10^{-5} F
Var: 50+

5) A parallel plate capacitor is made using two square plates, 6.38 cm on a side, spaced 0.380 cm apart. An electron is sent through the plates with speed 1.74×10^6 m/s and is deflected $30.0°$. Find the charge on each plate. ($\varepsilon_0 = 8.85 \times 10^{-12} C^2/N \cdot m^2$, $e = 1.60 \times 10^{-19}$ C.)

Answer: 5.6×10^{-12} C
Var: 50+

Chapter 25   Current, Resistance, and Electromotive Force

Multiple Choice Questions

1) The density of free electrons in gold is 5.90 x 10^{28} m^{-3}. The resistivity of gold is 2.44$_*$ x 10^{-8} Ω • m at a temperature of 20°C and the temperature coefficient of resistivity is 0.004 (°C)$^{-1}$. A gold wire, 0.8 mm in diameter and 49 cm long, carries a current of 510 ma. The number of electrons per second passing a given cross section of the wire, is closest to:

   A) 3.2 x 10^{18} B) 3.2 x 10^{17} C) 3.0 x 10^{22} D) 7.2 x 10^{14} E) 6.3 x 10^{15}

   Answer: A
   Var: 50+

2) The density of free electrons in gold is 5.90 x 10^{28} m^{-3}. The resistivity of gold is 2.44$_*$ x 10^{-8} Ω • m at a temperature of 20°C and the temperature coefficient of resistivity is 0.004 (°C)$^{-1}$. A gold wire, 0.9 mm in diameter and 12 cm long, carries a current of 240 ma. The drift velocity of the electrons in the wire is closest to:

   A) 4.0 x 10^{-5} m/s

   B) 4.6 x 10^{-5} m/s

   C) 5.2 x 10^{-5} m/s

   D) 5.8 x 10^{-5} m/s

   E) 6.4 x 10^{-5} m/s

   Answer: A
   Var: 50+

3) The density of free electrons in gold is 5.90 x 10^{28} m^{-3}. The resistivity of gold is 2.44$_*$ x 10^{-8} Ω • m at a temperature of 20°C and the temperature coefficient of resistivity is 0.004 (°C)$^{-1}$. A gold wire, 0.8 mm in diameter and 47 cm long, carries a current of 500 ma. The electric field in the wire is closest to:

   A) 0.024 V/m

   B) 0.0061 V/m

   C) 0.019 V/m

   D) 0.031 V/m

   E) 0.061 V/m

   Answer: A
   Var: 50+

4) The density of free electrons in gold is 5.90×10^{28} m^{-3}. The resistivity of gold is $2.44* \times 10^{-8}$ $\Omega \cdot$ m at a temperature of 20°C and the temperature coefficient of resistivity is 0.004 (°C)$^{-1}$. A gold wire, 0.9 mm in diameter and 44 cm long, carries a current of 990 ma. The power dissipated in the wire is closest to:

A) 17 mW   B) 4.1 mW   C) 7.2 mW   D) 10 mW   E) 13 mW

Answer: A
Var: 50+

5) In a certain electroplating process gold is deposited by using a current of 10.0 A for 41 minutes. An Au$^+$ ion has a mass of approximately 3.3×10^{-22} g. How many grams of gold are deposited in this process?

A) 51   B) 25   C) 34   D) 43   E) 150

Answer: A
Var: 50+

Table 25.1

	Electrical Resistivity	Temperature Coefficient of Resistivity (°C)$^{-1}$
nichrome	1.0×10^{-6} (Ω-m)	+0.0004
carbon	3.5×10^{-5}	-0.0005

6) Electrical properties of nichrome and carbon at 20°C are given in the table. Nichrome and carbon are available in rods which have a cross–sectional area of 2.8×10^{-6} m^2. At a temperature of 20°C, the sum of the resistances of a section of nichrome rod and a section of carbon rod is 0.53 ohms. When the temperature is increased, the increase in the resistance of the nichrome section is exactly offset by the decrease in the resistance of the carbon section. In Table 25.1, the length of the nichrome section, in cm, is closest to:

A) 83   B) 68   C) 97   D) 110   E) 130

Answer: A
Var: 50+

7) Electrical properties of nichrome and carbon at 20°C are given in the table. Nichrome and carbon are available in rods which have a cross–sectional area of 6.0×10^{-6} m^2. At a temperature of 20°C, the sum of the resistances of a section of nichrome rod and a section of carbon rod is 0.94 ohms. When the temperature is increased, the increase in the resistance of the nichrome section is exactly offset by the decrease in the resistance of the carbon section. In Table 25.1, the length of the carbon section, in mm, is closest to:

A) 72   B) 89   C) 110   D) 120   E) 140

Answer: A
Var: 50+

The voltage and power ratings of a light bulb, which are the normal operating values, are 110 V and 60 W. Assume the filament resistance of the bulb is constant and is independent of operating conditions.

8) In Situation 25.1, the light bulb is operated with a current which is one half of the current rating of the bulb. The actual power drawn by the bulb is closest to:

   A) 10 W   B) 15 W   C) 20 W   D) 25 W   E) 30 W

   Answer: B
   Var: 1

9) In Situation 25.1, the light bulb is operated at a reduced voltage and the power drawn by the bulb is 36 W. The operating voltage of the bulb is closest to:

   A) 66 V   B) 72 V   C) 78 V   D) 85 V   E) 90 V

   Answer: D
   Var: 1

10) The heater element of a 120 V toaster is a 6.4 m length of nichrome wire, whose diameter is 0.68 mm. The resistivity of nichrome at the operating temperature of the toaster is $1.3 \times 10^{-6}\ \Omega \cdot m$. The toaster is operated at a voltage of 120 V. The power drawn by the toaster is closest to:

   A) 630 W   B) 610 W   C) 650 W   D) 670 W   E) 690 W

   Answer: A
   Var: 50+

11) The heater element of a 120 V toaster is a 9.7 m length of nichrome wire, whose diameter is 0.30 mm. The resistivity of nichrome at the operating temperature of the toaster is $1.3 \times 10^{-6}\ \Omega \cdot m$. The nichrome wire is replaced by a 5.5 m length of tungsten wire. The power of the toaster, when operated at a voltage of 120 V, remains unchanged when the wire replacement is made. The resistivity of tungsten, at the operating temperature of the toaster, is $2.4 \times 10^{-7}\ \Omega \cdot m$. The diameter of the tungsten wire is closest to:

   A) 0.13 mm   B) 0.11 mm   C) 0.081 mm   D) 0.057 mm   E) 0.15 mm

   Answer: A
   Var: 50+

12)   Figure 25.1a

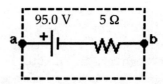

   The emf and the internal resistance of a battery are as shown. In Figure 25.1a, a current of 8.3 A is drawn from the battery when a resistor is connected across the terminals. The power dissipated by the resistor is closest to:

   A) 440 W   B) 700 W   C) 620 W   D) 530 W   E) 790 W

   Answer: A
   Var: 50+

13)

Figure 25.1b

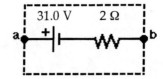

The emf and the internal resistance of a battery are as shown. In Figure 25.1b, when the terminal voltage V_{ab} is equal to 17.4 V, the current through the battery, including direction, is closest to:

  A) 6.8 A, from b to a

  B) 8.7 A, from b to a

  C) 6.8 A, from a to b

  D) 8.7 A, from a to b

  E) 16 A, from b to a

Answer: A
Var: 50+

14)

Figure 25.1c

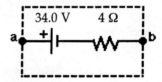

The emf and the internal resistance of a battery are as shown. In Figure 25.1c, the battery is charged by an external 47.6 V source. The rate at which chemical energy is being stored in the battery is closest to:

  A) 120 W   B) 330 W   C) 260 W   D) 190 W   E) 400 W

Answer: A
Var: 50+

15)

Figure 25.1d

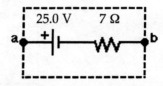

The emf and the internal resistance of a battery are as shown. In Figure 25.1d, a current of 7.8 A is established through the battery from b to a. The terminal voltage V_{ab} is closest to:

  A) –30 V   B) 80 V   C) 30 V   D) –80 V   E) zero

Answer: A
Var: 50+

16)

Figure 25.1e

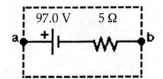

The emf and the internal resistance of a battery are as shown. In Figure 25.1e, the power dissipated within the battery is 9.5 W when a resistor is connected across the terminals. The power dissipated by the resistor is closest to:

A) 120 W   B) 180 W   C) 240 W   D) 300 W   E) 350 W

Answer: A
Var: 50+

17) In an electroplating process, copper (ionic charge +2e, atomic weight 63.6) is deposited using a current of 10 A. What mass of copper is deposited in 10 minutes?

A) 3.96   B) 2.52   C) 0.99   D) 2.52   E) 1.98

Answer: E
Var: 1

18) Building codes usually limit the current carried by a No. 14 copper wire to 15 A. Many household circuits are wired with this size wire. What is the drift velocity of the electrons in this case? The diameter of No. 14 wire is 1.6 mm. Assume one conduction electron per atom in copper. The atomic weight of copper is 63.3 and its density is 8900 kg/m^3.

A) 5.52 x 10^{-4} m/s

B) 4.56 x 10^{-4} m/s

C) 1.65 x 10^{-3} m/s

D) 4.44 x 10^{-2} m/s

E) 4.89 x 10^{-5} m/s

Answer: A
Var: 1

Figure 25.2

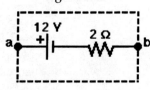

The emf and the internal resistance of a battery are as shown.

19) In Figure 25.2, a current of 6.0 A is drawn from the battery. The terminal voltage of the battery V_{ab} is closest to:

A) zero   B) +12 V   C) +24 V   D) –12 V   E) –24 V

Answer: A
Var: 1

20) In Figure 25.2, a 3.0 ohm cable is connected across the battery. The rate at which chemical energy in the battery is depleted is closest to:

A) 24 W   B) 27 W   C) 29 W   D) 32 W   E) 34 W

Answer: C
Var: 1

21) In Figure 25.2, when the terminal voltage of the battery V_{ab} is equal to 20 V, the current which passes through the battery, including direction, is closest to:

A) 4 A, from a to b

B) 5 A, from a to b

C) 6 A, from a to b

D) 4 A, from b to a

E) 5 A, from b to a

Answer: A
Var: 1

22) In Figure 25.2, an external power source charges the battery with a current of 2.0 A. The rate at which the external source delivers energy to the battery is closest to:

A) 16 W   B) 20 W   C) 24 W   D) 28 W   E) 32 W

Answer: E
Var: 1

23) In Figure 25.2, the power dissipated in an external resistor, which is connected across the terminals of the battery, is equal to 18 W. The terminal voltage of the battery V_{ab} is closest to:

A) 6.0 V   B) 7.2 V   C) 8.4 V   D) 9.6 V   E) 10.8 V

Answer: A
Var: 1

Figure 25.3

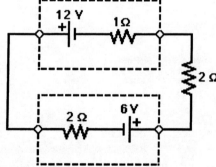

A circuit has two batteries and a resistor as shown.

24) In Figure 25.3, the terminal voltage of the 6 V battery is closest to:

A) +1.2 V   B) +2.4 V   C) +3.6 V   D) –1.2 V   E) –2.4 V

Answer: D
Var: 1

25) In Figure 25.3, the terminal voltage of the 12 V battery is closest to:

A) 8.4 V   B) 9.6 V   C) 10.8 V   D) 13.2 V   E) 15.6 V

Answer: A
Var: 1

Figure 25.4

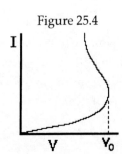

26) In Figure 25.4, a plot of current versus voltage for a semiconductor device is called a thermistor. Observe that there are two different currents which can correspond to a given potential difference across the device for some values of the voltage. Which of the following explanations best accounts for this curious (and useful) behavior?

A) The supply of charge carriers in the device becomes depleted when the voltage approaches the value V_0.

B) The device becomes super conducting when V reaches V_0.

C) The device has a large negative temperature coefficient of resistivity that varies greatly with temperature (i.e. resistivity decreases with increasing temperature).

D) The device has a large positive temperature coefficient of resistivity that varies greatly with temperature.

E) The device has negative coefficient of thermal expansion for some temperature ranges (i.e.its cross–section decreases as it gets hotter for some temperature range).

Answer: C
Var: 1

27) If the length and diameter of a wire of circular cross section are both doubled, the resistance is

A) unchanged.

B) doubled.

C) increased fourfold.

D) halved.

E) None of these are true.

Answer: D
Var: 1

28) Nichrome wire, often used for heating elements, has resistivity of 1.0×10^6 $\Omega \cdot$ m at room temperature. What length of No. 30 wire (diameter 0.250 mm) is needed to wind a resistor that has 50 ohms at room temperature?

A) 3.66 m   B) 2.45 m   C) 0.61 m   D) 6.54 m   E) 22.4 m

Answer: B
Var: 1

29) In an oceanographic experiment two long, coaxial electrodes are inserted into sea water and the resistance between them is measured. If the inner cylinder has diameter a and the outer cylinder has diameter 3a, the resistance can be expressed as $R = f\rho/r$ where L = length of the cylinders and r = resistivity of sea water. What is the value of the numerical factor f?

    A) 0.22   B) 0.17   C) 2.13   D) 3.14   E) 1.60

Answer: B
Var: 1

30) A current density of J is flowing in a resistor of resistivity ρ. We can thus recognize $J_2\rho$ as the

    A) electric field in the resistor.

    B) total power dissipated in the resistor.

    C) heat generated per unit volume in the resistor.

    D) electrical energy stored in the resistor.

    E) potential drop across the resistor.

Answer: C
Var: 1

Short Answer Questions

1) The current in a wire varies with time according to $I(t) = 1.00 \text{ A} + (3.40 \text{ A}/\text{s})t$. How many coulombs of charge pass a cross section of the wire in the time period between $t = 0$ and $t = 3.00$ s?

Answer: 18.3 coulombs
Var: 50+

2) A wire of radius 1.1 mm carries a current of 2.5 A. The potential difference between points on the wire 49 m apart is 2.6 V. What are
a) the electric field in the wire and
b) the resistivity ρ of the material of which the wire is made?

Answer: a) 0.053 V/m
           b) $8.1 \times 10^{-8} \, \Omega \cdot \text{m}$
Var: 50+

Figure 25.5

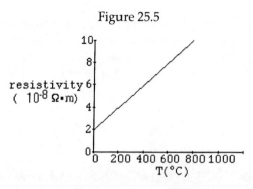

3) In Figure 25.5, a piece of wire 9.5 cm long carries a current I when a voltage V is applied across its ends at a temperature of $0°C$. If the resistivity of the material of which the wire is made varies with temperature as shown, what length of the same diameter wire is needed so that the same current flows when the same voltage is applied at temperature $400°C$?

Answer: 3.2 cm
Var: 50+

4) A heating element of resistance (at its operating temperature) 325 Ω is connected to a battery of emf 785 V and unknown internal resistance r. It is found that heat energy is being generated in the heater element at a rate of 72.0 W. What is the rate at which heat energy is being generated in the internal resistance of the battery?

Answer: 297 watts
Var: 50+

5) When a thin copper wire of length 178.0 m is connected between the terminals of a 1.2 V battery, of negligible internal resistance, a current of 2.0 amps is produced. What is the diameter of the wire? (The resistivity of copper is 1.72×10^{-8} $\Omega \cdot$ m.)

Answer: 2.5×10^{-3} m
Var: 1

6) When an external resistor of resistance $R_1 = 14$ Ω is connected to the terminals of a battery, a current of 6.0 A flows through the resistor. When an external resistor of resistance R = 64.4 Ω is connected instead, the current is 2.0A. Calculate:
(a) the emf of the battery and
(b) the internal resistance of the battery.

Answer: (a) 150 volts
         (b) 11 Ω
Var: 1

Chapter 26   Direct-Current Circuits

Multiple Choice Questions

Figure 26.1

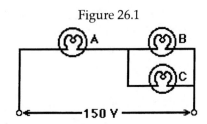

1) Three light bulbs, A, B, and C, have electrical ratings as follows:
   Bulb A - 85 W, 3.1 A
   Bulb B - 80 V, 205 W
   Bulb C - 120 V, 0.1 A
   The three bulbs are connected in a circuit, which is across a 150-V line, as shown. Assume the filament resistances of the light bulbs are constant and independent of operating conditions. In Figure 26.1, the equivalent resistance of the circuit is closest to:

   A) 39 Ω   B) 31 Ω   C) 47 Ω   D) 55 Ω   E) 63 Ω

   Answer: A
   Var: 50+

2) Three light bulbs, A, B, and C, have electrical ratings as follows:
   Bulb A - 80 W, 4.2 A
   Bulb B - 80 V, 205 W
   Bulb C - 120 V, 0.6 A
   The three bulbs are connected in a circuit, which is across a 150-V line, as shown. Assume the filament resistances of the light bulbs are constant and independent of operating conditions. In Figure 26.1, the actual power drawn by bulb A is closest to:

   A) 100 W   B) 110 W   C) 120 W   D) 130 W   E) 140 W

   Answer: A
   Var: 50+

3) Three light bulbs, A, B, and C, have electrical ratings as follows:
   Bulb A - 91 W, 2.2 A
   Bulb B - 80 V, 205 W
   Bulb C - 120 V, 0.1 A
   The three bulbs are connected in a circuit, which is across a 150-V line, as shown. Assume the filament resistances of the light bulbs are constant and independent of operating conditions. In Figure 26.1, the current through bulb B is closest to:

   A) 3.0 A   B) 3.4 A   C) 3.8 A   D) 4.3 A   E) 4.7 A

   Answer: A
   Var: 50+

4) Three light bulbs, A, B, and C, have electrical ratings as follows:
Bulb A – 98 W, 1.3 A
Bulb B – 80 V, 205 W
Bulb C – 120 V, 0.7 A
The three bulbs are connected in a circuit, which is across a 150–V line, as shown. Assume the filament resistances of the light bulbs are constant and independent of operating conditions. In Figure 26.1, the voltage across bulb C is closest to:

A) 47 V   B) 50 V   C) 44 V   D) 41 V   E) 38 V

Answer: A
Var: 50+

Figure 26.2

A galvanometer G deflects full scale when a potential difference of 0.500 V is applied. The internal resistance of the galvanometer r_g is 25 ohms. An ammeter is constructed by incorporating the galvanometer and an additional resistance R_S. The ammeter deflects full scale when a measurement of 2.0 A is made.

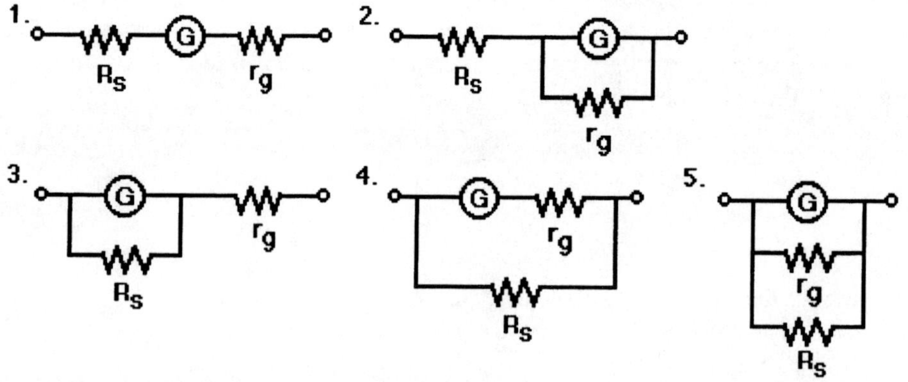

5) In Figure 26.2, the resistance R_S is closest to:

A) 0.244 Ω   B) 0.247 Ω   C) 0.250 Ω   D) 0.253 Ω   E) 0.256 Ω

Answer: D
Var: 1

6) In Figure 26.2, the most appropriate circuit diagram for the ammeter is:

A) 1   B) 2   C) 3   D) 4   E) 5

Answer: D
Var: 1

7) In Figure 26.2, the resistance R_S is closest to:

A) 475 Ω   B) 488 Ω   C) 500 Ω   D) 512 Ω   E) 525 Ω

Answer: A
Var: 1

Figure 26.3

A galvanometer G deflects full scale when a potential difference of 0.500 V is applied. The internal resistance of the galvanometer r_g is 25 ohms. A voltmeter is constructed by incorporating the galvanometer and an additional resistance Rs. The voltmeter deflects full scale when a measurement of 10 V is made.

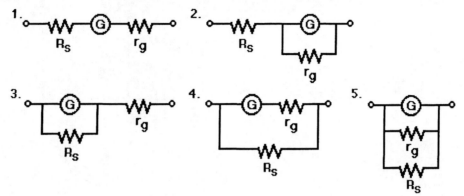

8) In Figure 26.3, the most appropriate circuit diagram for the voltmeter is:

   A) 1   B) 2   C) 3   D) 4   E) 5

Answer: B
Var: 1

9)

Figure 26.4a

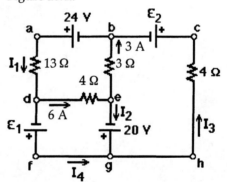

A multiloop circuit is given. It is not necessary to solve the entire circuit. In Figure 26.4a, the current I_1 is closest to:

   A) –0.7 A   B) 0.7 A   C) 4 A   D) –4 A   E) zero

Answer: A
Var: 50+

269

10)

Figure 26.4b

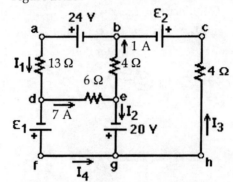

A multiloop circuit is given. It is not necessary to solve the entire circuit. In Figure 26.4b, the current I_2 is closest to:

A) –6 A   B) 6 A   C) 8 A   D) –8 A   E) zero

Answer: A
Var: 50+

11)

Figure 26.4c

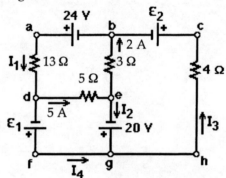

A multiloop circuit is given. It is not necessary to solve the entire circuit. In Figure 26.4c, the emf ε_1 is closest to:

A) –5 V   B) 5 V   C) 45 V   D) 51 V   E) –51 V

Answer: A
Var: 50+

12)

Figure 26.4d

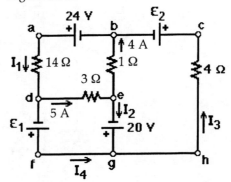

A multiloop circuit is given. It is not necessary to solve the entire circuit. In Figure 26.4d, the potential difference V_{ag} is closest to:

A) 0 V   B) 40 V   C) –40 V   D) –48 V   E) 48 V

Answer: A
Var: 50+

Figure 26.5

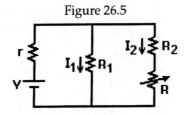

13) In Figure 26.5, the circuit R is a variable resistance. As R is decreased

A) I_1 remains unchanged, I_2 increases.

B) I_1 decreases, I_2 decreases.

C) I_1 decreases, I_2 increases.

D) I_1 increases, I_2 decreases.

E) I_1 increases, I_2 increases.

Answer: C
Var: 1

Figure 26.6

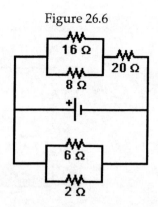

14) In Figure 26.6, the current of the circuit in the 8 ohm resistor is 0.5A. What is the current in the 2 ohm resistor?

   A) 2.25 A   B) 0.75 A   C) 4.5 A   D) 9.5 A   E) 6.4 A

   Answer: D
   Var: 1

Figure 26.7

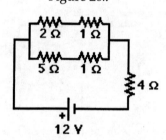

15) In Figure 26.7, what is the power dissipated in the 2 ohm resistance in the circuit ?

   A) 5.33 W   B) 8.0 W   C) 6.67 W   D) 2.67 W   E) 3.56 W

   Answer: E
   Var: 1

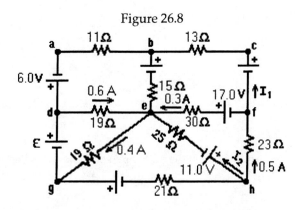

Figure 26.8

A multiloop circuit is given. Some circuit quantities are not labeled. It is not necessary to solve the entire circuit.

16) In Figure 26.8, the current I_1 is closest to:

A) zero B) +0.2 A C) +0.4 A D) –0.2 A E) –0.4 A

Answer: B
Var: 1

17) In Figure 26.8, the emf ε is closest to:

A) +3 V B) +18 V C) –3 V D) –10 V E) –18 V

Answer: B
Var: 1

18) In Figure 26.8, the current I_2 is closest to:

A) +0.1 A B) +0.3 A C) +0.5 A D) –0.1 A E) –0.3 A

Answer: E
Var: 1

19) In Figure 26.8, the potential difference V_{fa} is closest to:

A) +10 V B) +22 V C) –4 V D) –12 V E) –24 V

Answer: D
Var: 1

20)

Figure 26.9a

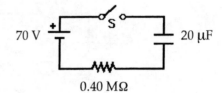

70 V $\quad$ S $\quad$ 20 μF

0.40 MΩ

Initially, for the circuit shown, the switch S is open and the capacitor is uncharged. The switch S is closed at time t = 0. In Figure 26.9a, when the charge on the capacitor is 700 μC, the current in the circuit, in μA, is closest to:

A) 88 $\qquad$ B) 96 $\qquad$ C) 79 $\qquad$ D) 70 $\qquad$ E) 61

Answer: A
Var: 50+

21)

Figure 26.9b

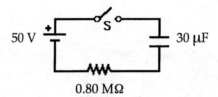

50 V $\quad$ S $\quad$ 30 μF

0.80 MΩ

Initially, for the circuit shown, the switch S is open and the capacitor is uncharged. The switch S is closed at time t = 0. In Figure 26.9b, when the time t is equal to 8.0 s, the charge on the capacitor, in μC, is closest to:

A) 430 $\qquad$ B) 340 $\qquad$ C) 510 $\qquad$ D) 600 $\qquad$ E) 680

Answer: A
Var: 50+

22)

Figure 26.9c

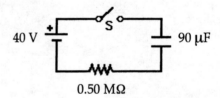

40 V $\quad$ S $\quad$ 90 μF

0.50 MΩ

Initially, for the circuit shown, the switch S is open and the capacitor is uncharged. The switch S is closed at time t = 0. In Figure 26.9c, when the energy stored in the capacitor is 50 mJ, the time t is closest to:

A) 81 s $\qquad$ B) 65 s $\qquad$ C) 97 s $\qquad$ D) 110 s $\qquad$ E) 130 s

Answer: A
Var: 50+

23)

Figure 26.9d

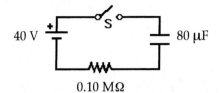

Initially, for the circuit shown, the switch S is open and the capacitor is uncharged. The switch S is closed at time t = 0. In Figure 26.9d, when the time t is equal to 20.0 s, the potential difference across the resistor is closest to:

A) 3.3 V   B) 3.9 V   C) 4.6 V   D) 5.3 V   E) 5.9 V

Answer: A
Var: 50+

24)

Figure 26.9e

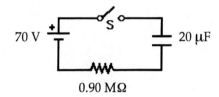

Initially, for the circuit shown, the switch S is open and the capacitor is uncharged. The switch S is closed at time t = 0. In Figure 26.9e, at a given instant, the potential difference across the capacitor is twice the potential difference across the resistor. At that instant, the charge on the capacitor, in μC, is closest to:

A) 930   B) 820   C) 700   D) 520   E) 350

Answer: A
Var: 50+

25)

Figure 26.10a

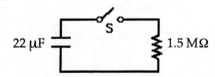

Initially, for the circuit shown, the switch S is open and the capacitor voltage is 80 V. The switch S is closed at time t = 0. In Figure 26.10a, the charge on the capacitor, when the current in the circuit is 33 μA, in μC, is closest to:

A) 1100   B) 1000   C) 960   D) 890   E) 830

Answer: A
Var: 50+

26)

Figure 26.10b

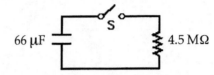

Initially, for the circuit shown, the switch S is open and the capacitor voltage is 80 V. The switch S is closed at time t = 0. In Figure 26.10b, when the energy stored in the capacitor is 20 mJ, the time t is closest to:

A) 350 s   B) 320 s   C) 390 s   D) 420 s   E) 460 s

Answer: A
Var: 50+

27)

Figure 26.10c

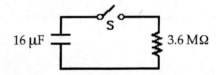

Initially, for the circuit shown, the switch S is open and the capacitor voltage is 80 V. The switch S is closed at time t = 0. In Figure 26.10c, the capacitor voltage when the time t is equal to 40.0 s is closest to:

A) 40 V   B) 45 V   C) 50 V   D) 55 V   E) 60 V

Answer: A
Var: 50+

28)

Figure 26.10d

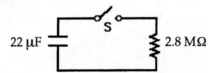

Initially, for the circuit shown, the switch S is open and the capacitor voltage is 80 V. The switch S is closed at time t = 0. In Figure 26.10d, the time t, when the current in the circuit is 7.0 μA, is closest to:

A) 87 s   B) 95 s   C) 78 s   D) 69 s   E) 61 s

Answer: A
Var: 50+

Figure 26.11

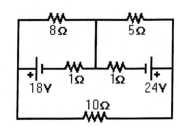

29) In Figure 26.11, what power is dissipated in the 10 ohm resistor in the circuit?

A) 3.33 W   B) 2.15 W   C) 6.84 W   D) 7.22 W   E) 5.17 W

Answer: C
Var: 1

30) Which of the following is an accurate statement?

A) An ammeter is constructed by placing a resistor in series with a galvanometer.

B) The resistance between the terminals of an ammeter should be as large as possible.

C) A "shunt" resistor is the name given the resistor placed in parallel with a galvanometer.

D) An ammeter disturbs a circuit, whereas a voltmeter does not.

E) When one attaches a resistor to a galvanometer to construct a voltmeter, the current through the galvanometer is typically much less than that through the resistor.

Answer: C
Var: 1

31) Which of the following is an accurate statement?

A) When a household circuit is rated at 20 A, this means the wires in the circuit will not carry more than 20 A.

B) When a lamp and a radio are plugged into a household receptacle, they are connected in series.

C) The wires which are grounded in household circuits carry no current.

D) Modern household plugs have three prongs. Two of these are connected to ground wires.

E) If any of the three wires leading to a household appliance were to have the insulation rubbed off, exposing the bare metal wire, touching one of these bare wires would expose you to the danger of electrocution (should you be standing barefoot on a damp concrete floor).

Answer: D
Var: 1

Figure 26.12

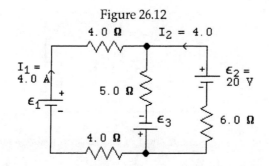

1) In Figure 26.12, consider the circuit sketched. Note that two currents are shown. Calculate the emf's ε_1 and ε_3.

Answer: ε_1 = 28 volts

ε_3 = 44 volts

Var: 1

Figure 26.13

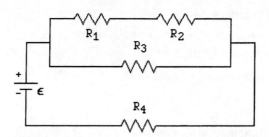

2) In Figure 26.13, consider the circuit sketched. The battery has emf ε = 10 volts and negligible internal resistance. The four resistors have resistances of R_1 = 15 Ω, R_2 = 17 Ω, R_3 = 33 Ω, and R_4 = 15 Ω. Calculate the rate at which heat is being generated in the resistor R_4.

Answer: 1.5 watts

Var: 50+

Figure 26.14

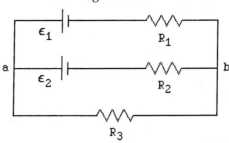

3) In Figure 26.14, consider the circuit sketched. The two batteries have negligible internal resistance and emf's ε_1 = 28.0 V and ε_2 = 42.0 V. The three resistors have resistances R_1 = 2.00 Ω, R_2 = 5.00 Ω, and R_3 = 1.00 Ω. Calculate the potential difference $V_a - V_b$ between points a and b.

Answer: 13.2 volts
Var: 1

Figure 26.15

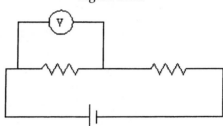

4) In Figure 26.15, two 360.0-Ω resistors are connected in series with a source of emf. A voltmeter with internal resistance if 6350 Ω is connected across one of the resistors and reads 3.23 V. Find the emf of the source.

Answer: 6.64 volts
Var: 1

5) A resistor with resistance 470 Ω is in a series with a capacitor of capacitance 8.5 x 10^{-6} F. What capacitance must be placed in parallel with the original capacitance to change the capacitive time constant of the combination to three times its original value?

Answer: 17 x 10^{-6} F
Var: 50+

Chapter 27   Magnetic Field and Magnetic Forces

Multiple Choice Questions

1) Alpha particles (charge = +2e, mass = 6.68 x 10^{-27} kg) are accelerated in a cyclotron to a final orbit radius of 0.90 m. The magnetic field in the cyclotron is 0.20 T. The period of circular motion of the alpha particles is closest to:

A) 0.66 μs   B) 1.0 μs   C) 1.3 μs   D) 1.6 μs   E) 2.0 μs

Answer: A
Var: 50+

2) Alpha particles (charge = +2e, mass = 6.68 x 10^{-27} kg) are accelerated in a cyclotron to a final orbit radius of 0.80 m. The magnetic field in the cyclotron is 0.50 T. The centripetal acceleration of the alpha particles in the final orbit radius is closest to:

A) 4.6 x 10^{14} m/s^2

B) 6.6 x 10^{14} m/s^2

C) 9.2 x 10^{14} m/s^2

D) 1.4 x 10^{15} m/s^2

E) 1.8 x 10^{15} m/s^2

Answer: A
Var: 50+

3) Alpha particles (charge = +2e, mass = 6.68 x 10^{-27} kg) are accelerated in a cyclotron to a final orbit radius of 0.80 m. The magnetic field in the cyclotron is 0.60 T. The kinetic energy of an alpha particle in the final orbit is closest to:

A) 11 MeV   B) 9.4 MeV   C) 13 MeV   D) 14 MeV   E) 16 MeV

Answer: A
Var: 50+

4) Alpha particles (charge = +2e, mass = 6.68 x 10^{-27} kg) are accelerated in a cyclotron to a final orbit radius of 0.60 m. The magnetic field in the cyclotron is 0.80 T. The magnetic flux enclosed by the final orbit is closest to:

A) 0.90 Wb   B) 0.75 Wb   C) 0.60 Wb   D) 1.0 Wb   E) 1.2 Wb

Answer: A
Var: 50+

5) If you were to cut a small permanent bar magnet in half,

    A) one piece would be a magnetic north pole and the other piece would be a south pole.

    B) neither piece would be magnetic.

    C) each piece would in itself be a smaller bar magnet with both north and south poles.

    D) each piece would contain both north and south poles, but on a given piece the intensity of the north and south poles would not necessarily be equal.

    E) None of these statements is true.

Answer: C
Var: 1

Figure 27.1

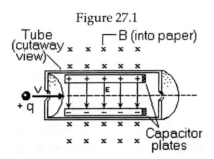

6) In Figure 27.1 is a velocity selector that can be used to measure the speed of a charged particle. A beam of particles is directed along the axis of the instrument. A parallel plate capacitor sets up an electric field E which is oriented perpendicular to a uniform magnetic field B. If the plates are separated by 2 mm and the value of the magnetic field is 0.1 T, what voltage between the plates will allow particles of speed 5×10^5 m/s to pass straight through without deflection?

    A) 100 V   B) 310 V   C) 630 V   D) 32 V   E) 16 V

Answer: A
Var: 50+

7) Which of the following is an accurate statement?

    A) Magnetic field lines have as their sources north and south poles.

    B) A magnetic field line is, by definition, tangent to the direction of the magnetic force on a moving charge at a given point in space.

    C) The magnetic force on a moving charge does not change its energy.

    D) The magnetic force on a current carrying wire is greatest when the wire is parallel to the magnetic field.

    E) A current carrying loop of wire tends to line up with its plane parallel to an external magnetic field in which it is positioned.

Answer: C
Var: 1

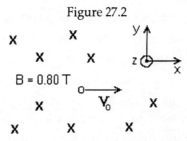

Figure 27.2

A uniform magnetic field of magnitude 0.80 T in the negative z–direction is present in a region of space. A uniform electric field is also present.

8) In Figure 27.2, an electron, projected with an initial velocity $v_0 = 2.6 \times 10^4$ m/s in the positive x–direction, traverses the region without deflection. The electric field vector, in kV/m, is closest to:

A) –21 j   B) +21 i   C) +33 i   D) +33 j   E) –33 j

Answer: A
Var: 50+

9) In Figure 27.2, the electric field is set at 77,600 V/m in the positive y-direction. An electron is projected with an initial velocity $v_0 = 9.7 \times 10^4$ m/s in the positive x-direction. The y-component of the initial force on the electron is closest to:

A) -2×10^{-14} N

B) $+2 \times 10^{-14}$ N

C) -1×10^{-14} N

D) $+1 \times 10^{-14}$ N

E) zero

Answer: A
Var: 50+

Figure 27.3

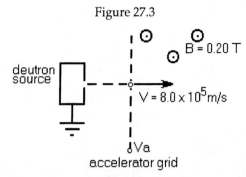

A mass spectrograph is operated with deuterons, which have a charge of +e and a mass of 3.34 x 10^{-27} kg. Deuterons emerge from the source, which is grounded with negligible velocity. The velocity of the deuterons as they pass through the accelerator grid is 8.0 x 105 m/s. A uniform magnetic field of magnitude B = 0.20 T, directed out of the plane, is present at the right of the grid.

10) In Figure 27.3, the electric potential of the accelerator grid V_a is closest to:

A) +7 kV   B) +9 kV   C) +11 kV   D) –7 kV   E) –9 kV

Answer: D
Var: 1

11) In Figure 27.3, the deuterons are in circular orbit in the magnetic field. The radius of the orbit and the initial sense of deflection are closest to:

A) 60 mm, upward

B) 70 mm, upward

C) 60 mm, downward

D) 70 mm, downward

E) 80 mm, downward

Answer: E
Var: 1

12) In Figure 27.3, the angular velocity of the deuterons in the magnetic field is closest to:

A) 1.6 x 10^6 rad/s

B) 4.0 x 10^6 rad/s

C) 1.0 x 10^7 rad/s

D) 2.5 x 10^7 rad/s

E) 6.3 x 10^7 rad/s

Answer: C
Var: 1

283

Figure 27.4

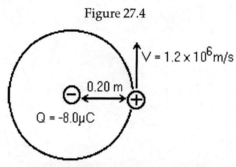

An ion of mass m and of charge +e is in circular orbit around a fixed point charge Q, with charge –8.0 µC. The radius of the orbit is 0.20 m, and the speed of the ion in the orbit is 1.2×10^6 m/s. A uniform external magnetic field, perpendicular to the plane of the orbit, is present. The magnetic force on the ion is equal to the electric force in magnitude and in direction at all points of the orbit.

13) In Figure 27.4, the external magnetic field and the direction relative to the plane of the orbit are closest to:

    A) 1.1 T, inward

    B) 1.3 T, outward

    C) 1.5 T, inward

    D) 1.7 T, outward

    E) 1.9 T, inward

Answer: C
Var: 1

14) In Figure 27.4, the mass m of the ion is closest to:

    A) 4×10^{-26} kg

    B) 5×10^{-26} kg

    C) 6×10^{-26} kg

    D) 7×10^{-26} kg

    E) 8×10^{-26} kg

Answer: E
Var: 1

Figure 27.5

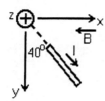

15) In Figure 27.5, a wire segment 1.2 m long carries a current I = 3.5 A, and is oriented. A uniform magnetic field of magnitude 0.50 T is present as shown. Right-handed coordinates are used. The magnetic force on the wire segment, in SI units, is closest to:

A) +1.3 j

B) –1.3 k

C) +1.3 k

D) +1.3 j – 1.6 k

E) –1.3 j + 1.6 k

Answer: C
Var: 1

Figure 27.6

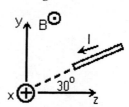

16) In Figure 27.6, a wire segment 1.2 m long carries a current I = 3.5 A, and is oriented. A uniform magnetic field of magnitude 0.50 T is present as shown. Right-handed coordinates are used. The magnetic force on the wire segment, in SI units, is closest to:

A) +1.1 j – 1.8 k

B) –1.1 j + 1.8 k

C) –1.1 j – 1.8 k

D) +1.8 j – 1.1 k

E) –1.8 j + 1.1 k

Answer: C
Var: 1

17)

Figure 27.7a

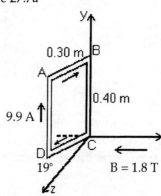

A rigid rectangular loop, which measures 0.30 m by 0.40 m, carries a current of 9.9 A, as shown. A uniform external magnetic field of magnitude 1.8 T in the negative x-direction is present. Segment CD is in the x-z plane and forms a 19° angle with the z-axis, as shown. In Figure 27.7a, the y-component of the magnetic force on segment AB is closest to:

A) +5.1 N   B) –5.1 N   C) +1.7 N   D) –1.7 N   E) zero

Answer: A
Var: 50+

18)

Figure 27.7b

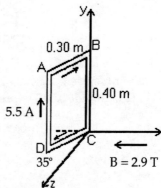

A rigid rectangular loop, which measures 0.30 m by 0.40 m, carries a current of 5.5 A, as shown. A uniform external magnetic field of magnitude 2.9 T in the negative x-direction is present. Segment CD is in the x-z plane and forms a 35° angle with the z-axis, as shown. In Figure 27.7b, an external torque applied to the loop keeps it in static equilibrium. The magnitude of the external torque is closest to:

A) 1.1 N • m   B) 0.73 N • m   C) 1.3 N • m   D) 1.4 N • m   E) 1.6 N • m

Answer: A
Var: 50+

286

19)

Figure 27.7c

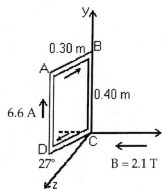

A rigid rectangular loop, which measures 0.30 m by 0.40 m, carries a current of 6.6 A, as shown. A uniform external magnetic field of magnitude 2.1 T in the negative x-direction is present. Segment CD is in the x-z plane and forms a 27° angle with the z-axis, as shown. In Figure 27.7c, the magnetic flux through the loop of the external field is closest to:

A) 0.22 Wb   B) 0.19 Wb   C) 0.15 Wb   D) 0.11 Wb   E) 0.28 Wb

Answer: A
Var: 50+

20)

Figure 27.7d

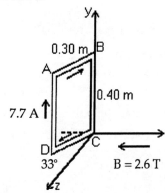

A rigid rectangular loop, which measures 0.30 m by 0.40 m, carries a current of 7.7 A, as shown. A uniform external magnetic field of magnitude 2.6 T in the negative x-direction is present. Segment CD is in the x-z plane and forms a 33° angle with the z-axis, as shown. In Figure 27.7d, the magnitude of the magnetic moment of the loop is closest to:

A) 0.92 A $\cdot$ m^2

B) 0.77 A $\cdot$ m^2

C) 0.62 A $\cdot$ m^2

D) 0.46 A $\cdot$ m^2

E) 0.31 A $\cdot$ m^2

Answer: A
Var: 50+

287

Figure 27.8

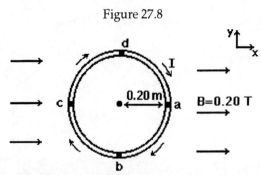

A rigid circular loop has a radius of 0.20 m and is in the x–y plane. A clockwise current I is carried by the loop, as shown. The magnitude of the magnetic moment of the loop is 0.75 A $\cdot$ m^2. A uniform external magnetic field, B = 0.20 T in the positive x–direction, is present.

21) In Figure 27.8, the current in the loop is closest to:

A) 3.0 A   B) 4.5 A   C) 6.0 A   D) 7.5 A   E) 9.0 A

Answer: C
Var: 1

22) In Figure 27.8, the magnitude of the magnetic torque exerted on the loop is closest to:

A) 0.15 N $\cdot$ m   B) 0.25 N $\cdot$ m   C) 0.35 N $\cdot$ m   D) 0.45 N $\cdot$ m   E) 0.55 N $\cdot$ m

Answer: A
Var: 1

23) In Figure 27.8, the loop is released from rest. The initial motion of the loop is described by:

A) points a, b, c, and d move clockwise

B) points a, b, c, and d, move counterclockwise

C) point a moves out of the plane; point c moves into the plane

D) point b moves out of the plane; point d moves into the plane

E) point c moves out of the plane; point a moves into the plane

Answer: C
Var: 1

24) In Figure 27.8, an external torque changes the orientation of the loop from one of lowest potential energy to one of highest potential energy. The work done by the external torque is closest to:

A) 0.2 J   B) 0.3 J   C) 0.4 J   D) 0.5 J   E) 0.6 J

Answer: B
Var: 1

25) An electron is projected along the positive z-axis, with an initial speed of 5.0×10^5 m/s. A uniform magnetic field is present, but there is no electric field. The electron experiences an initial acceleration whose components are $a_x = -7.0 \times 10^{16}$ m/s^2, $a_y = -3.5 \times 10^{16}$ m/s^2, $a_z = 0$. The components of the uniform magnetic field, in SI units, are closest to:

A) $B_x = +0.4$, $B_y = +0.8$, $B_z = 0.0$

B) $B_x = +0.4$, $B_y = -0.8$, $B_z = 0.0$

C) $B_x = +0.4$, $B_y = +0.8$, B_z is indeterminate

D) $B_x = +0.4$, $B_y = -0.8$, B_z is indeterminate

E) $B_x = -0.4$, $B_y = +0.8$, B_z is indeterminate

Answer: D
Var: 1

26) A 10 meter length of wire carrying a current of 7 A lies on a horizontal table with a rectangular top of dimensions 0.600 m x 0.800 m. The ends of the wire are attached to opposite ends of a diagonal of the rectangle. A vertical magnetic field of 0.10 T is present. What magnetic force acts on this segment of wire?

A) 0.70 N

B) 0.98 N

C) 7.0 N

D) zero

E) The force cannot be determined without knowing the shape of the length of wire.

Answer: A
Var: 50+

27) A circular coil of wire of 200 turns and diameter 5 cm carries a current of 4 A. It is placed in a magnetic field of 0.70 T with the plane of the coil making an angle of 30° with the magnetic field. What is the torque on the coil?

A) 0.95 N • m   B) 0.55 N • m   C) 1.8 N • m   D) 2.5 N • m   E) 0.48 N • m

Answer: A
Var: 50+

Short Answer Questions

1) A wire along the z-axis carries a current of 3.1 A in the positive z direction. Find the force (magnitude and direction) exerted on a 8.0 cm long length of the wire by a uniform magnetic field with magnitude 0.30 T in the –x direction.

Answer: 0.074 N, –y direction
Var: 50+

2) A proton, with mass 1.67×10^{-27} kg and charge $+1.6 \times 10^{-19}$ C, is sent with velocity 4.7×10^4 m/s in the x–direction into a region where there is a uniform electric field of magnitude 720 V/m in the y direction. What is the magnitude and direction of the uniform magnetic field in the region, if the proton is to pass through undeflected? Assume that the magnetic field has no x-component. Neglect gravitational effects.

Answer: 1.5×10^{-2} T, +z direction

Var: 50+

Figure 27.9

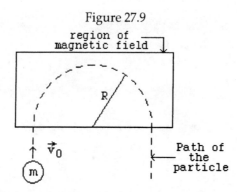

3) In Figure 27.9, a small particle of charge $q = -8.5 \times 10^{-6}$ C and mass $m = 3.1 \times 10^{-12}$ kg has velocity $v_0 = 2.5 \times 10^3$ m/s as it enters a region of uniform magnetic field. The particle is observed to travel in the semicircular path shown, with radius R = 5.0 cm. Calculate the
(a) magnitude and
(b) direction of the magnetic field in the region.

Answer: (a) B = 0.018 T
(b) directed into the paper

Var: 50+

Figure 27.10

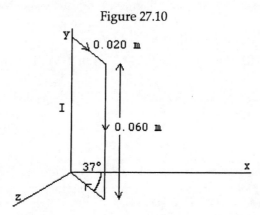

4) In Figure 27.10, the rectangular loop is pivoted about one side (of length 0.060 m), that coincides with the y-axis. The end (length 0.020 m) of the loop that lies in the xz-plane makes an angle of $37°$ with the x-axis, as shown in the sketch. The loop carries a current of I = 77 A in the direction shown. (In the side of the loop that is along the y-axis the current is in the +y direction.) If there is a uniform magnetic field of magnitude 5.9 T in the –x direction, find the magnitude of the torque that the magnetic field exerts on the loop.

Answer: 4.4×10^{-1} N • m

Var: 50+

Figure 27.11

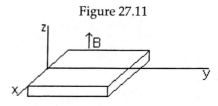

5) In Figure 27.11, a metal strip is oriented as shown. It is 0.40 cm wide (in the x–direction), 0.80 cm long (in the y–direction) and 0.10 cm thick (in the z–direction). The strip is in a magnetic field of 1.0 T that is in the +z direction as shown. If the density of free electrons in the metal is 3.9×10^{28} electrons per m^3, what will be the Hall emf, the potential difference between the two edges of the strip?

Answer: 3.4×10^6 volts
Var: 1

Chapter 28   Sources of Magnetic Field

Multiple Choice Questions

1) A point charge Q moves on the x–axis in the positive direction with a speed of 440 m/s. A field point is on the y–axis at y = +50 mm. The magnetic field produced at the field point, as the charge moves through the origin, is equal to –0.70 k μT. The charge Q is closest to:

   A) –40 μC   B) +40 μC   C) –30 μC   D) +30 μC   E) +20 μC

Answer: A
Var: 50+

2) A point charge Q moves on the x–axis in the positive direction with a speed of 460 m/s. A field point is on the y–axis at y = +40 mm. The magnetic field produced at the field point, as the charge moves through the origin, is equal to –0.80 k μT. When the charge is at x = +40 mm, the magnitude of the magnetic field at the field point is closest to:

   A) 0.28 μT   B) 0.37 μT   C) 0.45 μT   D) 0.54 μT   E) 0.62 μT

Answer: A
Var: 50+

3) A point charge Q moves on the x–axis in the positive direction with a speed of 230 m/s. A field point is on the y–axis at y = +60 mm. The magnetic field produced at the field point, as the charge moves through the origin, is equal to –0.60 k μT. The moving charge is replaced by a current on the x–axis that produces a magnetic field at the field point that is equal to –0.60 k μT. The current and its sense along the x–axis are closest to:

   A) 180 mA, negative

   B) 180 mA, positive

   C) 270 mA, positive

   D) 360 mA, positive

   E) 360 mA, negative

Answer: A
Var: 50+

Figure 28.1

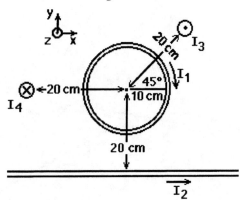

4) A circular loop of radius 10 cm and three long straight wires carry currents of $I_1 = 60$ A, $I_2 = 20$ A, $I_3 = 10$ A, and $I_4 = 10$ A, respectively, as shown. Each straight wire is 20 cm from the center of the loop. In Figure 28.1, the y–component of the resultant magnetic field at the center of the loop is closest to:

A) –17 μT   B) –20 μT   C) –15 μT   D) +20 μT   E) +15 μT

Answer: A
Var: 50+

5) A circular loop of radius 10 cm and three long straight wires carry currents of $I_1 = 60$ A, $I_2 = 80$ A, $I_3 = 10$ A, and $I_4 = 50$ A, respectively, as shown. Each straight wire is 20 cm from the center of the loop. In Figure 28.1, the z–component of the resultant magnetic field at the center of the loop is closest to:

A) –300 μT   B) +300 μT   C) –20 μT   D) +20 μT   E) –110 μT

Answer: A
Var: 50+

Figure 28.2

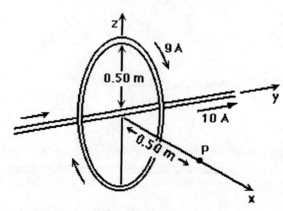

A long straight wire on the y–axis carries a 10 A current in the positive y–direction. A circular loop 0.50 m in radius, which is in the y–z plane, carries a 9 A current, as shown.

6) In Figure 28.2, a field point P is on the positive x-axis, at a distance of 0.50 m from the center of the loop. The magnetic field at the field point P is closest to:

A) zero

B) $(-8.0 \times 10^{-6}\text{T})$ k

C) $(+4.0 \times 10^{-6}\text{T})$ i $- (4.0 \times 10^{-6}\text{T})$ k

D) $(-4.0 \times 10^{-6}\text{T})$ i $- (4.0 \times 10^{-6}\text{T})$ k

E) $(-4.0 \times 10^{-6}\text{T})$ i $- (8.0 \times 10^{-6}\text{T})$ k

Answer: D
Var: 1

7)

Figure 28.3a

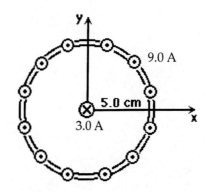

A long cylindrical shell 5.0 cm in radius is coaxial with a long thin wire. The shell carries a current of 9.0 A, uniformly distributed over the shell, and the wire carries a current of 3.0 A, as shown. In Figure 28.3a, a field point is on the positive x-axis, 3.0 cm from the wire. The y-component of the magnetic field at this point is closest to:

A) -2.0×10^{-5} T

B) $+2.0 \times 10^{-5}$ T

C) -6.7×10^{-6} T

D) $+6.7 \times 10^{-6}$ T

E) -4.7×10^{-5} T

Answer: A

Var: 36

8)

Figure 28.3b

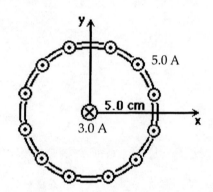

A long cylindrical shell 5.0 cm in radius is coaxial with a long thin wire. The shell carries a current of 5.0 A, uniformly distributed over the shell, and the wire carries a current of 3.0 A, as shown. In Figure 28.3b, a field point is on the positive y-axis, 8.0 cm from the wire. The x-component of the magnetic field at this point is closest to:

A) -5.0×10^{-6} T

B) $+5.0 \times 10^{-6}$ T

C) -1.8×10^{-5} T

D) $+1.3 \times 10^{-5}$ T

E) -1.3×10^{-5} T

Answer: A
Var: 36

Figure 28.4

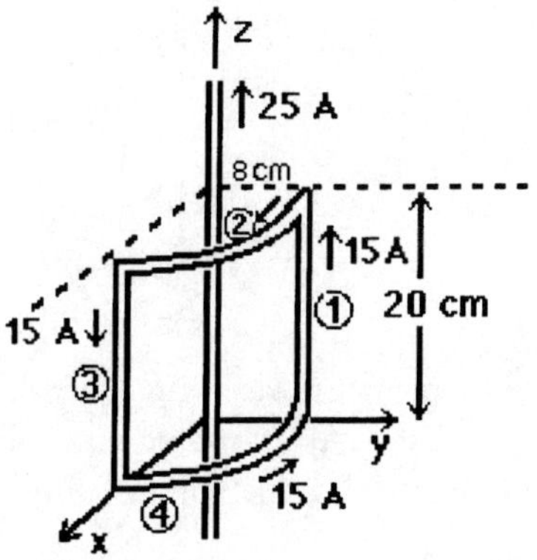

A non–planar rigid loop has two vertical sections, numbered 1 and 3, which are 20 cm long. It also has two 90 degree arc sections, numbered 2 and 4. The curved sections have a radius of 8 cm, and the centers are on the z–axis. The loop carries a current of 15 A, as shown. A straight wire lies on the z–axis and carries a current of 25 A, as shown.

9) In Figure 28.4, the force exerted on section 1 due to the 25 A current is closest to:

A) zero

B) $(+2 \times 10^{-4}\,N)\,i$

C) $(-2 \times 10^{-4}\,N)\,j$

D) $(-4 \times 10^{-4}\,N)\,i$

E) $(+4 \times 10^{-4}\,N)\,j$

Answer: C
Var: 1

10) In Figure 28.4, the force exerted on section 2 due to the 25 A current is closest to:

A) zero

B) $(+1.2 \times 10^{-4}\,N)\,i$

C) $(-1.2 \times 10^{-4}\,N)\,j$

D) $(+1.7 \times 10^{-5}\,N)\,i \; + (1.7 \times 10^{-5}\,N)\,j$

E) $(+1.7 \times 10^{-5}\,N)\,i \; - (1.7 \times 10^{-5}\,N)\,j$

Answer: A
Var: 1

11) In Figure 28.4, the vertical axis that passes through the center of mass of the loop has coordinates of x = y = 4.42 cm. The magnitude of the torque on the loop, about this vertical axis is closest to:

A) zero

B) $6 \times 10^{-6}\,N \cdot m$

C) $6 \times 10^{-6}\,N \cdot m$

D) $6 \times 10^{-6}\,N \cdot m$

E) $6 \times 10^{-6}\,N \cdot m$

Answer: E
Var: 1

Figure 28.5

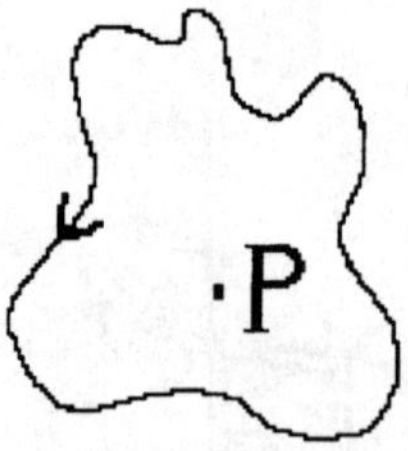

12) In Figure 28.5, an irregular loop of wire carrying a current lies in the plane of the paper here. Suppose that now the loop is distorted into some other shape while remaining in the same plane. Point P is still within the loop. Which of the following is a true statement concerning this situation?

A) The magnetic field at point P will always lie in the plane of the paper.

B) It is possible that the magnetic field at point P is zero.

C) The magnetic field at point P will not change in magnitude when the loop is distorted.

D) The magnetic field at P will not change in direction when the loop is distorted.

E) None of these are true.

Answer: D
Var: 1

13) When using the equation $\vec{B} = \dfrac{\mu_0 d\vec{\ell} \times \vec{r}}{4\pi r^2}$ to find the magnetic field due to a current in a wire, it is important to recognize that

A) this expression must be integrated over all values of r to find the total magnetic field.

B) this expression must be integrated over the length of the wire to find the total magnetic field.

C) $\vec{d\ell}$ is a small element of displacement along an imaginary path surrounding the wire.

D) $\vec{r}$ is a vector directed from the point at which the field is to be found toward a small element of length $\vec{d\ell}$ on the wire.

E) $\vec{dB}$ is the change in magnetic field when one moves an additional distance $\vec{dr}$ from the wire.

Answer: B
Var: 1

14)

Figure 28.6a

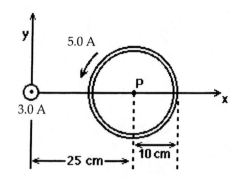

A long straight wire on the z–axis carries a current of 3.0 A in the positive direction. A circular loop in the x–y plane, of radius 10 cm, carries a 5.0 A current, as shown. Point P, at the center of the loop, is 25 cm from the z–axis. In Figure 28.6a, a circular coil of four turns, 2 cm in diameter, is placed in the x–y plane with its center at P. The magnetic flux through the coil is closest to:

A) 9.9×10^{-9} Wb

B) 4.9×10^{-9} Wb

C) 2.0×10^{-8} Wb

D) 1.5×10^{-8} Wb

E) 4.0×10^{-8} Wb

Answer: A
Var: 50+

15)

Figure 28.6b

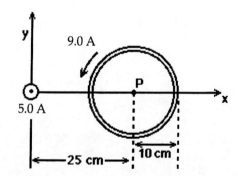

A long straight wire on the z–axis carries a current of 5.0 A in the positive direction. A circular loop in the x–y plane, of radius 10 cm, carries a 9.0 A current, as shown. Point P, at the center of the loop, is 25 cm from the z–axis. In Figure 28.6b, the angle that the magnetic field at P forms with the positive y–direction is closest to:

A) 86°   B) 65°   C) 45°   D) 25°   E) 4.0°

Answer: A
Var: 50+

16)

Figure 28.6c

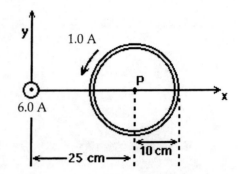

A long straight wire on the z-axis carries a current of 6.0 A in the positive direction. A circular loop in the x-y plane, of radius 10 cm, carries a 1.0 A current, as shown. Point P, at the center of the loop, is 25 cm from the z-axis. In Figure 28.6c, a current element I dl, equal to 8.00×10^{-3} A • m in the positive z-direction, is placed at P. The x-component of the force on the current element is closest to:

A) -3.8×10^{-8} N

B) $+3.8 \times 10^{-8}$ N

C) -1.9×10^{-8} N

D) $+1.9 \times 10^{-8}$ N

E) zero

Answer: A
Var: 50+

17)

Figure 28.6d

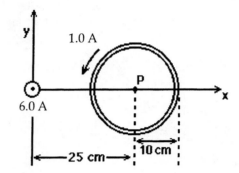

A long straight wire on the z-axis carries a current of 6.0 A in the positive direction. A circular loop in the x–y plane, of radius 10 cm, carries a 1.0 A current, as shown. Point P, at the center of the loop, is 25 cm from the z-axis. In Figure 28.6d, an electron is projected from P with a velocity of 4.0×10^6 m/s in the negative x-direction. The y-component of the force on the electron is closest to:

A) -4.0×10^{-18} N

B) $+4.0 \times 10^{-18}$ N

C) -2.0×10^{-18} N

D) $+2.0 \times 10^{-18}$ N

E) zero

Answer: A
Var: 50+

Figure 28.7

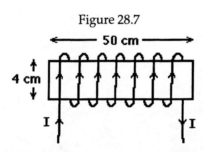

18) A solenoid is wound with 110 turns on a form 4 cm in diameter and 50 cm long. The windings carry a current in the sense that is shown. The current produces a magnetic field, of magnitude 2.5 mT, at the center of the solenoid. In Figure 28.7, the current in the solenoid windings is closest to:

A) 9.0 A   B) 7.9 A   C) 6.8 A   D) 11 A   E) 10 A

Answer: A
Var: 50+

19) A solenoid is wound with 690 turns on a form 4 cm in diameter and 50 cm long. The windings carry a current in the sense that is shown. The current produces a magnetic field, of magnitude 2.6 mT, at the center of the solenoid. In Figure 29.7, the magnetic flux in the solenoid is closest to:

A) 3.3×10^{-6} Wb

B) 1.6×10^{-6} Wb

C) 2.6×10^{-5} Wb

D) 6.5×10^{-6} Wb

E) 1.3×10^{-5} Wb

Answer: A
Var: 50+

Figure 28.8

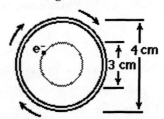

20) In Figure 28.8, a view of the solenoid, showing the clockwise sense of the current in the windings, is given. An electron is in circular motion near the center of the solenoid, with an orbital diameter of 3.0 cm. The speed of the electron and the sense of the orbital motion are closest to:

A) 4×10^6 m/s, clockwise

B) 6×10^6 m/s, clockwise

C) 8×10^6 m/s, clockwise

D) 4×10^6 m/s, counterclockwise

E) 10×10^6 m/s, counterclockwise

Answer: A
Var: 1

Figure 28.9

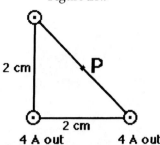

21) Three very long, straight, parallel wires each carry currents of 4 A, directed out of the page in the drawing in Figure 28.9. The wires pass through the vertices of a right isosceles triangle of side 2 cm. What is the magnitude of the magnetic field at point P at the midpoint of the hypotenuse of the triangle?

    A) 4.42×10^{-6} T

    B) 1.77×10^{-5} T

    C) 5.66×10^{-5} T

    D) 1.26×10^{-4} T

    E) 1.77×10^{-6} T

Answer: C
Var: 1

22) A metallic weight is suspended from a metal spring. If now a current is passed through the spring,

    A) the spring will contract, raising the weight.

    B) the spring will extend, lowering the weight.

    C) the weight will not move.

    D) whether or not the weight moves up or down depends on what the weight is made of (i.e. whether or not it is magnetizable).

    E) None of these are true.

Answer: A
Var: 1

Figure 28.10

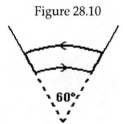

23) In Figure 28.10, what is the magnetic field at the center of the two concentric arcs? The inner arc is of radius 4 cms and the outer arc is of radius 6 cms. The loop carries a current of 4 A.

    A) 2.09×10^{-5} T

    B) 4.45×10^{-5} T

    C) 3.49×10^{-6} T

    D) 7.14×10^{-4} T

    E) 7.95×10^{-6} T

Answer: C
Var: 1

Figure 28.11

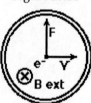

A conducting ring of radius R = 0.040 m carries a current of unknown magnitude and sense. A uniform external magnetic field B_{ext} = 90 μT, directed into the plane, is applied as shown. An electron is projected from the center of the ring, with an initial velocity u = 5.0×10^5 m/s towards the right. The electron experiences an initial force F = 1.2×10^{-17} N in the upward direction, as shown.

24) In Figure 28.11, the magnetic field, produced by the current, at the center of the ring, in μT, is closest to:

    A) 60   B) 150   C) 150   D) 240   E) 240

Answer: D
Var: 1

25) In Figure 28.11, the current in the ring is changed, but the magnetic field is unchanged. The electron, projected as before with the same initial velocity, experiences zero force at the center of the ring. This new current in the ring, and its sense, are closest to:

    A) 6 A, clockwise

    B) 10 A, clockwise

    C) 15 A, clockwise

    D) 6 A, counterclockwise

    E) 10 A, counterclockwise

Answer: D
Var: 1

Figure 28.12

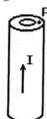

26) In Figure 28.12, consider a long hollow cylindrical metal pipe of inner radius a and outer radius b in which flows a current I uniformly distributed over the cross section of the conductor. In order to calculate the magnetic field at a point P a distance R from the axis, where $a < r < b$, i.e. P is within the metal,

A) it would be easiest to use the Biot Savart Law.

B) we carry out a line integral along a path which encloses all of the current in the conductor.

C) we recognize that B is directed radially outward because of the cylindrical radial symmetry of problem.

D) we evaluate $\int \vec{B} \cdot \vec{d\ell}$, where $\vec{d\ell}$ is directed along the direction of current flow.

E) we evaluate a line integral along a path that passes through the point P.

Answer: E
Var: 1

27) A type of transmission line for electromagnetic waves consists of two parallel conducting planes (assumed infinite in width) separated by a distance A. Each carries the same uniform current antiparallel surface current density of 16 A/m. What is the value of the magnetic field 1 mm from one of the planes if a = 0.8 cm?

A) 3.20 x 10^{-3} T

B) 1.00 x 10^{-5} T

C) 4.63 x 10^{-5} T

D) 2.01 x 10^{-5} T

E) 7.07 x 10^{-4} T

Answer: D
Var: 1

305

Figure 28.13

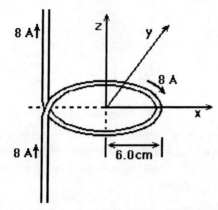

28) In Figure 28.13, an insulated wire is bent into a circular loop of radius 6.0 cm and has two long straight sections. The loop is in the x–y plane, with the center at the origin. The straight sections are parallel to the z-axis. The wire carries a current of 8 A. The magnitude of the magnetic field at the origin, in μT, is closest to:

A) 70   B) 80   C) 90   D) 100   E) 110

Answer: C
Var: 1

Figure 28.14

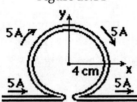

29) In Figure 28.14, a wire is bent into the shape of an Omega, with a circular loop of radius 4.0 cm and two long straight sections. The loop is in the x–y plane, with the center at the origin. The straight sections are parallel to the x-axis. The wire carries a 5 A current, as shown. The magnitude of the magnetic field at the center of the loop, in μT, is closest to:

A) 25   B) 40   C) 55   D) 80   E) 105

Answer: C
Var: 1

Figure 28.15

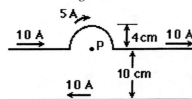

30) In Figure 28.15, the upper wire has two long straight sections and a semicircular arc of radius 4.0 cm. The lower wire is long and straight. The upper sections are parallel to the lower wire and are 10 cm above it. The upper straight sections are parallel to the lower wire and are 10 cm above it. The upper wire carries a current of 10 A and the lower wire carries the return current. The magnitude of the magnetic field at P, which is at the center of the semicircular arc, in μT, is closest to:

A) 60   B) 80   C) 100   D) 140   E) 180

Answer: C
Var: 1

31) Which of the following would be most useful if you were to attempt to calculate the magnetic field at the center of a square loop of wire?

A) $\overrightarrow{dF} = i \, \overrightarrow{d\ell} \times \overrightarrow{B}$

B) $\int \overrightarrow{B} \cdot \overrightarrow{d\ell} = \mu_o \, i$

C) $dB = \dfrac{\mu_o \, i}{4\pi} \dfrac{d\ell \sin \theta}{4^2}$

D) $B = \dfrac{\mu_o \, i}{2\pi r}$ for a long straight wire.

E) $B = \dfrac{\mu_o \, i}{2r}$ at the center of a circular loop.

Answer: C
Var: 1

32) A 2 μF capacitor is connected in series with a 500 kΩ resistor. What is the displacement current through the capacitor 500 ms after the combination begins to be charged by a 12 volt battery?

A) 4.66×10^{-5} A

B) 1.20×10^{-5} A

C) 2.19×10^{-5} A

D) 8.80×10^{-6} A

E) 9.44×10^{-6} A

Answer: E
Var: 1

Short Answer Questions

Figure 28.16

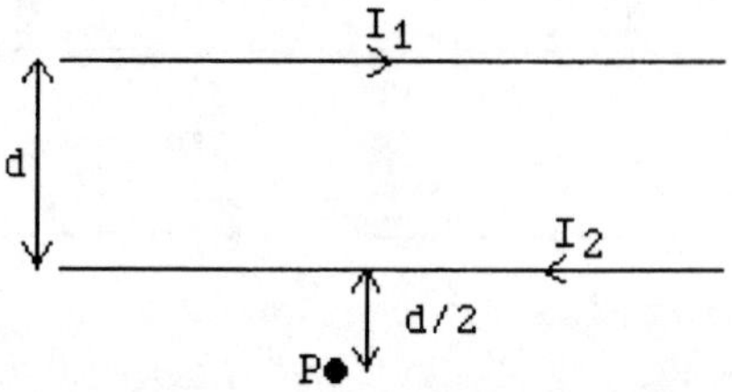

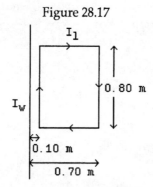

1) In Figure 28.16, the two long straight wires are separated by a distance of d = 0.60 m. The currents are I_1 = 5.0 A to the right in the upper wire and I_2 = 6.0 A to the left in the lower wire. What is the magnitude and direction of the magnetic field at point P, that is a distance d/2 = 0.30 m below the lower wire?

(NOTE: μ_0 = 4π x 10^{-7}T • m/A.)

Answer: B = 2.9 x 10^{-6} T, directed out of the plane of the paper.
Var: 50+

Figure 28.17

I_1

I_w

0.80 m

0.10 m

0.70 m

2) In Figure 28.17, a rectangular current loop is carrying current I_1 = 8.0 A, in the direction is located near a long wire carrying a current I_w. The long wire is parallel to the sides of the rectangle. The rectangle loop has length 0.80 m and its sides are 0.10 m and 0.70 m from the wire. If the net force on the loop is to have magnitude 2.3 x 10^{-6} N and is to be directed towards the wire, what must be the (a) magnitude and (b) direction (from top to bottom or from bottom to top in the sketch) of the current I_w in the wire? (NOTE:

μ_0 = 4π x 10^{-7} T • m/A.)

Answer: (a) 0.21 A
         (b) from bottom to top
Var: 50+

3) A student needs to make a solenoid that produces 1.08 T at its center. He will wrap a wire around a solid cylinder of iron with a relative permeability K_m of 1400, a length of 16.3 cm, and a radius of 1.92 cm. If the wire can carry a maximum current of 1.28 amp, how many turns of wire are needed along the entire cylinder to produce the desired B field?

Answer: 78.2 turns
Var: 50+

Figure 28.18

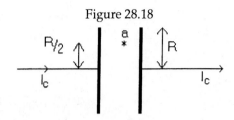

4) In Figure 28.18, a parallel-plate capacitor with circular plates of radius $R = 99.00$ cm and separated by a distance of 4.00 mm is being charged. The conduction current in the wires is $I_c = 6.40$ A. Calculate the magnitude and direction of the induced magnetic field at point a, which is 3.00 cm above the center of the plates. (NOTE: $\mu_o = 4\pi \times 10^{-7}$ T $\cdot$ m/A.)

Answer: 3.92×10^{-8} T, directed out of the plane of the paper
Var: 50+

5) A coaxial cable consists of an inner cylindrical conductor of radius $R_1 = 0.040$ m on the axis of an outer hollow cylindrical conductor of inner radius $R_2 = 0.080$ m and outer radius $R_3 = 0.090$ m. The inner conductor carries current $I_1 = 3.00$ A in one direction, and the outer conductor carries current $I_2 = 8.10$ A in the opposite direction. What is the value of the magnetic field at the following distances from the axis of the cable:
(a) at r = 0.060 m (in the gap midway between the two conductors), and
(b) at r = 0.150 m (outside the cable)?
(NOTE: $U_o = 4\pi \times 10^{-7}$ T $\cdot$ m/A.)

Answer: (a) $B = 1.00 \times 10^{-5}$ T
(b) $B = 6.80 \times 10^{-6}$ T
Var: 50+

Chapter 29   Electromagnetic Induction

Multiple Choice Questions

Figure 29.1

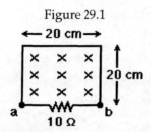

1) In Figure 29.1, a wire and a 10 ohm resistor are used to form a circuit in the shape of a square, 20 cm by 20 cm. A uniform but non–steady magnetic field is directed into the plane of the circuit. The magnitude of the magnetic field is decreased from 1.20 T to 0.40 T in a time interval of 55 ms. The average induced current and its direction through the resistor, in this time interval, are closest to:

A) 58 mA, from b to a

B) 35 mA, from b to a

C) 58 mA, from a to b

D) 35 mA, from a to b

E) 87 mA, from a to b

Answer: A
Var: 50+

2) A search coil is tightly wound on a plastic form, 4.40 cm in diameter. The coil has 60 turns and a resistance of 5.8 ohms. The coil is placed between the poles of magnet, and is snatched away in a time interval of 0.20 s. The charge displaced during this time interval is 0.020 C. The magnetic field between the poles of the magnet is closest to:

A) 1.3 T   B) 1.1 T   C) 1.5 T   D) 0.87 T   E) 0.67 T

Answer: A
Var: 50+

Figure 29.2

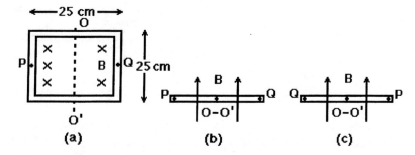

(a)   (b)   (c)

3) In Figure 29.2, a coil of 8 turns is wound on a square frame, 25 cm by 25 cm. The resistance of the coil is 4.1 ohms. The coil is initially in a horizontal plane and a uniform vertical magnetic field B is present. Two views of the initial orientation of the coil are given in figs (a) and (b). Points P and Q are initially of the left and right sides of the frame, respectively. The coil is flopped over about axis O-O', through 180 degrees, to the final horizontal orientation, shown in fig (c). The time interval, during which the coil is flipped over, is 0.50 s. The average induced current in the coil during the 0.50 s time interval is 96 ma. The magnitude of the magnetic field which is present is closest to:

A) 0.20 T   B) 0.39 T   C) 0.79 T   D) 1.6 T   E) 3.1 T

Answer: A
Var: 50+

4)   Figure 29.3a

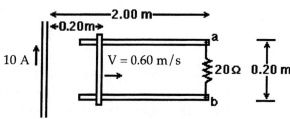

A long vertical wire carries a steady 10 A current. A pair of rails are horizontal and are 0.20 m apart. A 20 ohm resistor connects points a and b, at the end of the rails. A bar is in contact with the rails, and is moved by an external force with a constant velocity of 0.60 m/s, as shown. The bar and the rails have negligible resistance. At a given instant t_1, the bar is 0.20 m from the wire, as shown. In Figure 29.3a, at time t_1, the induced current and its direction through the resistor are closest to:

A) 0.060 μA, from a to b
B) 0.060 μA, from b to a
C) 0.030 μA, from a to b
D) 0.030 μA, from b to a
E) 0.18 μA, from b to a

Answer: A
Var: 50+

5)

Figure 29.3b

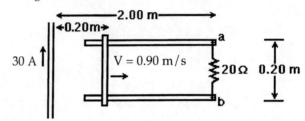

A long vertical wire carries a steady 30 A current. A pair of rails are horizontal and are 0.20 m apart. A 20 ohm resistor connects points a and b, at the end of the rails. A bar is in contact with the rails, and is moved by an external force with a constant velocity of 0.90 m/s, as shown. The bar and the rails have negligible resistance. At a given instant t_1, the bar is 0.20 m from the wire, as shown. In Figure 29.3b, at a later instant t_2, the potential difference across the resistor is 0.86 μV. The time interval, $\Delta t = t_2 - t_1$ is closest to:

A) 1.2 s   B) 1.3 s   C) 1.4 s   D) 1.5 s   E) 1.6 s

Answer: A
Var: 50+

6)

Figure 29.4a

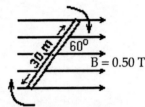

Wire is wound on a square frame, 30 cm by 30 cm, to form a coil of 6 turns. The frame is mounted on a horizontal shaft through its center (perpendicular to the plane of the diagram). The coil is in clockwise rotation, with a period of 0.020 s. A uniform, horizontal, magnetic field of 0.50 T is present. At a given instant, the plane of the coil forms a 60° angle with the horizontal, as shown. In Figure 29.4a, at that instant, the flux through the coil is closest to:

A) 0.039 Wb   B) 0.031 Wb   C) 0.023 Wb   D) 0.015 Wb   E) 0.046 Wb

Answer: A
Var: 50+

312

7)   Figure 29.4b

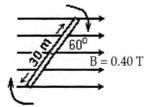

Wire is wound on a square frame, 30 cm by 30 cm, to form a coil of 7 turns. The frame is mounted on a horizontal shaft through its center (perpendicular to the plane of the diagram). The coil is in clockwise rotation, with a period of 0.060 s. A uniform, horizontal, magnetic field of 0.40 T is present. At a given instant, the plane of the coil forms a $60°$ angle with the horizontal, as shown. In Figure 29.4b, at that instant, the emf induced in the coil is closest to:

A) 13 V   B) 23 V   C) 2.1 V   D) 3.6 V   E) 26 V

Answer: A
Var: 50+

Figure 29.5

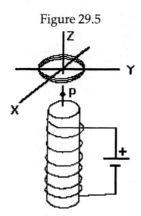

8) In Figure 29.5, a coil of wire is placed on the axis of a solenoid carrying a DC current. Which of the following will NOT result in an EMF being induced in the coil?

A) Rotate the coil about the x–axis.

B) Rotate the coil about the y–axis.

C) Rotate the coil about the z–axis.

D) Move the coil toward point P.

E) Change the current in the solenoid.

Answer: C
Var: 1

9) A circular coil of 30 turns and radius 5 cms is placed with its plane oriented at $90°$ to a magnetic field of 0.1 T. The field is now increased at a steady rate, reaching a value of 0.4 T after 4 seconds. What EMF is induced in the coil?

A) 0.018 V   B) 0.023 V   C) 0.029 V   D) 0.035 V   E) 0.040 V

Answer: A
Var: 50+

Figure 29.6

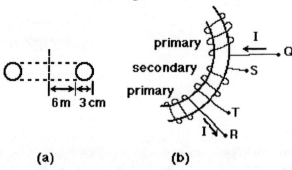

(a)   **(b)**

10) The cross section of a toroidal form is shown in fig (a). A primary coil has 900 turns, which are wound completely around the toroidal form. The terminals of the primary coil are Q and R. A secondary circular coil of 7 turns is tightly wound around the form, with terminals S and T. The primary and secondary windings are shown in fig (b). A steady current of 810 mA is supplied to the primary windings by a battery which is not shown. A switch (not shown) is opened, which disconnects terminals Q and R from the battery. The current in the primary coil falls to zero in a time interval of 0.80 s. In Figure 29.6, the average emf in the primary coil, in the 0.8 s time interval, is closest to:

   A) 19 μV   B) 11 μV   C) 15 μV   D) 23 μV   E) zero

   Answer: A
   Var: 50+

11) The cross section of a toroidal form is shown in fig (a). A primary coil has 500 turns, which are wound completely around the toroidal form. The terminals of the primary coil are Q and R. A secondary circular coil of 8 turns is tightly wound around the form, with terminals S and T. The primary and secondary windings are shown in fig (b). A steady current of 300 mA is supplied to the primary windings by a battery which is not shown. A switch (not shown) is opened, which disconnects terminals Q and R from the battery. The current in the primary coil falls to zero in a time interval of 0.10 s. In Figure 29.6, the average emf in the secondary coil, in the 0.1 s time interval, is closest to:

   A) 0.28 μV   B) 0.16 μV   C) 0.22 μV   D) 0.34 μV   E) 0.40 μV

   Answer: A
   Var: 50+

12) The polarities of the induced emf's in the primary and secondary coils are:

   A) Q and R are at the same potential; S is positive and T is negative

   B) Q is positive and R is negative; S is positive and T is negative

   C) Q is positive and R is negative; T is positive and S is negative

   D) R is positive and Q is negative; S is positive and T is negative

   E) R is positive and Q is negative; T is positive and S is negative

   Answer: E
   Var: 1

Figure 29.7

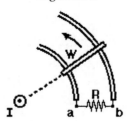

13) In Figure 29.7, a straight wire carries a steady current I. A bar is in contact with a pair of circular rails, and rotates about the straight wire. The induced current through the resistor R is:

A) zero   B) from a to b   C) from b to a

Answer: A
Var: 1

Figure 29.8

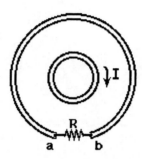

14) In Figure 29.8, the inner loop carries a current I that is increasing. The resistor R is in the outer loop. The induced current through the resistor R is:

A) zero   B) from a to b   C) from b to a

Answer: B
Var: 1

Figure 29.9

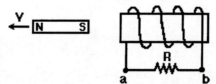

15) In Figure 29.9, a bar magnet moves away from the solenoid. The induced current through the resistor R is:

A) zero   B) from a to b   C) from b to a

Answer: B
Var: 1

Figure 29.10

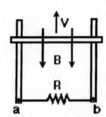

16) In Figure 29.10, a bar is in contact with a pair of parallel rails and is in motion with velocity v. A uniform magnetic field is present. The induced current through the resistor R is:

    A) zero   B) from a to b   C) from b to a

Answer: A
Var: 1

Figure 29.11

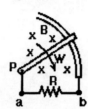

17) In Figure 29.11, one end of a bar is in contact with a circular rail and the other end is pivoted at P. A steady, uniform, magnetic field B is present. The bar rotates about P. The induced current through the resistor R is:

    A) zero   B) from a to b   C) from b to a

Answer: C
Var: 1

Figure 29.12

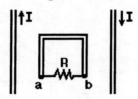

18) In Figure 29.12, two parallel wires carry a current I in opposite directions. A rectangular loop is midway between the wires. The current I is decreasing. The induced current through the resistor R is:

    A) zero   B) from a to b   C) from b to a

Answer: B
Var: 1

Figure 29.13

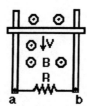

19) In Figure 29.13, a bar is in contact with a pair of parallel rails. A steady, uniform, magnetic field, perpendicular to the plane of the rails, is present. The bar is in motion with velocity v. The induced current through the resistor R is:

A) zero   B) from a to b   C) from b to a

Answer: B
Var: 1

Figure 29.14

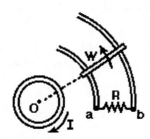

20) In Figure 29.14, a loop carries a steady current I. A bar is in contact with a pair of circular rails, and rotates about the center of the loop. The induced current through the resistor R is:

A) zero   B) from a to b   C) from b to a

Answer: C
Var: 1

Figure 29.15

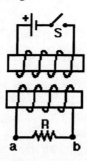

21) In Figure 29.15, two solenoids are side by side. The switch S, initially open, is closed. The induced current through the resistor R is:

A) zero   B) from a to b   C) from b to a

Answer: C
Var: 1

Figure 29.16

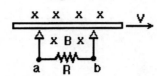

22) In Figure 29.16, a long bar slides on two contact points and is in motion with velocity **v**. A steady, uniform, magnetic field B is present. The induced current through the resistor R is:

    A) zero   B) from a to b   C) from b to a

Answer: A
Var: 1

Figure 29.17

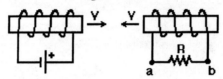

23) In Figure 29.17, a battery supplies a steady current to the solenoid on the left. The two solenoids are moving towards each other. The induced current through the resistor R is:

    A) zero   B) from a to b   C) from b to a

Answer: B
Var: 1

Figure 29.18

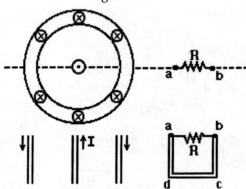

24) In Figure 29.18, a long straight wire carries a steady current I, and a long coaxial cylinder returns the same current. A rectangular loop *abcd* is outside the cylinder. A top view, and a cross–section view, through the dotted line. The current I is increasing. The induced current through the resistor R is:

    A) zero   B) from a to b   C) from b to a

Answer: A
Var: 1

Figure 29.19

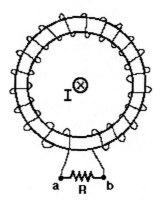

25) In Figure 29.19, a straight wire carries a current I. The wire passes through the center of a toroidal coil. The current is quickly reduced to zero. The induced current through the resistor R is:

   A) zero   B) from a to b   C) from b to a

Answer: C
Var: 1

26) The EMF produced by a generator is $V = V_0 \cos \omega t$. If the angular velocity of the generator is doubled, and everything else remains the same, the new EMF will be

   A) $V_0 \cos 2\omega t$

   B) $V_0 \cos 1/2\omega t$

   C) $2V_0 \cos \omega t$

   D) $2V_0 \cos 2\omega t$

   E) $V_0 \cos \omega t$

Answer: D
Var: 1

27) A coil of 100 turns, area 3.0 cms^2 and resistance 71 ohms is placed in a magnetic field with the plane of the coil perpendicular to the magnetic field. The coil is connected to a galvanometer that measures the total charge that flows through the coil. The coil is jerked out of the magnetic field in 100 ms and a charge of 7.6 μC is observed to flow through the galvanometer. What is the magnitude of the magnetic field?

   A) 0.018 T   B) 0.036 T   C) 0.090 T   D) 0.13 T   E) 0.17 T

Answer: A
Var: 50+

319

Figure 29.20

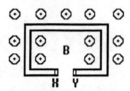

28) In Figure 29.20, a C-shaped conductor is in a uniform magnetic field B, which is increasing. The polarity of the induced emf in terminals X and Y is:

A) X and Y are at the same potential

B) X is positive and Y is negative

C) Y is positive and X is negative

Answer: C
Var: 1

Figure 29.21

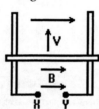

29) In Figure 29.21, a bar is in contact with a pair of parallel rails. A steady, uniform, magnetic field B is present. The bar is in motion with velocity v. The polarity of the induced emf in terminals X and Y is:

A) X and Y are at the same potential

B) X is positive and Y is negative

C) Y is positive and X is negative

Answer: A
Var: 1

Figure 29.22

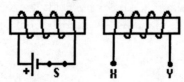

30) In Figure 29.22, two solenoids are in line. The switch S, initially closed, is opened. The polarity of the induced emf in terminals X and Y is:

A) X and Y are at the same potential

B) X is positive and Y is negative

C) Y is positive and X is negative

Answer: B
Var: 1

Figure 29.23

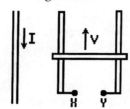

31) In Figure 29.23, a straight wire carries a steady current I. A bar is in contact with a pair of rails and is in motion with velocity **v**. The polarity of the induced emf in terminals X and Y is:

A) X and Y are at the same potential

B) X is positive and Y is negative

C) Y is positive and X is negative

Answer: C
Var: 1

Figure 29.24

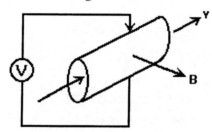

32) In Figure 29.24, an electromagnetic flowmeter is useful when it is desirable not to interrupt the system in which the fluid is flowing (e.g. for the blood in an artery during heart surgery). Such a device is illustrated. The conducting fluid moves with velocity v in a tube of diameter d perpendicular to which is a magnetic field B. A voltage V is induced between opposite sides of the tube. Given B = 0.120 T, d = 1.2 cm, and a measured voltage of 6.78 mV, determine the speed of the blood.

A) 4.7 m/s

B) 25 m/s

C) 0.18 m/s

D) 2.5 m/s

E) 1.8×10^3 m/s

Answer: A
Var: 50+

33) It is known that birds can detect the earth's magnetic field, but the mechanism of how they do this is not known. It has been suggested that perhaps they detect a motional EMF as they fly north to south, but it turns out that the induced voltages are small compared to the voltages normally encountered in cells, so this is probably not the mechanism involved. To check this out, calculate the induced voltage for a wild goose with a wingspan of 1.2 m flying due south at 23 m/s at a point where the earth's magnetic field is 5×10^{-5} directed downward from horizontal by $37°$. The expected voltage would be about

A) 0.83 mV   B) 1.1 mV   C) 1.4 mV   D) 0.11 mV   E) 0.42 mV

Answer: A
Var: 50+

34) At its normal operating speed, an electric fan motor draws a current of 3.1 A when plugged into a 120 V outlet. However, if the blade is held and prevented from rotating, the current drawn rises to 24.8 A. What back EMF does the motor generate under normal operating conditions?

A) 105 V   B) 15.0 V   C) 37.5 V   D) 60.0 V   E) 82.5 V

Answer: A
Var: 50+

35) An important feature of induced electric fields is that they

A) are not conservative.

B) act only on moving electric charges, not on static ones.

C) are characterized by having sources and sinks.

D) have a potential function associated with them that is time dependent.

E) are parallel to the changing magnetic field that induces them.

Answer: A
Var: 1

36) If you hold a sheet of copper in a strong permanent magnet, with the plane of the sheet perpendicular to the magnetic field, and quickly jerk it out,

A) you will experience a magnetic force opposing your action.

B) you will experience a magnetic force assisting your action.

C) you will feel no magnetic force.

D) any force you feel will be due mainly to iron impurities in the copper, since copper itself is not magnetic.

E) None of these are true.

Answer: A
Var: 1

322

Short Answer Questions

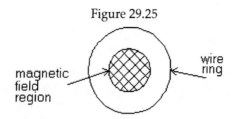

Figure 29.25

1) In Figure 29.25, a uniform magnetic field B is confined to a cylindrical volume of radius 0.03 m. B is directed into the plane of the paper and is increasing at a constant rate of $\Delta B/\Delta t = 0.100$ T/s. Calculate the magnitude and direction of the current induced in a circular wire ring of radius 0.16 m and resistance 5.1 Ω that encircles the magnetic field region.

Answer: 5.5×10^{-5} A, counterclockwise

Var: 50+

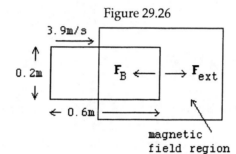

Figure 29.26

2) In Figure 29.26, there is a uniform magnetic field of magnitude B = 2.2 T and directed into the plane of the paper in the region shown. Outside this region the magnetic field is zero. A rectangular loop 0.20 m by 0.60 m and of resistance 3 Ω is being pulled into the magnetic field by an external force, as shown.
(a) What is the direction (clockwise or counterclockwise) of the current induced in the loop?
(b) Calculate the magnitude of the external force F_{ext} required to move the loop at a constant speed of v = 3.9 m/s. The mass of the loop is 0.008 kg.

Answer: (a) counterclockwise
(b) 3×10^{-1} N

Var: 50+

Figure 29.27

3) In Figure 29.27, a large cylindrical loop of 227 turns and radius 67.0 cm carries a current of 54.0 A. A small square loop of 27 turns and 1.00 cm on a side is placed at the center of the large loop. If the current in the large loop drops to 0 in 0.0470 s, find the induced emf in the small loop. (Assume that the magnetic field in the region of the square loop is uniform.)

Answer: 6.60×10^{-4} V

Var: 50+

Figure 29.28

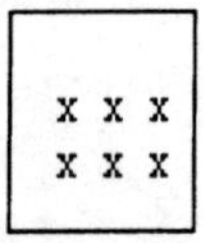

x x x
x x x

4) In Figure 29.28, a flexible square loop 0.700 m on a side is made of wire of resistance 0.200 Ω. A magnetic field with magnitude 1.70 T is directed onto the plane of the loop. A student crushes the wires together forming a loop of zero area in 0.350 s. Find the total amount of charge flowing through the wire.

Answer: 4.17 C
Var: 50+

Figure 29.29

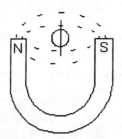

5) In Figure 29.29, a circular loop of area 0.010 m^2 with 62 turns and resistance 1.0 Ω is placed between the poles of a large U–shaped horseshoe magnet, where the magnetic field is 0.11 T. The loop is being rotated about a diameter. How much charge flows through the wire in 1/4 of a revolution.

Answer: 0.068 C
Var: 50+

Chapter 30   Inductance

Multiple Choice Questions

1) An 99 mH solenoid inductor is wound on a form 0.80 m in length and 0.10 m in diameter. A coil is tightly wound around the solenoid at its center. The coil resistance is 7.5 ohms. The mutual inductance of the coil and solenoid is 26 μH. At a given instant, the current in the solenoid is 680 mA, and is decreasing at the rate of 2.5 A/s. The number of turns in the winding of the solenoid is closest to:

   A) 2800   B) 2700   C) 2900   D) 3100   E) 3200

Answer: A
Var: 50+

2) An 86 mH solenoid inductor is wound on a form 0.80 m in length and 0.10 m in diameter. A coil is tightly wound around the solenoid at its center. The coil resistance is 8.0 ohms. The mutual inductance of the coil and solenoid is 12 μH. At a given instant, the current in the solenoid is 120 mA, and is decreasing at the rate of 2.5 A/s. At the given instant, the induced emf in the solenoid is closest to:

   A) 220 mV   B) 240 mV   C) 190 mV   D) 170 mV   E) 150 mV

Answer: A
Var: 50+

3) An 27 mH solenoid inductor is wound on a form 0.80 m in length and 0.10 m in diameter. A coil is tightly wound around the solenoid at its center. The coil resistance is 8.3 ohms. The mutual inductance of the coil and solenoid is 91 μH. At a given instant, the current in the solenoid is 420 mA, and is decreasing at the rate of 2.5 A/s. At the given instant, the flux linkage NΦ for the solenoid is closest to:

   A) 1.1×10^{-2} Wb

   B) 3.8×10^{-3} Wb

   C) 7.6×10^{-3} Wb

   D) 1.5×10^{-2} Wb

   E) 1.9×10^{-2} Wb

Answer: A
Var: 50+

4) An 51 mH solenoid inductor is wound on a form 0.80 m in length and 0.10 m in diameter. A coil is tightly wound around the solenoid at its center. The coil resistance is 6.1 ohms. The mutual inductance of the coil and solenoid is 50 μH. At a given instant, the current in the solenoid is 930 mA, and is decreasing at the rate of 2.5 A/s. At the given instant, the magnetic energy of the solenoid, in μJ, is closest to:

   A) 22,000   B) 19,000   C) 17,000   D) 14,000   E) 11,000

Answer: A
Var: 50+

5) An 49 mH solenoid inductor is wound on a form 0.80 m in length and 0.10 m in diameter. A coil is tightly wound around the solenoid at its center. The coil resistance is 3.8 ohms. The mutual inductance of the coil and solenoid is 53 μH. At a given instant, the current in the solenoid is 680 mA, and is decreasing at the rate of 2.5 A/s. At the given instant, the induced current in the coil is closest to:

A) 35 μA   B) 28 μA   C) 42 μA   D) 49 μA   E) 56 μA

Answer: A
Var: 50+

6)   Figure 30.1a

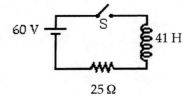

An R–L circuit has a 60 V battery, a 41 H inductor, a 25 ohm resistor, and a switch S, in series, as shown. Initially, the switch is open, and there is no magnetic flux in the inductor. At time t = 0 s, the switch is closed. In Figure 30.1a, when the time t = 1.31 s, the current in the circuit is closest to:

A) 1.3 A   B) 1.1 A   C) 0.88 A   D) 1.9 A   E) 2.4 A

Answer: A
Var: 50+

7)   Figure 30.1b

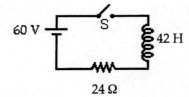

An R–L circuit has a 60 V battery, a 42 H inductor, a 24 ohm resistor, and a switch S, in series, as shown. Initially, the switch is open, and there is no magnetic flux in the inductor. At time t = 0 s, the switch is closed. In Figure 31.1b, when the inductor voltage is 24 V, the time t is closest to:

A) 1.6 s   B) 1.4 s   C) 1.8 s   D) 1.9 s   E) 2.1 s

Answer: A
Var: 50+

8)

Figure 30.1c

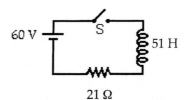

An R–L circuit has a 60 V battery, a 51 H inductor, a 21 ohm resistor, and a switch S, in series, as shown. Initially, the switch is open, and there is no magnetic flux in the inductor. At time t = 0 s, the switch is closed. In Figure 30.1c, when the resistor voltage is equal to the inductor voltage, the current in the circuit is closest to:

A) 1.4 A   B) 0.57 A   C) 1.1 A   D) 0.86 A   E) 1.7 A

Answer: A
Var: 50+

9)

Figure 30.1d

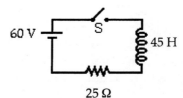

An R–L circuit has a 60 V battery, a 45 H inductor, a 25 ohm resistor, and a switch S, in series, as shown. Initially, the switch is open, and there is no magnetic flux in the inductor. At time t = 0 s, the switch is closed. In Figure 30.1d, the rate of change of the current when the current is 1.5 A is closest to:

A) 0.50 A/s   B) 0.75 A/s   C) 0.67 A/s   D) 0.58 A/s   E) 0.83 A/s

Answer: A
Var: 50+

10)

Figure 30.1e

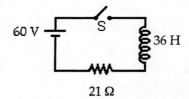

An R–L circuit has a 60 V battery, a 36 H inductor, a 21 ohm resistor, and a switch S, in series, as shown. Initially, the switch is open, and there is no magnetic flux in the inductor. At time t = 0 s, the switch is closed. In Figure 30.1e, when the magnetic energy of the inductor is equal to one half of its terminal value, the time t is closest to:

A) 2.1 s   B) 1.2 s   C) 2.4 s   D) 1.7 s   E) 2.8 s

Answer: A
Var: 50+

11)   Figure 30.2a

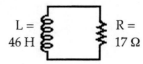

An R–L circuit is shown, with a 17 ohm resistor and an ideal 46 H inductor, that has zero
resistance. At time t = 0 s, there is a 12A current in the circuit. In Figure 30.2a, at time t = 0 s, the
rate of change of the current is closest to:

A) –4.4 A/s   B) –11 A/s   C) –18 A/s   D) –25 A/s   E) –32 A/s

Answer: A
Var: 50+

12)   Figure 30.2b

An R–L circuit is shown, with a 25 ohm resistor and an ideal 46 H inductor, that has zero
resistance. At time t = 0 s, there is a 12A current in the circuit. In Figure 30.2b, when the
magnetic energy of the inductor is 1600 J, the rate of dissipation in the resistor is closest to:

A) 1700 W   B) 430 W   C) 870 W   D) 1300 W   E) 2200 W

Answer: A
Var: 50+

13)   Figure 30.2c

An R–L circuit is shown, with a 10 ohm resistor and an ideal 32 H inductor, that has zero
resistance. At time t = 0 s, there is a 12A current in the circuit. In Figure 30.2c, when the current
is decreasing at the rate of 2.0 A/s, the time t is closest to:

A) 2.0 s   B) 1.2 s   C) 2.8 s   D) 3.6 s   E) 4.4 s

Answer: A
Var: 50+

14)   Figure 30.2d

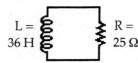

An R–L circuit is shown, with a 25 ohm resistor and an ideal 36 H inductor, that has zero resistance. At time t = 0 s, there is a 12A current in the circuit. In Figure 30.2d, when the time t is equal to 5.0 s, the inductor emf is closest to:

   A) 9.3 V   B) 8.5 V   C) 7.8 V   D) 10 V   E) 11 V

Answer: A
Var: 50+

15)   Figure 30.2e

An R–L circuit is shown, with a 23 ohm resistor and an ideal 42 H inductor, that has zero resistance. At time t = 0 s, there is a 12A current in the circuit. In Figure 30.2e, when the magnetic energy of the inductor is 800 J, the time t is closest to:

   A) 1.2 s   B) 1.5 s   C) 0.97 s   D) 0.73 s   E) 0.49 s

Answer: A
Var: 50+

16) Two coils are connected in series. To obtain the maximum mutual inductance,

   A) the coils should be far apart.

   B) the axes of the coils should be perpendicular.

   C) one coil should be wound clockwise and one counterclockwise about the same axis.

   D) it makes no difference how the coils are oriented, as long as they are in series.

   E) None of these are true.

Answer: E
Var: 1

17) A 5 H inductor carries a current of 2 amps. How can a self–induced EMF of 50 volts be made to appear across the inductor?

   A) Change the current at the rate of 10 amps/sec.

   B) Change the current to 10 amps.

   C) Break the circuit instantaneously.

   D) Change the current uniformly to zero in 20 seconds.

   E) None of these.

Answer: A
Var: 1

Figure 30.3

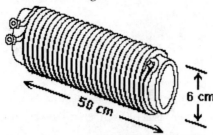

A graduate student wished to construct a furnace for heat treating small metal castings. Using a ceramic tube as a core, he wraps 1000 turns of nichrome resistance wire over a length of 50 cms. The tube diameter is 6 cms. He first solders one end of the resistance wire to a terminal post, then wraps 500 turns of wire along the tube. At the end of the tube he bends the wire around a binding post and then wraps a second layer of 500 turns on top of the first 500 turns. The details of how this is done is shown carefully in the sketch above. The total wire resistance used is 12 ohms (resistance measured when in operation).

18) In Figure 30.3, consider the following: the student's thesis advisor suggests that perhaps it would be wise to run the furnace on DC to see if this has any effect on diffusion rates in the materials under study. In view of this, the student decides he should give some consideration to whether or not the inductance of his furnace will be a factor in its utilization. Which of the following is the most accurate statement with respect to this question?

A) The inductance of the furnace will depend on whether AC or DC is used.

B) The furnace will have approximately zero inductance.

C) The inductance will depend on the frequency of AC used.

D) The inductance will be approximately 1.78 mh.

E) The inductance will be approximately 3.56 mh.

Answer: B
Var: 1

Situation 30.1

A series circuit contains an 80 μF capacitor, a 20 mH inductor, and a switch. The resistance of the circuit is negligible. Initially, the switch is open, the capacitor voltage is 50 V, and the magnetic energy of the inductor is zero. At time t = 0 s, the switch is closed.

19) In Situation 30.1, the time t at which the magnetic energy of the inductor first reaches its maximum value is closest to:

A) 2 ms   B) 4 ms   C) 6 ms   D) 8 ms   E) 10 ms

Answer: A
Var: 1

20) In Situation 30.1, the maximum current in the circuit is closest to:

A) 2.2 A   B) 2.4 A   C) 2.8 A   D) 3.0 A   E) 3.2 A

Answer: E
Var: 1

21) In Situation 30.1, when the current is 1.5 A, the charge on the capacitor, in μC, is closest to:

A) 2000   B) 2500   C) 3000   D) 3500   E) 4000

Answer: D
Var: 1

22) In Situation 30.1, when the capacitor voltage is 30 V, the rate of change of the current is closest to:

A) 1000 A/s   B) 1500 A/s   C) 2000 A/s   D) 2500 A/s   E) 3000 A/s

Answer: B
Var: 1

23) In Situation 30.1, at a given instant, the magnetic energy of the inductor is twice the electrostatic energy of the capacitor. At that instant, the current is closest to:

A) 2.0 A   B) 2.2 A   C) 2.4 A   D) 2.6 A   E) 2.8 A

Answer: D
Var: 1

Situation 30.2

A real inductor and a 50 μF capacitor are the elements of a L–R–C circuit. The real inductor has an inductance of 80 mH and a resistance of 48 ohms. The circuit is in a state of underdamped oscillation.

24) In Situation 30.2, the angular frequency of the oscillation of the circuit is closest to:

A) 300 rad/s   B) 350 rad/s   C) 400 rad/s   D) 450 rad/s   E) 500 rad/s

Answer: C
Var: 1

25) In Situation 30.2, a series resistor is added to the circuit in order to make it critically damped. The resistance of the added resistor is closest to:

A) 16 Ω   B) 32 Ω   C) 48 Ω   D) 64 Ω   E) 80 Ω

Answer: B
Var: 1

26) In Situation 30.2, the real inductor is replaced by an ideal inductor that has zero resistance, but the original capacitor is retained. The circuit then oscillates without any damping, with an angular frequency of 600 rad/s. The inductance of the ideal inductor is closest to:

A) 50 mH   B) 55 mH   C) 60 mH   D) 65 mH   E) 70 mH

Answer: B
Var: 1

27) What is the significance of the minus sign in the equation $\varepsilon = \dfrac{-d\phi}{dt}$?

    A) An inductive element does not absorb energy in a circuit; instead it delivers energy.

    B) An inductive element does not deliver energy to a circuit; instead it absorbs energy.

    C) The current and voltage in an inductive element are $180°$ out of phase.

    D) Inductive effects always act in a sense to oppose the change which caused them.

    E) An induced EMF always acts to reduce the current in the circuit in which the EMF is induced.

Answer: D
Var: 1

28) Consider a solenoid whose length is three times its diameter.

    A) The stored energy density is greater at the center than at the ends.

    B) The stored energy density is greater at the ends than at the center.

    C) The stored energy density is constant throughout the solenoid.

    D) Energy in the solenoid may be considered to be stored in the windings of the solenoid, rather than in the empty volume inside.

    E) None of these.

Answer: A
Var: 1

29) An LRC circuit has L = 0.600 H, C = 5 x 10^{-5} F and resistance R. What resistance must be used to cause the resonant frequency to be 70% of what it would have been with no resistance in the circuit?

    A) 72 ohms   B) 216 ohms   C) 102 ohms   D) 156 ohms   E) 122 ohms

Answer: D
Var: 1

Short Answer Questions

Figure 30.4

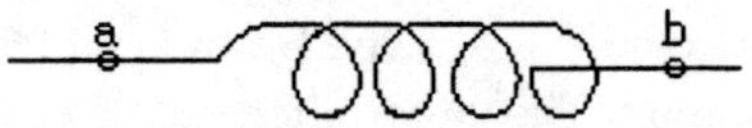

1) In Figure 30.4, the current in a solenoid is decreasing at a rate of –9.8 A/s. The self-induced emf in the solenoid is found to be 8.1 volts.
(a) What is the self-inductance of the solenoid?
(b) If the current is in the direction from b to a in the sketch, which point, a or b is at higher potential? The solenoid has negligible resistance.

Answer: (a) 0.83 H
        (b) point a
Var: 50+

Figure 30.5

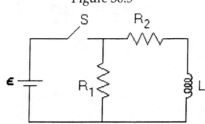

2) Consider the circuit sketched above. The battery has emf $\varepsilon = 15$ volts and negligible internal resistance. The inductance is $L = 0.50$ H and the resistances are $R_1 = 12\ \Omega$ and $R_2 = 9.0\Omega$. Use Figure 30.5 to answer the following questions:

(a) Initially the switch S is open and no currents flow. Then the switch is closed. What is the current in the resistor R_1 just after the switch is closed?

(b) After leaving the switch closed for a long time, it is opened again. Just after it is opened, what is the current in R_1?

Answer: (a) 1.3 A
         (b) 1.7 A
Var: 50+

3) An LC circuit consists of a capacitor with $C = 3.4 \times 10^{-6}$ F and an inductor with $L = 0.080$ H. At $t = 0$ the capacitor has charge 5.4×10^{-6} C and the current in the inductor is zero. The circuit oscillates at its resonant frequency.

(a) How long after $t = 0$ will the current in the circuit be maximum?

(b) What will be this maximum current?

Answer: (a) 8.2×10^{-4} seconds
         (b) 1.0×10^{-2} A
Var: 1

4) A toroidal solenoid has a mean radius of 0.210 m, a cross-sectional area of 2.00×10^{-3} m and 631 turns. What current is required to produce a stored energy of 0.0300 J? (NOTE: $\mu_o = 4\pi \times 10^{-7}$T • m/A.)

Answer: 8.89 A
Var: 1

5) The mutual inductance between two coils is 0.0100 H. The current in the first coil changes uniformly from 2.70 A to 5.00 A in 0.160 s. If the second coil has a resistance of 0.600 Ω, what is the magnitude of the induced current in the second coil?

Answer: 0.344 A
Var: 1

Chapter 31   Alternating Current

Multiple Choice Questions

1)

Figure 31.1a

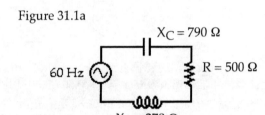

$X_C = 790 \ \Omega$

$R = 500 \ \Omega$

60 Hz

$X_L = 270 \ \Omega$

The 60 Hz ac source of a series circuit has a voltage amplitude of 120 V. The capacitive and inductive reactances are 790 Ω and 270 Ω, respectively. The resistance is 500 Ω. In Figure 31.1a, the capacitance, in μF, is closest to:

A) 3.4   B) 6.5   C) 9.7   D) 13   E) 20

Answer: A
Var: 50+

2)

Figure 31.1b

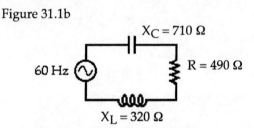

$X_C = 710 \ \Omega$

$R = 490 \ \Omega$

60 Hz

$X_L = 320 \ \Omega$

The 60 Hz ac source of a series circuit has a voltage amplitude of 120 V. The capacitive and inductive reactances are 710 Ω and 320 Ω, respectively. The resistance is 490 Ω. In Figure 31.1b, the inductance, in mH, is closest to:

A) 850   B) 1900   C) 3200   D) 4000   E) 5300

Answer: A
Var: 50+

3)   Figure 31.1c

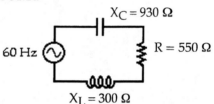

The 60 Hz ac source of a series circuit has a voltage amplitude of 120 V. The capacitive and inductive reactances are 960 Ω and 230 Ω, respectively. The resistance is 490 Ω. In Figure 31.1c, the rms current in the circuit is closest to:

   A) 0.097 A   B) 0.11 A   C) 0.12 A   D) 0.14 A   E) 0.17 A

Answer: A
Var: 50+

4)   Figure 31.1d

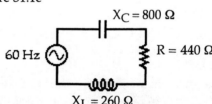

The 60 Hz ac source of a series circuit has a voltage amplitude of 120 V. The capacitive and inductive reactances are 930 Ω and 300 Ω, respectively. The resistance is 550 Ω. In Figure 31.1d, the phase angle is closest to:

   A) –49°   B) 49°   C) –72°   D) 72°   E) –18°

Answer: A
Var: 50+

5)   Figure 31.1e

The 60 Hz ac source of a series circuit has a voltage amplitude of 120 V. The capacitive and inductive reactances are 800 Ω and 260 Ω, respectively. The resistance is 440 Ω. In Figure 31.1e, the resistance is changed from its original value so that the power factor is now 0.80. The original values of capacitance, inductance, and frequency remain unchanged. The new resistance is closest to:

   A) 720 Ω   B) 650 Ω   C) 580 Ω   D) 490 Ω   E) 410 Ω

Answer: A
Var: 50+

6)

Figure 31.2a

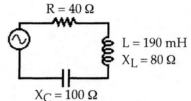

R = 40 Ω

L = 190 mH
X_L = 80 Ω

X_C = 100 Ω

A series ac circuit is shown. The inductor has a reactance of 80 ohms and an inductance of 190 mH. A 40 ohm resistor and a capacitor whose reactance is 100 ohms, are also in the circuit. The rms current in the circuit is 2.2 A. In Figure 31.2a, the rms voltage of the source is closest to:

A) 98 V   B) 96 V   C) 93 V   D) 91 V   E) 88 V

Answer: A
Var: 50+

7)

Figure 31.2b

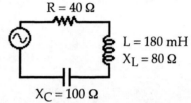

R = 40 Ω

L = 180 mH
X_L = 80 Ω

X_C = 100 Ω

A series ac circuit is shown. The inductor has a reactance of 80 ohms and an inductance of 180 mH. A 40 ohm resistor and a capacitor whose reactance is 100 ohms, are also in the circuit. The rms current in the circuit is 1.8 A. In Figure 31.2b, the capacitance of the capacitor is closest to:

A) 23 μF   B) 24 μF   C) 21 μF   D) 19 μF   E) 18 μF

Answer: A
Var: 50+

8)

Figure 31.2c

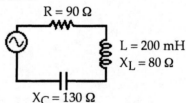

R = 90 Ω

L = 200 mH
X_L = 80 Ω

X_C = 130 Ω

A series ac circuit is shown. The inductor has a reactance of 80 ohms and an inductance of 200 mH. A 90 ohm resistor and a capacitor whose reactance is 130 ohms, are also in the circuit. The rms current in the circuit is 1.3 A. In Figure 31.2c, the phase angle of the circuit is closest to:

A) –29°   B) 29°   C) +90°   D) –61°   E) 61°

Answer: A
Var: 50+

9)

Figure 31.2d

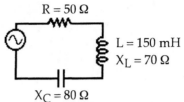

R = 50 Ω
L = 150 mH
$X_L = 70$ Ω
$X_C = 80$ Ω

A series ac circuit is shown. The inductor has a reactance of 70 ohms and an inductance of 150 mH. A 50 ohm resistor and a capacitor whose reactance is 80 ohms, are also in the circuit. The rms current in the circuit is 2.2 A. In Figure 31.2d, the voltage amplitude across the capacitor is closest to:

A) 250 V   B) 180 V   C) 320 V   D) 390 V   E) 110 V

Answer: A
Var: 50+

10)

Figure 31.2e

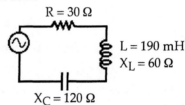

R = 30 Ω
L = 190 mH
$X_L = 60$ Ω
$X_C = 120$ Ω

A series ac circuit is shown. The inductor has a reactance of 60 ohms and an inductance of 190 mH. A 30 ohm resistor and a capacitor whose reactance is 120 ohms, are also in the circuit. The rms current in the circuit is 1.3 A. In Figure 31.2e, the peak magnetic energy in the inductor is closest to:

A) 0.32 J   B) 0.16 J   C) 0.48 J   D) 0.64 J   E) 0.80 J

Answer: A
Var: 50+

11)

Figure 31.2f

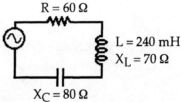

R = 60 Ω
L = 240 mH
$X_L = 70$ Ω
$X_C = 80$ Ω

A series ac circuit is shown. The inductor has a reactance of 70 ohms and an inductance of 240 mH. A 60 ohm resistor and a capacitor whose reactance is 80 ohms, are also in the circuit. The rms current in the circuit is 1.3 A. In Figure 31.2f, the capacitor is changed so that the circuit is in resonance. The voltage of the source is adjusted so that the rms current of 1.3 A is maintained. The new voltage amplitude of the source is closest to:

A) 110 V   B) 95 V   C) 79 V   D) 130 V   E) 140 V

Answer: A
Var: 50+

12) With the aid of a phasor diagram one can show that the impedance of a 2 μF capacitor connected in parallel with a 160 Ω resistor is, when used at a frequency of 500 Hz,

A) 104 Ω   B) 88.1 Ω   C) 113 Ω   D) 24.4 Ω   E) 94.2 Ω

Answer: C
Var: 1

13) The inductor in a radio receiver carries a current of amplitude 200 mA when a voltage of amplitude 2.4 V is across it at a frequency of 1400 kHz. What is the value of the inductance?

A) 1.43 mH   B) 1.36 mH   C) 9.20 mH   D) 4.42 mH   E) 1.97 mH

Answer: B
Var: 1

14) When a mass is suspended from a spring and immersed in liquid it can be made to undergo forced damped harmonic oscillations. The behavior is in many ways analogous to that of a driven RLC series circuit to which is applied a sinusoidal EMF. To which of the following is the kinetic energy of the mass analogous?

A) The energy dissipated as heat in the resistor.

B) The energy stored in the capacitor.

C) The magnetic energy stored in the inductor.

D) The total energy provided by the source of EMF.

E) The current in the circuit.

Answer: C
Var: 1

15)

Figure 31.3a

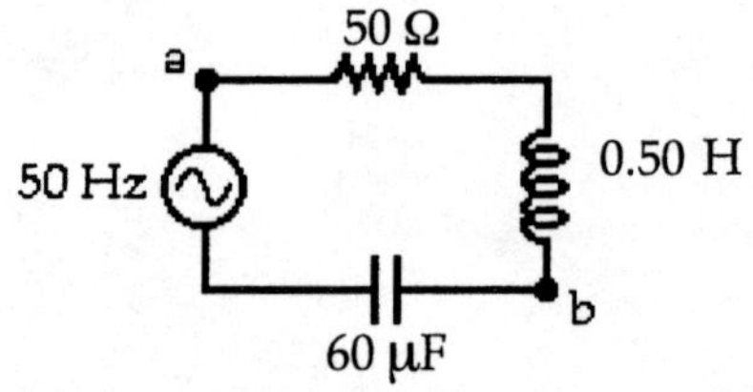

A series circuit has a 50 Hz ac source, a 50 ohm resistor, a 0.50 H inductor, and an 60 μF capacitor, as shown. The rms current in the circuit is 1.9 A. In Figure 31.3a, the voltage amplitude of the source is closest to:

A) 310 V   B) 270 V   C) 220 V   D) 180 V   E) 160 V

Answer: A
Var: 50+

16)

Figure 31.3b

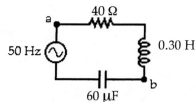

A series circuit has a 50 Hz ac source, a 40 ohm resistor, a 0.30 H inductor, and an 60 μF capacitor, as shown. The rms current in the circuit is 1.6 A. In Figure 31.3b, the power factor of the circuit is closest to:

A) 0.70   B) 0.66   C) 0.63   D) 0.59   E) 0.56

Answer: A
Var: 50+

17)

Figure 31.3c

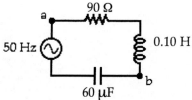

A series circuit has a 50 Hz ac source, a 90 ohm resistor, a 0.10 H inductor, and an 60 μF capacitor, as shown. The rms current in the circuit is 2.4 A. In Figure 31.3c, the rms voltage across points a and b in the circuit is closest to:

A) 229 V   B) 291 V   C) 206 V   D) 162 V   E) 19 V

Answer: A
Var: 50+

18)

Figure 31.3d

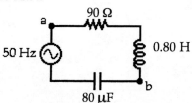

A series circuit has a 50 Hz ac source, a 90 ohm resistor, a 0.80 H inductor, and an 80 μF capacitor, as shown. The rms current in the circuit is 3.4 A. In Figure 31.3d, the frequency of the source is changed so that the capacitive reactance is equal to twice the inductive reactance. The original circuit elements are retained. The new frequency of the source, in Hz, is closest to:

A) 14   B) 13   C) 16   D) 17   E) 19

Answer: A
Var: 50+

19)

Figure 31.3e

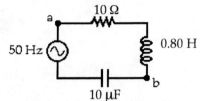

10 Ω

0.80 H

50 Hz

10 μF

A series circuit has a 50 Hz ac source, a 10 ohm resistor, a 0.80 H inductor, and an 10 μF capacitor, as shown. The rms current in the circuit is 1.5 A. In Figure 31.3e, the capacitance is changed so that the circuit is in resonance. The original resistor and inductor are retained. The voltage and frequency of the source are kept at the original values. The new capacitance, in μF, is closest to:

A) 13   B) 14   C) 15   D) 16   E) 18

Answer: A
Var: 50+

Figure 31.4

R = 100 Ω

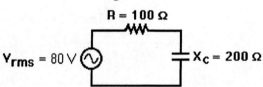

V_{rms} = 80 V

X_C = 200 Ω

An ac source whose rms voltage is 80 V is in series with a 100 ohm resistor and a capacitor, whose reactance is 200 ohms at the frequency of the source.

20) In Figure 31.4, the rms voltage across the capacitor is closest to:

A) 66 V   B) 68 V   C) 70 V   D) 72 V   E) 74 V

Answer: D
Var: 1

21) In Figure 31.4, the instantaneous voltage of the source when the current is a maximum is closest to:

A) 35 V   B) 50 V   C) 70 V   D) 100 V   E) 115 V

Answer: B
Var: 1

22) In Figure 31.4, the instantaneous current, when the voltage of the source is zero and is increasing, is closest to:

A) zero   B) 0.16 A   C) 0.23 A   D) 0.32 A   E) 0.45 A

Answer: E
Var: 1

23) In a series RLC circuit suppose V_C, V_L, V_R are the potential differences across the three elements. Then for such a circuit

   A) equal amounts of power will be dissipated in the inductor, the capacitor and the resistor.

   B) equal amounts of power will be dissipated in the resistor, the inductor and the capacitor only when the circuit is at resonance.

   C) the current in the inductor will not necessarily be in phase with the current in the other two elements.

   D) the voltage across the resistor will always be in phase with the applied EMF.

   E) None of these is true.

Answer: E
Var: 1

24) Which of the following is an accurate statement?

   A) The ratio of the maximum EMF applied to a circuit to the maximum resulting current is called the impedance of the circuit.

   B) Impedance is the term used to refer to resistance in an AC circuit.

   C) Impedance, reactance and resistance all have the same meaning, but they are applied to different types of circuit elements.

   D) Since impedance is frequency dependent, it is not strictly correct to measure it in ohms.

   E) In an RLC circuit, power is dissipated in resistive, inductive and capacitive elements, but not necessarily in equal amounts.

Answer: A
Var: 1

Figure 31.5

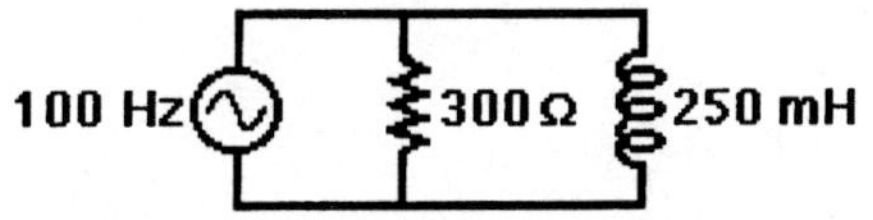

A 300 ohm resistor and a 200 mH inductor are connected in parallel across a 100 Hz ac source, as shown. The rms current through the inductor is 0.50A.

25) In Figure 31.5, the rms current through the resistor is closest to:

   A) 0.21 A   B) 0.23 A   C) 0.26 A   D) 0.28 A   E) 0.31 A

Answer: C
Var: 1

26) In Figure 31.5, the rms voltage of the source is closest to:

   A) 79 V   B) 83 V   C) 88 V   D) 92 V   E) 97 V

Answer: A
Var: 1

27) In Figure 31.5, the impedance of the circuit is closest to:

　A) 100 Ω　　　　B) 140 Ω　　　　C) 210 Ω　　　　D) 270 Ω　　　　E) 340 Ω

Answer: B
Var: 1

28) In Figure 31.5, the angle by which the source voltage leads the source current (negative if it lags) is closest to:

　A) +28°　　　　B) +62°　　　　C) +90°　　　　D) –28°　　　　E) –62°

Answer: B
Var: 1

29) In Figure 31.5, for the circuit to be in resonance, a capacitor is connected in parallel across the ac source. The capacitance of this capacitor is:

　A) 10 μF　　　　B) 20 μF　　　　C) 30 μF　　　　D) 40 μF　　　　E) 50 μF

Answer: A
Var: 1

Figure 31.6

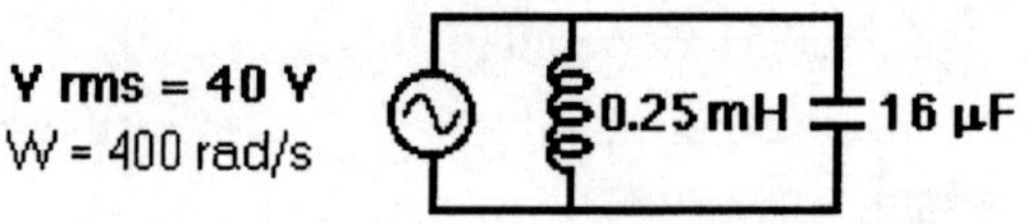

Y rms = 40 Y
W = 400 rad/s
0.25 mH 　16 μF

A 0.25 H inductor and a 16 μF capacitor are connected in parallel across an ac source. The rms voltage of the source is 40 V, and the angular frequency is 400 rad/s. The resistance of the circuit is negligible.

30) In Figure 31.6, the rms inductor current is closest to:

　A) 0.36 A　　　　B) 0.40 A　　　　C) 0.44 A　　　　D) 0.48 A　　　　E) 0.52 A

Answer: B
Var: 1

31) In Figure 31.6, the rms source current is closest to:

　A) 0.14 A　　　　B) 0.18 A　　　　C) 0.22 A　　　　D) 0.26 A　　　　E) 0.30 A

Answer: A
Var: 1

32) In Figure 31.6, the angle by which the source voltage leads the source current (negative if it lags) is closest to:

　A) +33°　　　　B) +57°　　　　C) +90°　　　　D) –33°　　　　E) –57°

Answer: D
Var: 1

33) In Figure 31.6, the impedance of the circuit is closest to:

　A) 260 Ω　　　　B) 270 Ω　　　　C) 280 Ω　　　　D) 290 Ω　　　　E) 300 Ω

Answer: C
Var: 1

34) In Figure 31.6, the angular frequency of the source is changed, so that the circuit is in resonance. The source voltage is unchanged. The new rms current through the capacitor is closest to:

A) 0.26 A   B) 0.28 A   C) 0.30 A   D) 0.32 A   E) 0.34 A

Answer: D
Var: 1

Figure 31.7

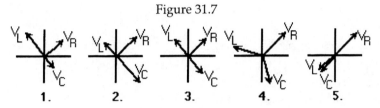

1.   2.   3.   4.   5.

35) In Figure 31.7, which of the phasor diagrams represents a series RLC circuit driven at resonance?

A) 1   B) 2   C) 3   D) 4   E) 5

Answer: C
Var: 1

36) Which of the following is a true statement?

A) All electromagnetic waves travel at the same speed in vacuum.

B) Light speeds up when it moves from air into water.

C) Some electromagnetic waves have electric charge.

D) In vacuum high frequency electromagnetic waves travel at higher speed than do low frequency electromagnetic waves.

E) Electrons are a kind of electromagnetic wave.

Answer: A
Var: 1

Short Answer Questions

1) A transformer is needed to step down a high-voltage, low-current input to a low-voltage, high-current output. The secondary voltage must not exceed 510 volts and the primary current must not exceed 0.17 amperes. If the power is to be 800 watts, what is the smallest possible ratio of turns (primary to secondary) in the transformer?

Answer: 9.2
Var: 50+

2) An ac series circuit consists of a voltage source, a resistance R = 270 Ω and an inductance L. (There is no capacitance in the circuit.) The current amplitude is 0.60 A, and the phase angle between the source voltage and the current has magnitude $|\Phi| = 31°$.
(a) Does the source voltage lag or lead the current?
(b) What is the voltage amplitude of the source?

Answer: (a) The source voltage leads the current.
        (b) 190 volts
Var: 50+

3) An ac series circuit consists of a voltage source of frequency f = 60 Hz and voltage amplitude V, a resistor of resistance R = 381 Ω, and a capacitor of capacitance C = 3.8 x 10^{-6} F. What must the source voltage amplitude V be for the average electrical power consumed in the resistor to be 333 watts? There is no inductance in the circuit.

Answer: 1100 volts
Var: 50+

4) A series ac circuit consists of a voltage source of frequency f = 60 Hz and source voltage amplitude 345 volts, a resistor of resistance R = 524 Ω, a capacitor of capacitance C = 8.2 x 10^{-6} F, and an inductor of inductance L.
(a) What must be the value of L for the phase angle Φ to be zero?
(b) When L has the value calculated in (a), what is the current amplitude in the circuit?

Answer: (a) 0.86 H (b) 0.658 A
Var: 50+

5) In an L–R–C series circuit L = 0.920 H, R =380.0 Ω, and C = 9.10 μF. The voltage amplitude of the source is 250.0 V. Find the rms voltage across the capacitor when the source operates at resonance.

Answer: 148 V
Var: 50+

Chapter 32   Electromagnetic Waves

Multiple Choice Questions

1) A 5.64×10^{14} Hz electromagnetic wave propagates in carbon tetrachloride with a speed of 2.05×10^8 m/s. The wavelength of the wave in carbon tetrachloride is closest to:

A) 363 nm   B) 403 nm   C) 452 nm   D) 483 nm   E) 532 nm

Answer: A
Var: 50+

2) A 5.26×10^{14} Hz electromagnetic wave propagates in carbon tetrachloride with a speed of 2.05×10^8 m/s. The wavelength of the wave in vacuum is closest to:

A) 570 nm   B) 390 nm   C) 456 nm   D) 513 nm   E) 627 nm

Answer: A
Var: 50+

3) A 3.49×10^{14} Hz electromagnetic wave propagates in carbon tetrachloride with a speed of 2.05×10^8 m/s. The relative magnetic permeability of carbon tetrachloride is 1.00. The dielectric constant of carbon tetrachloride at a frequency of 3.49×10^{14} Hz is closest to:

A) 2.14   B) 2.53   C) 1.75   D) 1.36   E) 0.97

Answer: A
Var: 50+

4) A planar electromagnetic wave is propagating in the positive x–direction. At a certain point P and at a given instant, the electric field of the wave is given by E = –j 80 mV/m. The magnetic vector of the wave, at the point P at that instant is closest to:

A) $(-2.7 \times 10^{-10}$ T) k
B) $(+2.7 \times 10^{-10}$ T) k
C) $(+2.7 \times 10^{-10}$ T) j
D) $(+6.7 \times 10^{-9}$ T) k
E) $(-6.7 \times 10^{-9}$ T) j

Answer: A
Var: 50+

5) A planar electromagnetic wave is propagating in the positive x–direction. At a certain point P and at a given instant, the electric field of the wave is given by $E = -j\,33\,mV/m$. The Poynting vector at the point P at that instant is closest to:

A) $(+2.9 \times 10^{-6}\,W/m^2)\,i$

B) $(-2.9 \times 10^{-6}\,W/m^2)\,i$

C) $(+1.4 \times 10^{-6}\,W/m^2)\,i$

D) $(-1.4 \times 10^{-6}\,W/m^2)\,i$

E) $(-1.4 \times 10^{-6}\,W/m^2)\,k$

Answer: A
Var: 50+

6) The magnitude of the Poynting vector of a planar electromagnetic wave has an average value of $918\,mW/m^2$. The maximum value of the magnetic field in the wave is closest to:

A) $8.77 \times 10^{-8}\,T$

B) $6.20 \times 10^{-8}\,T$

C) $4.38 \times 10^{-8}\,T$

D) $1.21 \times 10^{-7}\,T$

E) $1.75 \times 10^{-7}\,T$

Answer: A
Var: 50+

7) The magnitude of the Poynting vector of a planar electromagnetic wave has an average value of $719\,mW/m^2$. The wave is incident upon a rectangular area, 1.5 m by 2.0 m, at right angles. The total energy that traverses the area in a time interval of one minute is closest to:

A) 130 J   B) 160 J   C) 190 J   D) 230 J   E) 260 J

Answer: A
Var: 50+

8) An 800 kHz radio signal is detected at a point 5.7 km distant from a transmitter tower. The electric field amplitude of the signal at that point is 120 mV/m. Assume that the signal power is radiated uniformly in all directions and that radio waves incident upon the ground are completely absorbed. The magnetic field amplitude of the signal at that point, in nT, is closest to:

A) 0.40   B) 0.32   C) 0.24   D) 0.48   E) 0.56

Answer: A
Var: 50+

9) An 800 kHz radio signal is detected at a point 4.4 km distant from a transmitter tower. The electric field amplitude of the signal at that point is 930 mV/m. Assume that the signal power is radiated uniformly in all directions and that radio waves incident upon the ground are completely absorbed. The average electromagnetic energy density at that point is closest to:

A) 3.8×10^{-12} J/m^3

B) 5.4×10^{-12} J/m^3

C) 7.7×10^{-12} J/m^3

D) 1.1×10^{-11} J/m^3

E) 1.5×10^{-11} J/m^3

Answer: A
Var: 50+

10) An 800 kHz radio signal is detected at a point 3.3 km distant from a transmitter tower. The electric field amplitude of the signal at that point is 430 mV/m. Assume that the signal power is radiated uniformly in all directions and that radio waves incident upon the ground are completely absorbed. The intensity of the radio signal at that point is closest to:

A) 2.5×10^{-4} W/m^2

B) 3.5×10^{-4} W/m^2

C) 4.9×10^{-4} W/m^2

D) 1.7×10^{-4} W/m^2

E) 1.2×10^{-4} W/m^2

Answer: A
Var: 50+

11) An 800 kHz radio signal is detected at a point 9.7 km distant from a transmitter tower. The electric field amplitude of the signal at that point is 660 mV/m. Assume that the signal power is radiated uniformly in all directions and that radio waves incident upon the ground are completely absorbed. The average total power radiated by the transmitter is closest to:

A) 6.8×10^5 W

B) 8.2×10^5 W

C) 9.8×10^5 W

D) 1.1×10^6 W

E) 1.3×10^6 W

Answer: A
Var: 50+

Figure 32.1

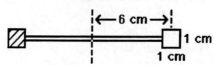

A radiometer has two square vanes (1 cm by 1 cm), attached to a light horizontal cross arm, and pivoted about a vertical axis through the center. The center of each vane is 6 cm from the axis. One vane is silvered and it reflects all radiant energy incident upon it. The other vane is blackened and it absorbs all incident radiant energy. Radiant energy, which has an intensity of 300 W/m^2, is incident normally upon the vanes.

12) In Figure 32.1, the radiant power absorbed by the blackened vane is closest to:

    A) 0.03 W   B) 0.04 W   C) 0.05 W   D) 0.06 W   E) 0.09 W

Answer: A
Var: 1

13) In Figure 32.1, the radiation pressure on the blackened vane is closest to:

    A) 1×10^{-10} Pa

    B) 1×10^{-9} Pa

    C) 1×10^{-8} Pa

    D) 1×10^{-7} Pa

    E) 1×10^{-6} Pa

Answer: E
Var: 1

14) In Figure 32.1, the torque on the vane assembly, about the vertical axis, is closest to:

    A) zero

    B) 6×10^{-12} N • m

    C) 1.2×10^{-11} N • m

    D) 1.8×10^{-11} N • m

    E) 2.4×10^{-11} N • m

Answer: B
Var: 1

15) A certain electromagnetic field traveling in vacuum has a maximum electric field of 1200 V/m. What is the maximum magnetic field of this wave?

    A) 3.4×10^{-4} T

    B) 4.0×10^{-5} T

    C) 2.2×10^{-5} T

    D) 9.6×10^{-6} T

    E) 8.7×10^{-6} T

Answer: B
Var: 1

16) What is the wavelength used by a radio station that broadcasts with a carrier frequency of 920 kHz?

A) 22.6 m   B) 226 m   C) 326 m   D) 175 m   E) 276 m

Answer: C
Var: 1

Situation 32.1

A microwave oven operates at a frequency of 2400 MHz. The height of the oven cavity is 25 cm and the base measures 30 cm by 30 cm. Assume that microwave energy is generated uniformly on the upper surface of the cavity and propagates directly downward towards the base. The base is lined with a material which completely absorbs microwave energy. The total microwave energy content of the cavity is 0.50 mJ.

17) In Situation 32.1, the power output of the microwave oven is closest to:

A) 500 W   B) 550 W   C) 600 W   D) 650 W   E) 700 W

Answer: C
Var: 1

18) In Situation 32.1, the intensity of the microwave beam is closest to:

A) 5200 W/m^2

B) 5700 W/m^2

C) 6200 W/m^2

D) 6700 W/m^2

E) 7200 W/m^2

Answer: D
Var: 1

19) In Situation 32.1, the electric field amplitude is closest to:

A) 1600 V/m   B) 1900 V/m   C) 2200 V/m   D) 2500 V/m   E) 2800 V/m

Answer: C
Var: 1

20) In Situation 32.1, the force on the base due to the radiation is closest to:

A) 1.5×10^{-6} N

B) 2.0×10^{-6} N

C) 2.5×10^{-6} N

D) 3.0×10^{-6} N

E) 3.5×10^{-6} N

Answer: B
Var: 1

21) A 5.6×10^{14} Hz laser emits a $4.3\ \mu s$ pulse, 5.0 mm in diameter, with a beam energy density of $0.32\ J/m^3$. The number of wavelengths in the length of the beam is closest to:

A) 2.4×10^9 B) 7.2×10^9 C) 7.2×10^8 D) 2.4×10^{10} E) 7.2×10^{10}

Answer: A
Var: 50+

22) A 3.3×10^{14} Hz laser emits a $9.6\ \mu s$ pulse, 5.0 mm in diameter, with a beam energy density of $0.28\ J/m^3$. The power emitted by the laser is closest to:

A) 1.7 kW   B) 3.3 kW   C) 5.0 kW   D) 6.6 kW   E) 8.3 kW

Answer: A
Var: 50+

23) A 8.3×10^{14} Hz laser emits a $5.3\ \mu s$ pulse, 5.0 mm in diameter, with a beam energy density of $0.67\ J/m^3$. The amplitude of the electric field of the emitted waves is closest to:

A) 3.9×10^5 V/m

B) 5.5×10^5 V/m

C) 2.8×10^5 V/m

D) 1.8×10^5 V/m

E) 1.4×10^5 V/m

Answer: A
Var: 50+

24) A 7.9×10^{14} Hz laser emits a $7.3\ \mu s$ pulse, 5.0 mm in diameter, with a beam energy density of $0.65\ J/m^3$. The average Poynting vector magnitude of the beam is closest to:

A) 2.0×10^8 W/m^2

B) 9.8×10^7 W/m^2

C) 1.4×10^8 W/m^2

D) 6.9×10^7 W/m^2

E) 4.9×10^7 W/m^2

Answer: A
Var: 50+

Situation 32.2

A standing planar electromagnetic wave is established in a resonant cavity formed by two parallel conducting plates that are 12 cm apart. The number of electric field antinoidal planes, including the cavity walls, in the standing wave is three.

25) In Situation 32.2, the frequency of the electromagnetic wave in GHz (G = giga = 10^9), is closest to:

A) 1.25   B) 2.50   C) 3.75   D) 5.00   E) 6.25

Answer: C
Var: 1

26) In Situation 32.2, the number of antinoidal planes for the magnetic field is:

A) 2 B) 3 C) 4 D) 5 E) 6

Answer: C
Var: 1

27) In Situation 32.2, the smallest distance between an electric field antinoidal plane and a magnetic field antinoidal plane, in cm, is closest to:

A) zero B) 1.0 C) 2.0 D) 3.0 E) 4.0

Answer: C
Var: 1

28) A certain glass has an index of refraction of 1.44 at a wavelength of 560 nm in vacuum. What is the effective dielectric constant at the corresponding frequency?

A) 1.98 B) 1.20 C) 2.07 D) 1.44 E) 3.66

Answer: C
Var: 1

29) Electromagnetic standing waves are set up in a conducting cavity resonator in the form of a hollow metal box. The waves bounce back and forth between two parallel surfaces separated by 0.80 cms. What is the minimum resonant frequency for such a resonator?

A) 4.42 GHz B) 12.4 GHz C) 3.30 GHz D) 18.8 GHz E) 15.5 GHz

Answer: D
Var: 1

30) What is the essential difference between microwaves and blue light?

A) One has an electric charge, the other does not.

B) One undergoes refraction, the other does not.

C) One is a form of radiation, the other is not.

D) Blue light is a beam of photons. Microwaves are not photons.

E) There is no essential difference in the nature of microwaves and blue light other than a difference in frequency and wavelength.

Answer: E
Var: 1

31) An electromagnetic wave polarized parallel to the z-axis is traveling in the positive direction along the x-axis. How can this wave best be detected using a straight wire antenna?

A) Orient the antenna parallel to the x-axis.

B) Orient the antenna parallel to the y-axis.

C) Orient the antenna parallel to the z-axis.

D) The antenna will work equally well for any of these orientations.

E) This wave cannot be detected with a straight wire antenna. A loop antenna must be used.

Answer: C
Var: 1

32) An electromagnetic wave is radiated by a straight wire antenna that is oriented vertically. Such a wave could be best detected by

    A) a loop antenna oriented with the plane of the loop horizontal.

    B) a loop antenna oriented with the plane of the loop vertical and parallel to the velocity vector of the wave.

    C) a loop antenna oriented with the plane of the loop perpendicular to the velocity vector of the wave.

    D) a straight wire antenna placed in a horizontal plane.

    E) More than one of these.

Answer: B
Var: 1

Short Answer Questions

1) A sinusoidal electromagnetic wave is propagating in vacuum.
(a) At a given point and at a particular time the electric field is in the +x direction and the magnetic field is in the –y direction. What is the direction of propagation of the wave?
(b) At the above point the intensity of the wave is 0.94 W $\cdot$ m^{-2}. What is the electric field amplitude at this point? (NOTE: $\mu_0 = 4\pi \times 10^{-7}$ T $\cdot$ m/A and c = 3.00 $\times 10^8$ m/s.)

Answer: (a) –z direction (b) 27 V/m
Var: 50+

2) An electromagnetic wave has a wavelength of 2.90 $\times 10^{-5}$ m in air and a wavelength of 2.50 $\times 10^{-5}$ m in a certain dielectric material. Find the dielectric constant for the material.

Answer: 1.35
Var: 50+

3) A source of light produces an electric field amplitude of 8.88 V/m 45.0 m from the source. What is the power output from the source?

Answer: 2660 W
Var: 50+

4) A totally absorbing surface of area A = 7.7 cm^2 faces a small source of sinusoidal electromagnetic radiation that is 2.2 m away. At the surface A the electric field amplitude of the radiation is 47 V/m. (Note: $\mu_0 = 4\pi \times 10^{-7}$ T $\cdot$ m/A and c = 3.00 $\times 10^8$ m/s.)
(a) What is the radiation pressure exerted on the surface?
(b) What is the total power output of the source, if it is assumed to radiate uniformly in all directions?

Answer: (a) 9.8 $\times 10^{-9}$ Pa
        (b) 1.8 $\times 10^2$ watts
Var: 50+

5) An electromagnetic standing wave is resonating in a cavity with n = 1. The nodal plane of the E field and the closest nodal plane of the B field are separated by 0.87 m.
(a) Find the length of the resonating cavity.
(b) Find the frequency of the electromagnetic wave.

Answer: (a) 1.74 m

(b) 8.6×10^7 Hz

Var: 1

Chapter 33   The Nature and Propagation of Light

Multiple Choice Questions

1) The doublet of the sodium spectrum, in the yellow band, has two constituents having lengths of 589.0 nm and 589.6 nm, respectively. Light of this doublet is propagated at normal incidence through a crystal slab. The index of refraction of the crystal at these wavelengths is 1.873. The number of waves of the 589.0 nm constituent that are present in a crystal 1.7 mm thick is closest to:

   A) 5400   B) 2900   C) 4000   D) 10,000   E) 7400

   Answer: A
   Var: 50+

2) The doublet of the sodium spectrum, in the yellow band, has two constituents having lengths of 589.0 nm and 589.6 nm, respectively. Light of this doublet is propagated at normal incidence through a crystal slab. The index of refraction of the crystal at these wavelengths is 1.516. The number of waves that are present in a crystal is different for each constituent. The difference in the number of waves, in a particular crystal, is one whole wave. The thickness of the crystal, in mm, is closest to:

   A) 0.38   B) 0.47   C) 0.58   D) 0.71   E) 0.88

   Answer: A
   Var: 50+

3) A ray in air is incident on a glass plate whose index of refraction is 1.60. The angle of refraction is one half the angle of reflection. The angle of refraction is closest to:

   A) 37°   B) 35°   C) 33°   D) 31°   E) 29°

   Answer: A
   Var: 50+

4) A ray in glass is incident onto a water–glass interface, at an angle of incidence equal to half the critical angle for that interface. The indices of refraction for water and the glass are 1.33 and 1.55, respectively. The angle that the refracted ray in the water makes with the normal is closest to:

   A) 35°   B) 40°   C) 45°   D) 30°   E) 25°

   Answer: A
   Var: 50+

5) The critical angle for an air–glass interface is 10.5 degrees. A ray in air is incident on the interface. The reflected ray is 100 percent polarized. The angle of refraction is closest to:

   A) 10.3°   B) 9.73°   C) 9.13°   D) 8.53°   E) 7.93°

   Answer: A
   Var: 50+

6) A glass plate whose index of refraction is 1.55 is immersed in a liquid. The surface of the glass is inclined at an angle of 54° with the vertical. A horizontal ray in the glass is incident on the interface. When the liquid is a certain alcohol, the incident ray arrives at the interface at the critical angle. The index of refraction of the alcohol is closest to:

A) 1.25   B) 1.23   C) 1.21   D) 1.19   E) 1.27

Answer: A
Var: 50+

7) A glass plate whose index of refraction is 1.68 is immersed in a liquid. The surface of the glass is inclined at an angle of 35° with the vertical. A horizontal ray in the glass is incident on the interface. The liquid is an oil whose index of refraction is 1.40. The incident horizontal ray refracts at the interface. The angle that the refracted ray, in the oil, makes with the horizontal is closest to:

A) 8.5°   B) 4.2°   C) 6.4°   D) 11°   E) 13°

Answer: A
Var: 50+

8)   Figure 33.1a

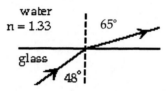

A ray in glass arrives at the glass–water interface at an angle of 48° with the normal. The refracted ray, in water, makes a 65° angle with the normal. The index of refraction of water is 1.33. In Figure 33.1a, the angle of incidence of a different ray in the glass is 12°. The angle of refraction in the water is closest to:

A) 15°   B) 13°   C) 11°   D) 17°   E) 19°

Answer: B
Var: 50+

9)   Figure 33.1b

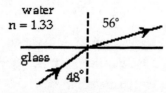

A ray in glass arrives at the glass–water interface at an angle of 48° with the normal. The refracted ray, in water, makes a 56° angle with the normal. The index of refraction of water is 1.33. In Figure 33.1b, the angle of incidence of a different ray in the glass is 11°. The angle of refraction in the water is closest to:

A) 64°   B) 62°   C) 60°   D) 66°   E) 68°

Answer: B
Var: 50+

10)

Figure 33.2a

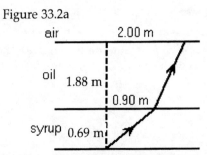

A tank holds a layer of oil, 1.88 m thick, which floats on a layer of syrup that is 0.69 m thick. Both liquids are clear and do not intermix. A ray, which originates at the bottom of the tank on a vertical axis, crosses the oil–syrup interface at a point 0.90 m from the axis. The ray continues and arrives at the oil–air interface, 2.00 m from the axis and at the critical angle. In Figure 33.2a, the index of refraction of the oil is closest to:

   A) 1.98   B) 1.96   C) 1.94   D) 2.00   E) 2.02

Answer: A
Var: 50+

11)

Figure 33.2b

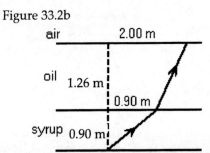

A tank holds a layer of oil, 1.26 m thick, which floats on a layer of syrup that is 0.90 m thick. Both liquids are clear and do not intermix. A ray, which originates at the bottom of the tank on a vertical axis, crosses the oil–syrup interface at a point 0.90 m from the axis. The ray continues and arrives at the oil–air interface, 2.00 m from the axis and at the critical angle. In Figure 33.2b, the index of refraction of the syrup is closest to:

   A) 1.41   B) 1.29   C) 2.06   D) 1.85   E) 1.62

Answer: A
Var: 50+

12) When light travels from air into water,

   A) its velocity, wavelength and frequency all change.

   B) its velocity changes, but its frequency and wavelength do not change.

   C) its frequency changes, but its velocity and wavelength do not change.

   D) its velocity and wavelength change, but its frequency does not change.

   E) its wavelength changes, but its velocity and frequency do not change.

Answer: D
Var: 1

13)

Figure 33.3

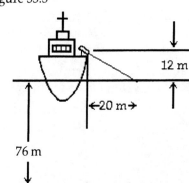

In Figure 33.3, a laser positioned on a ship is used to communicate with a small two man research submarine resting on the bottom of a lake. The laser is positioned 12 meters above the surface of the water, and it strikes the water 20 meters from the side of the ship. The water is 76 meters deep and has an index of refraction of 1.33. How far is the submarine from the side of the ship?

A) 84.1 m   B) 64.1 m   C) 104 m   D) 74.1 m   E) 94.1 m

Answer: A
Var: 50+

14) Carbon disulfide (n = 1.63) is poured to a depth of 4 cms in a flask, and a layer of water (n = 1.33) is poured on top of it to an additional depth of 6 cms. What would be the apparent depth of an object resting on the bottom of the flask when viewed by an observer looking straight down?

A) 5.64 cms   B) 8.24 cms   C) 6.97 cms   D) 7.76 cms   E) 6.90 cms

Answer: C
Var: 1

15)

Figure 33.4

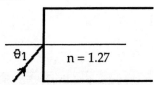

In Figure 33.4, in the investigation of a new type of optical fiber (index of refraction n = 1.27), a laser beam is incident on the flat end of a straight fiber in air. What is the maximum angle of incidence θ_1 if the beam is not to escape from the fiber?

A) 51.5°   B) 48.4°   C) 45.3°   D) 42.2°   E) 39.1°

Answer: A
Var: 30

Situation 33.1

A tank holds a 1.44 m thick layer of oil that floats on a 0.96 m thick layer of brine. Both liquids are clear and do not intermix. Point O is at the bottom of the tank, on a vertical axis. The indices of refraction of the oil and the brine are 1.40 and 1.52, respectively.

16) In Situation 33.1, a ray originating at O, crosses the brine–oil interface at a point 0.60 m from the axis. The ray continues and emerges into the air. The angle that the ray in the air makes with the vertical is closest to:

    A) 48°   B) 51°   C) 54°   D) 57°   E) 60°

Answer: A
Var: 1

17) In Situation 33.1, a ray originating at O reaches a point on the brine–oil interface at the critical angle. The distance of this point from the axis is closest to:

    A) 1.5 m   B) 1.7 m   C) 1.9 m   D) 2.1 m   E) 2.3 m

Answer: E
Var: 1

18) In Situation 33.1, a ray originating at O reaches a point on the oil–air interface at the critical angle. The distance of this point from the axis is closest to:

    A) 1.5 m   B) 1.7 m   C) 1.9 m   D) 2.1 m   E) 2.3 m

Answer: E
Var: 1

Situation 33.2

A bichromatic source produces light having wavelengths in vacuum of 450 nm and 650 nm. The indices of refraction are 1.440 and 1.420, respectively.

19) In Situation 33.2, a ray of the bichromatic light, in air, is incident upon the oil at an angle of incidence of 50.0°. The angle of dispersion between the two refracted rays in the oil is closest to:

    A) 0.5°   B) 0.7°   C) 0.9°   D) 1.1°   E) 1.3°

Answer: A
Var: 1

20) In Situation 33.2, a ray of the bichromatic light, in the oil, is incident on the oil–air interface, at an angle of incidence of 40.0 degrees. The angle of dispersion between the two refracted rays in air is closest to:

    A) 1.6°   B) 1.9°   C) 2.2°   D) 2.5°   E) 2.8°

Answer: B
Var: 1

21) Dispersion of electromagnetic waves

   A) refers to the fact that waves radiate out in all directions from a point source.

   B) results from the fact that waves of different frequencies travel at different speeds in matter.

   C) refers to the phenomenon wherein a ray changes direction when it passes from one material into another.

   D) is the underlying phenomenon utilized in some types of sun glasses.

   E) accounts for the fact that the sky is blue.

Answer: B
Var: 1

Figure 33.5

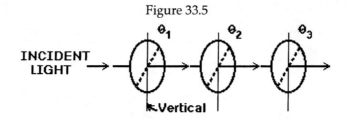

22) In Figure 33.5, the orientation of the transmission axis for each of three polarizing sheets is labeled relative to the vertical direction. A beam of light, polarized in the vertical direction, is incident on the first polarized with an intensity of $1000/Wm^2$. What is the intensity of the beam after it has passed through the three polarizing sheets when $\theta_1 = 30°$, $\theta_2 = 30°$, and $\theta_3 = 60°$?

   A) $141 \ W/m^2$

   B) $316 \ W/m^2$

   C) $433 \ W/m^2$

   D) $563 \ W/m^2$

   E) $188 \ W/m^2$

Answer: D
Var: 1

23) Which of the following is an accurate statement?

A) Light which comes directly toward you directly from the sun is more strongly polarized than is sunlight which has been scattered and comes toward you from some other direction.

B) Red light tends to be scattered more effectively than is blue light.

C) The reason sunsets tend to look red in color is that the red component of the sunlight is coherently scattered in the forward direction, whereas other colors are not scattered as much.

D) Light with its electric field vibrating in the plane of incidence is said to be polarized, whereas light whose electric field is not vibrating in the plane of incidence is said to be unpolarized.

E) None of these is true

Answer: E
Var: 1

Figure 33.6

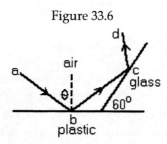

A ray ab, of natural light in air, makes an angle of incidence q at *b* on a plastic plate. The reflected ray *bc* is incident onto a glass surface at *c*, is reflected again, and continues as ray cd. The index of refraction of the plastic is 1.48. The glass surface forms a 60° angle with the plastic surface.

24) In Figure 33.6, ray *bc* and ray *cd* are both 100 percent polarized. The angle of incidence q is closest to:

A) 55.0°   B) 55.5°   C) 56.0°   D) 56.5°   E) 57.0°

Answer: C
Var: 1

25) In Figure 33.6, the angle of incidence q is set at 62°. Ray *cd* is 100 percent polarized but ray *bc* is not. The index of refraction of the glass is closest to:

A) 1.52   B) 1.54   C) 1.56   D) 1.58   E) 1.60

Answer: E
Var: 1

Situation 33.3

The following are positioned in sequence: A source of a beam of natural light of intensity I_0; three ideal polarizers A, B, and C; and an observer. Polarizer axis angles are measured clockwise from the vertical, from the perspective of the observer. The axis angle of polarizer A is set at zero degrees (vertical), and the axis angle of polarizer C is set at 50 degrees.

26) In Situation 33.3, polarizer B is set so that the beam intensity is zero at the observer. The two possible axis angle settings of polarizer B are:

A) $40°$ and $90°$

B) $40°$ and $130°$

C) $40°$ and $140°$

D) $90°$ and $130°$

E) $90°$ and $140°$

Answer: E
Var: 1

27) In Situation 33.3, polarizer B is set so that the beam intensity at the observer is a maximum. The axis angle of polarizer B is:

A) $0°$ B) $25°$ C) $50°$ D) $75°$ E) $100°$

Answer: B
Var: 1

28) In Situation 33.3, the axis angle of polarizer B is set at $120°$. The ratio of the intensity of the beam at the observer to the intensity of the source is closest to:

A) 0.015   B) 0.020   C) 0.025   D) 0.030   E) 0.035

Answer: A
Var: 1

Situation 33.4

A beam of light is linearly polarized in a vertical plane and has an intensity I_0. The beam passes through an ideal polarizer and then through an ideal analyzer whose axis is set horizontally.

29) In Situation 33.4, the axis of the polarizer is set at $60°$ with the vertical. The ratio of the intensity of the final beam to I_0 is closest to:

A) 0.19   B) 0.25   C) 0.31   D) 0.37   E) 0.43

Answer: A
Var: 1

30) In Situation 33.4, the axis of the polarizer is set at $40°$ with the vertical. The ratio of the electric field in the final beam to that of the initial beam is closest to:

A) 0.24   B) 0.32   C) 0.40   D) 0.49   E) 0.57

Answer: D
Var: 1

Short Answer Questions

Figure 33.7

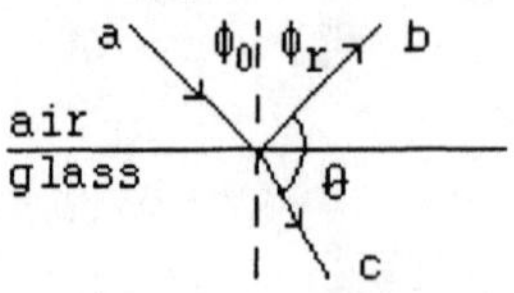

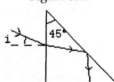

1) In Figure 33.7, a ray of light in air is incident on a flat piece of glass, at an angle of $\phi_o = 67°$ with respect to the normal. The glass has an index of refraction n = 1.5. What is the angle θ between the reflected (ray b) and refracted (ray c) rays?

Answer: 75°
Var: 50+

Figure 33.8

2) In Figure 33.8, the corner of a prism (n = 1.24) is a 45° angle. The incident light makes an angle i with respect to the normal, as shown. If i is larger than some angle i_o, the light is totally reflected at the second face of the prism. Find i_o.

Answer: 10.9°
Var: 39

3) A ray of light traveling in air makes a 63.0° angle with respect to the normal of the surface of a liquid. It travels in the liquid at a 40.3° angle with respect to the normal. Find the critical angle for total internal reflection. (Assume n = 1 for air.)

Answer: 46.5°
Var: 50+

4) When unpolarized light from air (n = 1) is incident on a piece of glass with index of refraction n = 1.23, the reflected light is found to be completely polarized when the angle of incidence is θ_B. What is the angle of refraction in this case? Give a numerical answer.

Answer: 39.1°
Var: 50+

5) Three linear polarizers are oriented as follows: The axis of the second is at an angle of $59.0°$ relative to the first. The axis of the third is at an angle of $31.0°$ relative to the second, so the axis of the third polarizer is perpendicular to the axis of the first. Unpolarized light of intensity $I_0 = 43.0 \text{ W}/\text{m}^2$ is incident on the first polarizer.

(a) What is the intensity of the light after it passes through all three polarizers?

(b) What is the intensity of the transmitted light if the second polarizer is removed?

Answer: (a) $4.19 \text{ W}/\text{m}^2$
 (b) 0

Var: 50+

Chapter 34   Geometric Optics and Optical Instruments

Multiple Choice Questions

1) A plane mirror is placed on the level bottom of a swimming pool which holds water (n = 1.33) to a depth of 2.5 m. A small toy is suspended 2.0 m above the mirror. An observer above the water looks vertically downward at the toy and its image in the mirror. The apparent difference in depth between the toy and its image in the mirror is closest to:

   A) 3.0 m   B) 2.7 m   C) 2.3 m   D) 2.0 m   E) 1.7 m

   Answer: A
   Var: 12

2) A plane mirror is placed on the level bottom of a swimming pool which holds water (n = 1.33) to a depth of 2.5 m. A small toy is suspended 1.1 m above the mirror. An observer above the water looks vertically downward at the toy and its image in the mirror. A swimmer whose head is in the water looks vertically downward at the toy and its image in the mirror. The apparent difference in depth of the toy and its image in the mirror is closest to:

   A) 2.2 m   B) 1.9 m   C) 1.7 m   D) 1.4 m   E) 1.1 m

   Answer: A
   Var: 12

3) A glass tumbler with a flat base 7.3 mm thick contains an alcoholic liquid 54 mm in height. The indices of refraction of the glass and the liquid are 1.50 and 1.34, respectively. The apparent thickness of the glass base, viewed at normal incidence from above the liquid, in mm, is closest to:

   A) 4.9   B) 5.0   C) 5.2   D) 5.4   E) 5.6

   Answer: A
   Var: 50+

4) A glass tumbler with a flat base 4.9 mm thick contains an alcoholic liquid 58 mm in height. The indices of refraction of the glass and the liquid are 1.50 and 1.34, respectively. The apparent thickness of the liquid, viewed at normal incidence from below the tumbler, in mm, is closest to:

   A) 43   B) 42   C) 40   D) 39   E) 45

   Answer: A
   Var: 50+

5) A glass tumbler with a flat base 5.9 mm thick contains an alcoholic liquid 47 mm in height. The indices of refraction of the glass and the liquid are 1.50 and 1.34, respectively. The tumbler is emptied. The apparent thickness of the glass base, viewed at normal incidence, in mm, is closest to:

   A) 3.9   B) 4.1   C) 4.2   D) 4.4   E) 4.5

   Answer: A
   Var: 50+

6)

Figure 34.1a

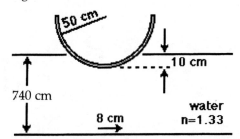

A thin hemispherical bowl of clear plastic floats on water in a tank. The radius of the bowl is 50 cm and the depth of the bowl in water is 10 cm. The depth of the water (n = 1.33) in the tank is 740 cm. An object 8.0 cm long is on the bottom of the tank directly below the bowl. The object is viewed from directly above the bowl. Ignore the refractive effects of the plastic. In Figure 34.1a, the position of the image below the water level, in cm, is closest to:

A) 130   B) 120   C) 220   D) 160   E) 210

Answer: A
Var: 50+

7)

Figure 34.1b

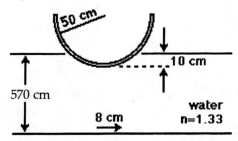

A thin hemispherical bowl of clear plastic floats on water in a tank. The radius of the bowl is 50 cm and the depth of the bowl in water is 10 cm. The depth of the water (n = 1.33) in the tank is 570 cm. An object 8.0 cm long is on the bottom of the tank directly below the bowl. The object is viewed from directly above the bowl. Ignore the refractive effects of the plastic. In Figure 34.1b, the character of the image is:

A) virtual and erect

B) real and inverted

C) real and erect

D) virtual and inverted

E) indeterminate

Answer: A
Var: 50+

8)

Figure 34.1c

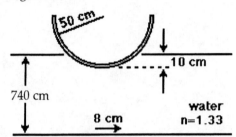

A thin hemispherical bowl of clear plastic floats on water in a tank. The radius of the bowl is 50 cm and the depth of the bowl in water is 10 cm. The depth of the water (n = 1.33) in the tank is 740 cm. An object 8.0 cm long is on the bottom of the tank directly below the bowl. The object is viewed from directly above the bowl. Ignore the refractive effects of the plastic. In Figure 34.1c, the size of the image, in cm, is closest to:

A) 1.7   B) 2.6   C) 3.4   D) 5.1   E) 6.0

Answer: A
Var: 50+

9)

Figure 34.2a

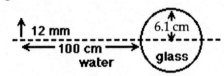

A glass sphere of radius 6.1 cm is immersed in water. An erect object that is 12 mm high is on a horizontal axis which passes through the center of the sphere. The object is 100 cm from the edge of the sphere. The indices of refraction of water and the glass are 1.33 and 1.55, respectively. In Figure 34.2a, the character of the intermediate image, with respect to the erect object, is:

   A) real and inverted

   B) real and erect

   C) virtual and erect

   D) virtual and inverted

   E) indeterminate

Answer: A
Var: 50+

10)

Figure 34.2b

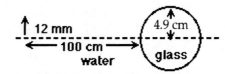

A glass sphere of radius 4.9 cm is immersed in water. An erect object that is 12 mm high is on a horizontal axis which passes through the center of the sphere. The object is 100 cm from the edge of the sphere. The indices of refraction of water and the glass are 1.33 and 1.55, respectively. In Figure 34.2b, the position of the final image, measured from the center of the sphere, in cm, is closest to:

A) 22, on the right

B) 22, on the left

C) 31, on the right

D) 31, on the left

E) 41, on the right

Answer: A

Var: 50+

11)

Figure 34.2c

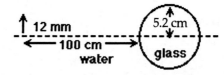

A glass sphere of radius 5.2 cm is immersed in water. An erect object that is 12 mm high is on a horizontal axis which passes through the center of the sphere. The object is 100 cm from the edge of the sphere. The indices of refraction of water and the glass are 1.33 and 1.55, respectively. In Figure 34.2c, the character of the final image, with respect to the erect object, is:

A) real and inverted

B) real and erect

C) virtual and erect

D) virtual and inverted

E) indeterminate

Answer: A

Var: 50+

367

12)

Figure 34.2d

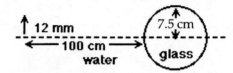

A glass sphere of radius 7.5 cm is immersed in water. An erect object that is 12 mm high is on a horizontal axis which passes through the center of the sphere. The object is 100 cm from the edge of the sphere. The indices of refraction of water and the glass are 1.33 and 1.55, respectively. In Figure 34.2d, the size of the final image, in mm, is closest to:

A) 3.7   B) 4.6   C) 5.9   D) 8.4   E) 14

Answer: A
Var: 50+

13) As you walk away from a plane mirror on a wall, your image

   A) gets smaller.

   B) may or may not get smaller, depending on where the observer is positioned.

   C) is always a real image, no matter how far you are from the mirror.

   D) changes from being a virtual image to a real image as you pass the focal point.

   E) is always the same size.

Answer: E
Var: 1

14) Suppose you place your face in front of a concave mirror.

   A) If you position yourself between the center of curvature and the focal point of the mirror, you will not be able to see your image.

   B) No matter where you place yourself, a real image will be formed.

   C) Your image will always be inverted.

   D) Your image will be diminished in size.

   E) None of these is true.

Answer: A
Var: 1

15) A compound lens is made by joining the plane surfaces of two thin plano-convex lenses of different glasses. The radius of each convex surface is 80 cm. The indices of refraction of the two glasses are 1.50 and 1.60. The focal length of the compound lens, in cm, is closest to:

A) 67   B) 69   C) 71   D) 73   E) 75

Answer: D
Var: 1

16) A doubly convex thin glass lens has equal radii of curvature. The focal length of the lens is + 70.6 cm and the index of refraction of the glass is 1.52. The radius of curvature of each convex surface, in cm, is closest to:

A) 73   B) 66   C) 59   D) 80   E) 88

Answer: A
Var: 50+

17) A doubly convex thin glass lens has equal radii of curvature. The focal length of the lens is + 31.2 cm and the index of refraction of the glass is 1.52. The lens is replaced with a plano–convex glass lens of the same focal length and thickness. The radius of curvature of the convex surface is 13.0 cm. The index of refraction of the glass of the plano–convex lens is closest to:

A) 1.42   B) 1.44   C) 1.40   D) 1.38   E) 1.36

Answer: A
Var: 50+

Figure 34.3

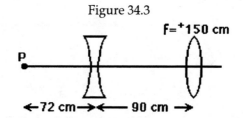

18) In Figure 34.3, a convex lens of focal length +150 cm is 90 cm to the right of a concave lens. A point source of paraxial rays is at P, 72 cm to the left of the concave lens. This point source produces a parallel beam to the right of the convex lens. The focal length of the concave lens, in cm, is closest to:

A) –33   B) –43   C) –60   D) –100   E) –360

Answer: E
Var: 1

Situation 34.1

An erect object is 50 cm from a concave mirror of radius 60 cm.

19) In Situation 34.1, the character of the image is:

     A) real and erect

     B) real and inverted

     C) virtual and erect

     D) virtual and inverted

     E) indeterminate

Answer: B
Var: 1

20) In Situation 34.1, the distance of the image from the mirror, in cm, is closest to:

A) 19   B) 35   C) 60   D) 75   E) 120

Answer: D
Var: 1

21) In Situation 34.1, the lateral magnification of the image is closest to:

A) +0.4   B) +0.7   C) +1.5   D) –0.7   E) –1.5

Answer: E
Var: 1

22) In Situation 34.1, the object is moved to a new position, such that the new lateral magnification is +2.5. The new object distance, in cm, is closest to:

A) 18   B) 24   C) 30   D) 36   E) 42

Answer: A
Var: 1

Figure 34.4

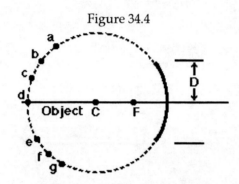

23) In Figure 34.4, a concave spherical mirror has a circular perimeter of diameter D. An object is placed in front of the mirror. The center of curvature C and the focal point F of the mirror are shown. You wish to view all of the image of the object by placing your eye at a point on the dashed circle shown. What is the greatest range of positions which will allow you to see all of the image in the mirror?

A) Any point on the circle from a to g.

B) Any point on the circle from b to f.

C) Any point on the circle from c to e.

D) Any point on the circle from d to g.

E) Any point on the circle from d to e.

Answer: B
Var: 1

Figure 34.5

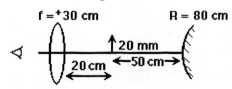

An optical system comprises in turn, from left to right: an observer, a lens of focal length +30 cm, an erect object 20 mm high, and a convex mirror of radius 80 cm. The object is between the lens and the mirror, 20 cm from the lens and 50 cm from the mirror. The observer views the image formed first by reflection and then by refraction.

24) In Figure 34.5, the character of the intermediate image formed by the mirror, with respect to the erect object, is:

   A) real and erect

   B) real and inverted

   C) virtual and erect

   D) virtual and inverted

   E) indeterminate

   Answer: C
   Var: 1

25) In Figure 34.5, the position of the final image, measured from the mirror, in cm, is closest to:

   A) 90   B) 102   C) 114   D) 126   E) 138

   Answer: C
   Var: 1

26) In Figure 34.5, the character of the final image, with respect to the erect object, is:

   A) real and erect

   B) real and inverted

   C) virtual and erect

   D) virtual and inverted

   E) indeterminate

   Answer: B
   Var: 1

27) In Figure 34.5, the size of the final image, in mm, is closest to:

   A) 4.3   B) 5.5   C) 6.7   D) 7.9   E) 9.1

   Answer: A
   Var: 1

28) Suppose you wanted to start a fire using sunlight and a mirror. Which of the following statements is most accurate?

  A) It would be best to use a plane mirror.

  B) It would be best to use a convex mirror.

  C) It would be best to use a concave mirror, with the object to be ignited positioned at the center of curvature of the mirror.

  D) It would be best to use a concave mirror, with the object to be ignited positioned halfway between the mirror and its center of curvature.

  E) One cannot start a fire using a mirror, since mirrors form only virtual images.

Answer: D
Var: 1

29) When an object is placed 30 cm from a converging lens, the image formed is positioned 60 cm from the lens. If the object is moved 5 cm closer to the lens, the position of the image changes by 40 cm. What is the focal length of the lens?

  A) 16 cm   B) 32 cm   C) 36 cm   D) 20 cm   E) 25 cm

Answer: D
Var: 1

30) An amateur astronomer grinds a convex–convex lens whose surfaces have radii of curvature of 40 cm and 60 cm. The glass has an index of refraction of 1.54. What is the focal length of this lens in air?

  A) 42.5 cm   B) 126 cm   C) 88.8 cm   D) 44.4 cm   E) 222 cm

Answer: D
Var: 1

31) A 35 mm camera equipped with a 80 mm focal length lens is used to photograph a tree 15 m tall. The aperture of the lens is set at $f/5.6$. The aperture diameter at $f/5.6$, in mm, is closest to:

  A) 14   B) 9   C) 11   D) 17   E) 20

Answer: A
Var: 50+

32) A 35 mm camera equipped with a 100 mm focal length lens is used to photograph a tree 23 m tall. The aperture of the lens is set at $f/8$. A 32 mm high image of the tree on the film is required. The required distance, between the tree and the camera, to take the photograph is closest to:

  A) 72 m   B) 75 m   C) 79 m   D) 83 m   E) 86 m

Answer: A
Var: 50+

33) A lens of focal length 70 mm is mounted on a 35 mm camera. The lens aperture is set at $f/4$ and the shutter speed set at 1/30 s. The aperture diameter, in mm, is closest to:

    A) 18   B) 12   C) 15   D) 20   E) 23

Answer: A
Var: 50+

34) A lens of focal length 40 mm is mounted on a 35 mm camera. The lens aperture is set at $f/5.6$ and the shutter speed set at 1/250 s. A different camera has a lens of focal length 56 mm in place. The shutter speed is set at 1/60 s. The lens aperture setting, for the closest matching film exposure, is:

    A) $f/5.6$ B) $f/8$ C) $f/11$ D) $f/16$ E) $f/22$

Answer: D
Var: 1

35) A lens of focal length 40 mm is used as a magnifier. The object being viewed is 5.1 mm long, and is positioned at the focal point of the lens. The angle subtended by the image at infinity, in milliradians, is closest to:

    A) 128   B) 85   C) 42   D) 170   E) 213

Answer: A
Var: 50+

36) A lens of focal length 45 mm is used as a magnifier. The object being viewed is 9.8 mm long, and is positioned at the focal point of the lens. The user of the magnifier has a near point at 25 cm. The angular magnification of the magnifier is closest to:

    A) 5.6   B) 5.0   C) 6.1   D) 6.7   E) 7.2

Answer: A
Var: 50+

37) A lens of focal length 105 mm is used as a magnifier. The object being viewed is 8.2 mm long, and is positioned at the focal point of the lens. The lens is moved closer to the object, so that the image is now 25 cm from the lens. The distance the lens has been moved, in cm, is closest to:

    A) 3.1   B) 3.4   C) 2.8   D) 2.5   E) 2.2

Answer: A
Var: 50+

38) A lens of focal length 100 mm is used as a magnifier. The object being viewed is 7.0 mm long, and is positioned at the focal point of the lens. The lateral magnification of the magnifier, when the image is 25 cm from the lens, is closest to:

    A) 3.5   B) 3.2   C) 3.0   D) 2.7   E) 3.8

Answer: A
Var: 50+

39) A farsighted boy has a near point at 0.9 m and requires eyeglasses to correct his vision. Corrective lenses are available in increments in power of 0.25 diopters. The eyeglasses should have lenses of the lowest power for which the near point is no further than 25 cm. The correct choice of lens power for eyeglasses, in diopters, is:

    A) +3.00   B) +2.75   C) +2.50   D) +3.25   E) +3.50

Answer: A
Var: 18

40) A farsighted boy has a near point at 1.4 m and requires eyeglasses to correct his vision. Corrective lenses are available in increments in power of 0.25 diopters. The eyeglasses should have lenses of the lowest power for which the near point is no further than 25 cm. The boy borrows eyeglasses that have a power of +2.25 diopters. With these eyeglasses, the near point of the boy, in cm, is closest to:

    A) 34   B) 31   C) 36   D) 40   E) 44

Answer: A
Var: 50+

41) A myopic girl wears eyeglasses that allow her to have clear distant vision. The power of the lenses of her eyeglasses is –0.25 diopters. Without eyeglasses, the far point of the girl is closest to:

    A) 4.0 m   B) 3.0 m   C) 2.0 m   D) 5.0 m   E) 6.0 m

Answer: A
Var: 12

42) A machinist with normal vision has a near point at 25 cm. The machinist wears eyeglasses in order to do close work. The power of the lenses is +3.25 diopters. With these eyeglasses, the near point of the machinist, in cm, is closest to:

    A) 14   B) 11   C) 8   D) 17   E) 19

Answer: A
Var: 14

43) In a 35 mm single lens reflex camera (SLR) the distance from the lens to the film is varied in order to focus on objects at varying distances. Over what range must a lens of 50 mm focal length vary if the camera is to be able to focus on objects ranging in distance from infinity down to 1.4 m from the camera?

    A) 1.85 mm   B) 1.48 mm   C) 5.56 mm   D) 7.41 mm   E) 2.59 mm

Answer: A
Var: 50+

44) Many people believe they can read better in bright light than in dim light. Is this true?

  A) No, this is a purely psychological effect, since the optical properties of the eye are not dependent on the light used. Bright light merely stimulates some visual neurons that are normally dormant.

  B) Yes, this is true because contraction of the pupil in bright light reduces spherical aberration.

  C) No, because contraction of the pupil in bright light means the same amount of light strikes the retina, and hence the nature of the image formed is unchanged.

  D) Yes, because bright light tends to reduce astigmatism due to excess contraction of the ciliary muscles.

  E) Yes, because bright light increases the magnification provided by the cornea and crystalline lens.

Answer: B
Var: 1

Situation 34.2

The objective of a microscope has a focal length of 2.4 mm and the eyepiece has an angular magnification of 15. The object is positioned 0.06 mm beyond the focal point of the objective. The focal point of the eyepiece is positioned at the real image formed by the objective.

45) In Situation 34.2, the overall magnification of the microscope is closest to:

  A) 400   B) 450   C) 500   D) 550   E) 600

Answer: E
Var: 1

46) In Situation 34.2, the separation between the objective and the eyepiece, in mm, is closest to:

  A) 98   B) 102   C) 107   D) 111   E) 115

Answer: E
Var: 1

Situation 34.3

The objective and the eyepiece of a microscope have focal lengths of 4.0 mm and 25 mm, respectively. The objective produces a real image 30 times the size of the object. The final image is viewed at infinity. The near point of the microscope user is at 25 cm.

47) In Situation 34.3, the distance between the object and the focal point of the objective, in mm, is closest to:

  A) 0.13   B) 0.18   C) 0.23   D) 0.28   E) 0.33

Answer: A
Var: 1

48) In Situation 34.3, the distance between the objective and the real image produced by it, in mm, is closest to:

  A) 116   B) 120   C) 124   D) 128   E) 132

Answer: C
Var: 1

49) In Situation 34.3, the overall magnification of the microscope is closest to:

A) 250   B) 300   C) 350   D) 400   E) 450

Answer: B
Var: 1

Situation 34.4

The angular magnification of a refracting telescope is 40. When the object and final image are both at infinity, the distance between the eyepiece and the objective is 143.5 cm. The telescope is used to view a distant radio tower. The real image of the tower, formed by the objective, is 6.0 mm in height. The focal point of the eyepiece is positioned at the real image.

50) In Situation 34.4, the focal length of the objective, in cm, is closest to:

A) 137   B) 138   C) 139   D) 140   E) 141

Answer: D
Var: 1

51) In Situation 34.4, the angle subtended by the final image of the tower is closest to:

A) 0.15 rad   B) 0.17 rad   C) 0.19 rad   D) 0.21 rad   E) 0.23 rad

Answer: B
Var: 1

Situation 34.5

The mirror of a reflecting telescope has a 2.4 m radius of curvature and the eyepiece has a focal length of 20 mm. The telescope is used to view a crater on the moon. The final image is viewed at infinity. The angle subtended by the final image of the crater is 12 m rad. The distance of the moon from the earth is 380,000 km.

52) In Situation 34.5, the distance between the eyepiece and the mirror, in cm, is closest to:

A) 122   B) 140   C) 162   D) 242   E) 260

Answer: A
Var: 1

53) In Situation 34.5, the diameter of the real image of the crater, formed by the mirror, in mm, is closest to:

A) 0.24   B) 0.36   C) 0.48   D) 0.60   E) 0.72

Answer: A
Var: 1

54) In Situation 34.5, the diameter of the crater, in km, is closest to:

A) 51   B) 76   C) 101   D) 127   E) 152

Answer: B
Var: 1

55) The objective and the eyepiece of a refracting astronomical telescope have focal lengths of 320 cm and 4.0 cm, respectively. The telescope is used to view Neptune and the final image is set at infinity. The diameter of Neptune is 4.96×10^7 m and the distance from Earth at the time of observation is 4.4×10^{12} m. The angle subtended by the final telescopic image of Neptune, in m rad, is closest to:

   A) 0.9   B) 1.1   C) 1.3   D) 1.5   E) 1.7

Answer: A
Var: 1

56) A refracting telescope has an objective focal length of 320 cm and an angular magnification of 75. The telescope is initially focused on a star. The telescope is then refocused on a mountain top, 10 km distant. The final telescopic image is at infinity in both cases. The change made, in the separation between the objective and the eyepiece, due to the refocusing, in mm, is closest to:

   A) +1.0 mm   B) +1.5 mm   C) +2.0 mm   D) –1.5 mm   E) –2.0 mm

Answer: A
Var: 1

57) As a treatment for cataracts (a cloudiness of the lens of the eye), the natural lens is removed and a plastic lens is implanted. After this is done a person can see distant objects clearly, but he cannot accommodate to focus on nearby objects. If for example such a person wanted to read a book at a distance of 25 cm, he would have to wear eyeglasses whose diopter power was approximately

   A) +2.78 diopters

   B) +3.33 diopters

   C) –1.78 diopters

   D) +4.00 diopters

   E) –4.00 diopters

Answer: D
Var: 1

58) In a compound microscope

   A) both the objective and the eyepiece form real images.

   B) magnification is provided by the objective lens and not by the eyepiece. The eyepiece merely increases the resolution of the image viewed.

   C) magnification is provided by the objective and not by the eyepiece. The eyepiece merely increases the brightness of the image viewed.

   D) The magnification is $m_1 + M_2$, where m_1 is the lateral magnification of the objective and M_2 is the angular magnification of the eyepiece.

   E) the image of the objective serves as the object for the eyepiece.

Answer: E
Var: 1

59) The eyepiece of a compound microscope has a focal length of 2.50 cm and the objective has a focal length of 1.30 cm. The two lenses are separated by 26.0 cm. The microscope is used by a person with normal eyes (near point at 25 cm). What is the angular magnification of the microscope?

A) 181   B) 200   C) 452   D) 500   E) 235

Answer: A
Var: 50+

60) If one were to cover the lower half of the objective lens of a telescope, what effect would this have on the image?

A) The lower half of the image would be blacked out.

B) The upper half of the image would be blacked out.

C) This would have no effect on the appearance of the image.

D) The image would appear as before, but dimmer.

E) The shape of the image would be somewhat distorted.

Answer: D
Var: 1

61) The objective lens of an astronomical telescope has a focal length of 60 cm and the eyepiece has a focal length of 2 cm. How far apart should the lenses be placed in order to form a final image at infinity?

A) 44 cm   B) 58 cm   C) 76 cm   D) 60 cm   E) 62 cm

Answer: E
Var: 1

62) Which of the following is an accurate statement?

A) A zoom lens of the type used in cameras and projectors functions by varying the distance between various combinations of lenses while keeping the focal length of the combination constant.

B) In a graded-index converging lens the index of refraction increases as the distance from the axis increases.

C) A Fresnel lens utilizes interference effects, as opposed to refraction.

D) An advantage of a Fresnel lens is that it is much lighter than a comparable ordinary lens.

E) A reason for using a Fresnel lens rather than an ordinary lens is that the Fresnel lens gives a much higher quality image.

Answer: D
Var: 1

Short Answer Questions

1) When an object is placed 136 cm from a diverging thin lens, its image is found to be 68 cm from the lens. The lens is removed, and replaced by a thin converging lens whose focal length is the same in absolute value as the diverging lens. This second lens is at the original position of the first lens. Where is the image of the object now?

Answer: at infinity
Var: 50+

2) An object 3.4 mm tall is placed 25 cm from the vertex of a convex spherical mirror. The radius of curvature of the mirror has magnitude 36 cm.
(a) How far is the image from the vertex of the mirror?
(b) What is the height of the image?

Answer: (a) 10 cm
         (b) 1.4 mm
Var: 50+

Figure 34.6

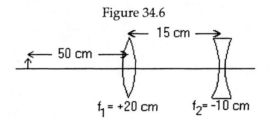

3) In Figure 34.6, an object of height 2.00 mm is placed 57 cm to the left of a converging lens of focal length $f_1 = +20$ cm. A diverging lens of focal length $f_2 = -10$ cm is 15 cm to the right of the first lens. Calculate the
(a) location (relative to the second lens),
(b) nature (real or virtual),
(c) orientation (erect or inverted), and
(d) height of the final image formed by the pair of lenses.

Answer: (a) 27 cm to the left of the second lens
         (b) virtual
         (c) erect
         (d) 1.9 mm
Var: 50+

4) The left–hand end of a glass rod is ground to a spherical surface. The glass has index of refraction 1.50. A small object 4.00 mm tall is placed in the axis of the rod, 25.0 cm to the left of the vertex of the spherical surface. The image is formed in the rod, 39.0 cm to the right of the vertex.
(a) What is the magnitude of the radius of curvature of the spherical surface at the end of the rod?
(b) What is the height of the image?

Answer: (a) 6.37 cm
         (b) 4.16 mm
Var: 50+

5) A tank contains benzene, which has index of refraction 1.50. A dime is on the bottom of the tank. When viewed at normal incidence the dime appears to be 54 cm below the surface of the benzene. What is the actual depth of the benzene?

Answer: 81 cm
Var: 50+

6) What power (in diopters) if corrective lens is required to correct the vision of a myopic eye whose far point is at 240 cm?

Answer: –0.42 diopters
Var: 29

7) A zoom lens is adjusted to change its focal length from 44 mm to 242 mm. If the same amount of light is to be admitted to the lens, what is the final f-number if the original f-number was 2.0?

Answer: 11
Var: 50+

8)   Figure 34.7

In Figure 34.7, a numismatist is examining a 1905 coin with a magnifying glass of focal length 31 cm. The numeral "5" appears to be 3.8 mm high when focused at a near point of 25 cm (that is, it appears to be the same size as an object 3.8 mm high on the same surface of the coin.) What is the actual size of the numeral "5"? (Assume nonastigmatic numismatist.)

Answer: 2.1 mm
Var: 50+

9) A sailboat on the ocean has a mast of height 19.2 m. When viewed through a pair of binoculars the mast has an angular size of 0.076 rad. If the eyepiece of the binoculars has a focal length of 1.15 cm and the objective lens has a focal length of 7.85 cm, what is the distance between the observer and the sailboat?

Answer: 1.7 km
Var: 50+

10) A compound microscope consists of an objective of focal length f_O and an eyepiece with magnification 25. The microscope is designed so that the object is focused in a plane 16.0 cm away from the focal point of the objective lens. When properly adjusted, the eyepiece and the objective are 17.4 cm apart. What is f_O? (Assume that the eyepiece magnification is based on an image at infinity and a near point at 25 cm.)

Answer: 0.4 cm
Var: 50+

Chapter 35   Interference

Multiple Choice Questions

1) Two radio antennas are 140 m apart on a north–south line. The two antennas radiate in phase at a frequency of 5.1 MHz. All radio measurements are made far from the antennas. The smallest angle, reckoned east of north from the antennas, at which constructive interference of two radio waves occurs, is closest to:

    A) $33°$ B) $36°$ C) $30°$ D) $26°$ E) $23°$

Answer: A
Var: 50+

2) Two radio antennas are 100 m apart on a north–south line. The two antennas radiate in phase at a frequency of 4.6 MHz. All radio measurements are made far from the antennas. The smallest angle, reckoned north of east from the antennas, at which destructive interference of the two radio waves occurs, is closest to:

    A) $19°$ B) $9.5°$ C) $14°$ D) $24°$ E) $29°$

Answer: A
Var: 50+

3) Two radio antennas are 130 m apart on a north–south line. The two antennas radiate in phase at a frequency of 3.5 MHz. All radio measurements are made far from the antennas. Point A is due east of the antennas and point B is $30°$ north of east from the antennas. Both points A and B are at the same large distance from the antennas. The ratio of the intensity of the radio signal at B to that at A is closest to:

    A) 0.53   B) 0.26   C) 0.79   D) 1.1   E) 1.6

Answer: A
Var: 50+

4) Two radio antennas are 10 km apart on a north–south axis on a seacoast. The antennas broadcast identical AM radio signals, in phase, at a frequency of 1.10 MHz. A steamship, 200 km offshore, travels due north at a speed of 15 km/hr and passes east of the antennas. A radio on board the ship is tuned to the broadcast frequency. The reception of the radio signal on the ship is a maximum at a given instant. The time interval until the next occurrence of maximum reception is closest to:

    A) 22 min   B) 16 min   C) 27 min   D) 33 min   E) 38 min

Answer: A
Var: 50+

5) Two radio antennas are 10 km apart on a north–south axis on a seacoast. The antennas broadcast identical AM radio signals, in phase, at a frequency of 3.70 MHz. A steamship, 200 km offshore, travels due north at a speed of 15 km/hr and passes east of the antennas. A radio on board the ship is tuned to the broadcast frequency. Four minutes after a radio signal of maximum intensity is received, the ratio of the intensity of the signal received to the maximum intensity is closest to:

A) 0.13   B) 0.18   C) 0.23   D) 0.077   E) 0.039

Answer: A
Var: 50+

6)

Figure 35.1a

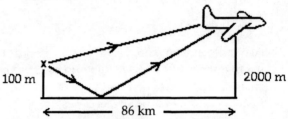

An FM radio transmitter, operating at a frequency of 120 MHz, is atop a 100 m tower. An airplane is in flight over the ocean at an altitude of 2000 m. Radio waves reach the airplane directly from the transmitter and by reflection from the surface of the ocean. When the airplane is 86 km from the tower, the pilot observes that radio reception has faded due to destructive interference of the waves in the two paths. Assume the wave reflected from the ocean surface has undergone a half wave phase shift. In Figure 35.1a, the waves of the reflected path arrive at the airplane delayed, with respect to the direct path. The time interval of this delay, in ns, is closest to:

A) 16   B) 14   C) 18   D) 20   E) 22

Answer: A
Var: 50+

7)

Figure 35.1b

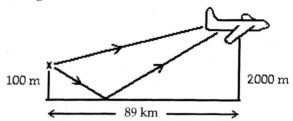

100 m   2000 m

←——— 89 km ———→

An FM radio transmitter, operating at a frequency of 120 MHz, is atop a 100 m tower. An airplane is in flight over the ocean at an altitude of 2000 m. Radio waves reach the airplane directly from the transmitter and by reflection from the surface of the ocean. When the airplane is 89 km from the tower, the pilot observes that radio reception has faded due to destructive interference of the waves in the two paths. Assume the wave reflected from the ocean surface has undergone a half wave phase shift. In Figure 35.1b, the ratio of the difference in the lengths of the two radio paths to the wavelength is closest to:

A) 1.8   B) 1.9   C) 2.0   D) 2.1   E) 2.2

Answer: A
Var: 50+

8)

Figure 35.2a

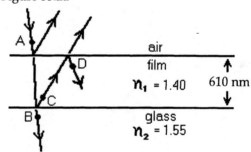

A 610 nm thick film, of index $n_1 = 1.40$, is on the surface of a glass plate, of index $n_2 = 1.55$. A ray of monochromatic light, of 500 nm wavelength, is incident normally upon the air–film interface, and undergoes reflections and transmissions. Consider points A, B, C, and D as being at a negligible distance from their nearest interfaces, respectively. In Figure 35.2a, the phase difference in the wave at B, with respect to the wave at A is closest to:

A) 11 rad   B) 8.7 rad   C) 8.6 rad   D) 9.6 rad   E) 12 rad

Answer: A
Var: 50+

9)

Figure 35.2b

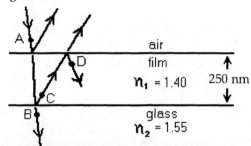

A 250 nm thick film, of index $n_1 = 1.40$, is on the surface of a glass plate, of index $n_2 = 1.55$. A ray of monochromatic light, of 500 nm wavelength, is incident normally upon the air–film interface, and undergoes reflections and transmissions. Consider points A, B, C, and D as being at a negligible distance from their nearest interfaces, respectively. In Figure 35.2b, the phase difference in the wave at C, with respect to the wave at A is closest to:

A) 1.3 rad　　　　B) 2.3 rad　　　　C) 3.3 rad　　　　D) 4.4 rad　　　　E) 5.5 rad

Answer: A
Var: 50+

10)

Figure 35.2c

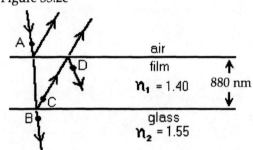

A 880 nm thick film, of index $n_1 = 1.40$, is on the surface of a glass plate, of index $n_2 = 1.55$. A ray of monochromatic light, of 500 nm wavelength, is incident normally upon the air–film interface, and undergoes reflections and transmissions. Consider points A, B, C, and D as being at a negligible distance from their nearest interfaces, respectively. In Figure 35.2c, the phase difference in the wave at D, with respect to the wave at A is closest to:

A) 28 rad　　　　B) 29 rad　　　　C) 30 rad　　　　D) 31 rad　　　　E) 33 rad

Answer: A
Var: 50+

11) Which of the following statements best states the principle which accounts for the phenomenon of interference?

  A) The necessary and sufficient condition for the interference of two waves is that they overlap in space and travel at the same velocity.

  B) When two or more waves overlap, the resultant displacement at any point and at any instant may be found by adding the instantaneous displacements that would be produced at the point by the individual waves if each were present alone.

  C) Since energy is conserved, for every region in which destructive interference occurs, there must be a corresponding region in which constructive interference occurs.

  D) Interference requires that the two interacting waves be in phase.

  E) It is not possible to observe interference effects using a single light source.

Answer: B
Var: 1

12) When an airplane flies by in the vicinity of your house, you may notice your television picture flicker. This effect is most likely due to

  A) diffraction.

  B) interference.

  C) phase incoherence.

  D) refraction.

  E) frequency modulation.

Answer: B
Var: 1

13) At most, how many bright fringes can be formed on one side of the central bright fringe (not counting the central bright fringe) when light of 625 nm falls on a double slit whose spacing is 4.74×10^{-6} m?

  A) 7 B) 6 C) 5 D) 8 E) 9

Answer: A
Var: 50+

Situation 35.1

A 360 nm thick oil film floats on the surface of the water. The indices of refraction of the oil and the water are 1.50 and 1.33, respectively. The surface of the oil is illuminated from above at normal incidence with white light.

14) In Situation 35.1, the two wavelengths of light in the 400 nm to 800 nm wavelength band that are most strongly reflected, in nm, are closest to:

  A) 410 and 700

  B) 430 and 720

  C) 450 and 740

  D) 470 and 760

  E) 490 and 780

Answer: B
Var: 1

385

15) In Situation 35.1, the wavelength of light in the 400 nm to 800 nm wavelength band that is most weakly reflected, in nm, is closest to:

A) 520   B) 540   C) 560   D) 580   E) 600

Answer: B
Var: 1

Situation 35.2

A pair of narrow slits, separated by 1.8 mm, is illuminated by a monochromatic light source. Light waves arrive at the two slits in phase. A fringe pattern is observed on a screen 4.8 m from the slits.

16) In Situation 35.2, there are 5.0 bright fringes/cm on the screen. The wavelength of the monochromatic light is closest to:

A) 550 nm   B) 600 nm   C) 650 nm   D) 700 nm   E) 750 nm

Answer: E
Var: 1

17) In Situation 35.2, monochromatic light of 450 nm wavelength is used. The angular separation between adjacent dark fringes on the screen, measured at the slits, in m rad, is closest to:

A) 0.15   B) 0.20   C) 0.25   D) 0.30   E) 0.36

Answer: C
Var: 1

Situation 35.3

Two optically flat glass plates, 16 cm long, are in contact at one end and separated by 0.020 mm at the other end. The space between the plates is occupied by oil with index of refraction 1.45. The index of the glass plates is 1.55. The plates are illuminated at normal incidence with monochromatic light, and fringes are observed.

18) In Situation 35.3, the monochromatic light has a wavelength of 580 nm. The number of bright fringes which are visible is closest to:

A) 60   B) 70   C) 80   D) 90   E) 100

Answer: E
Var: 1

19) In Situation 35.3, the spacing of the dark fringes is 2.0 mm. The wavelength of the monochromatic light, in nm, is closest to:

A) 425   B) 475   C) 525   D) 675   E) 725

Answer: E
Var: 1

Situation 35.4

The curved surface of a plano-convex glass lens is placed on an optically flat glass plate. The radius of curvature of the convex surface is 40 cm. The plane surface of the lens is illuminated at normal incidence with monochromatic light and Newton's rings are observed by reflection. Do not consider the center spot as a ring.

20) In Situation 35.4, the light has a wavelength of 720 nm. The radius of the third bright ring, in mm, is closest to:

A) 0.66   B) 0.76   C) 0.85   D) 0.93   E) 1.00

Answer: C
Var: 1

21) In Situation 35.4, the radius of the third dark ring is 0.80 mm. The wavelength of the light, in nm, is closest to:

A) 490   B) 530   C) 580   D) 620   E) 650

Answer: B
Var: 1

Figure 35.3

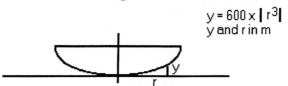

$$y = 600 \times |r^3|$$
$$y \text{ and } r \text{ in m}$$

A plano-convex glass lens is ground to a special non-spherical surface. The lens is placed on an optically flat glass plate for testing. The equation for the curved surface of the lens is $y = 600 \times |r^3|$ where y and r are both in m. Newton's rings are observed by reflection when the lens is illuminated normally from above, with monochromatic light whose wavelength is 600 nm. Do not consider the center spot as a ring.

22) In Figure 35.3, the radius of the second bright ring is closest to:

A) 0.79 mm   B) 0.91 mm   C) 1.00 mm   D) 1.08 mm   E) 1.14 mm

Answer: B
Var: 1

23) In Figure 35.3, the radius of the second dark ring is closest to:

A) 0.79 mm   B) 0.91 mm   C) 1.00 mm   D) 1.08 mm   E) 1.14 mm

Answer: C
Var: 1

Situation 35.5

The mirrors of a Michelson interferometer are 5.0 cm wide. Monochromatic light of 450 nm wavelength is used and 12.0 fringes are observed.

24) In Situation 35.5, the angle formed by the plane of the movable mirror and the plane of the image of the fixed mirror, in mrad, is closest to:

A) 36   B) 45   C) 54   D) 63   E) 72

Answer: C
Var: 1

25) In Situation 35.5, the movable mirror is moved toward the observer and 12.0 fringes travel across the field of view. The distance the movable mirror was moved, in mm, is closest to:

A) 1.8 B) 2.7 C) 3.6 D) 4.5 E) 5.4

Answer: B
Var: 1

Figure 35.4

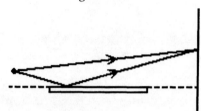

26) In Figure 35.4, Lloyd's Mirror is an apparatus that can be used to form interference fringes using a single source. Light from the source is reflected off a plane mirror and viewed on a screen. A reflected ray and a direct ray can interfere to form a fringe pattern on the screen. In the arrangement drawn here, the screen is 2.4 m from the source, and the separation between fringes on the screen is 1.3 mm. The light has wavelength 580 nm. How high above the reflecting plane is the source positioned?

A) 1.64 mm B) 1.08 mm C) 0.54 mm D) 1.22 mm E) 0.27 mm

Answer: C
Var: 1

27) An oil film (n = 1.48) of thickness 290 nm floating on water is illuminated with white light at normal incidence. What is the wavelength of the dominant color in the reflected light?

A) Green (541 nm)

B) Blue-green (493 nm)

C) Violet (404 nm)

D) Yellow (572 nm)

E) Blue (470 nm)

Answer: D
Var: 1

28) If light traveling in material of index n_1 is reflected from a material of index n_2, then in the case where $n_2 > n_1$ the light undergoes a 180° phase shift on reflection. This helps us to understand

A) why the central spot in Newton's rings is dark.

B) why the separation of fringes due to two slit interference increases with increasing angle of deviation.

C) why a dark fringe appears on the axis ($\theta = 0°$) in a double slit interference pattern.

D) why no factor of two appears in the equation d sin θ = mλ.

E) why nonreflective coatings on lenses are made using coating material with a greater index of refraction than that of the glass they are coating.

Answer: A
Var: 1

29) The main reason the Michelson–Morley experiment is considered important is that

    A) it demonstrated that light was an electromagnetic wave.

    B) it gave strong experimental support to the special theory of relativity.

    C) it demonstrated the existence of the ether.

    D) it showed that light could exhibit interference effects.

    E) it provided an accurate measurement of the speed of light.

Answer: B
Var: 1

30) A spaceship utilizes a large sail of highly reflecting aluminum foil as an auxiliary propulsion system. If the sail area is 1.6 km^2 and is oriented for maximum efficiency in starlight of intensity 500 W/m^2 and wavelength 550 nm, the resulting acceleration of a ship of mass 120,000 kg would be about

    A) $1.2 \times 10^{-6} \, m/s^2$

    B) $3.46 \times 10^{-4} \, m/s^2$

    C) $2.2 \times 10^{-5} \, m/s^2$

    D) $7.5 \times 10^{-6} \, m/s^2$

    E) $4.4 \times 10^{-5} \, m/s^2$

Answer: E
Var: 1

Short Answer Questions

1) Light of wavelength 519 nm passes through two slits. In the interference pattern on a screen 4.6 m away, adjacent bright fringes are separated by 2.3 mm. What is the separation of the two slits?

Answer: 1.0 mm
Var: 50+

2) Light is incident perpendicularly from air onto a liquid film that is on a glass plate. The liquid film is 197 nm thick, and the liquid has index of refraction 1.60. The glass has index of refraction n = 1.50. Calculate the longest visible wavelength (as measured in air) of the light for which there will be totally destructive interference between the rays reflected from the top and bottom surfaces of the film. (Note: Assume that the visible spectrum lies between 400 and 700 nm.)

Answer: 630 nm
Var: 50+

3) A soap bubble, when illuminated with light of 584 nm, appears to be especially reflective. If the index of refraction of the film is 1.35, what is the thinnest thickness the soap film can be?

Answer: 108 nm
Var: 50+

4) Light of wavelength λ = 525 nm passes through two slits separated by 0.500 mm and produces an interference pattern on a screen 7.80 m away. Let the intensity at the central maximum be I_0. What is the distance on the screen from the center of this central maximum to the point where the intensity has fallen to $1/2\, I_0$? (Assume that the slits are sufficiently narrow that diffraction effects may be ignored.)

Answer: 2.05×10^{-3} m

Var: 50+

5) A helium–neon laser emits light of wavelength 632.8 nm directed at a black piece of paper of mass 0.050 g. The power output of the laser is 33.0 mW, and all of the emitted light strikes the paper.
(a) How many photons strike the paper in one second?
(b) What is the recoil velocity of the paper assuming the beam strikes the paper for only one second and the beam is totally absorbed by the paper?

Answer: (a) 1.05×10^{17} photons
   (b) 2.2×10^{-6} m/s

Var: 50+

Chapter 36   Diffraction

Multiple Choice Questions

1) A single slit forms a diffraction pattern, with the first minimum at an angle of 40° from central maximum. Monochromatic light of 440 nm wavelength is used. The same slit, illuminated by a different monochromatic light source, produces a diffraction pattern with the second minimum at a 60° angle from the central maximum. The wavelength of this light, in nm, is closest to:

   A) 297   B) 314   C) 332   D) 349   E) 367

   Answer: A
   Var: 33

2) A single slit forms a diffraction pattern, with the first minimum at an angle of 40° from central maximum. Monochromatic light of 530 nm wavelength is used. The width of the slit, in nm, is closest to:

   A) 825   B) 791   C) 757   D) 723   E) 689

   Answer: A
   Var: 33

3) A single slit, 2100 nm wide, forms a diffraction pattern when illuminated by monochromatic light of 670 nm wavelength. The largest angle from the central maximum at which the intensity is zero is closest to:

   A) 73°   B) 70°   C) 67°   D) 64°   E) 61°

   Answer: A
   Var: 50+

4) A single slit, 1600 nm wide, forms a diffraction pattern when illuminated by monochromatic light of 670 nm wavelength. At an angle of 10° from the central maximum, the phase angle between wavelets originating at the far edge of the slit, relative to wavelets originating at the near edge, is closest to:

   A) 2.6 rad   B) 1.3 rad   C) 2.0 rad   D) 3.3 rad   E) 3.9 rad

   Answer: A
   Var: 50+

5) A single slit, 1400 nm wide, forms a diffraction pattern when illuminated by monochromatic light of 430 nm wavelength. At an angle of 10° from the central maximum, the ratio of the intensity to that of the central maximum is closest to:

   A) 0.30   B) 0.34   C) 0.38   D) 0.42   E) 0.46

   Answer: A
   Var: 50+

6) A single slit forms a diffraction pattern with monochromatic light. The 6-th minimum of the pattern occurs at an angle of 26° from the central maximum. The number of bright bands on either side of the central band is closest to:

A) 12   B) 11   C) 13   D) 14   E) 15

Answer: A
Var: 50+

7) A single slit forms a diffraction pattern with monochromatic light. The fourth minimum of the pattern occurs at an angle of 25° from the central maximum. The angle at which the fifth minimum of the pattern occurs is closest to:

A) 31.9°   B) 31.4°   C) 30.9°   D) 32.4°   E) 32.9°

Answer: A
Var: 40

8) An 18 mm wide diffraction grating has rulings of 580 lines per mm. Light is incident normally on the grating. Monochromatic light of 487 nm wavelength is used. The largest angle from the normal at which an intensity maximum is formed is closest to:

A) 58   B) 56   C) 54   D) 52   E) 50

Answer: A
Var: 50+

9) An 47 mm wide diffraction grating has rulings of 550 lines per mm. Light is incident normally on the grating. Two spectral lines have wavelengths close to 580 nm and the difference in their wavelengths is small. The smallest difference in the wavelengths of the two spectral lines that can be resolved by the grating in the highest order is closest to:

A) 0.007   B) 0.01   C) 0.02   D) 0.03   E) 0.04

Answer: A
Var: 50+

10) An 11 mm wide diffraction grating has rulings of 410 lines per mm. Light is incident normally on the grating. The longest wavelength that forms an intensity maximum in the fifth order is closest to:

A) 488 nm   B) 463 nm   C) 513 nm   D) 538 nm   E) 563 nm

Answer: A
Var: 50+

11) The spacing of ruled lines on a diffraction grating is 1820 nm. The grating is illuminated at normal incidence with a parallel beam of white light in the 400 nm to 700 nm wavelength band. The angular width of the gap between the first order spectrum and the second order spectrum is closest to:

A) 3.5°   B) 4.5°   C) 5.5°   D) 6.5°   E) 2.5°

Answer: A
Var: 50+

12) The spacing of ruled lines on a diffraction grating is 1830 nm. The grating is illuminated at normal incidence with a parallel beam of white light in the 400 nm to 700 nm wavelength band. The second order spectrum and the third order spectrum overlap. The angular width of the overlap is closest to:

A) 8.9°　　　　B) 7.9°　　　　C) 6.9°　　　　D) 5.9°　　　　E) 4.9°

Answer: A
Var: 50+

13) The spacing of ruled lines on a diffraction grating is 1520 nm. The grating is illuminated at normal incidence with a parallel beam of white light in the 400 nm to 700 nm wavelength band. The longest wavelength that appears in the third order spectrum is closest to:

A) 507 nm　　　　B) 487 nm　　　　C) 467 nm　　　　D) 447 nm　　　　E) 527 nm

Answer: A
Var: 50+

Situation 36.1

A metallic sheet has a large number of slits, 5.0 mm wide and 20 cm apart, and is used as a diffraction grating for microwaves. A wide parallel beam of microwaves is incident normally on the grating.

14) In Situation 36.1, the microwave wavelength is 6.0 cm. The largest angle from the normal, at which an intensity maximum occurs, is closest to:

A) 64°　　　　B) 69°　　　　C) 74°　　　　D) 79°　　　　E) 84°

Answer: A
Var: 1

15) In Situation 36.1, the smallest microwave frequency for which only the central maximum occurs is closest to:

A) 0.5 GHz　　　　B) 0.7 GHz　　　　C) 1.0 GHz　　　　D) 1.5 GHz　　　　E) 2.0 GHz

Answer: D
Var: 1

16) In Situation 36.1, intensity maxima occur two degrees apart in the central region. The wavelength of the microwaves is closest to:

A) 5 mm　　　　B) 6 mm　　　　C) 7 mm　　　　D) 8 mm　　　　E) 9 mm

Answer: C
Var: 1

17) Light of wavelength 560 nm illuminates a single slit placed 60 cm from a screen. The separation between the first and third minima in the diffraction pattern is 2.8 mm. What is the slit width?

    A) 0.72 mm

    B) 0.24 mm

    C) 1.16 mm

    D) 3.8×10^{-5} m

    E) 0.082 mm

Answer: B
Var: 1

18) If the intensity of the central maximum in a single slit diffraction pattern has intensity I_o, what is the approximate intensity of the first secondary maximum?

    A) $0.22\ I_o$ B) $0.25\ I_o$ C) $0.50\ I_o$ D) $0.045\ I_o$ E) $0.090\ I_o$

Answer: D
Var: 1

19) Consider the interference pattern formed by 12 equally spaced narrow slits. How many minima are there between adjacent maxima?

    A) 12   B) 6   C) 13   D) 11   E) 5

Answer: D
Var: 1

Situation 36.2

Certain planes of a crystal of halite have a spacing of 0.399 mm. The crystal is irradiated by a beam of x-rays. First order constructive interference occurs when the beam makes an angle of 20° with the planes.

20) In Situation 36.2, the wavelength of the x-rays, in nm, is closest to:

    A) 0.14   B) 0.17   C) 0.21   D) 0.24   E) 0.27

Answer: E
Var: 1

21) In Situation 36.2, the angle the beam makes with the planes for second order constructive interference to occur is closest to:

    A) 37°   B) 40°   C) 43°   D) 46°   E) 49°

Answer: C
Var: 1

22) A diffraction grating has 450 lines per mm. What is the highest order that contains the entire visible spectrum from 400 nm to 700 nm?

    A) m = 2   B) m = 3   C) m = 4   D) m = 5   E) m = 6

Answer: B
Var: 1

23) Which of the following changes would increase the separation between the bright fringes in the diffraction pattern formed by a diffraction grating?

A) Increase the wavelength of the light used.

B) Increase the separation between the slits.

C) Immerse the apparatus in water.

D) None of these.

E) More than one of these.

Answer: A
Var: 1

24) The lattice spacing of the principal Bragg planes in sodium chloride is 0.282 nm. For what wavelength will the first order diffracted beam be deviated by 70°?

A) 0.323 nm   B) 0.530 nm   C) 0.662 nm   D) 0.150 nm   E) 0.680 nm

Answer: A
Var: 1

25) A camera set with f-number f/4 has a focal length of 50 nm. What is the minimum spacing of two objects positioned 12 meters from the lens if the objects are barely resolved in the image? Assume the light wavelength is 500 nm.

A) 1.66 mm

B) 4.72 mm

C) 0.024 mm

D) 4.9×10^{-5} m

E) 0.58 mm

Answer: E
Var: 1

26) Suppose that a spherical object of diameter R is placed in a beam of light which is incident on a screen a distance d >> R from the object. What will be seen at the center of the "shadow" region of the screen?

A) The center of the shadow may be bright or dark, depending on the magnitudes of R, d and the wavelength of the light, λ.

B) The center of the shadow will be bright only if $\frac{2R^2}{d} = 1.22\lambda$

C) The center of the shadow will be dark only if $\frac{2R^2}{d} = 1.22\lambda$

D) The center of the shadow will be dark in all cases.

E) The center of the shadow will be bright in all cases.

Answer: E
Var: 1

27) Which of the following does not accurately describe a hologram?

A) It is a photographic image of an interference pattern.

B) It forms a true three dimensional image of an object.

C) The light used to form the hologram must be coherent.

D) The hologram image looks the same when viewed from all perspectives or directions.

E) It must be viewed with light of the same wavelength as that used to make the hologram.

Answer: D
Var: 1

Situation 36.3

A camera used for aerial surveillance has a lens with a 30 cm maximum aperture and a 42 cm focal length. Assume light of 550 nm wavelength is used and that the resolution of the camera is limited solely by diffraction.

28) In Situation 36.3, the angular resolution of the camera at maximum aperture, in mrad, is closest to:

A) 1.6   B) 2.2   C) 3.2   D) 4.5   E) 6.3

Answer: B
Var: 1

29) In Situation 36.3, the lens has a minimum aperture of 3.8 cm. For this aperture, the radius of the Airy disk in the focal plane is closest to:

A) 1.9 μm   B) 2.6 μm   C) 3.7 μm   D) 5.2 μm   E) 7.4 μm

Answer: E
Var: 1

Short Answer Questions

Figure 36.1

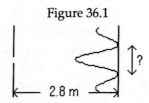

2.8 m

1) In Figure 36.1, a slit 0.3×10^{-3} m wide is illuminated by light of wavelength 403 nm. A diffraction pattern is seen on a screen 2.8 m from the slit. What is the linear distance on the screen between the first two diffraction minima on either side of the central diffraction maximum?

Answer: 7.5×10^{-3} m
Var: 50+

2) A diffraction grating is to be used to find the wavelength of the emission spectrum of a gas. The grating spacing is not known, but a light of a known wavelength of 632.8 nm is deflected by 43.2° in the second order by this grating. Light of the wavelength to be measured is deflected by 48.4° in the second order. What is the wavelength of this light?

Answer: 691 nm
Var: 50+

3) Treat each of your eyes as a circular aperture of diameter 3.5 mm. Light of wavelength 500 nm is used to view two point sources that are 712 m distant from you. How far apart must these two point sources be if they are to be just resolved by your eye? Assume that the resolution is diffraction limited and use Rayleigh's criterion.

Answer: 1.2×10^{-1} m
Var: 50+

4) In a diffraction pattern produced by a single slit, the phase angle β (the phase difference between wavelets from the top and bottom of the slit) is 9.60 π rad at an angle of 0.770° from the central maximum. If the light used has a wavelength of 555 nm, find the slit width.

Answer: 1.98×10^{-4} m
Var: 50+

5) A researcher is investigating a cubic crystal with x rays. He is looking at Bragg reflection from the planes parallel to the cube faces. He finds that when using x rays of 0.165 nm a strong first maximum occurs when the beam makes an angle of 23.5° with the planes. What is the spacing of adjacent atoms in the crystal?

Answer: 0.207 nm
Var: 1

Chapter 37   Relativity

Multiple Choice Questions

1) Two fixed navigation beacons mark the approach lane to a star. The beacons are in line with the star and are 36 Mm apart. A spaceship approaches the star with a relative velocity of 0.20 c and passes the beacons. The passage of the ship between the beacons is timed by observers on the beacons. The time interval of the passage is closest to:

   A) 600 ms   B) 610 ms   C) 590 ms   D) 350 ms   E) 230 ms

   Answer: A
   Var: 50+

2) Two fixed navigation beacons mark the approach lane to a star. The beacons are in line with the star and are 28 Mm apart. A spaceship approaches the star with a relative velocity of 0.80 c and passes the beacons. The passage of the ship between the beacons is timed by an observer on the ship. The time interval of the passage is closest to:

   A) 70 ms   B) 120 ms   C) 190 ms   D) 42 ms   E) 28 ms

   Answer: A
   Var: 50+

3) Two fixed navigation beacons mark the approach lane to a star. The beacons are in line with the star and are 78 Mm apart. A spaceship approaches the star with a relative velocity of 0.50 c and passes the beacons. As the ship passes the first beacon the ship emits a short radar pulse toward the second beacon, and the radar echo is received at the ship. The time interval between the emission of the radar pulse and the reception of the radar echo is closest to:

   A) 350 ms   B) 400 ms   C) 450 ms   D) 300 ms   E) 180 ms

   Answer: A
   Var: 50+

4)   Figure 37.1a

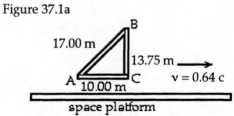

space platform

A right-angled construction frame ABC, when measured at rest, has dimensions as follows: AB = 17.00 m, AC = 10.00 m, and BC = 13.75 m. The frame is given a velocity of 0.64 c, relative to the space platform, in a direction parallel to AC. The dimensions of the moving frame are measured simultaneously by observers on the platform. In Figure 37.1a, the length BC measured by these observers is closest to:

   A) 14 m   B) 12 m   C) 10 m   D) 8 m   E) 16 m

   Answer: A
   Var: 50+

5)

Figure 37.1b

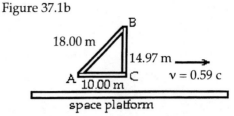

A right-angled construction frame ABC, when measured at rest, has dimensions as follows: AB = 18.00 m, AC = 10.00 m, and BC = 14.97 m. The frame is given a velocity of 0.59 c, relative to the space platform, in a direction parallel to AC. The dimensions of the moving frame are measured simultaneously by observers on the platform. In Figure 37.1b, the length AB measured by these observers is closest to:

A) 17.0 m   B) 17.5 m   C) 16.5 m   D) 16.0 m   E) 18.0 m

Answer: A
Var: 50+

6)

Figure 37.2a

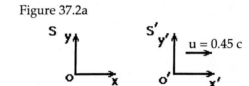

System S' has a velocity u = +0.45 c relative to system S, as shown. The clocks of S and S' are synchronized at t = t' = 0 s when the origins 0 and 0' coincide. An event is observed in both systems. The event takes place at x = 600 m and at time t = 1.9 μs, as measured by an observer in S. In Figure 37.2a, the x'-coordinate of the event, measured by an observer in S' is closest to:

A) 380   B) 340   C) 360   D) 350   E) 310

Answer: A
Var: 50+

7)

Figure 37.2b

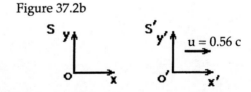

System S' has a velocity u = +0.56 c relative to system S, as shown. The clocks of S and S' are synchronized at t = t' = 0 s when the origins 0 and 0' coincide. An event is observed in both systems. The event takes place at x = 800 m and at time t = 3.0 μs, as measured by an observer in S. In Figure 37.2b, the time t' of the event, measured by an observer in S' is closest to:

A) 1.8 μs   B) –4.9 μs   C) 1.7 μs   D) 1.3 μs   E) 1.5 μs

Answer: A
Var: 50+

8)

Figure 37.2c

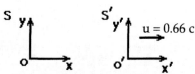

System S' has a velocity u = +0.77 c relative to system S, as shown. The clocks of S and S' are synchronized at t = t' = 0 s when the origins 0 and 0' coincide. An event is observed in both systems. The event takes place at x = 400 m and at time t = 8.7 μs, as measured by an observer in S. In Figure 37.2c, a rod which is stationary in S has a proper length of 137 m. The length of the rod measured by an observer in S' is closest to:

A) 87 m   B) 210 m   C) 79 m   D) 61 m   E) 54 m

Answer: A
Var: 50+

9)

Figure 37.2d

System S' has a velocity u = +0.66 c relative to system S, as shown. The clocks of S and S' are synchronized at t = t' = 0 s when the origins 0 and 0' coincide. An event is observed in both systems. The event takes place at x = 800 m and at time t = 3.8 μs, as measured by an observer in S. In Figure 37.2d, a stopwatch which is stationary in S' records a proper time interval of 17 s. The time interval, measured by an observer in S is closest to:

A) 23 s   B) 13 s   C) 25 s   D) 29 s   E) 31 s

Answer: A
Var: 50+

10)

Figure 37.3a

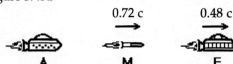

The captain of spaceship A observes enemy spaceship E escaping with a relative velocity of 0.48 c. A missile M is fired from ship A, with a velocity of 0.72 c relative to ship A. In Figure 37.3a, the relative velocity of approach of missile M, observed by the crew on ship E, is closest to:

A) 0.37 c   B) 0.24 c   C) 0.34 c   D) 0.30 c   E) 0.27 c

Answer: A
Var: 50+

11)   Figure 37.3b

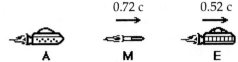

The captain of spaceship A observes enemy spaceship E escaping with a relative velocity of 0.52 c. A missile M is fired from ship A, with a velocity of 0.72 c relative to ship A. In Figure 37.3b, the captain of ship A observes missile M closing in on ship E with a relative velocity that is closest to:

A) 0.20 c   B) 0.32 c   C) 0.29 c   D) 0.26 c   E) 0.23 c

Answer: A
Var: 50+

12) If you were in a spaceship traveling at a speed close to the speed of light (with respect to earth) you would notice that

A) some of your physical dimensions were smaller than normal.

B) your mass is different than normal.

C) your pulse rate is different than normal.

D) None of these effects occur.

E) More than one of these effects occur.

Answer: D
Var: 1

13) A spaceship approaching an asteroid at a speed of 0.6 c launches a scout rocket with speed 0.4 c. At what speed is the scout rocket approaching the asteroid?

A) 0.81 c   B) 1.00 c   C) 0.76 c   D) 0.64 c   E) 0.96 c

Answer: A
Var: 1

14)   Figure 37.4a

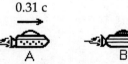

Three spaceships A, B, and C are in motion. The commander on ship B observes ship C approaching with a relative velocity of 0.78 c. The commander also observes ship A, advancing in the rear, with a relative velocity of 0.31 c. In Figure 37.4a, the velocity of ship C, relative to an observer on ship A, is closest to:

A) 0.88 c   B) 0.38 c   C) 1.4 c   D) 0.62 c   E) 1.1 c

Answer: A
Var: 50+

15)

Figure 37.4b

0.48 c 0.83 c

A B C

Three spaceships A, B, and C are in motion. The commander on ship B observes ship C approaching with a relative velocity of 0.83 c. The commander also observes ship A, advancing in the rear, with a relative velocity of 0.48 c. In Figure 37.4b, the commander on ship B observes ship A and ship C approaching each other, with a relative velocity that is closest to:

A) 1.3 c   B) 0.94 c   C) 0.25 c   D) 0.58 c   E) 2.2 c

Answer: A
Var: 50+

Situation 37.1

A navigational beacon in deep space broadcasts at a radio frequency of 50 MHz. A spaceship approaches the beacon with a relative velocity of 0.40 c.

16) In Situation 37.1, the frequency of the beacon radio signal that is detected on the ship is closest to:

A) 55 MHz   B) 60 MHz   C) 66 MHz   D) 71 MHz   E) 76 MHz

Answer: E
Var: 1

17) In Situation 37.1, the space ship passes the beacon and departs from it with a different relative velocity. The beacon signal is now detected at a frequency of 40 MHz. The new velocity of the spaceship, relative to the beacon, is closest to:

A) 0.20 c   B) 0.22 c   C) 0.24 c   D) 0.26 c   E) 0.28 c

Answer: B
Var: 1

Situation 37.2

A proton (rest energy = 938 MeV) has a speed of 0.80 c.

18) In Situation 37.2, the ratio of the kinetic energy of the proton to its rest energy is closest to:

A) 0.60   B) 0.67   C) 0.80   D) 1.2   E) 1.7

Answer: B
Var: 1

19) In Situation 37.2, the momentum of the proton is closest to:

A) 4.0×10^{-19}

B) 4.4×10^{-19}

C) 5.0×10^{-19}

D) 5.8×10^{-19}

E) 6.7×10^{-19}

Answer: E
Var: 1

Situation 37.3

An electron has a kinetic energy equal to twice its rest energy.

20) In Situation 37.3, the speed of the electron is closest to:

A) 0.84 c   B) 0.87 c   C) 0.89 c   D) 0.91 c   E) 0.94 c

Answer: E
Var: 1

21) In Situation 37.3, the relativistic mass of the electron is closest to:

A) 1.8×10^{-30} kg

B) 2.3×10^{-30} kg

C) 2.7×10^{-30} kg

D) 3.2×10^{-30} kg

E) 3.6×10^{-30} kg

Answer: C
Var: 1

22) Consider three galaxies, Alpha, Beta and Gamma. An observer in Beta sees the other two galaxies each moving away from him in opposite directions at speed 0.7 c. At what speed would an observer in Alpha see the galaxy Beta moving?

A) 0.82 c   B) 0.70 c   C) 0.94 c   D) 0.35 c   E) 0.57 c

Answer: B
Var: 1

23) Consider three galaxies, Alpha, Beta and Gamma. An observer in Beta sees the other two galaxies each moving away from him in opposite directions at speed 0.7 c. At what speed would an observer in Alpha see the galaxy Gamma moving?

A) 0.7 c   B) 1.4 c   C) 0.82 c   D) 0.94 c   E) 0.98 c

Answer: D
Var: 1

24) Free neutrons (unlike those in the nucleus of an atom) decay spontaneously into a proton, an electron and an antineutrino. The masses of these particles are (approx.)

$m_n = 1.67492 \times 10^{-27}$ kg

$m_p = 1.67262 \times 10^{-27}$ kg

$m_e = 9.10939 \times 10^{-31}$ kg

The mass of the neutrino is zero (or nearly so). How much energy is released in this decay?

A) 1.01×10^{-14} J

B) 1.25×10^{-13} J

C) 4.66×10^{-12} J

D) 7.08×10^{-13} J

E) 5.61×10^{-12} J

Answer: B
Var: 1

Situation 37.4

A relativistic proton has a momentum of 1.0×10^{-18} kg $\cdot$ m/s. The rest energy of a proton is 0.150 nJ.

25) In Situation 37.4, the kinetic energy of the proton, in nJ, is closest to:

| A) 0.13 | B) 0.16 | C) 0.19 | D) 0.22 | E) 0.25 |

Answer: C
Var: 1

26) In Situation 37.4, the speed of the proton is closest to:

| A) 0.87 c | B) 0.89 c | C) 0.91 c | D) 0.93 c | E) 0.95 c |

Answer: B
Var: 1

27) The special theory of relativity predicts that there is an upper limit to the speed of a particle. It thus follows that there is also an upper limit on the following property of a particle.

A) The kinetic energy.

B) The total energy.

C) The linear momentum.

D) More than one of these.

E) None of these.

Answer: E
Var: 1

Situation 37.5

A spaceship moves with velocity 0.6 c with respect to the earth. At midnight it passes the earth, and observers on both the spaceship and on earth agree that their clocks read midnight. At 12:50 a.m. (spaceship time) the spaceship passes an interplanetary navigational station and sends a radio signal back to earth. The receiving antenna on earth, immediately on receiving this signal, responds by sending a signal back to the spaceship. The following questions refer to this series of events.

28) In Situation 37.5, how far from earth (as measured by an earth based observer) is the navigational station?

A) 6.75×10^{-11} m

B) 5.40×10^{-11} m

C) 8.44×10^{-11} m

D) 7.25×10^{-11} m

E) 6.50×10^{-11} m

Answer: A
Var: 1

29) In Situation 37.5, at what time (earth based clock) did the spaceship pass the navigational station?

    A) 12:50 a.m.

    B) 12:45:30 a.m.

    C) 12:40 a.m.

    D) 1:02:30 a.m.

    E) 1:10 a.m.

Answer: D
Var: 1

30) In Situation 37.5, at what time does the receiver on earth detect the signal from the spaceship (earth based time)?

    A) 1:30 a.m.   B) 1:42 a.m.   C) 1:36 a.m.   D) 1:48 a.m.   E) 1:40 a.m.

Answer: E
Var: 1

Short Answer Questions

1) An unstable particle is moving at a speed of 2.0×10^8 m/s relative to a laboratory. Its lifetime is measured by a stationary observer in the laboratory to be 9.8×10^{-6} seconds. What is the lifetime of the particle, measured in the rest frame of the particle? (Use 3.00×10^8 m/s for the speed of light.)

Answer: 7.3×10^{-6} seconds
Var: 50+

2) A spacecraft is measured by an observer on the ground to have a length of 25 m as it flies overhead with a speed 2.4×10^8 m/s. The spacecraft then lands and its length is again measured by the observer on the ground, this time while the spacecraft is at rest relative to him. What result does he now get for the length? (Use 3.00×10^8 m/s for the speed of light.)

Answer: 4.2×10^1 m
Var: 50+

3) An experimenter is observing the inelastic collision of two rather rapid objects in order to test the predictions of relativistic momentum conservation. Particle A has a known rest mass of 3.1×10^{-25} kg and moves with speed (in the lab) 2.4×10^8 m/s. Particle B's mass is unknown, but it moves with speed (also in the lab) 1.8×10^8 m/s. Initially the particles are moving in precisely opposite directions. After the collision (a near miss), the particles, to the experimenter's amazement, are each moving perpendicular to the original direction of motion. For this to happen, what must be the rest mass of particle B? (Like the experimenter, you should use 3.00×10^8 m/s as the speed of light.)

Answer: 5.5×10^{-25} kg
Var: 50+

4) How much work must be done to accelerate a particle of mass 6.5×10^{-14} kg (rest mass) from a speed of 1.5×10^8 m/s to a speed of 2.5×10^8 m/s? (Use c = 3.00×10^8 m/s for the speed of light.)

Answer: 3800 J
Var: 50+

5) Two spaceships are approaching one another, each at a speed of 0.79 c relative to a stationary observer on earth. What speed does an observer on one spaceship record for the other approaching spaceship?

Answer: 0.97 c
Var: 50+

Chapter 38   Quantum Physics I: Photon's, Electrons, and Atoms

Multiple Choice Questions

1) A photo cathode whose work function is 2.9 eV, is illuminated with white light that has a continuous wavelength band from 400 nm to 700 nm. The range of the wavelength band in this white light illumination for which photoelectrons are not produced, in nm, is closest to:

   A) 430 to 700   B) 400 to 480   C) 430 to 480   D) 400 to 430   E) 480 to 700

   Answer: A
   Var: 10

2) A photo cathode whose work function is 1.0 eV, is illuminated with white light that has a continuous wavelength band from 350 nm to 700 nm. The stopping potential for this white light illumination is closest to:

   A) 2.5 V   B) 2.3 V   C) 2.8 V   D) 3.1 V   E) 3.3 V

   Answer: A
   Var: 50+

3) A photocathode has a work function of 2.1 eV. The photocathode is illuminated with monochromatic radiation whose photon energy is 3.2 eV. The wavelength of the illuminating radiation is closest to:

   A) 390 nm   B) 360 nm   C) 330 nm   D) 420 nm   E) 450 nm

   Answer: A
   Var: 50+

4) A photocathode has a work function of 2.4 eV. The photocathode is illuminated with monochromatic radiation whose photon energy is 3.0 eV. The maximum kinetic energy of the photoelectrons produced is closest to:

   A) 9.6×10^{-20} J

   B) 3.8×10^{-19} J

   C) 4.2×10^{-19} J

   D) 4.5×10^{-19} J

   E) 4.8×10^{-19} J

   Answer: A
   Var: 50+

5) A photocathode has a work function of 3.3 eV. The photocathode is illuminated with monochromatic radiation whose photon energy is 3.8 eV. The threshold frequency for photoelectron production is closest to:

A) 8.0×10^{14} Hz

B) 1.2×10^{14} Hz

C) 8.3×10^{14} Hz

D) 8.7×10^{14} Hz

E) 9.2×10^{14} Hz

Answer: A
Var: 50+

6) A phototube has a stopping potential of 1.60 V when the cathode is illuminated with bichromatic light of 400 nm and 600 nm wavelengths. The maximum speed of the emitted photoelectrons, in SI units, is closest to:

A) 7.5×10^5 B) 7.0×10^5 C) 8.3×10^5 D) 8.8×10^5 E) 1.0×10^6

Answer: A
Var: 50+

7) A phototube has a stopping potential of 2.18 V when the cathode is illuminated with bichromatic light of 360 nm and 600 nm wavelengths. The threshold frequency of this phototube for photoelectron production is closest to:

A) 3.1×10^{14} Hz

B) -2.7×10^{13} Hz

C) 9.9×10^{13} Hz

D) 5.7×10^{14} Hz

E) 8.3×10^{14} Hz

Answer: A
Var: 50+

8) A stopping potential of 0.50 V is required when a phototube is illuminated with monochromatic light of 490 nm wavelength. The wavelength of a different monochromatic illumination for which the stopping potential is 1.50 V is closest to:

A) 350 nm   B) 330 nm   C) 380 nm   D) 400 nm   E) 450 nm

Answer: A
Var: 50+

9) A 100 W arc lamp operates with an efficiency of 5% for emitting light. It emits light of wavelength 657 nm. How many photons per second does it emit?

A) 1.7×10^{19} B) 3.3×10^{20} C) 3.3×10^{19} D) 1.0×10^{19} E) 3.4×10^{18}

Answer: A
Var: 50+

10) A beam of alpha particles (q = +2 e) is directed at a uranium (Z = 92) target. The radius of a uranium nucleus is 7.4 fm. The closest approach between centers of an alpha particle to a uranium is 30.0 fm. The kinetic energy of the incident alpha particles is closest to:

A) 4.5 MeV   B) 6.0 MeV   C) 7.5 MeV   D) 9.0 MeV   E) 10.5 MeV

Answer: D
Var: 1

11) A beam of 2.0 MeV protons is directed at a tungsten (Z = 74) target. The radius of a tungsten nucleus is 6.8 fm. The closest approach of a proton to the center of a tungsten nucleus is closest to:

A) 33 fm   B) 38 fm   C) 43 fm   D) 48 fm   E) 53 fm

Answer: E
Var: 1

12) A 29.0 pm photon is scattered by a stationary electron. The maximum energy loss of the photon is closest to:

A) 4 KeV   B) 7 KeV   C) 10 KeV   D) 12 KeV   E) 12 KeV

Answer: D
Var: 1

13) An 18.0 pm photon is scattered by a stationary electron through an angle of 120°. The wavelength of the scattered photon, in pm, is closest to:

A) 19.2   B) 20.4   C) 21.6   D) 22.9   E) 24.1

Answer: C
Var: 1

14) A large number of 30.0 pm photons are scattered twice by stationary electrons. The range of wavelengths of the doubly-scattered photons, in pm, is closest to:

A) 30 to 35   B) 30 to 40   C) 30 to 50   D) 35 to 40   E) 40 to 50

Answer: B
Var: 1

15) A 35.0 pm photon undergoes multiple Compton scattering by stationary electrons until the final wavelength of the photon is 75.0 pm. The minimum number of times that the photon was scattered is:

A) 8   B) 9   C) 10   D) 11   E) 12

Answer: B
Var: 1

Situation 38.1

An electric current through a tungsten filament maintains its temperature at 2800 K. Assume the tungsten filament behaves as an ideal radiator at that temperature.

16) In Situation 38.1, the wavelength at which the maximum in spectral emittance occurs is closest to:

    A) 1000 nm   B) 1200 nm   C) 1400 nm   D) 1600 nm   E) 1800 nm

Answer: A
Var: 1

17) In Situation 38.1, the effective radiating area of the filament, as an ideal radiator, is 2.0×10^{-6} m^2. The total power radiated by the filament is closest to:

    A) 5.5 W   B) 7.0 W   C) 8.5 W   D) 10.0 W   E) 11.5 W

Answer: B
Var: 1

18) The particle nature of light is best illustrated by which of the following?

    A) The scattering of alpha particles from gold foil

    B) The fact that hot objects emit electromagnetic radiation.

    C) The diffraction pattern observed when a beam of electrons is scattered by a crystal.

    D) The fact that a rainbow consists of a continuous spectrum of colors.

    E) The ejection of electrons from a metal surface illuminated by light.

Answer: E
Var: 1

Short Answer Questions

1) A hot object in a furnace can be viewed through a small hole in the furnace. The radiation from the interior of the furnace can be treated as blackbody radiation. When the radiation is brightest at wavelength $\lambda = 540$ nm, the temperature is 5370 K. After the object and the furnace interior have cooled, the radiation is brightest at $\lambda = 681$ nm. What is the new temperature?

Answer: 4260 K
Var: 50+

2) A photoelectric surface has a work function of 2.10 eV. Calculate the maximum kinetic energy, in eV, of electrons ejected from this surface by electromagnetic radiation of wavelength 314 nm. (Note: $h = 6.63 \times 10^{-34}$ J $\bullet$ s, $e = 1.60 \times 10^{-19}$ C, and $c = 3.00 \times 10^8$ m/s.)

Answer: 1.86 eV
Var: 50+

3) X-rays of energy 4.4×10^4 eV are Compton-scattered through an angle of 136°. What is the energy of the scattered X-rays, in electron volts? (Note: $h = 6.63 \times 10^{-34}$ J $\bullet$ s, $c = 3.00 \times 10^8$ m/s, $e = 1.60 \times 10^{-19}$ C, and the mass of the electron is 9.11×10^{-31} kg.)

Answer: 3.8×10^4 eV
Var: 50+

4) When a photoelectric surface is illuminated with light of wavelength 437 nm, the stopping potential is 1.67 V.
(a) What is the work function of the metal in eV?
(b) What is the maximum speed of the ejected electrons?
(Note: $h = 6.626 \times 10^{-34}$ J • s, $m_e = 9.110 \times 10^{-31}$ kg, $e = 1.602 \times 10^{-19}$ c)

Answer: (a) 1.17 Ev

(b) 7.66×10^5 m/s

Var: 1

Chapter 39   Quantum Physics II:
The Wave Nature of Particles

Multiple Choice Questions

1) An electron has the same de Broglie wavelength as an 830 nm photon. The speed of the electron is closest to:

A) 880 m/s   B) 960 m/s   C) 780m/s   D) 700 m/s   E) 250 m/s

Answer: A
Var: 50+

2) A proton has a speed of 1.4×10^4 m/s. The energy of a photon that has the same de Broglie wavelength as the proton is closest to:

A) 44 keV   B) 30 keV   C) 58 keV   D) 72 keV   E) 86 keV

Answer: A
Var: 50+

3) An electron has the same de Broglie wavelength as a 5.5 eV photon. The speed of the electron is closest to:

A) 3200 m/s   B) 3000 m/s   C) 2800 m/s   D) 2600 m/s   E) 2300 m/s

Answer: A
Var: 50+

4) An electron has a kinetic energy of 5.8 eV. The energy of a photon that has the same de Broglie wavelength as the electron is closest to:

A) 2.4 keV   B) 2.2 keV   C) 2.0 keV   D) 2.6 keV   E) 2.8 keV

Answer: A
Var: 50+

5) The neutrons in a beam have energies ranging from 0.05 eV to 0.15 eV. The beam is incident normally on the surface of a crystal. The neutrons diffract from surface planes of the crystal whose spacing is 227 pm. The range of angles from the normal, at which maximum intensity of diffracted neutrons occurs, is closest to:

A) 19° to 34°   B) 15° to 34°   C) 19° to 36°   D) 15° to 36°   E) 12° to 36°

Answer: A
Var: 50+

6) The neutrons in a beam have energies ranging from 0.04 eV to 0.13 eV. The beam is incident normally on the surface of a crystal. The neutrons diffract from surface planes of the crystal whose spacing is 292 pm. Neutrons diffracted at an angle of 31° from the normal are allowed to pass through slits to form a new beam. The energy of the neutrons in this new beam is closest to:

A) 0.036 eV   B) 0.031 eV   C) 0.027 eV   D) 0.023 eV   E) 0.019 eV

Answer: A
Var: 50+

7) A 560 eV electron beam is directed normally at the surface of a crystal. The first order intensity maximum of diffracted electrons occurs at an angle of 25° from the normal. The spacing of the surface planes of the crystal is closest to:

A) 120 pm   B) 110 pm   C) 97 pm   D) 84 pm   E) 72 pm

Answer: A
Var: 50+

8) A 690 eV electron beam is directed normally at the surface of a crystal. The first order intensity maximum of diffracted electrons occurs at an angle of 23° from the normal. The angle from the normal of the second order intensity maximum is closest to:

A) 51°   B) 53°   C) 49°   D) 47°   E) 45°

Answer: A
Var: 50+

9) The spacing of the surface planes of a crystal is 291 pm. A beam directed normally at the surface of the crystal undergoes first order diffraction at an angle of 32° from the normal. The diffraction is done with a beam of monochromatic x-rays. The energy of the photons is closest to:

A) 8.1 keV   B) 7.4 keV   C) 8.7 keV   D) 9.4 keV   E) 10 keV

Answer: A
Var: 50+

10) The spacing of the surface planes of a crystal is 298 pm. A beam directed normally at the surface of the crystal undergoes first order diffraction at an angle of 23° from the normal. The diffraction is done with a beam of monoenergetic electrons. The energy of the electrons is closest to:

A) 110 eV   B) 130 eV   C) 96 eV   D) 81 eV   E) 66 eV

Answer: A
Var: 50+

11) The spacing of the surface planes of a crystal is 194 pm. A beam directed normally at the surface of the crystal undergoes first order diffraction at an angle of 41° from the normal. The diffraction is done with a beam of monoenergetic neutrons. The energy of the neutrons is closest to:

A) 0.050 eV   B) 0.044 eV   C) 0.056 eV   D) 0.063 eV   E) 0.069 eV

Answer: A
Var: 50+

12) A single slit is illuminated at normal incidence with a parallel beam of 450 nm light. The entire central band of the diffraction pattern is observed at 90 degrees. The illumination is replaced by a 810 eV electron beam, which is directed at the slit at normal incidence. The angle at which the first minimum of the electron diffraction pattern occurs is closest to:

A) 0.096 mrad

B) 0.071 mrad

C) 0.046 mrad

D) 0.12 mrad

E) 0.15 mrad

Answer: A
Var: 50+

13) A molecule of roughly spherical shape has a mass of 7.70×10^{-25} kg and a diameter of 0.4 nm. The uncertainty in the measured position of the molecule is equal to the molecular diameter. The minimum speed of the molecule is closest to:

A) 0.3 m/s   B) 3 m/s   C) 30 m/s   D) 0.03 m/s   E) 0.003 m/s

Answer: A
Var: 50+

14) In an important experiment in 1927 a beam of electrons was scattered off a crystal of nickel. The intensity of the scattered beam varied with the angle of scattering, and analysis of these results lead to confirmation of

A) the particle nature of light.

B) the Bohr model of the atom.

C) the wave nature of electrons.

D) the Rutherford model of the nucleus.

E) the quantization of energy levels.

Answer: C
Var: 1

15) Electrons initially at rest (approximately) are accelerated along the z-axis by a uniform electric field. They fall through a potential difference of 600 V in a distance of 30 cms, at which point they strike a fluorescent screen. What will be the minimum uncertainty in locating the position where the electrons strike the screen (as determined by the uncertainty principle)? Note that the uncertainty in where the beam strikes results from both an initial uncertainty in the x position of the electron and the initial uncertainty in vx.

A) 5.25×10^{-5} m

B) 4.37×10^{-6} m

C) 1.66×10^{-5} m

D) 9.08×10^{-4} m

E) 7.70×10^{-5} m

Answer: B
Var: 1

16) An electron is confined to a length of 500 pm on the x-axis. The minimum kinetic energy of the electron is closest to:

A) 0.0015 eV   B) 0.015 eV   C) 0.15 eV   D) 1.5 eV   E) 15 eV

Answer: C
Var: 1

17) A proton is confined to a length of 2.0 pm on the x-axis. The minimum kinetic energy of the proton is closest to:

A) 0.5 eV   B) 5 eV   C) 50 eV   D) 500 eV   E) 5000 eV

Answer: B
Var: 1

18) A laser produces a beam of 4000 nm light. A shutter allows a pulse of light, 30 ps in duration, to pass. The uncertainty in the energy of a photon in the pulse is closest to:

A) 2×10^{-6} eV

B) 2×10^{-5} eV

C) 2×10^{-4} eV

D) 2×10^{-3} eV

E) 2×10^{-2} eV

Answer: B
Var: 1

19) An ultraviolet source produces a monochromatic beam of 200 nm light. A shutter allows a pulse to pass which is 10,000 wavelengths long. The uncertainty in the energy of a photon in this pulse is closest to:

A) 10^{-6} eV   B) 10^{-5} eV   C) 10^{-4} eV   D) 10^{-3} eV   E) 10^{-2} eV

Answer: C
Var: 1

20) A 440 nm spectral line is produced by a transition from an excited state to the ground state. The natural line width of the spectral line is 0.020 pm. The average time the atom spends in the excited state is closest to:

A) 5×10^{-6} s

B) 5×10^{-7} s

C) 5×10^{-8} s

D) 5×10^{-9} s

E) 5×10^{-10} s

Answer: D
Var: 1

21) The Ξ (1530) particle has a rest energy of 1530 MeV and an energy width (uncertainty) of 9 MeV. The average lifetime of the Ξ (1530) particle is closest to:

A) 7×10^{-24} s

B) 2×10^{-23} s

C) 7×10^{-23} s

D) 2×10^{-22} s

E) 7×10^{-22} s

Answer: C
Var: 1

22) The $\Sigma(1385)$ particle has a rest energy of 1385 MeV and its average lifetime is 1.9×10^{-23} s. The energy width (uncertainty) of the $\Sigma(1385)$ particle is closest to:

A) 0.35 MeV   B) 1.1 MeV   C) 3.5 MeV   D) 11 MeV   E) 35 MeV

Answer: E
Var: 1

23) The kinetic energy of the neutrons, considered as non-relativistic, in a neutron beam is 2.0 MeV. The de Broglie wavelength of the neutrons is closest to:

A) 2×10^{-14} m

B) 3×10^{-14} m

C) 11×10^{-14} m

D) 5×10^{-14} m

E) 6×10^{-14} m

Answer: A
Var: 1

24) The de Broglie wavelength of the electrons, considered as non-relativistic, in the electron beam of a television video tube is 7.55 pm. The accelerating potential used in the tube is closest to:

A) 20 kV   B) 22 kV   C) 24 kV   D) 26 kV   E) 28 kV

Answer: D
Var: 1

25) An electron microscope produces a beam of relativistic electrons whose de Broglie wavelength is 4.0 pm. The accelerating potential at which the microscope operates is closest to:

A) 84 keV   B) 87 keV   C) 91 keV   D) 94 keV   E) 98 keV

Answer: B
Var: 1

26) A linear accelerator produces a beam of relativistic electrons which have a kinetic energy of 10 MeV. The de Broglie wavelength of these electrons is closest to:

A) 0.12 pm   B) 0.18 pm   C) 0.27 pm   D) 0.39 pm   E) 0.59 pm

Answer: A
Var: 1

27) A major advantage of an electron microscope over a visible light microscope is that the electron microscope

A) has much greater magnification.

B) operates with much lower intensity.

C) can penetrate opaque samples.

D) can have much better resolution.

E) requires no lenses for its operation.

Answer: D
Var: 1

28) The longest wavelength of a photon that can be emitted by a hydrogen atom, for which the final state is n = 5, is closest to:

A) 7500 nm   B) 4700 nm   C) 2300 nm   D) 2600 nm   E) 4100 nm

Answer: A
Var: 10

29) The shortest wavelength of a photon that can be emitted by a hydrogen atom, for which the initial state is n = 4, is closest to:

A) 97 nm   B) 87 nm   C) 76 nm   D) 65 nm   E) 55 nm

Answer: A
Var: 10

30) The longest wavelength of a photon that can be emitted by a hydrogen atom, for which the initial state is n = 3, is closest to:

A) 550 nm   B) 575 nm   C) 600 nm   D) 625 nm   E) 650 nm

Answer: E
Var: 1

31) The shortest wavelength of a photon that can be emitted by a hydrogen atom, for which the initial state is $n = 3$, is closest to:

    A) 820 nm   B) 850 nm   C) 880 nm   D) 910 nm   E) 940 nm

Answer: A
Var: 1

32) The energy required to remove the electron from a hydrogen atom in the $n = 10$ state is closest to:

    A) 0.14 eV   B) 0.11 eV   C) 0.094 eV   D) 0.21 eV   E) 0.17 eV

Answer: A
Var: 9

33) A doubly-ionized lithium atom $3Li^{++}$ undergoes a state transition from $n = 5$ to $n = 4$. The wavelength of the photon which is emitted is closest to:

    A) 350 nm   B) 450 nm   C) 550 nm   D) 650 nm   E) 750 nm

Answer: B
Var: 1

34) What is the longest wavelength radiation that will emit photoelectrons from sodium metal for which the work function is 2.28 eV?

    A) 580 nm   B) 499 nm   C) 633 nm   D) 668 nm   E) 544 nm

Answer: E
Var: 1

35) A laser pulse of duration 25 ms has a total energy of 1.1 J. If the wavelength of this radiation is 438 nm, how many photons are emitted in one pulse?

    A) 2.4×10^{18} B) 6.0×10^{19} C) 2.9×10^{19} D) 9.6×10^{16} E) 1.9×10^{17}

Answer: A
Var: 50+

36) In order for an atom to emit light, it

    A) must be in the gaseous state.

    B) must be stimulated by external radiation.

    C) must be in the ground state.

    D) must be in an excited state.

    E) must be fluorescent.

Answer: D
Var: 1

Situation 39.1
A system of atoms has three energy levels as shown.

_____ 0.08 eV

_____ 0.06

_____ 0.00

37) In Situation 39.1, the system is in thermal equilibrium at a temperature of 300 K. The ratio of the number atoms in the middle state to that of the lowest state is closest to:

A) 0.10   B) 0.12   C) 0.14   D) 0.16   E) 0.18

Answer: A
Var: 1

38) In Situation 39.1, when the system is in thermal equilibrium at a given temperature, the number of atoms in the middle state equals 1.60 times the number of atoms in the highest state. The temperature of the system is closest to:

A) 410 K   B) 430 K   C) 450 K   D) 470 K   E) 490 K

Answer: E
Var: 1

39) The Bohr model of the hydrogen atom predicts an ionization energy of 13.6 eV. With this model one would expect the ionization energy of the Li^{++} ion to be

A) 122.4 eV   B) 40.8 eV   C) 54.4 eV   D) 27.2 eV   E) 79.6 eV

Answer: A
Var: 1

40) An important observation that led Bohr to formulate his model of the hydrogen atom was the fact that

A) a low density gas emitted a series of sharp spectral lines.

B) neutrons formed a diffraction pattern when scattered from a nickel crystal.

C) electrons were found to have a wave nature.

D) the peak of the blackbody radiation moved to shorter wavelengths as the temperature was increased.

E) the emission of light by an atom does not appear to conserve energy.

Answer: A
Var: 1

Short Answer Questions

1) Calculate the energy in eV of a neutron (mass 1.675×10^{-27} kg) that has de Broglie wavelength of 2.8×10^{-12} m

(Note: h = 6.626×10^{-34} J • s, c = 3.00×10^8 m/s, and e = 1.602×10^{-19} C.)

Answer: 100 eV
Var: 50+

2) An unstable particle produced in a high–energy collision is measured to have an energy of 483 MeV and an uncertainty in energy of 39 KeV. Use the Heisenberg uncertainty principle to estimate the lifetime of this particle.
(Note: h = 6.626 x 10^{-34} J • s, c = 3.00 x 10^8 m/s, and e = 1.602 x 10^{-19} C.)

Answer: 1.1 x 10^{-19} seconds
Var: 50+

3) A small dust particle m = 9.50 x 10^{-6} g is being observed under a magnifying lens. Its position is determined to be within 0.0080 mm.
(a) Find the velocity limit implied by the uncertainty of its position.
(b) Assuming the dust particle is moving at this speed, how many years would it take for the particle to move 1 mm?

Answer: (a) 2.4 x 10^{-21} m/s
          (b) 1.3 x 10^{10} yrs
Var: 50+

4) An electron, bound to a certain atom, has an ionization energy of 6.53 eV. Assuming that this energy is due to the size of the atom that contains it, estimate the size of the atom.
(Note: h = 6.626 x 10^{-34} J • s and m$_e$ = 9.11 x 10^{-31} kg.)

Answer: 7.63 x 10^{-11} m
Var: 50+

5) A beam of electrons, accelerated through a voltage of 76 V, is directed normally at the surface of a metal. An intensity maximum occurs when the reflected angle θ is 26° with respect to the incident beam. Find the spacing, d, between the crystal planes.
(Note: h = 6.626 x 10^{-34} J • s, m$_e$ = 9.11 x 10^{-31} kg, and e = 1.602 x 10^{-19} C.)

Answer: 3.2 x 10^{-10} m
Var: 50+

6) Recall that the energy levels of the hydrogen atom are given by
$$E_n = \frac{Rch}{n^2},$$ where R = 1.097 x 10^{-1} m.

What wavelength photon is emitted when the atom undergoes a transition from the n = 5 to the n = 8 level?

Answer: 3.74 x 10^{-6} meters
Var: 21

Chapter 40 Quantum Physics III: Quantum Mechanics

Multiple Choice Questions

1) A wave function is given by

$$\Psi(x) = 0 \qquad\qquad x < 0$$
$$\Psi(x) = Ax\,(L-x) \qquad 0 \geq x \geq L$$
$$\Psi(x) = 0 \qquad\qquad x > L$$

The product of the normalization constant A and the quantity $L^{5/2}$ is equal to:

A) $\sqrt{12}$ B) $\sqrt{15}$ C) $\sqrt{20}$ D) $\sqrt{24}$ E) $\sqrt{30}$

Answer: E
Var: 1

Situation 40.1

A particle is confined to a one-dimensional box on the x-axis between $x = 0$ and $x = L$. The potential height of the walls of the box is infinite. The normalized wave function of the particle, which is in the ground state, is given by

$$\Psi(x) = \sqrt{2/L}\,\sin \pi x / L \qquad\qquad 0 \leq x \leq L$$

2) In Situation 40.1, the probability of finding the particle between $x = 0$ and $x = L/3$, is closest to:

A) 0.20   B) 0.22   C) 0.24   D) 0.26   E) 0.28

Answer: A
Var: 1

3) In Situation 40.1, the maximum probability per unit length of finding the particle is equal to:

A) $1/\sqrt{L}$ B) $\sqrt{2}/\sqrt{L}$ C) $2/\sqrt{L}$ D) $1/L$ E) $2/L$

Answer: E
Var: 1

4) An electron is in an infinite square well that is 9.9 nm wide. The ground state energy of the electron is closest to:

A) 0.0038 eV   B) 0.0046 eV   C) 0.0054 eV   D) 0.0061 eV   E) 0.0069 eV

Answer: A
Var: 50+

5) An electron is in an infinite square well that is 2.5 nm wide. The electron makes the transition from the $n = 11$ to the $n = 6$ state. The wavelength of the emitted photon is closest to:

A) 240 nm   B) 210 nm   C) 170 nm   D) 280 nm   E) 320 nm

Answer: A
Var: 50+

6) An electron is in an infinite square well that is 5.5 nm wide. The smallest value of the state quantum number n for which the energy level exceeds 100 eV is closest to:

    A) 90   B) 91   C) 92   D) 89   E) 88

Answer: A
Var: 50+

7) An electron is bound in an infinite square-well potential on the x-axis. The width of the well is L and the well extends from x = 0 nm to x = 6.9 nm. In a given state, the normalized wave function of the electron is given by:

$$\Psi(x) = \sqrt{2/L}\sin(2\pi x/L)$$

The energy of the state is closest to:

    A) 0.032 eV   B) 0.016 eV   C) 0.039 eV   D) 0.024 eV   E) 0.0080 eV

Answer: A
Var: 50+

8) An electron is bound in an infinite square-well potential on the x-axis. The width of the well is L and the well extends from x = 0 nm to x = 5.6 nm. In a given state, the normalized wave function of the electron is given by:

$$\Psi(x) = \sqrt{2/L}\sin(2\pi x/L)$$

The probability per nm of finding the electron at x = 2.80 nm is closest to:

    A) zero   B) 0.4   C) 0.8   D) 1.1   E) 1.3

Answer: A
Var: 50+

9) An electron is bound in an infinite square-well potential on the x-axis. The width of the well is L and the well extends from x = 0 nm to x = 2.1 nm. In a given state, the normalized wave function of the electron is given by:

$$\Psi(x) = \sqrt{2/L}\sin(2\pi x/L)$$

The probability per nm of finding the electron at x = 0.30 nm is closest to:

    A) 0.58   B) zero   C) 0.20   D) 0.41   E) 0.79

Answer: A
Var: 50+

Situation 40.2

A particle of mass m is bound in a square-well potential of finite height. The well is on the x-axis and extends from x = -L/2 to x = +L/2. There is only a single bound state, whose normalized wave function is given by:

$$\Psi(x) = 1/\sqrt{L} \; \sqrt{\pi/4 + \pi} \; \exp(\pi/4) \; \exp(+\pi x/2L) \qquad x \le -L/2$$
$$\Psi(x) = 1/\sqrt{L} \; \sqrt{2\pi/4 + \pi} \; \cos(\pi x/2L) \qquad -L/2 \le x \le +L/2$$
$$\Psi(x) = 1/\sqrt{L} \; \sqrt{\pi/4 + \pi} \; \exp(\pi/4) \; \exp(-\pi x/2L) \qquad x \ge L/2$$

10) In Situation 40.2, denote the energy of the state by E. The ratio EmL^2/h^2 is closest to:

A) 0.03   B) 0.06   C) 0.09   D) 0.12   E) 0.15

Answer: A
Var: 1

11) In Situation 40.2, the probability per unit length of finding the particle at the center of the well is closest to:

A) 0.76/L   B) 0.80/L   C) 0.84/L   D) 0.88/L   E) 0.92/L

Answer: D
Var: 1

12) In Situation 40.2, the smallest probability per unit length of finding the particle inside the well is closest to:

A) 0.44/L   B) 0.50/L   C) 0.55/L   D) 0.61/L   E) 0.66/L

Answer: A
Var: 1

13) In Situation 40.2, the probability of finding the particle outside the well is closest to:

A) 0.20   B) 0.22   C) 0.24   D) 0.26   E) 0.28

Answer: E
Var: 1

14) An electron with kinetic energy 2.80 eV encounters a potential barrier of height $U_o = 5.40$ eV. If the barrier width is 0.4 nm, what is the probability that the electron will tunnel through the barrier?

A) 5.5×10^{-3} B) 1.1×10^{-2} C) 2.2×10^{-2} D) 4.4×10^{-2} E) 5.5×10^{-2}

Answer: A
Var: 50+

15) How does the probability of an electron tunneling through a potential barrier vary with the thickness of the barrier?

A) It decreases linearly with thickness.

B) It decreases sinusoidally with thickness.

C) It decreases exponentially with thickness.

D) It decreases inversely with thickness.

E) It is independent of the barrier thickness.

Answer: C
Var: 1

16) Which of the following is an accurate statement concerning the simple harmonic oscillator?

A) The spacing between energy levels increases with increasing energy.

B) The spacing between energy levels decreases with increasing energy.

C) The number of nodes of the wave function increases with increasing energy.

D) The wave functions are sinusoidal functions.

E) The potential energy varies linearly with displacement from equilibrium.

Answer: C
Var: 1

17) A low density beam of 40 eV electrons is directed at a potential barrier 130 eV high and 0.12 nm wide. The transmission coefficient is closest to:

A) 3.1×10^{-5} B) 6.2×10^{-5} C) 6.2×10^{-6} D) 3.1×10^{-6} E) 1.5×10^{-6}

Answer: A
Var: 50+

18) A low density beam of 8.0 eV electrons is incident on a potential barrier 14.0 eV in height and 0.80 nm in width. The fraction of the beam that is transmitted through the barrier is closest to:

A) 8.2×10^{-9} B) 1.2×10^{-7} C) 2.5×10^{-6} D) 8.2×10^{-6} E) 1.6×10^{-4}

Answer: A
Var: 50+

Situation 40.3

A free electron which has a kinetic energy of 3.0 eV is incident on a square-well potential. The depth of the well is 5.0 eV and the width is 4.0 nm.

19) In Situation 40.3, the wavelength of the wave function for the electron outside the well is closest to:

A) 330 pm   B) 430 pm   C) 550 pm   D) 710 pm   E) 870 pm

Answer: D
Var: 1

20) In Situation 40.3, the wavelength of the wave function for the electron inside the well is closest to:

A) 330 pm   B) 430 pm   C) 550 pm   D) 710 pm   E) 870 pm

Answer: B
Var: 1

Situation 40.4

The atoms in a nickel crystal vibrate as harmonic oscillators with an angular frequency of 2.3×10^{13} rad/s. The mass of a nickel atom is 9.75×10^{-26} kg.

21) In Situation 40.4, the effective interatomic force constant for nickel is closest to:

A) 37 N/m   B) 42 N/m   C) 47 N/m   D) 52 N/m   E) 57 N/m

Answer: D
Var: 1

22) In Situation 40.4, the spacing of the vibrational energy levels of nickel is closest to:

A) 0.015 eV   B) 0.019 eV   C) 0.023 eV   D) 0.027 eV   E) 0.031 eV

Answer: A
Var: 1

Short Answer Questions

1) The lowest energy level of a particle confined to a one–dimensional region of space with fixed dimension L is E_O (i.e., a "particle in a box"). If an identical particle is confined to a similar region with fixed distance $(1/4)L$, what is the energy of the lowest energy level that the particles have in common? Express your answer in terms of E_O.

Answer: $16E_O$
Var: 9

2) Consider a particle in a box of width L and let the particle be in a state $n = 11$. What is the first value of x, larger than 0, where the probability of finding the particle is highest?

Answer: L/22
Var: 18

3) An electron is bound in an infinite well of width 0.30 nm. If the electron is initially in $n = 9$ and falls to $n = 4$, find the wavelength of the emitted photon.
Note: ($c = 3.0 \times 10^8$ m/s, $m_e = 9.11 \times 10^{-31}$ kg, and $h = 6.626 \times 10^{-34}$ j • s)

Answer: 4.6×10^{-9} m
Var: 50+

4) A lithium atom, mass 1.17×10^{-26} kg, is vibrating with simple harmonic motion in a crystal lattice, where the force constant k is 71.0 N/m.
(a) What is the ground state energy of this system in eV?
(b) What would be the wavelength of the photon that could excite this system to the n = 1 level?

Answer: (a) 2.57×10^{-2} eV

(b) 2.42×10^{-5} m

Var: 50+

Chapter 41   Atomic Structure

Multiple Choice Questions

Situation 41.1
An atom has completely filled inner shells and a single valence electron in an excited p state. The filled inner shells have an orbital momentum equal to zero.

1) In Situation 41.1, the magnitude of the orbital angular momentum of the atom is closest to:

    A) 1.0 h   B) 1.2 h   C) 1.4 h   D) 1.7 h   E) 2.0 h

Answer: C
Var: 1

2) In Situation 41.1, a magnetic field is applied. The set of possible angles between the magnetic field and the orbital angular momentum is:

    A) 45°

    B) 90°

    C) 45°, 90°

    D) 45°, 135°

    E) 45°, 90°, 135°

Answer: E
Var: 1

3) The total number of electron states (including spin states), for which $\ell = 1$ in the K, L, and M shells is equal to:

    A) 6   B) 8   C) 10   D) 12   E) 16

Answer: D
Var: 1

4) The only valid electron state and shell designation among the following is:

    A) 1p, K   B) 2s, K   C) 1s, L   D) 2p, L   E) 3f, M

Answer: D
Var: 1

5) The only invalid electron state and shell designation among the following is:

    A) 1s, K   B) 2s, L   C) 2d, L   D) 3s, M   E) 3d, M

Answer: C
Var: 1

6) The correct ground state electron configuration of boron (Z = 5) is:

    A) $1s^2 2s^2 2p$ B) $1s^2 2s^2 p^3$ C) $1s^2 1p^2 2s$ D) $1s^2 2p^2 3s$ E) $1s^2 2p^3$

Answer: A
Var: 1

7) The only valid ground state electron configuration among the following is:

   A) $1s^2 2s^2 2p^6 3s$

   B) $1s^2 2s^2 2p^5$

   C) $1s^2 2s^2 2p^4 3s^2$

   D) $1s^2 2s^2 2p^3$

   E) $1s^2 2s^2 2p^6 3s^2 3p$

Answer: C
Var: 1

8) The normalized wave function for a hydrogen atom in the 1s state is given by:

$$\Psi(r) = 1/\sqrt{\pi \alpha_0^3} \, \exp(-r/\alpha_0)$$

where α_0 is the Bohr radius. The probability of finding the electron at a distance greater than $2.2\alpha_0$ from the proton is closest to:

   A) 1.9×10^{-1} B) 9.3×10^{-2} C) 1.4×10^{-1} D) 3.7×10^{-1} E) 2.8×10^{-1}

Answer: A
Var: 50+

9) An s state ($\ell = 0$) energy level is split into two levels by an applied magnetic field. A photon of 97 GHz microwave radiation induces a transition between the two levels. The applied magnetic field is closest to:

   A) 3.5 T   B) 0.55 T   C) 2.0 T   D) 4.5 T   E) 22 T

Answer: A
Var: 50+

10) An alkali metal atom is in the ground state. The orbital angular momentum equals zero and the spin angular momentum is entirely due to the single valence electron. A magnetic field is applied which splits the ground state energy level into two levels, 26 µeV apart. The applied magnetic field, in SI units, is closest to:

   A) 0.22   B) 0.17   C) 0.28   D) 0.33   E) 0.38

Answer: A
Var: 50+

11) An alkali metal atom is in the ground state. The orbital angular momentum equals zero and the spin angular momentum is entirely due to the single valence electron. A magnetic field is applied which splits the ground state energy level into two levels, 51 µeV apart. A photon, absorbed by the atom, induces a transition between the two levels. The wavelength of the photon is closest to:

   A) 24 mm   B) 32 mm   C) 40 mm   D) 48 mm   E) 52 mm

Answer: A
Var: 50+

12) An atom in a state with $\ell = 1$ decays to its ground state (with $\ell = 0$). A photon of wavelength 870 nm is emitted in the process. When the same process takes place in the presence of an intense magnetic field a change in the spectrum is observed. With the magnetic field present, one of the emitted lines observed has a wavelength of 870.018 nm. Which of the following wavelengths would you expect to be present also?

A) 869.982 nm

B) 870.036 nm

C) 870.054 nm

D) 870.072 nm

E) 869.946 nm

Answer: A
Var: 50+

13) Perhaps the most famous observation in spectroscopy was the recognition that the yellow-orange line in the spectrum of sodium is in fact a narrowly separated doublet. The explanation of this splitting is most closely related to

A) the de Broglie wavelength of the electron.

B) the existence of quantized orbital angular momentum of the electron.

C) the exclusion principle.

D) solution of the Schrodinger equation.

E) the existence of spin angular momentum of the electron.

Answer: E
Var: 1

14) Consider an atom with the electron configuration $1s^2 2s^2 2p^6 3s^2 3p^6$. Which of the following is an accurate statement concerning this atom?

A) The atomic number of this atom is $Z = 11$.

B) This atom is in an excited state.

C) This atom has a non-zero angular momentum.

D) This atom is most likely to give rise to an ion with charge +2e.

E) This atom would probably be very inert chemically.

Answer: E
Var: 1

15) A potassium atom ($Z = 19$) in the ground state has filled K, L, and M shells and a 4 s electron. The inner shells have zero total angular momentum. A magnetic field of 2.1 T is applied. The magnitude of the total angular momentum of the atom is closest to:

A) zero   B) 0.5 h   C) 0.7 h   D) 0.9 h   E) 1.0 h

Answer: D
Var: 42

16) A potassium atom (Z = 19) in the ground state has filled K, L, and M shells and a 4 s electron. The inner shells have zero total angular momentum. A magnetic field of 0.3 T is applied. The angle between the total angular momentum and the axis of the magnetic field is closest to:

A) 40°   B) 45°   C) 50°   D) 55°   E) 60°

Answer: D
Var: 11

17) A potassium atom (Z = 19) in the ground state has filled K, L, and M shells and a 4 s electron. The inner shells have zero total angular momentum. A magnetic field of 0.9 T is applied. The ground energy of a potassium atom is –4.339 eV. This energy level is split by the applied magnetic field into two levels. The difference in energy of these two levels is closest to:

A) 100 μeV   B) 120 μeV   C) 86 μeV   D) 68 μeV   E) 50 μeV

Answer: D
Var: 11

18) The ground state for the single valence electron of a gold atom (Z = 79) is 6 s and its energy is –9.22 eV. The effective nuclear charge for this 6 s electron is closest to:

A) 3.0   B) 3.5   C) 4.0   D) 4.5   E) 5.0

Answer: E
Var: 1

19) The ground state for the single valence electron of a rubidium atom (Z = 37) is 5 s and its energy is –4.18 eV. The valence electron is excited into the 5 g state. Assume this 5 g electron is entirely outside the electron cloud of the 36 other electrons in the atom. The energy of the 5 g electron is closest to:

A) –0.21 eV   B) –0.30 eV   C) –0.41 eV   D) –0.54 eV   E) –0.69 eV

Answer: D
Var: 1

Situation 41.2
A barium atom (Z = 56) has two outer electrons in the 6 s state when the atom is on the ground configuration. A singly charged Ba+ ion is formed when one of the 6 s electrons is removed. The energy required to remove this electron is 5.21 eV.

20) In Situation 41.2, the energy required to remove the remaining 6 s electron is 10.00 eV. The effective nuclear charge for the remaining 6 s electron of a Ba$^+$ ion is closest to:

A) 3.7   B) 4.1   C) 4.4   D) 4.8   E) 5.1

Answer: E
Var: 1

21) In Situation 41.2, the single outer electron of a Ba$^+$ ion is excited into the 6 h state (l = 5). Assume this 6 h electron is entirely outside the electron cloud of the 54 electrons in the inner shells. The energy of this 6 h electron is closest to:

A) –0.4 eV   B) –0.7 eV   C) –1.1 eV   D) –1.5 eV   E) –1.9 eV

Answer: D
Var: 1

22) The target of an x-ray tube is a metallic element. The smallest wavelength produced in the continuous x-ray spectrum is 118 pm. The K_α line of the characteristic x-ray spectrum is barely observed at the same wavelength of 118 pm. The potential difference used to accelerate the electron beam is closest to:

A) 10.5 kV   B) 12.6 kV   C) 14.6 kV   D) 16.7 kV   E) 18.7 kV

Answer: A
Var: 19

23) The target of an x-ray tube is a metallic element. The smallest wavelength produced in the continuous x-ray spectrum is 154 pm. The K_α line of the characteristic x-ray spectrum is barely observed at the same wavelength of 154 pm. The atomic number of the element of the target, is:

A) 29   B) 28   C) 27   D) 26   E) 25

Answer: A
Var: 19

24) The target material of an x-ray tube is an alloy with atomic numbers Z = 26 and 27. The electron beam is accelerated by a 11 kV potential difference. The smallest wavelength of the continuous x-ray spectrum produced is closest to:

A) 110 pm   B) 95 pm   C) 130 pm   D) 150 pm   E) 170 pm

Answer: A
Var: 50+

25) The target material of an x-ray tube is an alloy with atomic numbers Z = 23 and 25. The electron beam is accelerated by a 84 kV potential difference. The larger wavelength of the two K_α lines in the characteristic x-ray spectrum is closest to:

A) 250 pm   B) 270 pm   C) 230 pm   D) 210 pm   E) 190 pm

Answer: A
Var: 50+

Short Answer Questions

1) Consider the n = 6 shell.
(a) What is the largest value of the angular momentum quantum number, ℓ, in this shell?
(b) How many electrons can be placed in this shell?

Answer: (a) 5
      (b) 72
Var: 9

2) The energy of an electron in the p–level of an atom is changed in the presence of a magnetic field of magnitude 3.4 T. What is the difference between the largest and smallest possible energies? Recall that the Bohr magneton is 9.274×10^{-24} J/T.

Answer: 6.3×10^{-23} J
Var: 49

3) Consider a hydrogen atom in the n = 1 state in a magnetic field. For what value of the magnetic field is the splitting between the s = +1 and s = -1 levels equal to 9.3×10^{-5} eV?
(Note: $h = 6.626 \times 10^{-34}$ J • s, $e = 1.602 \times 10^{-19}$ C, and $m = 9.110 \times 10^{-31}$ kg.)

Answer: 0.80 T
Var: 50+

4) An atom with atomic number 5 is in its ground state. How many electrons are in its outermost shell?

Answer: 3
Var: 8

5) The ionization energy of the outermost electron in Li is 5.390 eV. What is the effective charge seen by this outermost electron? (Li has 2 energy levels.)

Answer: 1.26 e
Var: 1

Chapter 42   Molecules and Condensed Matter

Multiple Choice Questions

Situation 42.1

The ionization energy of lithium (Li) is 5.39 eV, the electron affinity of fluorine (F) is 3.45 eV, and the electrostatic potential energy of a lithium fluoride (LiF) molecule is -7.90 eV.

1) In Situation 42.1, the binding energy of a lithium fluoride molecule is closest to:

    A) -0.9 eV   B) -4.1 eV   C) -6.0 eV   D) -7.9 eV   E) -9.8 eV

Answer: C
Var: 1

2) In Situation 42.1, assume the electrostatic potential energy of the LiF molecule is entirely due to two point charges +e and -e. The separation of the nuclei under this assumption is closest to:

    A) 0.18 nm   B) 0.20 nm   C) 0.22 nm   D) 0.24 nm   E) 0.26 nm

Answer: A
Var: 1

3) The longest wavelength in the microwave absorption spectrum of LiI due to a rotational transition is 11.28 mm. The energy difference, between the $\ell = 4$ and $\ell = 3$ rotational energy levels is closest to:

    A) 440 μeV   B) 340 μeV   C) 250 μeV   D) 150 μeV   E) 55 μeV

Answer: A
Var: 33

4) The longest wavelength in the microwave absorption spectrum of LiI due to a rotational transition is 11.28 mm. The reduced mass of a LiI molecule is 1.093 x 10^{-26} kg. The Li-I bond length (internuclear separation) is closest to:

    A) 0.20 nm   B) 0.22 nm   C) 0.24 nm   D) 0.26 nm   E) 0.28 nm

Answer: C
Var: 1

5) The longest wavelength in the microwave absorption spectrum of LiI due to a rotational transition is 11.28 mm. The absorption frequency of LiI, for the transition between the $\ell = 5$ and the $\ell = 8$ rotational levels is closest to:

    A) 560 GHz   B) 390 GHz   C) 210 GHz   D) 40 GHz   E) 620 GHz

Answer: A
Var: 28

6) The vibrational frequency of an HF molecule is 8.72×10^{13} Hz and the reduced mass of the molecule is 1.589×10^{-27} kg. The ground state vibrational energy of an HF molecule is closest to:

A) 0.12 eV   B) 0.18 eV   C) 0.24 eV   D) 0.30 eV   E) 0.36 eV

Answer: B
Var: 1

7) The vibrational frequency of an HF molecule is 8.72×10^{13} Hz and the reduced mass of the molecule is 1.589×10^{-27} kg. The force constant k of the H–F bond is closest to:

A) 400 N • m   B) 440 N • m   C) 480 N • m   D) 520 N • m   E) 560 N • m

Answer: C
Var: 1

8) The vibrational frequency of an HF molecule is 8.72×10^{13} Hz and the reduced mass of the molecule is 1.589×10^{-27} kg. The energy required to break the H–F molecular bond (the dissociation energy) is 5.86 eV. Assume that all the vibrational energies of an HF molecule are those of a quantized harmonic oscillator. The maximum value of the vibrational quantum number for which the vibrational energy does not exceed the dissociation energy is equal to:

A) 12   B) 13   C) 14   D) 15   E) 16

Answer: D
Var: 1

Situation 42.2

The centroidal moment of inertia of a fluorine (F_2) molecule is 3.167×10^{-46} kg m^2. The mass of a fluorine molecule is 3.155×10^{-26} kg.

9) In Situation 42.2, the F–F bond length (internuclear separation) of the fluorine molecule is closest to:

A) 0.07 nm   B) 0.10 nm   C) 0.14 nm   D) 0.17 nm   E) 0.20 nm

Answer: C
Var: 1

10) In Situation 42.2, the rotational energy of a fluorine molecule for the $\ell = 20$ state is closest to:

A) 4.6×10^{-2} eV

B) 2.2×10^{-3} eV

C) 5.1×10^{-2} eV

D) 5.6×10^{-2} eV

E) 6.1×10^{-2} eV

Answer: A
Var: 23

434

11) A hydrogen deuteride (HD) molecule is formed by a bond between a hydrogen (H) atom and a deuterium (D) atom. The masses of hydrogen and deuterium atoms are 1.674×10^{-27} kg and 3.344×10^{-27} kg, respectively. The H–D bond length (separation of the nuclei) is 0.07414 nm. The centroidal moment of inertia of hydrogen deuteride is closest to:

A) 5.3×10^{-48} kg • m^2

B) 6.1×10^{-48} kg • m^2

C) 6.9×10^{-48} kg • m^2

D) 7.7×10^{-48} kg • m^2

E) 8.5×10^{-48} kg • m^2

Answer: B
Var: 1

12) Which of the following is an accurate statement?

A) A Van der Walls bond is an example of what is called a strong bond.

B) A hydrogen bond can occur in compounds not containing hydrogen.

C) The bonding in sodium chloride is an example of an ionic bond.

D) The bonding in sodium chloride is an example of a polarization bond.

E) A covalent bond occurs only in systems that have a net charge.

Answer: C
Var: 1

13) The energy levels of a rotating molecule are given by
$E = 1/2\ell \, (\ell + 1)C$ where $C = h^2 / 4\pi^2 I$
The spacing between the ℓ and $\ell - 4$ levels is thus

A) $(4\ell - 6)C$ B) $4\ell \, C$ C) $(4\ell - 4)C$ D) $(4\ell - 10)C$ E) $4\ell(\ell+1) \, C$

Answer: A
Var: 7

14) The energy band gap in in Sb is 0.23 eV. What is the minimum photon wavelength of a photon which will cause intrinsic photoconductivity in this material?

A) 1900 nm   B) 2670 nm   C) 5400 nm   D) 1600 nm   E) 178 nm

Answer: C
Var: 1

15) A semiconductor p–n diode has a current of 3.1mA when a forward bias of 90 mV is applied and the operating temperature is 300 K. The saturation current of the diode is closest to:

A) 99 μA   B) 30 μA   C) 9.9 μA   D) 3.0 μA   E) 0.99 μA

Answer: A
Var: 50+

16) A semiconductor p–n diode has a current of 2.7mA when a forward bias of 80 mV is applied and the operating temperature is 300 K. The operating temperature is increased to 310 K. The same forward bias voltage is applied. The new diode current is closest to:

    A) 2.4 mA   B) 2.2 mA   C) 2.7 mA   D) 2.9 mA   E) 3.2 mA

Answer: A
Var: 50+

17) The saturation current of a p–n junction diode is 270 mA and the operating temperature is 295 K. The bias voltage for which the current is 730 mA is closest to:

    A) 33 mV   B) 10 mV   C) 16 mV   D) 24 mV   E) 46 mV

Answer: A
Var: 50+

18) The saturation current of a p–n junction diode is 550 mA and the operating temperature is 295 K. The bias voltage for which the current is – 250 mA is closest to:

    A) –15 mV   B) –12 mV   C) –9.4 mV   D) –22 mV   E) –18 mV

Answer: A
Var: 50+

19) The saturation current of a p–n junction diode is 280 mA and the operating temperature is 295 K. The diode current when a forward bias voltage of 8.3 mV is applied is closest to:

    A) 110 mA   B) 120 mA   C) 130 mA   D) 140 mA   E) 150 mA

Answer: A
Var: 50+

20) A diatomic gas is at a temperature of 790 K. The spacing of the vibrational energy levels of the molecules is 0.1 eV. The average vibrational energy of a molecule at that temperature is closest to:

    A) 8.0×10^{-2} eV

    B) 7.6×10^{-2} eV

    C) 6.8×10^{-2} eV

    D) 8.4×10^{-2} eV

    E) 8.8×10^{-2} eV

Answer: A
Var: 50+

21) A diatomic gas is at a temperature of 900 K. The spacing of the vibrational energy levels of the molecules is 0.13 eV. The vibrational molar heat capacity in units of R at that temperature is closest to:

    A) 8.0×10^{-1} B) 7.2×10^{-1} C) 6.4×10^{-1} D) 5.6×10^{-1} E) 8.8×10^{-1}

Answer: A
Var: 50+

22) The Fermi energy of rubidium at a temperature of 5 K is 1.85 eV. An electron state in rubidium is 0.005 eV above the Fermi level. The probability that this state is occupied at T = 9K is closest to:

A) 2×10^{-3} B) 3×10^{-4} C) 6×10^{-5} D) 1×10^{-5} E) 3×10^{-6}

Answer: A
Var: 50+

23) The Fermi energy of a metallic material at a temperature of 7K is found to be 1.44 eV. The electron contribution to the molar heat capacity of this material in units of R, at T = 7K, is closest to:

A) 2×10^{-3} B) 4×10^{-3} C) 6×10^{-3} D) 8×10^{-3} E) 1×10^{-2}

Answer: A
Var: 50+

24) Lead telluride is a semiconductor with an energy gap of 0.30 eV between the valence and conduction bands. Assume the Fermi level is in the middle of the gap. At a temperature of 300 K, the probability that a state at the bottom of the conduction band is occupied is closest to:

A) 1×10^{-5} B) 4×10^{-5} C) 2×10^{-4} D) 7×10^{-4} E) 3×10^{-3}

Answer: E
Var: 1

25) Which of the following is an accurate statement?

A) A material in which the uppermost occupied band is half full will be a conductor.

B) When a group V element (like arsenic) is added to germanium, a group IV element, the result is a p-type semiconductor.

C) The Fermi level for a heavily doped p-type or n-type semiconductor is midway between the top of the valence band and the bottom of the conduction band.

D) A material in which a completely full valence band is separated from the conduction band by 5 eV would be a semiconductor.

E) Hole conductivity results in silicon when some of the silicon atoms are removed, leaving vacant lattice sites behind.

Answer: A
Var: 1

Short Answer Questions

1) When a certain diatomic molecule undergoes a transition from the l = 5 to the l = 3 rotational level, the emitted photon has wavelength 6.89×10^{-4} m. Calculate the moment of inertia of the molecule.
(Note: h = 6.626×10^{-34} J • s, e = 1.602×10^{-19} C, and c = 2.998×10^{-8} m • s.)

Answer: 3.47×10^{-46} kg • m^2
Var: 50+

2) A diatomic molecule, with each atom having 18 nucleons, has its $\ell = 0$ vibrational levels known. A hypothetical molecule, consisting of the same elements but with nuclear isotopes of mass numbers 16 and 20, would have different $\ell = 0$ vibrational energy levels. For a given vibration level n, find the ratio of the vibrational energy of the original molecule to that of the hypothetical molecule. (Assume all nucleons have a mass of 1 μ.)

Answer: 0.994
Var: 38

3) At 5000 K, the ratio of the number of N_2 molecules in the $n = 1$, $\ell = 0$ state to the number in the $n = 0$, $\ell = 0$ state is 0.0792. At another temperature, this ratio is found to be 0.17. What is this temperature?

Answer: 7200 K
Var: 1

4) For a solid in which the occupation of the energy states is given by the Fermi–Dirac distribution, the probability that a certain state is occupied at a temperature T_0 is 0.70. If the temperature is doubled to $2T_0$, what is the probability that the same state is occupied? Assume that the Fermi energy E_F does not change with temperature.

Answer: 0.60
Var: 1

5) When a voltage V_0 is applied in the forward direction across a diode, a current I is measured. When the same voltage is applied in the reverse direction, the magnitude of the current is decreased by a factor of 11. What is the voltage V_0? Assume room temperature (T = 300 K), and recall that k = 1.38 x 10^{-23} J/K and that the electron charge is 1.602 x 10^{19} C.

Answer: 62 mV
Var: 1

Chapter 43   Nuclear Physics

Multiple Choice Questions

1) The following masses are known:

$^1_0 n$ 1.008665 u

$^1_1 H$ 1.007825 u

$^{62}_{38} Ni$ 61.928349 u

The binding energy of $^{62}_{38} Ni$, in MeV, is closest to:

A) 540   B) 600   C) 650   D) 710   E) 770

Answer: A
Var: 12

2) The binding energy per nucleon for $^{222}_{86} Rn$, calculated from the liquid drop model, in MeV, is

closest to:

A) 7.7   B) 7.6   C) 7.4   D) 7.2   E) 7.0

Answer: A
Var: 13

3) A proton is projected at a stationary $^{226}_{88} Ra$ aluminum target. The proton momentarily comes

to a halt at a distance from the center of an aluminum nucleus, equal to twice the nuclear
radius. Assume that the nucleus retains its spherical shape and that the nuclear force on the
proton is negligible. The initial kinetic energy of the proton, in MeV, is closest to:

A) 8.7   B) 5.8   C) 2.9   D) 13   E) 17

Answer: A
Var: 14

4) Rubidium $^{87}_{37} Rb$ is a naturally-occurring nuclide which undergoes beta-minus decay. The

nuclide, which is the product of the decay, is:

A) $^{87}_{36} Kr$ B) $^{87}_{38} Kr$ C) $^{88}_{37} Rb$ D) $^{87}_{36} Sr$ E) $^{87}_{38} Sr$

Answer: E
Var: 1

5) Naturally-occurring tellurium, $^{123}_{52}$Te, transforms by electron capture, according to the reaction

$$^{123}_{52}\text{Te} + e^- \rightarrow X + \nu_e$$

The product nuclide, denoted by X, is:

A) $^{123}_{51}$Sb   B) $^{123}_{53}$Sb   C) $^{123}_{52}$Te   D) $^{123}_{51}$I   E) $^{123}_{53}$I

Answer: A
Var: 1

6) Neodymium ^{144}Nd is a nuclide which undergoes alpha decay. The nuclide which is the product of the decay is:

A) $^{142}_{56}$Ba   B) $^{140}_{58}$Ce   C) $^{140}_{559}$Pr   D) $^{148}_{62}$Sm   E) $^{146}_{64}$Gd

Answer: B
Var: 1

7) Scandium ^{44}Sc decays by emitting a positron. The nuclide which is the product of the decay is:

A) $^{43}_{21}$Sc   B) $^{45}_{21}$Sc   C) $^{44}_{20}$Ca   D) $^{43}_{21}$Ca   E) $^{44}_{22}$Ti

Answer: A
Var: 1

8) Neptunium $^{239}_{93}$Np has a decay constant of 3.40×10^{-6} s^{-1}. A 3.0 mg sample of Np-239 is prepared. The activity of the Np-239 sample, in Ci, is closest to:

A) 22   B) 70   C) 220   D) 700   E) 2200

Answer: D
Var: 1

9) A radioactive source of a single nuclide emits 2.4 MeV neutrons at the rate of 5600 neutrons per second. The number of atoms in the source is 4.6×10^9. The activity of the source, in nCi, is closest to:

A) 150   B) 1500   C) 15   D) 56   E) 560

Answer: A
Var: 50+

10) A radioactive source of a single nuclide emits 2.4 MeV neutrons at the rate of 4600 neutrons per second. The number of atoms in the source is 5.0×10^9. The mean lifetime of the nuclide is closest to:

A) 1.1×10^6 B) 8.7×10^5 C) 1.3×10^6 D) 1.5×10^6 E) 1.7×10^6

Answer: A
Var: 50+

11) The decay constant of a radioactive nuclide is 2.4×10^{-3} s^{-1}. The half-life of the nuclide, in minutes, is closest to:

A) 4.8   B) 7.0   C) 5.9   D) 2.8   E) 3.8

Answer: A
Var: 50+

12) The decay constant of a radioactive nuclide is 2.1×10^{-3} s^{-1}. At a given instant, the activity of a specimen of the nuclide is 60 mCi. The time interval required for the activity to decline to 50 mCi is closest to:

A) 87 s   B) 96 s   C) 100 s   D) 110 s   E) 120 s

Answer: A
Var: 50+

13) The decay constant of a radioactive nuclide is 1.6×10^{-3} s^{-1}. At a given instant, the number of atoms of the radioactive nuclide is 1.85×10^{12}. The number of atoms of the nuclide that remain after a time interval of 30 minutes is closest to:

A) 1.04×10^{11}
B) 1.14×10^{11}
C) 1.26×10^{11}
D) 1.38×10^{11}
E) 1.52×10^{11}

Answer: A
Var: 1

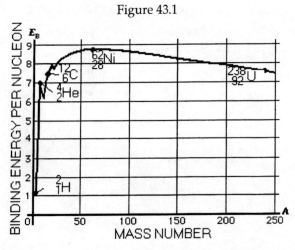

Figure 43.1

14) In Figure 43.1, the curve graphed here helps us to understand

A) why scintillation counters are used in nuclear physics.

B) why eventually the universe will be entirely composed of heavy elements like uranium.

C) the nature of the process called beta decay.

D) how energy is generated in a nuclear reactor.

E) how radioactive dating is accomplished.

Answer: D
Var: 1

15) Which of the following is not true of the nuclear force?

A) The nuclear force has a short range, of the order of nuclear dimensions.

B) For two protons in close proximity, the nuclear force and the electric force have comparable magnitudes.

C) The nuclear force does not depend on charge.

D) A nucleon in a large nucleus interacts via the nuclear force only with nearby nucleons, not with ones far away in the nucleus.

E) The nuclear force favors binding of pairs of protons or neutrons with opposite spin angular momenta.

Answer: B
Var: 1

16) The stability of $^{11}_{6}$C with respect to alpha, beta–plus and beta- 6 minus decay is to be determined. Do not consider the possibility of decay by electron capture. The following atomic masses are known:

$^{4}_{2}$He	4.002603
$^{7}_{4}$Be	7.016928
$^{11}_{5}$B	11.009305
$^{11}_{6}$C	11.011433
$^{11}_{7}$N	11.026742

The $^{11}_{6}$C nuclide is:

A) not subject to alpha, beta–plus or beta-minus decay

B) subject to alpha decay only

C) subject to beta–plus decay only

D) subject to beta-minus decay only

E) subject to beta–plus or beta-minus decay, but not to alpha decay

Answer: C
Var: 1

17) The stability of $^{36}_{17}Cl$ with respect to alpha, beta–plus, and beta–minus decay is to be determined. Do not consider the possibility of decay by electron capture. The following atomic masses are known:

$^{4}_{2}He$	4.002603
$^{32}_{15}P$	31.973907
$^{36}_{16}S$	35.967081
$^{36}_{17}Cl$	35.968307
$^{36}_{18}Ar$	35.967546

The $^{36}_{17}Cl$ nuclide is:

A) not subject to alpha, beta–plus or beta–minus decay

B) subject to alpha decay only

C) subject to beta–plus decay only

D) subject to beta–minus decay only

E) subject to beta–plus or beta–minus decay, but not to alpha decay

Answer: E
Var: 1

444

18) The stability of $^{47}_{21}$Sc with respect to alpha, beta–plus, and beta– 21 minus decay is to be determined. Do not consider the possibility of decay by electron capture. The following atomic masses are known:

$^{4}_{2}$He	4.002603
$^{43}_{19}$K	42.960717
$^{47}_{20}$Ca	46.954543
$^{47}_{21}$Sc	46.952409
$^{47}_{22}$Ti	46.951764

The $^{47}_{21}$Sc nuclide is:

A) not subject to alpha, beta–plus or beta–minus decay

B) subject to alpha decay only

C) subject to beta–plus decay only

D) subject to beta–minus decay only

E) subject to beta–plus or beta–minus decay, but not to alpha decay

Answer: D
Var: 1

19) The stability of $^{56}_{26}$Fe with respect to alpha, beta–plus, and beta– 26 minus decay is to be determined. Do not consider the possibility of decay by electron capture. The following atomic masses are known:

$^{4}_{2}$He	4.002603
$^{52}_{24}$Cr	51.944768
$^{56}_{25}$Mn	55.938907
$^{56}_{26}$Fe	55.934939
$^{56}_{27}$Co	55.939841

The $^{56}_{26}$Fe nuclide is:

A) not subject to alpha, beta–plus or beta–minus decay

B) subject to alpha decay only

C) subject to beta–plus decay only

D) subject to beta–minus decay only

E) subject to beta–plus or beta–minus decay, but not to alpha decay

Answer: A
Var: 1

20) Bismuth $\overset{212}{83}$ Bi is known to be radioactive. The stability of $\overset{212}{83}$ Bi with respect to alpha,

beta–plus, and beta–minus decay is 83 to be determined. Do not consider electron capture. The following atomic masses are known:

$\overset{4}{2}$He   4.002603

$\overset{208}{81}$Tl   207.981998

$\overset{212}{82}$Pb   211.991871

$\overset{212}{83}$Bi   211.991255

$\overset{212}{84}$Po   211.988842

The $\overset{212}{83}$ Bi nuclide is:

A) subject to alpha decay only

B) subject to beta–plus decay only

C) subject to beta–minus decay only

D) subject to alpha or beta–plus decay, but not beta–minus decay

E) alpha or beta–minus decay, but not beta–plus decay

Answer: E
Var: 1

21) The maximum permissible workday dose for occupational exposure to radiation is 11 mrem. A 69 kg laboratory technician absorbs 2.2 mJ of 0.3 MeV gamma rays in a work day. The relative biological efficiency (RBE) for gamma rays is 1.00. The ratio of the equivalent dosage received by the technician to the maximum permissible equivalent dosage is closest to:

A) 0.29   B) 0.32   C) 0.35   D) 0.38   E) 0.41

Answer: A
Var: 50+

22) The maximum permissible workday dose for occupational exposure to radiation is 20 mrem. A 70 kg laboratory technician absorbs 1.5 mJ of 0.4 MeV gamma rays in a work day. The relative biological efficiency (RBE) for gamma rays is 1.00. The number of gamma-ray photons absorbed by the technician in a workday is closest to:

A) 2×10^{10} B) 2×10^{9} C) 2×10^{8} D) 8×10^{8} E) 8×10^{7}

Answer: A
Var: 50+

23) A 72 kg researcher absorbs 8.9×10^8 neutrons in a work day. The energy of the neutrons is 3.7 MeV. The relative biological efficiency (RBE) for fast neutrons is 10. The equivalent dosage of the radiation exposure, in mrem, is closest to:

    A) 7.3   B) 2.3   C) 4.6   D) 22   E) 73

Answer: A
Var: 50+

24) A beryllium-8 atom at rest undergoes double alpha decay as follows:

$$ {}^{8}_{4}\text{Be} \rightarrow {}^{4}_{2}\text{He} + {}^{4}_{2}\text{He} $$

The atomic masses are:

$$ {}^{4}_{2}\text{He} \quad 4.002603 $$

$$ {}^{8}_{4}\text{Be} \quad 8.005305 $$

The kinetic energy of each departing alpha particle, in keV, is closest to:

    A) 46   B) 65   C) 92   D) 130   E) 180

Answer: A
Var: 1

25) One of the fusion reactions that occurs in the sun is:

$$ {}^{3}_{2}\text{He} + {}^{3}_{2}\text{He} \rightarrow {}^{4}_{2}\text{He} + {}^{1}_{1}\text{H} + {}^{1}_{1}\text{H} $$

The following atomic masses are known:

$$ {}^{1}_{1}\text{H} \quad 1.007825 $$

$$ {}^{3}_{2}\text{He} \quad 3.016029 $$

$$ {}^{4}_{2}\text{He} \quad 4.002603 $$

The reaction energy, in MeV, is closest to:

    A) 11   B) 13   C) 15   D) 17   E) 19

Answer: B
Var: 1

Situation 43.1

An excited $^{236}_{92}U*$ nucleus undergoes fission into two fragments.

$$^{236}_{92}U* \rightarrow {}^{144}_{56}Ba + {}^{92}_{36}Kr$$

The following atomic masses are known:

$^{92}_{36}Kr$ 91.926270

$^{144}_{56}Ba$ 143.922845

$^{236}_{92}U*$ 236.045563

26) In Situation 43.1, the reaction energy, in MeV, is closest to:

   A) 150   B) 160   C) 170   D) 180   E) 190

Answer: D
Var: 1

27) In Situation 43.1, assume, at a given instant, that the two fragments are spherical and barely in contact. At that instant, the electrostatic interaction energy of the two fragments, in MeV, is closest to:

   A) 230   B) 240   C) 250   D) 260   E) 270

Answer: C
Var: 1

Table 43.1

Time (days)	0	2	6	11	19	30
Counts per Minute	1000	899	726	556	556	200

28) In Table 43.1, in a laboratory accident a work area is contaminated with radioactive material. Health physicists monitor the area during a 30–day period and obtain the data shown here. The accident occurred at t = 0. They determine that it will not be safe for workers to enter the area until the radioactivity level has dropped to 52 counts per minute. Of the choices listed, which is the earliest time that workers could safely return?

   A) 55 days   B) 64 days   C) 73 days   D) 46 days   E) 35 days

Answer: A
Var: 50+

449

29) The radioactive nuclei ^{60}Co is widely used in medical applications. It undergoes beta decay, and the total energy of the decay process is 2.82 MeV per decay event. The half life of this nucleus is 272 days. Suppose that a patient is given a dose of 3.5 microCurie of ^{60}Co. If all of this material decayed while in the patient's body, what would be the total energy deposited there?

(1 Ci = 3.70×10^{10} decays/sec.)

A) 2.0 J

B) 5.8 J

C) 4.38×10^{12} J

D) 12 J

E) 2.11×10^6 J

Answer: A
Var: 50+

30) In the nuclear reaction here, which of the following is the missing nuclear product?

$$^{10}_{5}B + ^{4}_{2}He \rightarrow ^{1}_{1}H + ?$$

A) $^{12}_{9}F$ B) $^{21}_{7}N$ C) $^{13}_{6}C$ D) $^{13}_{7}N$ E) $^{14}_{7}N$

Answer: C
Var: 1

Short Answer Questions

1) If the radius of a nucleus is given by $R = R_0 A^{1/3}$ where $R_O = 1.20 \times 10^{-15}$ m, calculate the density of a nucleus that has A = 233. The mass of a nucleon (proton or neutron) is 1.67×10^{-27} kg.

Answer: 2.31×10^{17} kg/m^3
Var: 50+

2) The unstable isotope ^{234}Th decays by β emission with a half-life of 24.5 days.

(a) What mass of ^{234}Th will produce 8.4×10^{17} decays per second? (Note: 1u = 1.66×10^{-27} kg.)

(b) If the initial decay rate of the sample is 8.4×10^{17} decays per second, what is the decay rate after 83 days?

Answer: (a) 1.0 kg

(b) 8.0×10^{16} decays per second

Var: 50+

3) Consider the fusion reaction:

$$^2_1H + ^2_1H + ^2_1H \rightarrow ^4_2He + ^1_1H + ^1_0n$$

The atomic masses are:

^2_1H, 2.01410 u ; ^4_2He, 4.00260 u; ^1_1H, 1.00783 u and ^1_0n, 1.008665 u,

where 1u = 1.6606 x 10^{-27} kg. What mass of deuterium {^2_1H} fuel is used up in producing

6.4 x 10^{13} J of energy by this reaction?

Answer: 1.9 x 10^{-1} kg

Var: 50+

4) A hypothetical particle has mass 471 MeV/c^2. If such a particle at rest decays into two gamma-ray photons, what is the wavelength of each photon?
(Note: e = 1.602 x 10^{-19} C, c = 2.998 x 10^8 m/s, and h = 6.626 x 10^{-34} J • s.)

Answer: 5.27 x 10^{-15} m

Var: 50+

5) What initial kinetic energy must a proton have in order to initiate a nuclear reaction with a $^{14}_7$N nucleus? Express your answer in MeV. (R_0 = 1.2 x 10^{-15} m)

Answer: 5.8 MeV

Var: 14

Chapter 44   Particle Physics and Cosmology

Multiple Choice Questions

1) The resonance particle $\Lambda(1410)$ has a rest mass of 1410 MeV/c^2 and an energy width of 50.0 MeV. The average lifetime of the $\Lambda(1410)$ particle, in SI units, is closest to:

A) 1.3×10^{-23}

B) 1.3×10^{-22}

C) 1.3×10^{-21}

D) 7.2×10^{-24}

E) 7.2×10^{-23}

Answer: A
Var: 11

2) The $\Lambda(1410)$ particle has a rest energy of 1410 MeV and an average lifetime of 1.3×10^{-23} s. The energy width of the $\Lambda(1410)$ particle, in MeV, is closest to:

A) 50   B) 17   C) 150   D) 5.0   E) 1.7

Answer: A
Var: 11

Situation 44.1

A moving proton is incident upon and collides with a stationary target proton. The following reaction occurs:

$$p + p \;\rightarrow\; p + p + \pi^+ + \pi^+$$

3) In Situation 44.1, the threshold kinetic energy of the incident proton for this reaction to occur, in MeV, is closest to:

A) 280   B) 380   C) 490   D) 600   E) 710

Answer: D
Var: 1

4) In Situation 44.1, the kinetic energy of the incident proton is 950 MeV. The total kinetic energy of the four particles after the collision, in the center of mass system, in MeV, is closest to:

A) 150   B) 220   C) 440   D) 660   E) 880

Answer: A
Var: 50+

5) A p - $\overline{p}$ collider is used to produce head-on collisions between 90 MeV protons and 90 MeV antiprotons. For one particular collision, the following reaction takes place:

$$p + \overline{p} \rightarrow \pi^+ + \pi^- + \pi^0 + \pi^0$$

The charged pions depart in opposite directions and the kinetic energy of each charged pion is 310 MeV. The kinetic energy of each neutral pion, in MeV, is closest to:

A) 440   B) 420   C) 400   D) 380   E) 360

Answer: A
Var: 50+

6) A negative Ω^- particle at rest decays as follows:

$$\Omega^- \rightarrow \Lambda^0 + K^-$$

The kinetic energy of either decay particle, obtained by a non-relativistic calculation, is sufficiently accurate in this case. The kinetic energy of the K^- meson, in MeV, is closest to:

A) 43   B) 45   C) 41   D) 39   E) 37

Answer: A
Var: 3

7) A Ξ^0 particle at rest decays according to:

$$\Xi^0 \rightarrow \Sigma^0 + \gamma$$

The kinetic energy of the Σ^0 particle, obtained by a non- relativistic calculation, is sufficiently accurate in this case. The kinetic energy of the Σ^0 particle, in MeV, is closest to:

A) 5.7   B) 4.2   C) 2.8   D) 7.9   E) 11

Answer: A
Var: 5

8) A π^0 particle at rest decays via the electromagnetic interaction:

$$\pi^0 \rightarrow \gamma + \gamma$$

The wavelength of each gamma ray, in fm, is closest to:

A) 18   B) 17   C) 15   D) 14   E) 12

Answer: A
Var: 2

9) Complete the characterization of decay given below. The decay is:

$$\eta \rightarrow \eta^o + \pi^o$$

    A) allowed

    B) forbidden; conservation of energy is violated

    C) forbidden; conservation of baryon number is violated

    D) forbidden; conservation of strangeness is violated

    E) forbidden; conservation of lepton numbers is violated

Answer: C
Var: 1

10) Complete the characterization of decay given below. The decay is:

$$\Omega^- \rightarrow \Xi^o + K^-$$

    A) allowed

    B) forbidden; conservation of energy is violated

    C) forbidden; conservation of baryon number is violated

    D) forbidden; conservation of strangeness is violated

    E) forbidden; conservation of lepton numbers is violated

Answer: B
Var: 1

11) Complete the characterization of decay given below. The decay is:

$$\pi^o \rightarrow \mu^- + e^+$$

    A) allowed

    B) forbidden; conservation of energy is violated

    C) forbidden; conservation of baryon number is violated

    D) forbidden; conservation of strangeness is violated

    E) forbidden; conservation of lepton numbers is violated

Answer: E
Var: 1

12) Complete the characterization of decay given below. The decay is:

$$\Sigma^- \rightarrow K^- + \eta^o$$

    A) allowed

    B) forbidden; conservation of energy is violated

    C) forbidden; conservation of baryon number is violated

    D) forbidden; conservation of strangeness is violated

    E) forbidden; conservation of lepton numbers is violated

Answer: C
Var: 1

13) Complete the characterization of decay given below. The decay is:

$$\eta^0 \rightarrow \pi^+ + \pi^- + e^+ + e^-$$

    A) allowed

    B) forbidden; conservation of energy is violated

    C) forbidden; conservation of baryon number is violated

    D) forbidden; conservation of strangeness is violated

    E) forbidden; conservation of lepton numbers is violated

Answer: A
Var: 1

14) Complete the characterization of decay given below. The decay is:

$$\Xi^0 \rightarrow p + \pi^-$$

    A) allowed

    B) forbidden; conservation of energy is violated

    C) forbidden; conservation of baryon number is violated

    D) forbidden; conservation of strangeness is violated

    E) forbidden; conservation of lepton numbers is violated

Answer: D
Var: 1

15) Complete the characterization of decay given below. The decay is:

$$\pi^+ \rightarrow \mu^+ + \gamma$$

    A) allowed

    B) forbidden; conservation of energy is violated

    C) forbidden; conservation of baryon number is violated

    D) forbidden; conservation of strangeness is violated

    E) forbidden; conservation of lepton numbers is violated

Answer: E
Var: 1

16) Complete the characterization of decay given below. The decay is:

$$\Sigma^- \rightarrow \Lambda^0 + e^+ + \bar{\nu}_e$$

    A) allowed

    B) forbidden; conservation of energy is violated

    C) forbidden; conservation of baryon number is violated

    D) forbidden; conservation of strangeness is violated

    E) forbidden; conservation of lepton numbers is violated

Answer: A
Var: 1

17) Complete the characterization of decay given below. The decay is:

$\Xi^- \rightarrow \Lambda^0 + K^-$

   A) allowed

   B) forbidden; conservation of energy is violated

   C) forbidden; conservation of baryon number is violated

   D) forbidden; conservation of strangeness is violated

   E) forbidden; conservation of lepton numbers is violated

Answer: B
Var: 1

18) Complete the characterization of decay given below. The decay is:

$\Omega^- \rightarrow \eta + K^-$

   A) allowed

   B) forbidden; conservation of energy is violated

   C) forbidden; conservation of baryon number is violated

   D) forbidden; conservation of strangeness is violated

   E) forbidden; conservation of lepton numbers is violated

Answer: D
Var: 1

19) A neutral η^0 (mass 0.642 u) decays into two gamma photons. What is the energy in MeV of each photon?

   A) 299 MeV   B) 597 MeV   C) 1190 MeV   D) 199 MeV   E) 149 MeV

Answer: A
Var: 2

20) Consider the possibility that a neutron could decay into two pions. What, if any, conservation law would this process violate?

   A) Conservation of baryon number.

   B) Conservation of lepton number.

   C) Conservation of energy.

   D) Conservation of charge.

   E) None of these.

Answer: A
Var: 4

21) The Σ^- particle has strangeness S = -1. What is its quark composition?

   A) uds   B) ssd   C) dds   D) ddu   E) sss

Answer: C
Var: 1

22) A neutral spin - 0 meson has a strangeness S= -1. The quark content of this meson is:

    A) u $\bar{s}$ B) $\bar{u}$ s   C) d $\bar{s}$ D) $\bar{d}$ s   E) s $\bar{s}$

Answer: D
Var: 1

23) A neutral spin - 3/2 baryon has a baryon number B = +1 and strangeness S = +1. The quark content of this particle is:

    A) u d s   B) $\bar{u}$ $\bar{d}$ s   C) $\bar{u}$ d $\bar{s}$ D) $\bar{u}$ d s   E) $\bar{u}$ $\bar{d}$ $\bar{s}$

Answer: E
Var: 1

24) A spin –3/2 baryon has a charge Q = –e, baryon number B = +1, and a strangeness S = –1. The quark content of this particle is:

    A) u u s   B) u d s   C) $\bar{u}$ d s   D) u $\bar{d}$ s   E) d d s

Answer: E
Var: 1

25) A star exploded 1.9 million years ago, forming a supernova. The event is observed on earth. The speed at which the supernova recedes from earth, obtained from Hubble's law, is closest to:

    A) 38 km/s   B) 19 km/s   C) 6 km/s   D) 76 km/s   E) 133 km/s

Answer: C
Var: 50+

26) A galaxy is observed receding from earth with a speed of 6500 km/s. Assume Hubble's law is applicable to this galaxy. The light from the galaxy reaching earth today originated in the galaxy at a time in the past, in years, that is closest to:

    A) 3.3×10^8 B) 9.8×10^8 C) 9.8×10^7 D) 3.3×10^7 E) 9.8×10^6

Answer: A
Var: 50+

27) A galaxy is observed receding from earth with a speed of 9600 km/s. A red–shifted spectral line originating in the galaxy is compared to the same spectral line originating in the laboratory. The ratio of the wavelength of the red–shifted line to that of the unshifted line is closest to:

    A) 1.032   B) 1.051   C) 1.070   D) 1.090   E) 1.128

Answer: A
Var: 50+

28) The H_α spectral line of hydrogen has a wavelength of 656.3 nm. The H_α spectral line is observed in light from a star at a red-shifted wavelength of 902.0 nm. Hubble's law is valid for this star. The distance of the star from earth, in light-years, is closest to:

A) 4.6×10^9　　B) 1.5×10^9　　C) 4.6×10^8　　D) 1.5×10^8　　E) 4.6×10^7

Answer: A
Var: 50+

29) In a crude cosmological model, the universe is "enclosed" in a sphere which expands in accordance with Hubble's law. Assume the spherical "boundary" of the universe advances "outward" with the speed of light. The "radius" of the universe, in this model, in light-years, is closest to:

A) 6×10^8　　B) 2×10^9　　C) 6×10^9　　D) 2×10^{10}　　E) 6×10^{10}

Answer: D
Var: 1

30) The attractive force between quarks is mediated by particles called

A) stickons.

B) gluons.

C) adhesivons.

D) chromons.

E) forcons.

Answer: B
Var: 1

31) Redshift measurements on a constellation show that it is receding with a velocity of 7600 km / s. How far away is the galaxy?

A) 3.6×10^{24} m

B) 1.3×10^{26} m

C) 1.3×10^{24} m

D) 4.3×10^{23} m

E) 2.1×10^{22} m

Answer: A
Var: 50+

Short Answer Questions

1) A new "supercollider" is designed to accelerate protons and antiprotons to kinetic energies of up to 4.1 Tev (4.1×10^{12} eV).
a) If two protons, each with energy 4.1 Tev collide and result in a single particle at rest in the lab frame, what would be its rest mass in kg?
b) At what absolute temperature would these protons be thermal protons?
c) If the protons annihilate to produce two photons of equal energy, what would be the frequency and wavelength of each?
(Note: the proton charge is 1.602×10^{-19} C, the speed of light is $3.00 \times 10\text{-}23$ m/s, the Boltzman constant is 1.38×10^{-23} J/K, and the Planck constant is 6.626×10^{-34} J • s.)

Answer: (a) 1.5×10^{-23} kg
(b) 3.2×10^{16} K
(c) 9.9×10^{26} Hz, 3.0×10^{-19} m
Var: 50+

2) A high energy beam of protons collides with a stationary proton target and the available energy is 18.0 GeV. What is the speed of the proton beam that would generate this available energy? (The rest–mass energy of the proton is 978.3 MeV.) Express your answer as a fraction of the speed of light.

Answer: 0.99998 c
Var: 15

3) A distant galaxy is emitting light from the Helium spectrum at 388.9 nm. On earth the wavelength is observed to be 505.9 nm. How far from earth is this galaxy?
($H_0 = 20$ (km/s)/Mly, $c = 3.0 \times 10^8$ m/s.)
Express your answer in light years.

Answer: 3.9×10^9 light–years
Var: 50+

4) If a Ξ^- at rest decays into an Λ^0 and π^-, what is the total kinetic energy of the decay products? (The masses of Ξ^-, Λ^0 and π^- are 1321, 1116, and 140 MeV/c^2 respectively.)

Answer: 65 MeV
Var: 4

5) A cyclotron has magnetic poles with radius 0.320 m. If the cyclotron is used to accelerate ^{6}Li nuclei with mass 9.99×10^{-27} kg and charge +3, what is the minimum strength of the magnetic field that would cause relativistic effects? (Assume relativity becomes important at 0.1 c.)

Answer: 1.95 T
Var: 50+